Politics, Policy, and Government in British Columbia

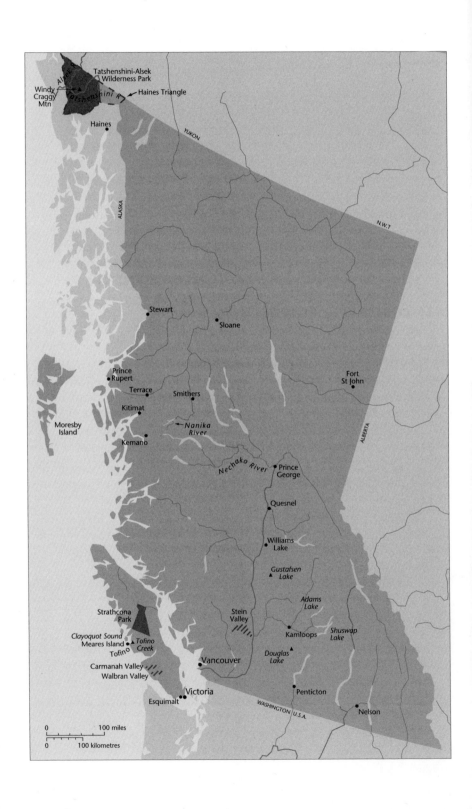

Edited by R.K. Carty

Politics, Policy, and Government
in British Columbia

UBCPress / Vancouver

Printed in Canada on acid-free paper ∞

ISBN 0-7748-0582-X

Canadian Cataloguing in Publication Data

Politics, policy, and government in British Columbia

   Includes bibliographical references and index.
   ISBN 0-7748-0582-X

   1. British Columbia – Politics and government – 1991- I. Carty, R. Kenneth, 1944-
FC3829.2.P64 1996   971.1'04   C96-910450-2
F1088.P64 1996

UBC Press gratefully acknowledges the ongoing support to its publishing program
from the Canada Council, the Province of British Columbia Cultural Services
Branch, and the Department of Communications of the Government of Canada.

UBC Press
University of British Columbia
6344 Memorial Road
Vancouver, BC V6T 1Z2
(604) 822-3259
Fax: 1-800-668-0821
E-mail: orders@ubcpress.ubc.ca
http://ubcpress.ubc.ca

Contents

Part 3: Governing the Province

Part 4: The Patterns of Public Policy

Acknowledgments

In the early stages of preparing this book, we were supported by the office of the Dean of Arts at the University of British Columbia, which provided us with the means to have a two-day meeting to discuss early drafts of the chapters. In particular, we would like to thank Professor Robert Kubicek who facilitated this meeting. We are also in the debt of Principal Richard Ericson and the members of Green College at UBC for hosting us. The college is quickly becoming central to the intellectual life of the province, and this book is one more thing to which it has contributed.

Lynda Erickson's chapter on the changing role of women in BC politics appeared in a comparative study edited by Jane Arscott and Linda Trimble entitled *In the Presence of Women*. We are grateful to the publishers, Harcourt Brace, for allowing us to use this work here and to Professor Erickson for a last-minute updating of the chapter to include the 1996 BC election results. All the other chapters were originally prepared for this book and represent the authors' latest thinking on their subjects. Though much of the text was initially drafted in 1995, and despite a tight publication schedule, several of the chapters have been able to incorporate references to the 1996 election that returned the NDP government. We appreciate the efforts of the staff at UBC Press to meet the demands that the election timetable imposed on us all.

The authors would all also like to thank Karen Murray, a UBC doctoral student, who has been a great help at many stages of this project, and Holly Keller-Brohman and Randy Schmidt, whose editorial skills have improved the manuscript. As faculty members in the province's universities and colleges, we know that students are often acutely aware of the cost of books, and so we appreciate the efforts of UBC Press to keep the price of this one as affordable as possible. Royalties from the book will go to the British Columbia Political Studies Association for use in student-related projects.

Introduction

R.K. Carty

British Columbia is a special place. Blessed by rich natural resources, favoured by a temperate climate on the quickly developing Pacific Rim, and enjoying the benefits of a diverse plural social base, the province thrives as the dynamic fifth region of a country widely regarded as among the most successful of contemporary industrial societies. Few people in history have been as fortunate as modern British Columbians, and so one might expect that governing such a society would be easy. This book explores the extent to which this is true by describing and explaining how British Columbians govern themselves. It asks how they engage in political competition, how they organize to make public decisions, and what the pattern of their public policy looks like.

The book is divided into four parts. In the first, 'Modern British Columbia,' are four essays that set the stage and paint the scenery for the play of the province's politics. Don Blake starts by noting that BC is often viewed as an exotic and turbulent place – at least by what are probably rather tame Canadian standards – but his careful portrayal of the province's political culture reveals the degree to which long-standing orientations to political organization and action persist. He describes these as populism and polarization, and the regularity with which they come up in subsequent chapters testifies to their impact as fundamental features of BC's political life. Michael Howlett and Keith Brownsey complement Blake's account of the political culture with their analysis of the province's political economy. Their provocative title – 'From Timber to Tourism' – stimulates reflection on the changing character of the province's economic base, and with that the material forces at work, and the dynamics they give rise to, in the province's political life. Howlett and Brownsey's theme and conclusions echo throughout the book and in particular animate the discussion in chapters like those on the making of environmental and forest policy.

Whatever British Columbians sometimes think, the province does not stand alone in the world. It is a Canadian province and its relationships with the rest of the country are the subject of Ed Black's chapter. Often considered a 'spoilt child' by Ottawa (itself thought of as a neglectful parent by BC), the province maintains a list of disputes that rarely shrinks. In good part this list reflects the fact of federalism and the reality that citizens live in, to borrow Don Blake's title of an earlier book, 'Two Political Worlds.' Black's chapter helps dissect these ongoing conflicts and assess their impact on the political life of the province. Of course, Native people and their concern for the land predate BC's 1871 entry into Confederation and any subsequent federal-provincial squabbling between white politicians. Paul Tennant's essay, which traces the history of the aboriginal peoples' land title claims, charts the place of Native communities in the life of the province and makes clear that large unresolved issues remain to be settled. They are complex, multidimensional problems that cast shadows over the constitutional, legal, economic, social, and moral life of the province. In contrast to political life during the province's first century, there is now little in BC's public life that is untouched by a concern for Native peoples and their issues.

The second part, entitled 'The Political Stage,' is also made up of four chapters. In it we see politicians and their parties competing with one another among the electorate, within the legislature, and through the media. Don Blake starts the section with an analysis of the patterns of party competition across electoral cycles in recent decades. He demonstrates that despite enduring divisions between social democrats (first as the Co-operative Commonwealth Federation, now the New Democratic Party) and those calling themselves 'free enterprisers,' the party system has been subject to periodic realignments. The story of the 1996 election, with its dramatic return of the NDP to a second term despite a lower percentage of the overall vote, is but the most recent chapter in this story. Norman Ruff's chapter on the legislature, which is the focus of much political conflict between elections, develops two quite distinct themes. He first demonstrates how much of BC's legislative practice and politics cannot be understood apart from an appreciation of the province's colonial heritage and ready acceptance of the British parliamentary tradition. The chapter then turns to questions of reform, and in particular how changing perspectives are challenging long-cherished, if traditional, notions and practices of representation.

The most long-delayed change to the political stage in BC has been the emergence of women as star players. As Lynda Erickson notes, the province was the first in the country to have a woman premier and, with the 1991 election, came to have a higher proportion of women in the legislature than any other Canadian province. Despite these changes, however, women are still far from having established parity with men in the political system, and feminist impulses in governmental decision-making processes remain rather fragile. The Harcourt government's creation of a Ministry of

Women's Equality marked a major attempt to change this, though it remains to be seen how much real difference it will make.

One element of politics that has endured since the development of a democratic franchise is the intimate connection between politics and the media. Politicians need the mass media to communicate with a mass electorate. The province's second premier was a man so enamoured with public life that he changed his name to Amor de Cosmos and founded a newspaper in 1860 to oppose Governor James Douglas. Politicians ever since have been wrestling with the communications media. Barbara McLintock, herself a working journalist, and Gerry Kristianson provide a lively account of the workings of the modern media in BC. But their chapter goes beyond a simple descriptive account to discuss a number of important normative issues that lie at the heart of any understanding of the role and impact of the media in liberal democracies.

In 'Governing the Province,' the third part of the book, there are chapters exploring the institutional core of public decision-making. Terence Morley leads off with a discussion of the system's political heart: the premier and his or her cabinet. This account reveals much about the structure and workings of BC governments, pointing to the great power they have and the real constraints they work under. Yet for all the formality of the system, different premiers bring stylistic differences to their governments, leading inevitably to a very personal style of governance. To balance this view of the political side of modern government, Norman Ruff provides a chapter on the provincial bureaucracy that supports the politicians and provides for the day-to-day delivery of public policies and government services. As he points out, over the past two decades the province has developed a modern, sophisticated public service to support expanded government activity. But that has, in turn, raised new problems, and Ruff explores the pressures that are now politicizing the senior levels of the bureaucracy and the consequences they bring in their wake. The final chapter in this part, again contributed by Terence Morley, deals with what is commonly referred to as the 'justice system.' In it Morley describes the constitutional and legal framework of life in the province, the attorney general, the police and correctional branches, the legal profession, and the judges and courts. This is the complex network of institutions and individuals responsible for enforcing the criminal law and for resolving, in an authoritative and enforceable way, private disputes.

The last part of the book is concerned with 'Patterns of Public Policy.' In the first of its six chapters, Gerry Kristianson notes that public policy is not solely the business of elected politicians or appointed bureaucrats. Every British Columbian has an interest – in fact, most have several interests – and they organize and work to influence those policy areas that concern them. Lobbying, per se, is not new, and Kristianson indicates how it has changed over the years. As a practitioner, he is able to draw on his intimate knowledge of the inner workings of the system to indicate, through a number of case studies, how influence is marshalled in this populist and polarized system. His chapter ends by asking a number of important questions about democratic politics.

Two chapters provide broad overviews of major policy areas. Brian Scarfe offers a masterful summary and explanation of the province's finances and fiscal policy. In it he first explains the federal-provincial financial system within which BC, like other provinces, operates. He then looks at expenditure and revenue patterns before considering the problems of debt management and the related issue of intergenerational equity. The chapter ends with a discussion of the province's budgeting system. Scarfe's contribution is a remarkably clear explanation of a very difficult and abstruse subject that is absolutely critical to understanding the realities of BC's governmental activity. Michael Prince's chapter provides an overview of the development and patterns of social policy and its making. As he points out, social policy and modern politics 'are inseparable,' and his developmental analysis of the patterns in BC reveals how these important policy areas are tied to constitutional and financial, as well as political, realities, and how social policy changes reflect the underlying dynamic of the province's political economy.

George Hoberg provides a chapter on forest policy. Given the vital importance of the forest industry to the development and modern economy of BC, an understanding of this policy area is critical. Hoberg's account takes readers into the policy-making process by examining a series of recent changes, especially the Clayoquot Sound imbroglio, that attracted worldwide attention, much to the government's discomfort. The chapter then goes beyond these descriptive case studies to explain the changes and to assess the extent to which they appear to have permanently transformed this policy area. By contrast, Kathryn Harrison's chapter explores the relatively new concerns raised by environmental politics. After considering the political system's 'green' impulses, Harrison turns to three case studies – the regulation of pulp mill effluents, the preservation of the Tatshenshini wilderness, and the Kemano Completion Project – to map the impact of changing values and polarized party competition on policy-making. Her analysis makes it clear that these kinds of issues are likely to continue to be important elements of the province's continuing public agenda.

The final chapter, by Richard Sigurdson, asks whether NDP governments are really any different from those of their opponents. In an important way, this chapter skilfully pulls together many of the themes raised throughout the book, asking whether parties, elections, and governments matter, and if so, how. It explores whether the patterns of governance and policy-making flow from party agendas or reflect more basic imperatives of the culture, economy, and history of the province. Sigurdson provides the reader with the added benefit of a review of Mike Harcourt's 1991-6 government, thus bringing the story of BC government and politics up to date.

Although we hope that this book will find an audience among all those interested in the politics, policies, and governments of the Canadian provinces, we realize that most who pore over its pages will have a primary interest in British Columbia. Perhaps the largest proportion of readers will be students, and it is largely with them in mind that the book has been conceived and for whom it has been written. We hope that they will find the descriptions, interpretations, and arguments interesting and stimulating. And we hope that these chapters will encourage readers to learn more about BC and move them to contribute to it, both as students and as citizens.

Part 1: Modern British Columbia

1
Value Conflicts in Lotusland: British Columbia Political Culture
Donald E. Blake

British Columbia is often viewed as a rather exotic or even eccentric place. During the 1950s and 1960s, editorial cartoonists had a field day with Social Credit supporters, portraying them as straitlaced, dark-suited men with halos or as equally sober women in flowery hats tut-tutting over the latest threat to their cosy existence from developers, immigrants, or leftists. When coupled with his grandiose schemes for economic development, puritanical lifestyle, and idiosyncratic behaviour at federal-provincial conferences, the initials of the premier at that time, W.A.C. Bennett, inevitably earned him the nickname 'Wacky Bennett.' Politicians on the left generated less colourful stereotypes, but contributed to the province's populist and polarized image through their links to a labour movement with a Marxist past and their unparalleled reputation for hostility to capitalism.

More recently, lifestyle images have come to predominate. BC is 'Lotusland,' where workplaces close early on Fridays and open late on Mondays to accommodate skiing, hiking, and the other activities of fitness fanatics. The province has spawned the most vigorous environmental movement in the country, the activities of which have led to dramatic confrontations with loggers and miners. Although the politics of environmental policy is explored in detail in Chapter 16, the examination of provincial political culture in this chapter includes a look at the value patterns linked to environmentalism.

Research in the 1970s and 1980s showed that the province's image as a battleground between left and right conducted by politicians with a keen awareness of the value of populist appeals is remarkably accurate. The picture is grounded in a political culture described as 'active, participative, populist, moralistic and striving,' where 'the choice among alternatives is seen by the actors as momentous and consequential, in short, worth fighting over.'[1] As demonstrated below, these divisions are still significant. However, they are crosscut by other value conflicts that have given 'new politics' issues, such as feminism and environmentalism, a prominent place on the political agenda. These divisions, together with economic restructuring and demographic changes produced by immigration, particularly from Asia, have profound implications for BC politics as the twentieth century draws to a close.

The 1970s: Populism and Polarization

The 1970s was a turbulent decade in BC politics. The NDP came into power in 1972 for the first time, with a political and economic agenda viewed by its opponents as a serious threat to the free enterprise system, precipitating a major realignment of the party system. In leading a successful drive to oust the NDP after only three years in office, Social Credit became the largest mass membership party in the province. Their success is partly attributable to a political culture with higher levels of citizen political efficacy – the belief that individuals can have a significant effect on political matters – than anywhere else in Canada. It also indicates the strength of populism in the province, 'the belief that "people like me" can get things done.'[2] The intensity of the reaction to the NDP victory is itself strong evidence of the mobilization potential of the competition between left and right.

In Canada, populism is rooted in the agrarian experience, particularly on the Prairies. Forced to cope with the vagaries of an international wheat economy in an uncertain climate, farmers came together for protection from the banks, the railroads, and a federal government viewed by turns as indifferent or hostile to their needs. Their activities gave rise to such parties as the Progressives, Social Credit, and the Co-operative Commonwealth Federation (CCF). While these parties differed in many respects and enjoyed varying degrees of success in national politics, all emphasized the importance of direct action and grassroots involvement in organizational activity and policy development, and were suspicious (and sometimes fearful) of the traditional elite, whether they be in business, the professions, or government. The parties based on these sentiments are not exclusively left-wing or right-wing, demonstrating that populist values have an appeal across the traditional ideological spectrum.

In BC during the 1970s, the populist legacy could be seen in both the NDP and Social Credit. Like the CCF before it, the NDP placed a heavy emphasis on democratic control within the party. Its leader, Dave Barrett, tie loosened and shirtsleeves rolled up, was just as capable of denouncing the pretensions of the highly educated, the insensitivity of the bureaucrats, and the evils of corporate finance as any stump speaker in the 1930s. His principal opponent, W.A.C. Bennett, had appropriated the Social Credit label from a small band of monetary reformers and used it to create a party based on small town BC, where the fitness of ordinary citizens for governing was taken for granted. Long after it became unfashionable in other parts of Canada, Bennett could be counted on to rally his troops at election time with the cry: 'The socialists are at the gates!' Even while implicitly challenging this view of the threat from the left, Bill Bennett, W.A.C. Bennett's successor as party leader and premier, acknowledged the importance of populism in the province's political culture. As he once put it, 'No party of the extreme right or the extreme left can survive. We are a populist party slightly to the right of centre. The NDP is a populist party slightly to the left.'[3]

The cross-party appeal of populist values at the time is apparent from data on public opinion taken from the 1979 BC Election Study.[4] Those in lower-status occupations, the less educated, and those living outside the major urban areas were more likely to endorse populist sentiments. However, each of the two major parties contained a mix of populists and non-populists, so that, on average, there was no significant difference between them in terms of populist appeal.[5]

Left/right differences between parties were much more clear cut. Social Credit was the party preferred by more 'individualistic' citizens, those more hostile to government regulation and more likely to believe that individuals rather than government must assume responsibility for their own economic well-being. Conversely, the NDP was favoured by those more willing to endorse collective, government-devised solutions to personal and societal economic problems. Significantly, however, and contrary to conventional wisdom at the time, the two major parties appealed across the 'class divide.' Working-class 'individualists' were just as important a part of Social Credit's electoral base as middle-class 'collectivists' were for the NDP's.[6]

Several developments over the past ten to fifteen years have profound implications for the province's political culture, as well as for the link between political values and partisanship. Immigration, especially from Asia, has altered the demographic profile, most significantly in Vancouver and the cities and suburbs to the east and south. According to the 1991 census, people of Asian ethnic origin accounted for an average of 17.5% of the population in thirty-three provincial electoral districts in the city of Vancouver and the adjacent suburbs. In one riding, Vancouver Kensington, people of Asian origin are a majority (51.3%).[7] The unevenness of the demographic changes may ultimately contribute to the reemergence of a form of regionalism, as less than 3% of the population outside the Lower Mainland is of Asian origin.

A significant portion of the province's population has moved there from other parts of the country, with less than half (47.9%) having been born in BC. Over a quarter (29.2%) were born elsewhere in Canada, and just under a quarter (22.9%) came from abroad. Together, these demographic developments have reduced the proportion of the population with ties to BC's past, and, especially in the case of international migration, have brought to the province thousands of individuals whose views of politics have been shaped by different experiences and value systems. The significance for provincial politics of issues such as environmental protection, affirmative action, and human rights also means that residents of the province, native born and newcomers alike, have been exposed to the forces behind the 'silent revolution' in values associated with decades of prosperity and peace.[8]

Finally, as discussed in detail in Chapter 2, the shift in emphasis in the provincial economy from resource extraction to services, especially through expansion of public sector employment, has accelerated. At the same time, the union movement, once the mainstay of the left, has become increasingly white collar and less based in private sector employment.

The parties themselves have changed, as has the pattern of party competition. At the leadership level in the NDP, populist rhetoric has been virtually eliminated. From 1987 to 1995, the party was led by a lawyer, Mike Harcourt, and it currently includes a substantial number of highly educated professionals in its legislative ranks. Glen Clark, the party's current leader, has a degree in urban planning. Like other parties of the left in the Western world, the NDP now places more emphasis on fiscal responsibility, partnership with the private sector, and the need to rein in the costs of social programs. Its principal opponent is a revitalized Liberal Party with no populist tradition, which, as detailed in Chapter 5, has attracted the bulk of the Social Credit Party's middle-class support. The Reform Party, the only other significant player in provincial politics, has siphoned off the most populist elements in the former Social Credit base. In other words, in policy terms the significance of the left/right division has been reduced and populist rhetoric pushed into the background.

None of these developments necessarily means that populist values or fundamental differences between left and right have been eliminated from the province's political culture. However, they do suggest that new perspectives have been added and that the balance between competing values has shifted. So, too, might their links with the party system. These possibilities are explored in the remainder of this chapter.

The 1990s: Populism and Polarization Revisited
According to a major study of value patterns conducted by the Angus Reid Group, British Columbians continue to exhibit higher levels of political efficacy than other Canadians. This conclusion is based on statistics showing that the proportion of British Columbians who believe that politics and government are too complicated for ordinary people to understand (47%) and that ordinary people do not have a say in what government does (45%) is substantially less than in the rest of Canada (66% and 50%, respectively). However, provincial residents were at least as likely as other Canadians to express cynical and distrustful views of politicians and the

political system.[9] This aspect of BC's political culture is essentially unchanged from the 1970s. Moreover, just as in the past, the highly educated are more trusting and more efficacious than the less well educated.

For an examination of contemporary populism and divisions between left and right political views, we turn to a survey conducted in June and July 1995 that contained several questions comparable to those used in previous studies. From this, it is clear that populism and polarization remain significant features of provincial political culture.

The 1995 survey contained four questions designed to measure the strength and distribution of populist sentiments. In particular, they identify those people who have significant concerns about personal empowerment in dealings with politicians and bureaucrats, and who believe in the importance of having ordinary people participate in political and economic decisions affecting their lives.[10] Respondents were asked to indicate the extent to which they agreed or disagreed with the following statements, which, when combined, yield a scale with possible scores from 0 through 6 depending on the number of statements a respondent agreed with and the strength of agreement:

- We could probably solve most of the big political problems if government could actually be brought back to people at the grassroots.
- Communities grow best through private decisions by individuals who know their own needs.
- A high priority should be placed on giving people more say in important government decisions.
- What we need is a government that protects the environment without all this red tape.

Although populist values continue to be widely shared (the average score is 4.4 on this scale), they remain more characteristic of the less educated and the less well off. As shown in Table 1.1, those with a secondary education or less have higher average scores (4.4 or higher compared to 4.2) on the populism scale than those with at least some postsecondary education. Moreover, 25.6% and 34.2%, respectively, of those with only an elementary education or some high school appear in the most populist group, compared to only 20% of those with higher educational levels.[11] Conversely, those with low scores on populism are over-represented among the best educated and under-represented among those with less education.

An even larger gap appears if we look at differences in the distribution of populist values within income groups. Only 18.2% of the wealthiest group in the population falls in the most populist group, compared to 30.5% of those in the lowest income category. Mean scores also differ significantly between income groups.

Table 1.1

Populism and social structure (horizontal percentages)

	Populism category				Mean score	Number of cases
	Lowest	2	3	Highest		
Income						
< $35,000	16.4	27.9	25.3	30.5	4.5	495
$35-$55,000	22.1	30.2	22.3	25.4	4.3	358
> $55,000	26.4	27.3	28.1	18.2	4.2	417
Education						
Elementary or less	20.5	25.6	28.2	25.6	4.4	39
Some secondary	16.1	21.7	28.0	34.2	4.6	535
Some postsecondary	24.9	31.4	23.6	20.1	4.2	907
Ethnic origin						
European	21.6	26.4	26.4	25.5	4.4	1,253
Asian	20.1	34.5	24.2	21.2	4.3	264
Other	14.5	29.0	21.7	34.8	4.5	69
Approximate total	21.1	27.9	25.9	25.2	4.4	

Notes: Populism was measured using a four-item scale with scores from 0 (low populism) to 6 (high populism). The four populism categories in the table were produced by dividing the range of scores for the sample as a whole approximately into quartiles. Results for ethnic origin include those from a supplementary sample of Mandarin-, Cantonese-, and Punjabi-speaking people in the Lower Mainland. Total frequencies differ slightly among the three parts of the table because of differences in the number of cases. The figures shown in the last row of the table are based on the distribution of populist values by ethnic origin.

Somewhat surprising, given BC's particular partisan history, is that birthplace – whether individuals were born in BC, elsewhere in Canada, or in a foreign country – made no difference. Table 1.1 does show that populism is slightly more common among British Columbians of European origin compared to those from Asian backgrounds (25.5% versus 21.2% are in the most populist group). However, the difference is well within sampling error, and the average scores (4.4 and 4.3, respectively) do not differ significantly.

During the 1970s and 1980s, provincial politics was suffused with the rhetoric of left versus right. From W.A.C. Bennett's final warning cry about 'socialists at the gates' through the economic restraint program of his successor, William Bennett, British Columbians on both sides of the ideological divide struggled to forward their own political and economic agendas. Ideological divisions among the mass public can be measured in a number of ways. In the 1979 election study, an 'individualism versus collectivism' scale was used to tap basic values about the degree of individual versus state responsibility for individual social and economic well-being, one of the key differences between contemporary conservative and liberal political philosophies. Examination of current value differences between left and right is based on responses to three questions in the 1995 survey dealing with government policy instruments in the area of the environment: taxation, regulation of business, and controls over land use.

Although all three questions focus specifically on environmental policy (that was the purpose of the survey itself), responses to them can be used to distinguish between those hostile to increased taxes versus those willing to accept higher taxes to achieve social objectives, between opponents and supporters of government regulation of business, and between hard-liners and their opponents on the issue of property rights. The particular pattern of responses would probably differ depending on what policy area was being considered, but more conservative individuals would be more likely to take a position against higher taxes, against increased regulation of business, and in favour of property rights than those with more liberal views.

The actual questions used to produce a 'neoconservatism' scale were the following, with scale scores ranging from 1 to 7 depending on the number of conservative responses (defined as those opposing government action in each case) and the intensity of the response:

• The government should do more to protect the environment, even if it leads to higher taxes.
• To prevent the destruction of natural resources, the government must have the right to control private land use.
• Protection of the environment requires more extensive regulation of business by government.

Table 1.2 presents the distribution of conservative values within categories defined on the basis of family income, education, and ethnic origin. Unlike the case for populism, differences on the left/right spectrum are only weakly related to socioeconomic status. There is no significant difference between income groups in average neoconservatism scores – all are within one decimal point of the overall average score of 3.4. If anything, those who are less well off are more likely to hold conservative views than those in the highest income group. Nearly 29% of those in the lowest income category fall into the most conservative group, compared to under 25% of those in the highest income category. Conservative views are also somewhat more common among those with less education. Although it would be unwise to make too much of a difference that is not statistically significant, the link between lower education and conservative values hints at the persistence of a working-class conservative streak in the province's political culture that was important in the cross-class appeal of political

Table 1.2

Neoconservatism and social structure (horizontal percentages)

	Neoconservatism category				Mean score	Number of cases
	Lowest	2	3	Highest		
Income						
< $35,000	29.6	25.0	17.3	28.2	3.4	504
$35-$55,000	27.9	27.3	19.1	25.7	3.3	366
> $55,000	27.3	30.4	18.0	24.3	3.3	444
Education						
Elementary or less	27.9	27.9	9.3	34.9	3.6	43
Some secondary	24.8	25.3	19.1	30.8	3.5	561
Some postsecondary	30.5	27.1	17.5	24.9	3.3	937
Ethnic origin						
European	28.4	26.3	17.8	27.6	3.4	1,310
Asian	26.7	27.8	21.9	23.6	3.3	288
Other	34.8	23.2	17.4	24.6	3.3	69
Approximate total	28.4	26.4	18.5	26.8	3.4	

Notes: Neoconservatism was measured using a three-item scale with possible scores from 1 (extreme liberal) to 7 (extreme conservative). The four categories of neoconservatism in the table were produced by dividing the range of scores in the sample as a whole approximately into quartiles. Results for ethnic origin include those from a supplementary sample of Mandarin-, Cantonese-, and Punjabi-speaking people in the Lower Mainland. Total frequencies differ slightly among the three parts of the table because of differences in the number of cases. The figures shown in the last row of the table are based on the distribution of neoconservative values by ethnic origin.

parties during the 1970s. This possibility is explored in more detail in Chapter 5.

Differences in neoconservatism by educational background are some-what more suggestive. Conservative values are considerably over-represented among the group with the least amount of education (34.9%) and some-what over-represented among those with only some high school education (30.8%). Conversely, those with the highest levels of education have the lowest average neoconservatism score (3.3) and proportionately the fewest (24.9%) in the most conservative group.

Differences by ethnic origin have been included in Table 1.2 in order to demonstrate that the increased presence of those with Asian cultural roots has, apparently, no implications for the division between left and right in the provincial political culture. Just as was the case with populism, within sampling error, there is no difference in the proportions of those from European or Asian backgrounds in the four neoconservatism categories.

Building upon the pioneering work of Ronald Inglehart, several studies have shown that Canadians, too, exhibit changes in value priorities linked to post-Second World War economic prosperity.[12] Generally speaking, those who came of age after the war give higher priority to values such as protecting the environment, having a say in governmental decisions, and freedom of speech than to values such as economic stability, law and order, and maintaining strong defence forces. This phenomenon has been shown to exist in all Western capitalist democracies. The explanation seems to be linked to the fact that younger age cohorts, having no direct experience of the Great Depression and the war that followed it, have come to take economic and military security for granted and therefore give higher priority to 'postmaterial' values.

Following Inglehart, the 1995 survey asked people to indicate whether they give high, medium, low, or no priority to each of twelve goals. Scale scores could range from -6 for those at the materialist end to +12 for those at the extreme postmaterialist position.[13] These twelve goals are:

Materialist
- maintain a high rate of economic growth
- make sure Canada has strong defence forces
- maintain a strong economy
- fight rising prices
- maintain order in the nation
- fight against crime

Postmaterialist
- give people more say in important government decisions
- progress toward a less impersonal, more humane society
- see that people have more say in how things get decided at work and in their community
- protect freedom of speech
- protect nature from being spoiled and polluted
- progress toward a society where ideas are more important than money.

The BC sample exhibits the expected relationship between age and the priority given to postmaterialist values. There is a sharp break in average scores on the postmaterialism scale between those born before 1940 compared to the younger group. The older cohort scores significantly lower on the postmaterialism scale. Postmaterialism is also clearly a distinctive attitudinal dimension. The postmaterialism scale is only weakly correlated (-.19) with neoconservatism and has no relationship at all with populism.

Table 1.3

Postmaterialism and social structure (horizontal percentages)

	Postmaterialism category					
	Lowest	2	3	Highest	Mean score	Number of cases
Income						
< $35,000	29.1	15.0	28.9	26.9	1.0	532
$35-$55,000	24.3	14.9	31.2	29.6	1.2	375
> $55,000	22.3	14.6	33.3	29.8	1.4	453
Education						
Elementary or less	34.0	21.3	36.2	8.5	0.3	47
Some secondary	28.5	18.8	32.3	20.4	0.8	592
Some postsecondary	23.1	13.5	31.1	32.3	1.4	969
Ethnic origin						
European	25.5	14.7	31.1	28.8	1.2	1,363
Asian	44.4	18.2	27.3	10.1	-0.1	297
Other	24.7	15.1	30.1	30.1	1.3	73
Approximate total	28.7	15.3	30.4	25.6	1.0	

Notes: Postmaterialism was measured using a twelve-item scale with scores from -6 (extreme materialism) to +8 (extreme postmaterialism). The four categories of postmaterialism in the table were produced by dividing the range of scores for the sample as a whole approximately into quartiles. Results for ethnic origin include those from a supplementary sample of Mandarin-, Cantonese-, and Punjabi-speaking people in the Lower Mainland. Total frequencies differ slightly among the three parts of the table because of differences in the number of cases. The figures shown in the last row of the table are based on the distribution of postmaterial values by ethnic origin.

More important for our purposes are the linkages between postmaterialism and other aspects of social structure. Our two measures of socioeconomic status – education and household income – are both related to postmaterialism. Those better educated and better off economically are significantly more likely to give priority to postmaterialist values (see Table 1.3). For example, 32.3% of those with some postsecondary education are found in the most postmaterialist group, compared to only 8.5% of those with an elementary education or less and 20.4% of those with some secondary education. Income differences are less stark, but also show that individuals from wealthier families are more likely than those from poorer backgrounds to be postmaterialists. This result also helps to validate the postmaterialism measure since one would expect those whose economic circumstances are less favourable to place a higher priority on material values.

The relationship with perhaps the greatest significance for BC political culture is that between postmaterialism and ethnic origin. Only about 10%

of those from Asian backgrounds are found in the group that places the greatest priority on postmaterialist values, compared to just under 30% of those whose roots are in Europe. Clearly, to the extent that new politics issues appear on the political agenda, they will have less resonance with the value priorities of an increasingly significant proportion of the population.

A substantial number (30.1%) of those in the 'other origin' category also fall into the most postmaterialist group, but the category is too small and too diverse to allow reliable generalizations. Interestingly, however, the most postmaterialist group in the sample (with an average score of 1.4) consists of those with a First Nations background. Unfortunately, there are only twenty-four of them in the study.

We now turn to the links between political culture and partisanship. Our partisanship measure uses provincial vote intention from the 1995 survey. As discussed above, during the 1970s groups of partisans were easier to distinguish in terms of left versus right rather than in terms of populism. The two major partisan groups at the time – Social Credit and the NDP – though differing significantly in ideology, had roughly equal proportions of populists and non-populists among their supporters. With three significant parties now vying for support – the NDP, Liberals, and BC Reform – the picture is more complicated. Left versus right remains a significant distinguishing feature among partisan groups; however, one party is clearly

Figure 1.1

Populism and partisanship

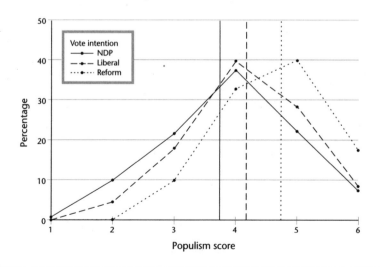

Note: Median position for each group marked with vertical line.

more dominated by populists than was true in the past. These observations are based on the patterns shown in Figures 1.1 and 1.2, which portray the distributions within groups, defined in terms of provincial vote intention, on the populism and neoconservatism scales.

The populism measure used here is not exactly the same as the one used in the 1979 election study, making precise comparisons impossible. However, it appears that populists may constitute a lower proportion of NDP voters than in the past. Using the same categories as in Table 1.1, fewer than 20% of NDP supporters are strong populists. This stands in sharp contrast to the pattern among BC Reform supporters, where 38.3% are from the most populist group. Liberal supporters are less distinct in this regard, with virtually the same proportion – around 22% – in the least populist and most populist groups. However, while the distributions of the populism scores within the Liberal and NDP groups shown in Figure 1.1 are rather similar, the median position (the score that divides a group in half) for Liberals is more populist than that for the NDP. There is no question, however, that Reform voters are much more concentrated in the most populist end of the spectrum. In other words, whereas the 1979 survey showed no significant difference between groups of partisans on this dimension, in the mid-1990s populism is more common among Reform voters than among supporters of its two major opponents.

Figure 1.2 reveals a similar alignment of partisans. Partisans form three distinctive groups along the left/right spectrum, with New Democrat voters

Figure 1.2

Neoconservatism and partisanship

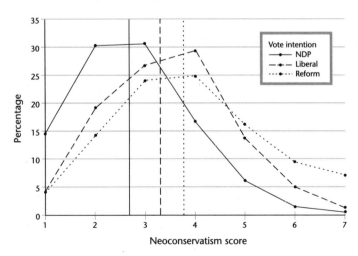

Note: Median position for each group marked with vertical line.

at one end, BC Reform supporters at the other, and Liberals in the middle. Using the same divisions as in Table 1.2, a substantial plurality (44.8%) of NDP supporters consist of people with the most liberal views, compared to only 23.2% for the Liberal Party and 18.1% for Reform. Conversely, the ranks of BC Reform contain a higher proportion with conservative views (39.5%), compared to 30.1% for the Liberals and a tiny proportion (11.4%) for the NDP.

We turn finally to an examination of postmaterialism, the value pattern associated with new politics issues (see Figure 1.3). The differentiation among partisan groups is similar to that associated with neoconservatism, with postmaterialists over-represented among New Democrats and under-represented among Reform voters, with Liberals in the middle but rather closer to Reform than to the NDP. Using the same categories as in Table 1.3, a substantial plurality of New Democrat voters (42.9%) can be classified as strong postmaterialists. The comparable figures for the Liberals and BC Reform are 20.7% and 15.7%, respectively. Conversely, roughly one-third of Liberal and Reform voters (32.0% and 31.0%, respectively) are strong materialists, compared to only 16.9% for the NDP.

Nevertheless, it is important to point out that none of these groups of voters is monolithic. As Figures 1.1 through 1.3 clearly illustrate, each contains a significant number of people who differ in some fashion from the dominant image conveyed by the overall average for the group. We know from observations of provincial politics that the clash between

Figure 1.3

Postmaterialism and partisanship

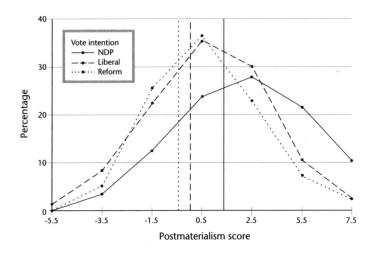

Note: Median position for each group marked with vertical line.

environmentalists and those favouring fewer restraints on economic activities with potentially harmful effects on the environment produces strains within the New Democratic Party, just as do differences over the role of government in economic management and social engineering. Similar divisions occur among Liberal and Reform activists. Hence, the single-minded pursuit of a particular ideological agenda by any party is potentially costly in terms of voter support. The nature of partisan alignments is explored more fully in Chapter 5.

Conclusion

Despite significant political and economic changes over the past ten to fifteen years, continuities in BC political culture are impressive. Ideological differences persist largely independently of class or other social group differences in the population. Populism, which in the 1970s was a prominent feature of the style of election campaigns and the conduct of debate in the provincial legislature, is an orientation that still has considerable appeal, especially among the less educated and less well off. However, the restructuring of the provincial party system has destroyed what were two partisan subcultures, whose members were committed to either the NDP or Social Credit.

Populism remains a significant feature of the provincial value pattern. The populist/non-populist division still exists independently of the cleavage between left and right. The link between social class and partisanship is still mediated by these value patterns. Nevertheless, changes in the pattern of party competition have altered the characteristics of partisan groups, sharpening some differences while reducing others. Moreover, the clash between materialist and postmaterialist values, which also distinguishes the parties' electoral bases, has emerged as an important feature of the province's political culture. It is also linked to differences in ethnic origin, a division that has been and will undoubtedly continue to be a source of social and political conflict.

The bulk of the NDP electorate is located left of centre, although the party is not exclusively their preserve. BC Reform, like Social Credit before it, is a mirror image of the NDP in terms of the left versus right division. Its supporters are, on average, more right-wing, but a substantial number are found at different places on the ideological spectrum. On the other hand, populism now serves to differentiate party supporters in a way it previously did not. While individuals with different levels of acceptance of populist values are found in both parties, populists are much more prominent among Reform supporters than among New Democrats.

Not surprisingly, given the Liberal Party's emergence as a major player in provincial politics and its role as official opposition to the NDP government following the 1991 election, Liberal supporters are significantly more right-wing than supporters of the NDP. However, they are more moderate than Reform voters. Liberal supporters are also midway between the NDP and Reform on the populism dimension. A third value dimension, postmaterialism, aligns the same three groups of party supporters in the same way.

In short, BC political culture exhibits considerable continuity. Populism and the clash between left-wing and right-wing political philosophies, which characterized the province's image in the heyday of Social Credit, still structure the political orientations of the electorate. Generational value differences linked to the increasing importance of postmaterialism and new politics issues have been added to the mix as well. However, the province's Asian ethnic minority, whose ranks have been swelled dramatically by immigration during the past decade, appears to attach much greater priority to traditional materialist values such as law and order and economic security. They represent an increasingly significant portion of the electorate in the Lower Mainland.

In one sense, given the political alignments associated with value differences, the stage appears to have been set for a reduction in the intensity of political conflict associated with fundamental value differences. Liberal Party supporters seem to occupy the middle ground on all three of the value dimensions explored in this chapter, giving the party the opportunity to play a moderating role between two extremes. However, for reasons outlined in greater detail in Chapter 5, that seems unlikely. Since the 1950s, the intensity of value disagreements, particularly over left/right issues, has forced political alignments in provincial politics into a two-party mould.

Further Reading
Blake, Donald E. *Two Political Worlds: Parties and Voting in British Columbia*. Vancouver: UBC Press 1985
Blake, Donald E., R.K. Carty, and Lynda Erickson. *Grassroots Politicians: Party Activists in British Columbia*. Vancouver: UBC Press 1991
Dyck, Rand. *Provincial Politics in Canada*. 2nd. ed. Toronto: Prentice Hall 1991
Morley, John T. 'Politics as Theatre: Paradox and Complexity in British Columbia.' *Journal of Canadian Studies* 25 (1990): 19-37
Simeon, Richard, and David J. Elkins. 'Provincial Political Cultures in Canada.' In *Small Worlds: Provinces and Parties in Canadian Political Life*, edited by David J. Elkins and Richard Simeon, 31-76. Toronto: Methuen 1980
Walker, R.B.J. 'Politics, Ideology and Everyday Life.' In *After Bennett: A New Politics for British Columbia*, edited by Warren Magnusson, Charles Doyle, R.B.J. Walker, and John De Marco, 325-35. Vancouver: New Star 1986

2

From Timber to Tourism: The Political Economy of British Columbia

Michael Howlett and Keith Brownsey

Although often viewed by journalists, pundits, and academics as a province characterized by a form of populist class conflict originating in the primary resource employment conditions of its inhabitants,[1] British Columbia has not conformed to this popular myth for some time. In fact, as early as 1911, over half of BC's labour force was employed in service sector activities,[2] reflecting the significant role played by transportation activities in the province's history from its entry into Confederation. Serving as the terminus of the transcontinental Canadian Pacific Railway (and the later Canadian Northern and Grand Trunk Pacific Railways), as well as enjoying the port of Vancouver's vital role in the export of all kinds of goods produced in the interior of the country, BC's employment has always reflected a diversity of sectoral occupations.

Even during the first major forest sector boom after 1911, primary sector employment declined as the expansion of the forestry industry resulted not so much in additional employment in logging and other primary industries but rather in an increase in secondary manufacturing in the sawmill and pulp and paper industries. Between 1951 and 1991, as mechanization overtook logging and fishing activities,[3] the primary sector declined even further to the point where just over 6 percent of the provincial labour force is now employed in these occupations.[4]

The political impact of the early dependence on resource-based economic activity was felt in a number of ways. Since these activities tended to take place in specific geographic locations determined by resource availability, they accentuated the regional structure of a province whose mountainous topography rendered communications and transportation expensive and difficult. As a result of both economy and geography, the economic and political centres in BC have always had some rivalry with each other, while the province's north has long resented what it believes is its subservient status to the population centres of the Lower Mainland and Vancouver Island.

Over the course of BC history, each of the regions has gained, and often lost, a certain amount of either political or economic power depending on the vagaries of international resource markets and prices, and the ebbs and flows of population to and from various regions in pursuit of high wages and work.[5] There has been competition between different groups or elites within the province over access to, and control over, resources and the course of local development. This competition has led to many confrontations between the different elements of provincial society over the proper role and purpose of government in the promotion of economic and social development.[6]

In the past, this regional tension was exacerbated by the rather stark social structure of mine, smelter, and forest towns in the rural areas of the province in which many workers had significant elements of their lives controlled by corporations headquartered in the Lower Mainland or outside the province.[7] Conflicts and confrontations over jobs and living and working conditions dovetailed with conflicts over local autonomy and control to produce a 'politics of exploitation' in which workers combated businesses in a heavily regionalized fashion.[8]

Although the legacies of the earlier era still persist, and many issues in the province are still defined in the popular press and political debate in regional terms,[9] this pattern of regionalized class conflict has changed over the past half century for a number of reasons. First, modern developments in transportation and communication technologies have overcome many of these 'natural' boundaries to provincial social cohesion and have greatly reduced the salience of regional conflicts in electoral terms.[10] Second, successive BC governments, like those of other Canadian provinces, have been engaged in a long process of institution-building, or 'province-building,' which has been designed, at least in part, to help overcome the fragmenting and decentralizing effects of geographic regionalism.[11] Provincial governments have constructed a sophisticated provincial bureaucracy that now provides the provincial population with a diversified economic base, performing many large and essential social services including the provision of uniform educational, health, and social welfare programs.[12] Scattered throughout the province, these services lessen the dependence of even remote areas on the health of the staples resource sector, and aid the socialization of the provincial populace in a common direction.

The strains imposed by the development of the service sector on a political system long dominated by interests associated with the production of staples products have been evident in the emergence of conflicts that have pitted logger against environmentalist and private capital against the public sector.[13] The expansion of the provincial state to accommodate the needs of both the staples and service sectors, the changing nature of economic activity as production has shifted from mill, mine, and factory to the office floor, and gender issues related to increasing numbers of women entering the service sector workforce have all helped to reshape the political life of the province in recent years.[14] From tourism to film to financial services, for the majority of the population this service economy has led to a pattern of provincial political life that differs greatly from that of the old resource-based economy.[15]

This chapter sets out the principal elements of the old and new BC political economies and outlines several of the most important implications that this shift in provincial occupational structures has had for contemporary BC politics.

The Old BC Political Economy: Frontier Exploitation

BC began its history as a settler colony based on resource exploitation. The first permanent European settlements in BC were in the northeastern corner of the province, established as outposts of the fur-trading empires of the Hudson's Bay Company and its rivals. Spanish explorers charted the southern coast and inland waters on expeditions mounted from Mexico and Peru, while Russian fur traders visited the coast from their stations in Alaska, Hawaii, and California. By the late eighteenth and early nineteenth centuries, most of these early explorers were replaced by British and American traders who wanted control of the Oregon Territory surrounding the Columbia River and access to the interior of the continent that the river provided.[16]

Together, these various adventurers created a small, fur-based economy that succeeded in disrupting long-established aboriginal hunting, trapping, and fishing methods, drawing the existing population into a primitive market economy.[17] The rudimentary institutions of government were established in this era and changed very little with the colony's entrance into Confederation in 1874.[18] In 1885, however, the character of the province changed completely with the completion of the Canadian Pacific Railway, which linked BC to the growing Canadian domestic market – and especially to the demand for large supplies of timber required to construct settlements in the Prairies.[19] The completion of the Panama Canal in 1917 further opened up European markets to BC fish and mineral exports, and contributed to the creation of the resource economy characteristic of the first half of the twentieth century in the province.

Dominated by local business elites, the provincial government granted large tracts of land to consortia planning to build railways. As a result of this policy, large amounts of timber and other resources fell into private hands.[20] Immediately upon completion of the CPR, eastern lumber interests, both Canadian and American, began to display an interest in largely untouched West Coast timber supplies. Local mills grew as the demand for timber in the expanding terminus city of Vancouver grew, and new mills were established by eastern interests to supply the BC, Manitoba, and Midwestern US markets.[21] Although its impact was great, this era of pure exploitation of the province's resources for company profits and government revenues was much shorter lived in BC than in central or eastern Canada. This was due to the late period in which the industry developed, and to the large size and relatively sophisticated nature of the companies that entered the province between 1888 and 1910.[22]

In the nineteenth and early twentieth centuries, political life in BC was focused on one issue: economic expansion through resource development. As governments collapsed and re-formed with great regularity, the one constant was an emphasis on the promotion of ever greater resource exploitation. Political parties began to take a recognized form, and party government was introduced in 1903, with a central pillar in party policy being various positions adopted on the future shape of the provincial economy.[23] At the same time, the amounts of capital needed in mining and forestry increased due to economies of scale in producing for an ever-expanding global market. In response, the Conservative government of Richard McBride sought to create a stable climate for resource investment, in part by modifying resource regulations to ensure that investors received a large return on their investments through guaranteed access to cheap resources.[24]

By 1908, however, the provincial government discovered that a 'laissez-faire' lumber industry policy, in the face of large, well-organized, and experienced private operators, quickly led to a crisis in which much of the timber on crown lands threatened to elude government control entirely, with no guarantee of any significant investment in resource development.[25] This resulted in the establishment of the Royal Commission of Inquiry on Timber and Forestry (the Fulton Commission) in 1910 and an end to unregulated resource exploitation.[26]

The Fulton Commission ushered in the beginnings of a new era in the province as the provincial government began to take the first steps toward a more prominent role in resource regulation. Marking the beginning of the creation of a modern administrative state in the province,[27] this new regulatory environment was resisted by different elements of provincial society and would take many years to alter the underlying structure of BC's political economy.

The Consolidation of the Staples Political Economy:
The Growth of the Public Sector and the Concentration of Capital

As the staples-based political economy moved from the era of relatively unfettered resource exploitation to one of resource management, the provincial government and public sector slowly came to take on most of the form of a modern welfare state. As it did, the traditional political party system broke down, and a new one emerged that centred on the politics of class. The 'new politics' of the old political economy, solidified during the Second World War as the Co-operative Commonwealth Federation (CCF), emerged as the electoral voice of the provincial labour movement and became a serious rival for political power at the polls. The emergence and strength of the CCF resulted in a series of coalitions on the part of the supporters and leaders of traditional political parties, who joined forces to keep the CCF from office.[28]

With the Second World War as a catalyst, the first coalition government oversaw a massive expansion in the primary exploitation and secondary processing of the province's natural resources – notably in pulp and paper, and aluminum smelting – and a parallel expansion in social services provided by the state. The province's submission to the 1950 Conference of Federal and Provincial Governments showed that the increases in economic activity were substantial. In the ten years from 1939 to 1949, the provincial population increased by more than 40 percent, while the gross value of forestry production tripled from $102.8 million in 1940 to $360.0 million in 1949. Mineral production almost doubled over the same period, growing from $75.7 million to $133.0 million. The gross value of total provincial production jumped from $311.0 million to $960.0 million by 1949.[29]

The period from 1941 to 1952 also witnessed the consolidation of many provincial resource companies into larger units, and the entrance into BC of large multinational resource companies such as Crown-Zellerbach, Anaconda, Bethlehem, Kaiser, and Alcan. In the forest sector, the Sloan Commission of 1945 set the tone for the future development of provincial forests by large capital. The commission recommended, and the government implemented, a modified tenure arrangement and imposed land management costs on forest companies. These two changes served as barriers to entry into the industry for small non-integrated producers and gave substantial cost advantages to vertically integrated firms.[30]

Significantly, during this period government expenditure as a percentage of the gross provincial product (GPP) also nearly doubled. Provincial spending on roads and bridges rose nearly 500 percent between 1940 and 1950, jumping from $2.9 million to $14.4 million. Outlays for education also increased dramatically. In 1940 the province spent $4.5 million on schools and universities; by 1950 the figure was almost $14.3 million. The government also introduced hospital insurance in 1948, providing coverage for all provincial residents and a ready method of financing massive hospital construction.[31]

In 1952 the anti-CCF coalition of Liberals and Conservatives collapsed due to internal squabbling among party leaders, but the coalition reemerged in the form of a provincial Social Credit Party.[32] W.A.C. Bennett's Social Credit government, however, merely continued the old coalition policy of consolidating the resource economy while expanding public services.

Extensions of the provincially owned railway system were announced annually in budget speeches, as were major highway developments and other improvements to the provincial economic infrastructure. While professing the importance of small business, Bennett assisted the expansion of large corporations and created a small business sector dependent on either transnational corporations or the state for its existence.[33] Tax concessions, royalty holidays, low stumpage rates, and inexpensive hydroelectricity for large resource companies were all features of Bennett's economic policy.[34]

Bennett also continued the coalitions' policy of countering CCF demands for 'provincialization' of the resource sector by providing a variety of social services through the public service. Employment in the public sector expanded as new schools, hospitals, and postsecondary institutions were built to serve the needs of the increased population. The number of highway and transportation workers also increased in order to construct and administer this new physical infrastructure.[35]

With the consolidation of the resource sector by large capital and the creation of a large public sector, the composition of the provincial workforce changed substantially between 1952 and 1972. As Table 2.1 shows, employment in the non-manual sector of the economy grew rapidly from 437,688 jobs in 1951 to 824,489 in 1971, an increase of almost 100 percent in absolute terms and an increase of 13 percent of the provincial labour force.

Many of the newly emerging technical and managerial jobs created during this period were directly dependent on public sector spending, as was a substantial proportion of the overall provincial labour force. From 1952 until 1972, when the W.A.C. Bennett Socreds were finally removed from office by the NDP, government expenditures doubled, rising from 6.5 to over 13 percent of the GPP.[36]

In 1972 the Social Credit coalition broke down and the renamed New Democratic Party – formed from the CCF – gained power under David Barrett. The Barrett government came to power promising reforms in education,

Table 2.1

Rise of non-manual labour in BC, 1941-71

Year	% of labour force	Number of non-manual jobs	% increase
1941	39	312,758	
1951	47	437,688	40
1961	55	560,462	28
1971	60	824,489	47

Source: Rennie Warburton and David Coburn, 'The Rise of Non-manual Work in British Columbia,' *BC Studies* 59 (1983): 5-27.

health care, and social services. Although it was subsequently criticized for its lack of commitment to socialist principles[37] and for its evident lack of managerial skills in putting its policies into operation,[38] the NDP nevertheless did manage to augment government control over the resource sector and to help consolidate the emerging provincial service sector society. This was apparent in its attempts to control profits and capture economic rents through the creation of government monopolies over the marketing of natural gas and oil through the BC Petroleum Corporation (BCPC), the provincialization of automobile insurance under the Insurance Corporation of BC (ICBC), and the implementation of an accelerated mineral royalty tax.[39] It cemented its support in the new middle class and the public sector working class by extending collective bargaining rights to the BC Government Employees' Union (BCGEU).[40] In a major blunder, however, it legislated striking lumber, ferry, and pulp and paper unions back to work, alienating some of its traditional working-class support just prior to the 1975 election.[41]

By 1975 the Social Credit Party had reemerged as a coalition of anti-NDP forces.[42] Under William Bennett – W.A.C. Bennett's son – the new coalition proved powerful enough in 1979, 1983, and 1986 to defeat a New Democratic Party supported by public and private sector labour and capable of securing about 40 percent of the popular vote.

The New Political Economy: The Rise of the Service Sector

The decline in the significance of the resource sector to the contemporary provincial economy is evident in the figures contained in Table 2.2 below. This table groups together primary and secondary resource-related activities in order to provide a better picture of the position of the resource sector in the contemporary provincial economy.

As these figures indicate, only about $12.5 billion of BC's total annual output of over $87 billion is directly accounted for by primary and secondary resource sector production. Even assuming that each dollar produced in these two sectors is linked to as many as two additional service sector dollars, resource activities account for less than half of BC's annual production. Although substantial, this represents a significant decline from earlier historical periods.

This is not to say that resource-based economic activity is not important to specific aspects of the provincial economy. The fact that BC's economy is neither large enough nor diversified enough to produce all that the province needs, nor to consume all that it produces, for example, has led to a tendency toward specialization in production for external markets. Much of this trade has always been, and remains today, resource related.

Despite much rhetoric about a Pacific outlook replacing the old reliance on markets in the US, the figures in Table 2.3 show that US markets

Table 2.2

British Columbia GDP, 1994 ($ millions)

Economic activity	GDP
Agriculture and related	2,158
Fishing and trapping	361
Forestry and related manufacturing	7,364
Mining and related manufacturing	3,108
Other manufacturing	3,292
Construction	6,509
Utilities	2,213
Transportation, storage, and communication	7,793
Retail and wholesale trade	11,246
Finance, insurance, real estate	18,527
Education	4,204
Health services	5,255
Other services	10,373
Public administration and defence	4,795
GDP at factor cost	87,198

Source: BC Stats, *Industry Accounts: Special Aggregations* (Victoria, 1996). Electronic document available at http://www.bcstats.gov.bc.ca/data/bus_stat/bcea/tab07.htm.

Table 2.3

British Columbia international trade flows, 1994

	Exports (%)	Imports (%)
United Kingdom	1.4	1.0
Germany	2.0	1.2
China	1.3	4.1
Hong Kong	0.8	1.2
Taiwan	1.6	2.6
Japan	24.8	18.9
South Korea	3.2	3.7
Australia	1.1	1.6
Mexico	0.3	0.9
United States	54.1	51.2
Other	8.9	13.6
Total value ($ billions)	22.8	18.2

Source: BC Stats, *Business Statistics* (Victoria, 1996). Electronic document available at http://www.bcstats.gov.bc.ca/data/bus_stat/trade/netbgeo.htm.

continue to be by far the most frequent destination for BC production, accounting for over half of all BC imports and exports.[43]

Traditional staples exports remain the most important in these markets. About two-thirds of BC's $22.8 billion in exports in 1994 originated in the forest sector, with approximately one-third resulting from softwood lumber sales.[44] Although it is true that 'soft products' are having an increasing impact, the province's international trade remains very much oriented toward the export of bulk resource commodities to the US.[45]

Even with respect to trade, however, it should be noted that the situation regarding exports from BC to the rest of Canada is much different from that of BC's international exports. The nature of BC interprovincial trade flows is set out in Table 2.4.

Total interprovincial trade amounts to around $28 billion, about two-thirds the amount of total international exports and imports. Unlike the international situation, where the province runs a $3.5 billion annual trade surplus, an $8 billion deficit is accrued interprovincially, mostly with Ontario. Much of this trade involves the exchange of manufactured goods (especially automobiles and parts from Ontario) and some services, notably tourism.[46]

While still significant in terms of overall production and in some specific areas of the economic life of the province, with respect to the occupation and employment of the provincial populace, the role of the resource sector pales in comparison to that of the service sector. Table 2.5 below

Table 2.4

British Columbia interprovincial trade flows, 1990 ($ millions)

	Imports	Exports	Balance
Newfoundland	35	73	38
Prince Edward Island	9	20	11
Nova Scotia	158	170	12
New Brunswick	304	157	(147)
Quebec	3,300	1,394	(1,906)
Ontario	9,357	3,086	(6,271)
Manitoba	700	581	(119)
Saskatchewan	409	797	388
Alberta	4,420	4,265	(155)
Yukon	61	229	168
NWT	156	105	(51)
Total	18,909	10,877	(8,052)

Source: BC Stats, *Interprovincial Trade* (Victoria, 1996). Electronic document available at http://www.bcstats.gov.bc.ca/data/bus_stat/trade/prov_tr.pdf.

shows the net absolute change in jobs by industry in the province between 1981 and 1991. As the table illustrates, BC now has a very large component of its labour force employed in the retail, wholesale, financial, transportation, communications, and public service occupations, which collectively comprise the service sector.[47]

Three factors account for most of the changes in provincial occupational structures. First, the economic and social changes at the provincial level have led to the large-scale expansion of the provincial public sector and the creation of a mini-welfare state in BC. By the late 1980s, all provincial governments spent on average 45 percent of provincial GDP. That is, almost one out of every two dollars generated in the provinces in a calendar year was spent by the public sector.[48] More significantly, in terms of employment, between 1941 and 1981 the BC provincial public service (narrowly defined to exclude educational or health workers, employees of crown corporations, and local government employees) grew from 1,851 employees to 43,152, an increase of 2,231 percent. Defined more broadly to include related service employment, teachers, and hospital and municipal workers, the public service grew by 542 percent between 1947 and 1975, from 35,851 workers to 229,855. The rate of growth in this sector was double that of the labour force over the same period.[49]

The second major factor has been the replacement of in-house production in firms by contracting out to other firms. This phenomenon of

Table 2.5

Employment growth by industry, 1981-91

Industry	Net absolute change
Total mining and forestry	(19,600)
Total resource manufacturing	(20,100)
Other manufacturing	7,000
Construction	9,600
Total transportation	600
Finance, insurance, and real estate	17,200
Total retail and wholesale trade	38,200
Total business services	37,800
Total health and services	46,100
Accommodation and food	32,300
Education	22,000
Other	48,200
Total economy	219,300

Source: R. Kunin and J. Knauf, *Skill Shifts in Our Economy: A Decade in the Life of British Columbia* (Vancouver: Canadian Employment and Immigration Commission 1992).

increased specialization and division of labour in private companies is not new, but it has progressed to the point where, for example, various forestry companies in BC now contract out virtually all of their financial and harvesting activities, remaining essentially contractors and product producers.[50] In most cases, the contracting firms are much smaller than their predecessors, resulting in small business employment growth as an aspect of service sector development.

The third factor contributing to the growth of the service sector has a more dramatic day-to-day impact on the lives of families and communities. This is growth in service sector employment due to the commercialization of former 'household' tasks such as day care, cleaning, haircuts, and food preparation. These activities have gradually come to be performed in the private small business sector. Although this transition has positively affected many households in that this work, traditionally undertaken by women, has been removed from the sphere of the family, these jobs tend to be low paid and remain predominantly female.[51]

These three activities – growth in the public sector, contracting out, and commercialization of personal services – account for much of the growth in service sector employment noted above. These changes in the basic occupational structure of the province have had a significant impact on provincial politics, as political parties have formed, fused, and failed in their effort to reflect shifting public concerns originating in the changing day-to-day life of a majority of the provincial population. Not surprisingly, these activities have generated several issues that have come, in one form or another, to dominate BC's contemporary political agenda.[52]

This became apparent after 1983 when the new service sector workforce flexed its political muscle for the first time in response to a Social Credit 'austerity' budget and related legislation.[53] Soon after the introduction of this administrative package, opposition groups – organized labour, teachers, civil servants, senior citizens, the disabled, environmentalists, and others – coalesced in the labour-led Operation Solidarity and the Solidarity Coalition, an alliance of many new social movements. Led by the large public sector unions and associations, including the BCGEU, the Hospital Employees' Union (HEU), and the BC Teachers Federation (BCTF), and the private sector International Woodworkers of America (IWA), a series of marches, rallies, and strikes were held throughout the province.[54] A province-wide general strike was averted only at the last moment when the government agreed to reconsider elements of its legislative package.

From 1983 to 1991, the major thrust of Social Credit government policy initiatives under Bennett and his successor, Bill Vander Zalm, was to attempt to limit the growth of this opposition coalition.[55] This was done through the replacement of a regulatory regime featuring direct government ownership or delivery of services with one featuring indirect government regulation, either through subsidies and tax incentives or through the establishment of quasi-judicial boards and commissions.[56]

In 1991, however, the NDP capitalized on the disarray of the Socreds following the resignation of Vander Zalm under a cloud of allegations of conflict of interest and finally regained control of the provincial government.[57] Once in office, the party moved quickly under Premier Mike Harcourt to consolidate its support, renegotiating previously frozen teachers' salaries, eliminating public sector wage freezes and restrictive labour legislation, and providing tax breaks and incentives for trade union members.[58] Still, the NDP's reliance on political appointments and affirmative action in the civil service has, as Norman Ruff suggests in Chapter 10, created an acrimonious situation between the government and the direct civil service. This discord threatened to undermine the NDP's base of electoral support just as the anti-NDP coalition appeared to be regrouping under the banner of the provincial Liberal Party,[59] contributing to their loss of twelve seats in their narrow 1996 reelection victory.

Conclusion: The Future of BC Politics in the New Political Economy

In BC a predominant political myth centres on the province being a resource hinterland whose politics revolve around the exploitation of natural resources. Although this view had a basis in fact in the early years of the province, and is perpetuated by every headline setting out the latest conflict between loggers and environmentalists, it has much less basis in present-day political-economic realities. Rather than face a set of political problems arising out of the old political economy, politicians in BC today must grapple with issues that have origins in the new service sector political economy that has emerged over the past half century.[60]

The NDP, as the traditional party of labour in the province, has aligned itself with the new service sectors that depend heavily on government spending. On the other hand, like former Social Credit governments, the Liberal Party has allied itself with large corporations as well as with elements of the traditional middle class of professionals and small businesses, all of which prefer a regime of privatization, deregulation, and tax and deficit reduction. Elections in the province are now fought over marginal support loosely adhering to each coalition. Public sector workers split off from the NDP when that party is forced to confront government spending issues,[61] and fragments of anti-NDP support will move to always-waiting third parties whenever the anti-NDP party is forced to confront regulatory or taxation issues that business does not favour.[62]

This is not to say, of course, that the old strains and conflicts associated with a resource-based economy have completely vanished from the province. In fact, much of the service sector growth and expansion have occurred in the heavily populated Lower Mainland and southern Vancouver

Island regions of the province, while various other regions of BC remain relatively more dependent on one or more of the traditional staples such as fur, fish, or forest products. Over 45 percent of business services as early as 1976 were 'exported' from the Lower Mainland to the rest of the province, while between one-quarter and one-third of service sector companies report 'exports' of greater than 25 percent of their sales to locations in the province outside the Lower Mainland.[63] This situation reflects the metropolitan-hinterland type linkages that continue to endure between the Lower Mainland and the rest of the province, and underscores the overlaps that exist between traditional staples production and urban service sector activities.[64]

Although significant, this variation in regional political economies should not be exaggerated. While there remains a relatively greater dependence on primary sector activities outside the Lower Mainland area – as approximately 13 percent of the labour force in 1986 was employed in these occupations compared to only 3 percent in the Vancouver region – both regions were dominated by service sector occupations. Fully 79 percent of employment in the Lower Mainland was in this sector, while 69 percent of employment in the rest of the province occurred in service sector occupations.

Many of the relevant aspects of BC's political life, including electoral competition, party structure, and systems of interest intermediation, are tied to the nature of the provincial political economy and change along with it. The result of the change in the political economy of BC outlined above, from a staples-led economy to one dependent on a variety of service industries, has been the emergence of a new set of issues with which the provincial political system now must deal.

Among the major sets of issues that will continue to occupy the future of BC politics, three deserve mention. First, BC faces several key gender issues. As women have moved into the public and private service sector workforce, this has raised a number of issues related to gender equality, such as demands for increased government action to ensure job and pay equity, an end to sexual harassment, and the provision of high quality and accessible day care.

Second, BC faces problems related to the growth of the small business sector and the critical role it now plays in employment creation and destruction. While small businesses can be successful, they often require either explicit subsidies such as low interest loans or implicit subsidies such as low minimum wage rates in order to succeed. Such firms have a high failure rate, with negative consequences not only for the owners but for employees faced with real or anticipated job losses. Small businesses also rarely have the wherewithal required to train their workers, meaning that provincial governments must also pick up an increasing amount of the responsibility and cost for education, training, and research and development.[65]

Both of these problems relate to a third service sector issue, which is how to finance any further increases in government spending required either to maintain existing levels of services or meet demands for new ones.[66] Whether this spending is funded through increased tax revenues or through deficit financing, it brings another set of concerns to bear on governments, including who to tax and at what rate, all of which have electoral implications for the government in power.

This is not to say that these are the only problems that future provincial governments will face. Others include a variety of issues related to the old political economy, such as dealing with the effects of globalization of forest industry production.[67] Others, such as concerns about ethnicity, sustainability, health, education, and other areas of social and cultural life, are connected to the new political economy but at one remove from it.[68] Still others, such as the fate of the nation and the constitution or the role of the province in the governance of the Cascadia region, exist at several removes. Nevertheless, many of the most common problems facing provincial politicians and officials are intricately bound to the day-to-day problems of provincial residents. These are people who are concerned, for the most part, with maintaining in the new service sector economy the same high standard of living and sociocultural development – a level as high as any prevailing in the most prosperous areas of North America, if not the industrialized world – as they enjoyed in the old staples.

Further Reading

Allen, Robert C. 'The BC Economy: Past, Present, Future.' In *Restraining the Economy: Social Credit Economic Policies for BC in the Eighties*, edited by Robert C. Allen and Gideon Rosenbluth, 9-42. Vancouver: New Star Books 1986

Black, E.R. 'British Columbia: The Politics of Exploitation.' In *Exploiting Our Economic Potential: Public Policy and the British Columbia Economy*, edited by R. Shearer, 23-41. Toronto: Holt Rinehart and Winston 1968

Blake, Donald E. 'The Electoral Significance of Public Sector Bashing.' *BC Studies* 62 (1984): 29-43

Blake, Donald, Richard Johnston, and David Elkins. 'Sources of Change in the BC Party System.' *BC Studies* 50 (1981): 3-28

Brownsey, K., and M. Howlett, eds. *The Provincial State: Politics in Canada's Provinces and Territories*. Toronto: Copp Clark Pitman 1992

Grubel, Herbert G., and Michael A. Walker. *Service Industry Growth: Causes and Effects*. Vancouver: Fraser Institute 1989

Kunin, R., and J. Knauf. *Skill Shifts in Our Economy: A Decade in the Life of British Columbia*. Vancouver: Canadian Employment and Immigration Commission 1992

MacKay, Donald. *Empire of Wood: The MacMillan-Bloedel Story*. Vancouver: Douglas and McIntyre 1981

Tomblin, Stephen G. 'W.A.C. Bennett and Province-Building in British Columbia.' *BC Studies* 85 (1990): 45-61

Warburton, R., and D. Coburn, eds. *Workers, Capital and the State in British Columbia: Selected Papers*. Vancouver: UBC Press 1988

3
British Columbia:
'The Spoilt Child of Confederation'
Edwin R. Black

Is British Columbia really the spoiled child of the Canadian federation? What are the causes of the many complaints and quarrels between the federal and provincial governments during the 1980s and 1990s? Were they all simply the result of petty politics on both sides, as the mass media so frequently claim? Or were there deeper issues, such as eastern Canada's persistent failure to understand BC's needs and accomplishments, or the self-centred nature of the provincial political culture? The list of problem cases is certainly extensive. It includes:

- Ottawa's 'arbitrary cuts' in payments for medical care, social welfare, and college and university education
- the disaster in salmon fisheries management
- land claims by First Nations
- foreign trade relations
- environmental protection and economic development
- constitutional rearrangements
- BC's lack of power in federal government and politics.

Investigating why these quarrels arise can tell us much about both the conduct of the BC government and the source of political conflict over what it does. There is one simple answer to why: trouble arises whenever the province wants something from the central government that is not being done for other provinces. Yet while there is much to this elementary approach, we need to probe deeper still.

The 'Contract' with Canada
The 'spoilt child' insult originated in eastern Canadian newspapers a century ago, but you can still hear it, and worse, today. Relations between the federal and provincial capitals have always been touchy. In the early 1990s,

Norman Ruff observed that 'Ottawa-Victoria relations ... have long been characterised by misunderstanding and bemusement, by suspicion and anger and, worst of all, by periods of mutual indifference and detachment.'[1] That lack of interest becomes particularly acute when political activists in the two different political systems are focused on radically different priorities.

Ottawa's habit of calling BC self-centred or spoiled began more than a century ago. Almost as soon as the West Coast settlements had joined the federation, eastern politicians and newspapers noticed a barrage of constant complaints coming from the new province.[2] Better-endowed with natural resources than most, BC's inhabitants nevertheless had a pesky habit of insisting that the rest of the country had made an enforceable contract in 1871: the railway was a paramount condition of Confederation. BC insisted time and time again that the Terms of Union[3] had to be kept, or 'the deal was off.' What the alternative might be was not clear, in either the last century or this, but there has always been a suspicion that the US was seen as a substitute partner.

The province that entered the Canadian federation in 1871 had been created only five years earlier from a disputatious union of two languishing British colonies, Vancouver Island and the mainland. The private and public buccaneers of both colonies carried their rivalries with them into the politics of the new province. The only time they considered setting aside that rivalry was to do battle with the far-off Dominion government. Even then the islanders and mainlanders fought over who should get whatever benefits could be extracted from Ottawa. The party-oriented elites who succeeded those early buccaneers were also in agreement on one further thing: not only was Ottawa wrong but so too were 'Bay Street and St. James Street.' That was where one traditionally found the moneylenders of the east who persisted, in the western view, in denying dynamic frontier economies the cash and credit that would soon bring prosperity to all if only those people would loosen their purse strings.

The initial and most important of the many Dominion-provincial struggles was about transportation connections: where they would be built, how soon, and who would pay how much to subsidize them. In the nineteenth century, politicians and business people, when discussing transportation connections, talked primarily about railways and occasionally about canals. Throughout the twentieth century, they still talked mostly about railways, but roads were becoming increasingly important, as were air, water, power, and pipeline transport. While later in the century, others worried about connecting BC to different communication systems, such as broadcasting and electronic networks, these concerns did not often surface in the muddied waters of intergovernmental relations.

Economic Factors in the Mix
The intimate connections between provincial politics and the major factors of the economy are explored in Chapters 2 (on political economy) and 15 (on the forest industry). As they point out, BC's natural resources have brought it not only relative wealth but an enormous dependence on foreign trade and world demand for those resources. Although now somewhat diminished by the elimination of federal transportation subsidies, the prosperity of several BC ports is still affected by world demand for prairie wheat. The other major resource in BC is, of course, the labour force – its size, education, skills, quality, and cost. All these factors are affected by Ottawa's trading relations with foreign states, as well as its immigration policies, training programs, labour laws, and economic management. Together, they provide fruitful ground in which intergovernmental differences can develop and fester.

Since the 'contract' for federation, BC has always been sensitive about getting its 'fair share' of economic development moneys. Whenever nineteenth-century federal governments questioned the desirability of building the long-promised railway to the Pacific, BC politicians never hesitated to threaten separation. The province saw the railway as its share of the Confederation pie, as well as being absolutely essential to its economic expansion, a view that ever since has set the tone for Ottawa-Victoria relations over development aid. The demand for a fair share has preoccupied many BC politicians. The threat of separation has mellowed somewhat in the last three decades, but a belief still lingers among some of the economic elites that if there were to be no obvious net economic benefit, then BC should go its own way by setting up independently, joining the United States, or even starting a new union. This financial-ledger style of relationship has frustrated federal politicians. A long continuing issue, the demand for economic development moneys has seldom been based on claimed needs but rather on a belief in strict apportionment. Saskatchewan or New Brunswick or any other province might very well need the money more, but that is no reason for denying BC voters their fair share.

Continuing Issues

Expansion
Even though BC is a large and resource-rich province, it has often elected political leaders who were devoted to territorial expansion and ever more economic growth. The early twentieth century saw the rise of demands that control of the Peace River Block be 'returned' to BC, a subject that became a major objective of the BC delegation to the Dominion-provincial conference of 1927 (together with railways). Such was the pressure from BC that Ottawa was forced to create a royal commission on the Peace

River Block, a move that finally, in 1930, resulted in BC securing control of the rich lands north and east of the continental divide that it had always considered its own.

After the Peace, the next 'natural' expansion was seen to be the Yukon, which was to be connected to Vancouver by rail. Every premier from Duff Pattullo in the 1930s to W.A.C. Bennett in the 1960s proposed such an annexation. Federal governments showed little interest in these ambitions and that particular expansionist fever began cooling off during the last quarter-century. As federal transportation spending steadily declined, railways looked more and more expensive and ever less attractive. Although the only feasible alternative for large-scale economic development, highway and road building attracted little or no funds from Ottawa, nor did they require the province to 'haggle with the feds' about conditional grant money. Throwing even more cold water on provincial territorial ambitions have been the ever-growing demands for resolution of the many Native land claims.

The focus in provincial expansion policy has consequently shifted to 'keeping' land – that is, keeping it in provincial hands and open for both resource exploitation and recreational use. The many conflicts that have arisen in this respect form an important segment of the discussions on forestry in this volume. Other conflicts, often neglected in the more urban parts of the province, have revolved around efforts to discover and exploit mineral deposits and hydroelectric generation projects. Wherever the latter has involved navigable waters, and that covers most generation projects, federal-provincial agreement has been absolutely essential before anything could be accomplished.

Economic Management

The economic depressions that followed the First World War and preceded the Second left Canadian federal governments determined to 'manage' the national economy so as to prevent such catastrophes in the future. Academic economic theories took hold in the federal Department of Finance in particular, and the central government began exercising all of its many constitutional authorities in the economic and financial fields. It undertook to maintain full employment, control inflation, stabilize the currency, attract low-cost foreign investment, reduce the cost of imports, and stimulate the export of natural and manufactured products. Many of these efforts were successful, and as long as the various regions of Canada suffered or prospered more or less uniformly, the BC government was content to endorse strong financial management from the centre.

Trouble came late in the century – after the province had worked its way through the recession of the early 1980s and Canada had moved into a much freer trading regime internationally. The rough economic times that developed during the early 1990s hit the various regions quite differently. The eastern half of Canada, where all federal governments find their electoral majorities, faced much more difficult situations than did BC, where the economy continued to grow rapidly. Ottawa's low inflation, high interest rate, and strong dollar policies were developed to deal with the 'overheated' Ontario economy, but they were in direct conflict with the economic situation in BC. Once again, BC's politicians said, Ottawa's policies were placing an unfair and unnecessary burden on BC's resource-based economy, and the province's representatives in Ottawa objected continuously. That nearly all economic specialists agreed on the virtual impossibility of regionally differentiated fiscal policies did nothing to reduce the complaints.[4]

The Free Trade Agreement (FTA) of 1988 was supposed to protect Canadian businesses from American protectionists and open up the US market. Special arrangements maintained the Ontario-Quebec auto industry and safeguarded Canadian cultural activities. For BC the FTA was a false promise. Many thought it would resolve a long-time trade dispute over softwood lumber. It did not. From BC's perspective, what happened was that American lumber producers stepped up their frontal attacks on BC's softwood lumber exporters.[5] The province consistently won the support of the federal government, as well as support from every international tribunal that heard the case. That, however, never seemed to discourage American lumber interests, who launched obstruction after obstruction and the dispute continued year after year. British Columbians had reason to feel that Ottawa's much-vaunted trade policy had left them badly used once again.

The ledger-book relationship between Ottawa and Victoria came to the fore once again in the 1980s with the demand that Ottawa invest in the Triumf/KAON[6] project at the University of British Columbia. Other provinces, most notably Quebec, had received moneys to stimulate high technology industries in their provinces. Because BC had 'fallen behind' in federal support for high technology funding, the BC government argued, Ottawa should pay for the KAON expansion project. At a time when the federal government was reducing its overall spending on research and development, Victoria was demanding support for a project that would devour $750 million, or more than three-quarters of the total federal research and development budget. It did not get the money, and provincial politicians felt they had a new and justifiable grievance with the central government.

Giant development schemes or megaprojects, such as the Triumf/KAON proposal, were for a long time vigorously promoted all across the country by the federal government; they formed an important part of its postwar economic management program. One of the most successful of these, and by far the most significant in BC, was the Kemano hydroelectric project in the northwestern part of the province. Its role as political football for different types of political combatants demonstrates how easily the federal division of regulatory authority can get tangled up in domestic political issues and cause intergovernmental discord.

The Kemano project, begun during the 1950s, provided Alcan Aluminium with the necessary inducements to build a giant aluminum smelter at Kitimat.[7] Both federal and provincial governments cooperated happily and hastily to negotiate three-way agreements with Alcan to provide water-right leases, hydroelectricity production permits, and protection for the fisheries of the Nechako and associated watersheds. The scheme provided jobs for thousands of workers from across BC and Canada and brought the northwest a major industry. After the first stage was built, Alcan decided in the early 1980s to exercise its rights to develop the Kemano Completion Project (KCP), the second phase of the massive enterprise. Both the federal and provincial governments approved the project, and Alcan began spending the hundreds of millions of dollars required. Apparently unnoticed by all, however, were significant changes in BC's political climate that turned the KCP into a dangerous political gamble. Megaprojects had lost public favour. Their job-producing potential was limited, their environmental costs were much more widely questioned, and environmental movements had grown greatly in political influence. The provincial government ordered a public inquiry, looked at the evidence, claimed that the federal regulatory measures were at fault, looked at its troubles with the salmon fishery generally, heeded numerous public objections, and cancelled the KCP. Victoria then claimed that Ottawa was liable for any compensatory damages to Alcan. Ottawa disagreed. All-out warfare between the two governments threatened. Then, at the critical moment, huge blocks of 'surplus' Columbia River electric power suddenly became available. Relief was felt in both political capitals as the power was made available to Alcan in pricing arrangements that satisfied almost everybody, and another federal-provincial crisis passed by.

Foreign Relations and the Fishery
The relationship between BC and the US has been much like that of Canada and the US. The US has been viewed sometimes as a suitor, other times as a competitor, and at yet other times as both. Over the years, American politicians' belief in the manifest destiny doctrine led to several boundary disputes. The Alaska Panhandle, Point Roberts, and southern Vancouver Island boundary disputes all went to international arbitration before being settled. The resolution of these disputes, in which BC usually saw itself as the loser, left provincial politicians persuaded that the central powers (British, then Canadian) cared more about appeasing the Americans than protecting BC. This mistrust of the federal government's ability, or willingness, to protect BC's interests in dealings with the Americans continues to

be a convenient whipping boy that is trundled out every time the provincial government feels slighted by Ottawa.

Today, the disputes between BC and the US are most often about resources, not land. Fish, fresh water, and hydroelectricity have become the primary points of contention. The combination of competing federal, state, and provincial governments means that disputes over who has the primary right to exploit resources crossing international boundaries are horribly complicated. The questions of which governments were responsible for what and which had what jurisdictional and economic rights long delayed agreement on the Columbia River dam and hydroelectric development projects. It took the agreement of many separate parties – BC, Ottawa, Washington, and the US states – to bring about an agreement.[8] Besides the obvious and huge power benefits involved, what worked strongly in the interest of this giant scheme was international agreement on financing, on its safeguarding of Fraser salmon runs (from the perils of hydroelectric dams), and on the provision of substantial 'downstream' flood control and power generation. That was more than a quarter-century ago. Such disputes over natural-resource sharing become even more contentious today with the inevitable adding in of significant environmental and conservation issues. The dreams of American entrepreneurs hoping to sell BC's ample fresh-water supplies to the thirsty cities of California led to a clause in the FTA specifically excluding such water from the permitted trading relations.

The great salmon runs of the Pacific Northwest have long been a source of wealth for BC and the Pacific states. They are also a splendid example of the complexity of the province's external relations. As long as salmon was abundant, there was relative peace among the stakeholders. The first great threat to the resource came in the early 1900s with the building of a railway through the Fraser River canyon. A blasting accident changed the course of the river at Hell's Gate. The result of changed water flows decimated the Fraser salmon stocks to the point that the fishery dependant on the Fraser run for its livelihood was almost wiped out. An agreement between the US and Canada provided for remedial work, financed jointly by both governments, that eventually restored the stocks. This agreement underlined the extremely close connections between the two countries' West Coast fisheries. Canada and the US recognized then the need for some kind of co-management of the salmon stocks.

In Canada salt-water fish stocks fall under federal legislative and regulatory authority. In the US they generally fall under the jurisdiction of the states up to the point where international treaties bring them into the federal sphere. The large number of players, each asserting some kind of ownership rights or sovereign authority, makes reaching any agreement in the area enormously complex. The West Coast local jurisdictions all suspect – with some justification – that the diplomatic departments in Ottawa and Washington would willingly sacrifice their fishery interests in the much wider game of international disputes. BC has complained in this vein ever since the 1871 Treaty of Washington. Other countries, most notably Japan, are also involved as parties to the Pacific Salmon Treaty. Yet another set of players was added to the mix in 1990, when the First Nations finally won legal recognition of their 'aboriginal right' to a fishery that they had long claimed in vain.[9]

The First Nations in BC were not to enjoy that right without protest for very long. Among other things, the resulting legal and political entitlements set in place different fishing regimes for aboriginals and non-aboriginals. The issue became critical when the salmon fisheries virtually collapsed during the mid-1990s. The result was a series of fierce accusations against Ottawa for incompetent management of the fishery and spinelessness in dealing with both Alaska and First Nations fishers. The governments of BC, Washington, and Oregon often had kinder things to say about each other than about their central governments.

First Nations and Land

Unlike other provinces, BC had never formally concluded treaties with most of its First Nations people. The Douglas Treaties, signed before Confederation, dealt with only a few bands, most of which were located on Vancouver Island. The result was that BC claimed over 80 percent of the province as crown land. This made BC ripe for the resource exploitation that would make the province, and many of its leading citizens, very wealthy.

For a century, the BC government steadfastly maintained that the First Nations, and by extension their land claims, were a purely federal responsibility. As a federal responsibility, Native land claims would not involve the province in demands for financial compensation or any transfers of land. Victoria maintained this position until the early 1990s, when the Harcourt government agreed to settle land claims on exactly the same fifty-fifty cost-sharing arrangement that other provinces had with the federal government. While that ended the quarrel on principle with Ottawa, disputes continued in individual cases on the appropriate valuation of lands turned over to various First Nations. Other quarrels with Ottawa continued to arise as the central government tried to work out Native self-government regimes that did not trespass on either provincial prerogatives or sensibilities.

Constitutional Issues

BC's premiers have often been accused of not representing the province well at the constitutional negotiating table. In most cases, however, the problem seems to have been that BC's leaders were seldom on the same wavelength as everyone else at the conference table.[10] For example, during the federal-provincial meetings in 1965 and 1966 on medicare and post-secondary education, the other leaders were focused on the issue at hand. Premier Bennett, however, insisted on talking about railways and high-ways. His interest seems to have been piqued only when the discussions turned to taxation, at which point he reiterated BC's long-held posi-tion that the province had not been receiving its fair share of the taxation pie.

During negotiations on the Meech Lake Accord in the 1980s, opponents accused the premier of the day, William Vander Zalm, of acquiescing once again to central Canada's wishes. At the same time, academics and politi-cians alike ridiculed him for arguing in favour of recognizing Canada as a union of ten distinct societies. In reality, he was only voicing a long-held belief in BC that the province was equal to, yet distinct from, all other provinces.

Different provinces have approached the question of defining the Cana-dian federation in a variety of ways. There can be little doubt that from the beginning BC held firmly to a contract theory of the association, even though the term bore a somewhat different sense than the contract views originally argued in Nova Scotia, New Brunswick, and Quebec. There is little evidence that British Columbians accepted the view that Confedera-tion was primarily a contract between two linguistic nationalities. Further, whatever the aberrations of occasional federal politicians elected from BC, no provincial government has held to the view often expressed in Ontario that the country should be dissolved into a more centralized political sys-tem. In pressing for fulfilment of BC's Terms of Union, both explicit and implicit, the province has always sought better transportation subsidies and links, as well as ever more control over its natural resources, fisheries, rivers, lands, and taxable assets in the province. When issues of decentrali-zation of power have been raised at federal-provincial conferences, BC pre-miers traditionally called on Ottawa to give BC more power. In the next breath would follow a demand that Ottawa compensate BC for the cost of exercising any new powers that it might get. BC has long been a strong advocate of national programs such as unemployment insurance. As long as Ottawa was willing to pay the bill for social programs, British Columbians would support them.

Discussion of the Charlottetown Accord in the 1990s found the premier of BC accused of being out of step both with other premiers and BC voters. Although the premier at that time, Mike Harcourt, approved of the Charlottetown agreement, the citizens of his province voted overwhelm-ingly against it – by the highest margin of any jurisdiction in Canada.[11] While political and media elites were quick to applaud proposed changes that would reduce the power of the central government, it was not enough. The perception persisted that too much was being given away to other distinct groups (mostly First Nations and Quebec) without BC receiving enough in return.

While asserting the constitutional equality of all provinces during the discussions of the 1980s and 1990s, BC from time to time also sought constitutional recognition as a distinctive fifth 'region' of the country. In early 1996 the Chrétien government gave that demand some legislative recognition.[12] Had this recognition been raised from the political to the formal constitutional level, the province would have attained a 'special status' very like that which the voters of BC had always opposed granting Quebec.

The Charlottetown Accord had proposed a formal embracing of much of the decentralism that had existed in Canada for some time. That many in the political elites of BC supported the proposal probably owed less to principle than to pragmatism. At least partial explanation can be found in the erosion of economic and social linkages caused by the federal budget retrenchments of the 1990s. Like other provinces, BC's east-west connections have often been weak compared to the north-south linkages. Indeed, instead of strengthening its links eastward, BC has in recent decades been working westward, trying hard to develop stronger ties with Asian countries on the Pacific Rim. The impetus for this owes much to recent changes in BC's socioeconomic composition, stimulated in large part by significant investment from Hong Kong and Japan, as well as substantial immigration from China and other countries of southeast Asia. Despite these changes, the US is, and will long continue to be, BC's largest trading partner and will doubtless remain the major source of BC's trade irritants. Any failure on Ottawa's part to intervene promptly and strongly on BC's behalf generates instant intergovernmental discussion and public complaint.

Social and Other Policy Areas

BC has long kept a careful ledger on what Robert Bourassa, a former premier of Quebec, called 'profitable federalism' – an accounting of economic and financial pluses and minuses from being a member of the Canadian federation. Intergovernmental finance is a complex affair that stimulates fierce debate among those who understand the arcane Canadian system. Some of these issues are explored and explained in detail in Chapter 13.

When the Chrétien government radically reduced federal transfer payments to the provinces in the early 1990s, loud moans were heard in all the right political circles. In BC, three programs – health insurance, social welfare, and postsecondary education – had accounted for fully half of all federal transfers to the province.[13] Slashing these payments was very unpopular in Victoria, but as one of the three most prosperous governments in the country, BC could do little more than join the others in ritual objection. Provincial objections became much more heated in late 1995 when the central government imposed a 'fine' on BC for introducing a three-month residence period for social welfare eligibility. Here, as with respect to medicare, BC protested that the federal government was claiming far more control over the system than the size of its subsidies warranted. Health and social welfare comprised two of the few issue areas where it could fairly be said that the probability of intergovernmental quarrelling depended significantly on the ideological outlooks of those involved.

The provision of staffed lighthouses, airport services, subsidies for new business, and new appointments to the office of lieutenant governor have all occasioned BC complaints about federal government activities. None, however, was as important in determining the quality of BC's relations with the federal government as one other factor that was not much discussed in the provincial mass media. Throughout the last half of the twentieth century, most of BC's representatives in the federal House of Commons were almost irrelevant in getting the province the things it wanted from Ottawa. For the most part, BC voters gave their votes (and presumably hearts) to members of third and fourth parties who never sat in the federal cabinet or its government caucus. While BC occasionally elected some MPs who formed part of the government, they were often weak and too few in number to be very effective. The provisions of national programs and the non-partisan, day-to-day activities of most federal public servants insulates much of the government's activities from the interparty battles of elected politicians, but not all of them. Regions such as BC, which persist in supporting non-governmental parties, suffer particular loss and inattention in all those sectors in which unique treatments or innovative policies are wanted.

This long-standing voting habit probably has its origins in immigration patterns that began changing fairly early in the twentieth century. An increasing proportion of the population originated in countries with no Liberal-Conservative Party traditions. The racial make-up of the provincial electorate began to change rapidly after the First World War and continued right through the twentieth century.[14] Changes in the general population were, however, very slow to be reflected in the political elites. As the demographics changed, so too did relationships with the central government and with the 'old-line' federal political parties. The continuing success of populist and radical 'third parties' at the provincial government level often produced elected politicians with little or no connection to federal counterparts, which in turn resulted in scant hope for Liberal or Conservative federalists hoping to establish strong party organizations in the province. Part of the price that British Columbians pay for their maverick voting is seen in the many public quarrels that break out between their two governments.

Those provincial politicians who attack the federal government tooth and nail do not represent the views of all British Columbians. Among those who refuse to see Ottawa as an adversary are many who enjoy or seek favours and protection from a central presence in such matters as environmental regulation, the financing of social services, and larger, more secure foreign markets. Others seek federal legal shelter from provincial laws, policies, and tax regimes they dislike. Federal government reduction of support for the social safety net does, however, seriously strain the loyalties of even its natural supporters in the province. Some in the economic and political elites have already declared that the time has come for a formal rethinking of the relationship.

BC Separatism

While BC lost its British colonial status a long time ago, its relations with Canada's semi-sovereign centre have long continued to exhibit many of the classic colonial attitudes. The influx of foreign capital late in the twentieth century radically reduced the old complaint about eastern financial capital, but it was replaced by a new theme: if Ottawa would only take its 'thieving tax fingers' out of the economy, BC could look after itself very well, thank you. Federalist discontent together with the separatist movement and referenda in Quebec gave rise to sporadic flights of mass media fancy about comparable independence for BC. The province's growing dependence on American capital and markets, however, raised the possibility that a different kind of shift in the dependence/independence relationship might already be well under way. BC and the neighbouring US states of Alaska, Oregon, and Washington share a number of common characteristics, including a common mistrust of central government and a feeling that they have often been denied their fair share. This has led to a small but persisting movement advocating the creation of Cascadia, a union of the these four jurisdictions. Despite the addition to the scheme, at various times, of Alberta and Montana, these discussions always seem to ignore the lumbering, fishery, and other fierce economic rivalries that so frequently put these jurisdictions at odds. The notion of Cascadia was, at least during the 1990s, hard to take seriously as anything more than a testament to the Pacific Northwest mind-set of always being mistreated by the centre.

Conclusion

As Norman Ruff has said, 'Global economic change has renewed the sense of a Pacific distinctiveness from the prairie neighbours beyond the Rockies, and has combined with national political changes to breed a determination to give an overriding priority to British Columbia's own agenda.'[15] The mass media revel in exaggerating the disputes that occur – they offer a Canadian version of a very civil war. The mass media are also fond of painting the pictures primarily in terms of rival politicians seeking popular favour. This is misleading; most contact between governments takes place at the civil servant level and the dominant theme there is cooperation. What brings politicians into the fray are much more persistent forces than personality clashes – it is the forces that arise from the divided jurisdictions imposed on all parties by the federal constitution of Canada. The merits of whatever provincial politicians ask – or demand – from their Ottawa counterparts seldom have much to do with the way those wishes are received. Far weightier are other factors, including:

- the number and importance of the province's MPs in the federal cabinet
- the timing of the next federal general election
- Ottawa's outlook on the Canadian economy as a whole
- how much attention the central government is giving to constitutional matters
- the state of the country's relations with the US and other trading partners.

In all, it must be remembered that, spoiled child or not, the way in which a community keeps its accounts and writes its law books will do nothing to increase its economic resources or its social cohesion. These can only come from renewed feelings of common purpose and fellow feeling.

Further Reading
Christensen, Bev. *Too Good to Be True: Alcan's Kemano Completion Project*. Vancouver: Talon Books 1995
Ormsby, Margaret A. *British Columbia: A History*. Toronto: Macmillan 1958
Roy, Patricia E., ed. *A History of British Columbia: Selected Readings*. Toronto: Copp Clark Pitman 1989
Swainson, Neil. *Conflict over the Columbia: The Canadian Background to an Historic Treaty*. Montreal: McGill-Queen's University Press 1979

4
Aboriginal Peoples and Aboriginal Title in British Columbia Politics
Paul Tennant

In establishing the foundations of British Columbia as a province within Canada, the early white politicians seemed to have solved the 'Indian problem.' By the 1880s they had rendered aboriginal land concerns illegitimate, and increasingly irrelevant, as far as the government and the non-Native public were concerned. The motto of the provincial politicians became, in effect, 'there is no problem and if there is a problem it is a federal responsibility.' For a century the province prevailed against Native demands. Then, commencing in the 1980s, political history reversed itself. Native land claims, along with the issue of aboriginal self-government, moved rapidly from the periphery to become highly contentious issues in BC politics.

My purpose in this essay is to examine the origin and political evolution of the issue of aboriginal title in BC, and to explain why and how the issue is now being dealt with. I will begin by saying something about colonialism and about the aboriginal peoples of BC.

Aboriginal Peoples and Colonialism
'Aboriginal' has political meaning only in a setting of colonialism, or in its aftermath. Aboriginal peoples are those who are already present and established when colonizers arrive. While racial differences are usually present between Natives and newcomers, such differences are incidental to, and in principle are irrelevant to, the concept of aboriginality. (In practice, however, white racism was a major factor in the treatment of aboriginal peoples throughout the European empires, and is still expressed today by those who assert that aboriginal rights are racial rights.) The essential difference relates to political power and influence, for by its very nature colonialism subjugates aboriginal peoples without their consent. This subjugation normally continues, and even intensifies, after a colony attains independence; it is typically marked by limitations of civil rights, restricted access to land and resources, and social controls exercised by government officials. If an

aboriginal people does survive, the subjugation can end only when it voluntarily enters into some form of comprehensive agreement, such as a treaty, with the contemporary regime.

Within the British Empire, Native peoples were typically recognized as having some continuing rights or interests in the land; that is, the exertion of British sovereignty was not regarded as erasing all previous land rights. The Royal Proclamation of 1763, for example, provided that 'Nations or Tribes of Indians' in North America were to be protected 'in the Possession of ... Parts of Our Dominions and Territories,' and that 'If at any Time any of the Said Indians should be inclined to dispose of the said Lands, the same shall be purchased only for Us [i.e., the Crown], in our Name, at some public Meeting or Assembly of the said Indians.'[1]

In acknowledging the Native tribes as in possession of lands and as able to dispose of such lands, the proclamation was undeniably treating them as having ownership. However, the stipulations that the Natives could dispose of the land only to the Crown, and then only collectively and in public, meant that aboriginal title was to be quite different in British law from the ordinary ownership individual settlers could acquire. In part for this reason, the terms Native 'interest' in the land or 'aboriginal land rights' are often used as other terms for Native or aboriginal title. Recognizing the validity of this title means acknowledging that the Native interest in the land continues, as a burden or encumbrance upon the Crown's basic underlying title, until it is voluntarily surrendered or formally extinguished in some other way.

The proclamation established the treaty process that was followed in advance of settlement in much of Canada east of the Rocky Mountains. Native nations surrendered their title to the Crown in return for various benefits, including the use of land reserves. In the Prairie treaties, reserves were made large enough for each Native family to have about the same amount of land (typically 640 acres) as a settler family would have. In what became Alberta and Saskatchewan, the treaties were negotiated before the provinces were even created, thus eliminating aboriginal title as a future provincial political issue.

In a few parts of the British Empire, aboriginal title was denied. In these cases, of which there were only two of significance, the doctrine of *terra nullius* was implemented; that is, the land was assumed to have lacked any significant previous human occupation, and so to be devoid of any aboriginal title. Australia provides the better known of the two cases, while BC provides the other.

The Aboriginal Peoples of BC

At the time of the first European contact, in 1774, several hundred thousand people inhabited what would become BC. There were some thirty separate peoples, each with its own name, language, culture, politics, and territory, and each composed of a number of local communities. Social and political organization was more intricate among the coastal peoples than among those of the interior, for the rich marine environment allowed aboriginal cultures to attain degrees of complexity found nowhere else on earth without agriculture. While each people was associated uniquely with one territory, it was common for neighbouring peoples to regard themselves as having equal rights to share in harvesting resources at particular places. Thus, peaceful 'overlaps' were common, although warfare over territory certainly occurred as well.

As yet there is no standard terminology in British Columbian English usage (among either Natives or non-Natives) that serves to designate and distinguish consistently between the peoples and their component local communities. 'Nation,' 'tribe,' and 'band' are the terms most commonly used. 'Band' is applied only to local communities but, because of its origin in the Indian Act, its use is increasingly confined to legalistic contexts. 'Nation' and 'tribe' have long been applied interchangeably to both peoples and communities, and thus do not serve to distinguish the two groupings. In recent years, 'tribal group' and 'tribal nation' have emerged as generic terms for peoples, and are not applied to local communities. 'First Nation' is most often applied to communities and bands, but it may also refer to tribal nations. In any case, distinguishing between a community and a tribal nation is often of major importance in political analysis, and failure to distinguish between the two is perhaps the most common deficiency in news reporting of aboriginal issues in the province.

Contact brought European diseases and a population decline that continued until the 1920s, when fewer than 30,000 registered,[2] or 'status,' Natives lived in the province. By 1995 the registered populations of BC First Nations was 98,000, of which 52 percent lived on reserves.[3] In addition there were perhaps half again as many persons having First Nations ancestry, but who were not registered Natives; these 'non-status' Natives tended to be urban dwellers.

Douglas, Trutch, and Confederation, 1849-71

Any understanding of the place of aboriginal issues in BC requires going back to the very beginnings, for no other contemporary concerns are so firmly rooted in the province's colonial past.[4] Vancouver Island was made a British colony in 1849, with the Hudson's Bay Company in charge of settlement. Both the British government and the company recognized aboriginal title, and in 1850 Chief Factor James Douglas proceeded to arrange purchase treaties with Native communities. The treaties explicitly provided that the land was being 'sold' and that, with the exception of village areas, 'the land itself ... becomes the entire property of the White people for ever.'⁵ Douglas soon became governor of the colony and continued making treaties, all with similar wording, until fourteen had been completed.

Douglas unilaterally abandoned treaty making, however, turning instead to what he described as his 'system': a policy of assimilating Natives through education, conversion to Christianity, and allowing them the same preemption (homesteading) rights as whites. As the very basis of preemption is the principle that vacant, unsurveyed crown land is not burdened in any way, it follows that offering preemption rights to Natives marked a de facto denial of aboriginal title. Although Douglas continued to request further funds from London for purchasing Native title, and white public opinion in the colony continued to support purchase of Native title in advance of settlement, no further treaties or purchases of Native title took place on the island.

The mainland became a colony in 1858, with Douglas as governor. Although his instructions from London assumed that there would be 'bargains or treaties with the natives for the cession of lands possessed by them,'⁶ the authorities in London were willing to allow Douglas a free hand, and in fact he took no steps whatsoever to purchase Native title. As on the island, he proceeded with his system, allocating reserves unilaterally without any formal Native agreement. As his intent was that Natives would leave their traditional villages to take up family farming, he granted only small land reserves (more than ten acres per family being unusual). Douglas retired in 1864. Two years later the two colonies were united as the colony of British Columbia.

With Douglas's departure, Joseph Trutch, in the role of Commissioner of Lands and Works, emerged as the most influential official in the colony. Unlike Douglas, who regarded Natives as morally equal to whites and entitled to equal political treatment, Trutch regarded them as inferior savages. Presumably, Trutch's views were shared by the majority of the white population and their elected legislators. Under his guidance, one of the first acts of the legislature of the united colony was to prohibit preemption by Natives. In the areas of white settlement, Natives were now restricted to their small reserves as far as land use was concerned. Henceforth in BC's development, an individual white male could typically preempt a piece of land larger than a nearby reserve occupied by more than a dozen Native families.

Besides restricting Native access to land, Trutch made two other notable and lasting contributions. First, in 1870, he became the first official to deny that aboriginal title had ever existed in BC. To get around the very obvious contradiction provided by the Douglas treaties, he revised history by depicting them as inconsequential friendship agreements. His denial of aboriginal title went hand in hand with the emerging white view that Natives had been primitive nomads so inferior to the civilized Europeans that they could not be regarded as having had rights in the land. From this time onward, indeed, it was common for whites to compare Natives to wild animals.

Legalistically, the new denial of title rested on the new belief that unencumbered crown title to the land had been created with the extension of British sovereignty. The doctrine of *terra nullius* had arrived in BC – and it would survive for 120 years. Believing that Native title had never existed, the supporters of the new doctrine could see no reason for treaties, nor for any other steps to extinguish something that did not exist.[7]

Trutch's other contribution was arranging the colony's entry into Canada in 1871. (In this regard, Trutch's abilities and outlook so impressed Prime Minister John A. Macdonald that he had Trutch knighted by Queen Victoria and then appointed him the province's first lieutenant governor.) Ottawa officials had virtually no knowledge of BC Native policy; there is even evidence that they took for granted that treaties had already been arranged. Thus, for different reasons, both governments assumed that crown land in the province was not encumbered by any Native title, and so the Terms of Union made no mention of such title or of any need for further treaties. Moreover, the terms provided that crown land in the province would be under provincial jurisdiction; thus, the federal authorities would have no power to compel the province to alter the status of such land, as would be required were treaties to be proceeded with. As for reserves, the terms provided that the province would give land to the federal Crown for use as Native reserves, but ensured that the province would not be obligated to exceed the ten acre per family figure already in effect.

Native Demands and Federal-Provincial Actions, 1871-1969

Under section 91 (24) of the Constitution Act of 1867, the Canadian Parliament had exclusive authority to enact laws pertaining to 'Indians, and Lands reserved for the Indians.' In other words, the federal division of powers did not apply. In regard to registered Natives and reserves, Parliament could proceed to enact laws under any of the headings otherwise reserved to the provinces under sections 92 and 93, as it did, for example, in establishing the system of church-operated Native residential schools. Provinces had no authority to pass legislation directed specifically at Natives or reserves. However, insofar as Parliament had not enacted laws in subject matters otherwise under provincial control, provincial laws of general application would apply to Natives and reserves. In practice, federal laws and regulations came to leave virtually no room for provincial laws to apply to reserve lands and activities upon them, but considerable room for provincial laws to apply to Native persons, especially when off reserves.

Nothing in the original Constitution Act obligated provinces to provide rights or services to Natives. In 1872 the BC legislature removed from

Natives, who still composed a majority of the population, the right to vote in provincial elections. Several decades later the legislature closed the minor loophole that had allowed Natives to purchase (as opposed to preempting) crown land. The major element of provincial Native policy after 1871, however, was resisting pressure from both the federal government and Natives for larger reserves and for provincial participation in treaty negotiation. As nothing in the Terms of Union or the Constitution Act compelled the province to accede to the pressure, and as the denial of the franchise had neutralized any Native political power, the province simply rejected the demands.

Federal pressure for treaties and larger reserves came mainly from Liberal governments. In 1876, in a speech in Victoria, Governor General Lord Dufferin expressed the federal Liberal government's views when he criticized BC's 'neglecting to recognize what is known as Indian title' and 'interfering with the prescriptive rights of the Queen's Indian subjects.' He pointed out that 'In Canada ... no government, whether central or provincial, has failed to acknowledge that the original title to the land existed in the Indian tribes and communities ... '[8] Federal Conservative governments, in contrast, were largely supportive of the province's stance in early decades.

Native complaints and protests about small reserves and failure to recognize aboriginal title emerged regularly as white settlement advanced. In the 1870s a number of tribal nations joined in protest meetings in the southern portions of the province, and in the 1880s a delegation of north coast chiefs came to Victoria and met with federal and provincial officials. The chiefs requested larger reserves, treaties, and self-government under British law. Premier William Smithe dismissed the demands, telling the chiefs that 'When the whites first came among you, you were little better than the wild beasts of the field.'[9]

Along with the Native demands in this period were frequent expressions of Native willingness to share land and resources with the white settlers. Treaties were seen by the Natives not only as vehicles for settling the issue of aboriginal title and allowing for larger reserves or land holdings, but also, and equally important, as means of establishing a legitimate relationship between Natives and whites, thus ending Native subjugation within BC and Canada. In demanding treaties, the Natives were recognizing the facts of postcontact reality: they were acknowledging that they could not regain control over their traditional territories.

As white settlement accelerated across the province after the turn of the century, Native anxiety rose apace, to the point that new Native political organizations were formed on the coast and in the interior, each linking a number of tribal nations, and each expressing similar political demands for treaties. In 1915 the coastal and interior groups united their existing organizations into the Allied Indian Tribes of BC, the first province-wide Native organization.

The Allied Tribes lobbied politicians in Victoria and Ottawa, seeking larger reserves and treaties, but now threatening the new tactic of going to court. By this time the terms 'Native claims' or 'land claims' were coming into common use in the province, indicating the increasingly legalistic emphasis Natives placed on their efforts as they realized that the federal and provincial governments were simply unwilling to resolve the old 'Native land question' by the political means of negotiating treaties.[10]

At this very time, the United Kingdom's highest court, which was still Canada's highest court of appeal, ruled in favour of aboriginal land rights. Although the case arose in Nigeria, the situation was similar to that in BC. To head off the danger that BC's Natives might get their claims into court, and also to diminish the seemingly perpetual political bother of having to deal with the Natives' claims, federal officials began considering a simple remedy: having Parliament amend the Indian Act to make claims activity illegal. This remedy was implemented in 1927 by Mackenzie King's Liberal government. The new amendment provided fines or jail for 'every person' who, without federal government permission, 'receives, obtains, solicits or requests from any Indian any payment or contribution ... for the prosecution of any claim ... '[11] In practical terms, no person, whether white 'agitator' or Native political activist, could now proceed with any Native land claim without government consent.

Parliament had rendered the federal and provincial governments safe from any court action concerning aboriginal title. After half a century of vacillation, the federal authorities had joined firmly with BC in upholding the view that Canada west of the continental divide had been *terra nullius*. For their part, BC Natives now abandoned any formal expression of their claims. Among them, indeed, there arose the widespread belief that even to *speak* publicly about land claims was a criminal act.

In 1947, essentially as an afterthought to the granting of the franchise to citizens of Asian ancestry, the provincial legislature returned the right to vote to registered Natives. (Natives did not obtain the federal franchise until 1960.) In 1951, by which time federal officials assumed that BC Natives had forsaken claims to aboriginal title, Parliament repealed the claims prohibition that had been in effect since 1927. Previously, in 1949, Parliament had abolished judicial appeals to England; Canada's own Supreme Court was now the country's highest appeal court. No thought was given to the role the Canadian judges might play should they be faced with the aboriginal title issue.

In the 1949 provincial election, Frank Calder, a Nisga'a hereditary chief, was elected as a Co-operative Commonwealth Federation MLA from the Atlin riding, in which Natives had suddenly become the majority among voters. For the next three decades, Calder would remain an MLA and be the most prominent Native rights and land claims advocate in the province. Through the 1950s and 1960s, Calder was the leading political spokesperson among the coastal peoples, while George Manuel, a Shuswap, played a similar role among interior peoples. The demands of each were the same, and they were virtually identical to those voiced by the coastal chiefs in the 1880s and by the Allied Tribes in the 1920s. They wanted recognition of Native title, they wanted treaties granting compensation and more extensive Native lands, and they wanted more self-government and less federal government tutelage.

In 1955 Calder organized his own people into the Nisga'a Tribal Council, the first in the province, and in 1969 he led the council in taking the Nisga'a land claim to court. Also in 1969, Prime Minister Trudeau's minister of Indian affairs, Jean Chrétien, issued an Native policy paper announcing the government's intent to complete the final assimilation of Natives by ending any special status for Natives. In the realm of federal Native policy, the paper promptly became known as *the* White Paper, and it stands to this day as a major symbol of white insensitivity.

From One Big Claim to Tribalism, 1969-90

The White Paper outraged Natives across Canada. In direct response in BC, the Union of British Columbia Indian Chiefs (UBCIC) was formed in late 1969. It was a reserve-based organization, representing the great majority of Native bands. Its express purpose was to gain settlement of the land claim. Its hope was that all BC bands would together present one collective land claim, or 'one big claim' as it was called, and that the union would negotiate the treaty to settle the claim. In response to the Native reaction, the federal government quickly abandoned its White Paper and began funding the UBCIC and other Native organizations. However, by 1975 it was evident that the UBCIC's grand hopes would not be fulfilled, partly because of its own internal difficulties, partly because the provincial NDP government (1972-5) had declined to participate, and partly because of the growing political strength of 'tribalism' among BC Natives.

Modern tribalism had begun with the forming of tribal councils by the Nisga'a and the Nuu-chah-nulth in the 1950s. As it developed in the early 1970s, tribalism was a social and political revivalist movement based upon the desire of many Natives to return to traditional collective identities and to reaffirm their personal roots in the cultures of their ancestors; it was initially a phenomenon of the coastal peoples. To some extent tribalism was a reaction to the subordination imposed by the Indian Act and to the pervasive negative effects of the Native residential schools. Tribalism meant that tribal nations, rather than bands or communities, were seen as the entities of primary political legitimacy and therefore as the preferred bases for political action.[12] Tribalism brought with it a renewed political confidence and a renewed emphasis upon pressing governments to resolve the land question; it gained a major boost when the Nisga'a won a partial victory in the Supreme Court of Canada in 1973 (the case is discussed below). Representing only status Natives and composed of local band chiefs selected under authority of the Indian Act, the UBCIC had resisted tribalism and as a result had lost much coastal support even before 1975. It never regained its original strength and most of its remaining support was concentrated in the south-central part of the province among the four Interior Salish tribal nations: the Lillooet, Nlaka'pamux, Shuswap, and Okanagan. Among these four, in turn, support for the UBCIC was strongest among the smaller and poorer bands.

By the late 1970s, the advocates of tribalism were seeking a means of coordinating their activities so as to maximize their political effectiveness, while avoiding the dangers associated with a centralized, overstaffed organization. The result was a series of loose umbrella organizations: the Provincial Regional Forum (1980), the Tribal Forum (1981-3), the Aboriginal People's Constitutional Convention (1982-8), and the BC First Nations Congress (1988-90).[13]

Federal treaty negotiations began with the Nisga'a in 1976, but, as the federal government would negotiate only one treaty at a time, and as the province (which controlled crown land) refused to participate, little progress could be made on the crucial question of land. By the early 1980s, most of the other coastal tribal councils had submitted formal statements of claim in the format (including a map of traditional territory) set by the federal government. Political frustration grew over the provincial government's refusal to negotiate, now emphatically reaffirmed by Bill Bennett, the Social Credit premier. From the Native perspective, the key irritant became provincially authorized resource development in claim areas outside reserves. It was in this context in 1984 that two Nuu-chah-nulth First Nations, the Clayoquot and the Ahousat, supported and coordinated by their tribal council, blockaded access to Meares Island to stop logging by MacMillan Bloedel. The blockade proved to be the event that led eventually to the province's abandoning its historic opposition to negotiations. The courts, however, played the decisive role in forcing the province's hand.

The Natives, the Courts, and the Province, 1969-90[14]

In 1969, led by Frank Calder and with Tom Berger as their lawyer, the Nisga'a took the land question to court. Calder and the Nisga'a sought a two-part judicial declaration concerning aboriginal title: first, that the Nisga'a had held title to their lands prior to British sovereignty, and second, given the absence of any formal transfer or other subsequent extinguishment of it, that the Nisga'a still held that title in the present day.

Compelled for the first time to present a developed argument against aboriginal title, the province, through its lawyers, argued essentially that aboriginality itself could imbue no practice or privilege with legal force sufficient to carry it forward into the new regime; in effect, the province was giving legalistic guise to the century-old white view that aboriginal people had been too primitive to be on a par with Europeans. The province argued further that to have legal meaning, any Native title or other rights would have had to be explicitly created *by the British* at the time of sovereignty.[15] But the province also argued that any such title that had been created in this way would have been extinguished, implicitly and automatically, by the colonial government's having passed land legislation that ignored Native title. Aboriginal title had never existed, had never been created, and could not have survived.

The BC Supreme Court and Court of Appeal upheld the province's arguments, and so gave judicial sanction to *terra nullius*.[16] The judges of the Supreme Court of Canada took a somewhat different view. The six judges who expressed opinions (none of whom was from BC) unanimously concluded that the Nisga'a had held aboriginal title when BC was created. Aboriginal title was thus recognized, and *terra nullius* rejected, by a majority of the judges of the country's highest court. The Nisga'a had gained a major philosophic victory and won half their case. On the other half, the one of practical importance, the six judges were divided. Three concluded that the title had been extinguished, implicitly, by the actions of the colony; three concluded that in the absence of any treaty or other formal extinguishment, aboriginal title still existed.

While the support of only three judges was insufficient for a Nisga'a legal victory,[17] it was, as has been indicated, sufficient to persuade the federal government to change its policy. The direct result was the modern round of treaty-making in northern Canada, and in BC the opening of federal negotiations with the Nisga'a.

In November 1984, the Supreme Court of Canada advanced the concept of aboriginal title significantly, this time in the *Guerin* case involving the Musqueam Reserve adjacent to Vancouver. Building on the opinions expressed in *Calder*, Chief Justice Brian Dickson wrote that the Natives' 'interest in their lands is a pre-existing legal right not created by the Royal Proclamation, by ... the Indian Act, or by any other executive order or legislative provision.' He went on to state that the legal right extended not only to reserve lands but also to 'traditional tribal lands' outside reserves.[18] Thus, present-day Natives now had legal rights in traditional territories outside reserves in non-treaty areas.

The Clayoquot and Ahousat First Nations, with substantial support from non-Native environmentalists, set up their Meares Island blockade against MacMillan Bloedel only weeks after the *Guerin* decision. Soon the company and the First Nations were before the provincial Supreme Court, each seeking an injunction to stop the activities of the other. The judge granted the company its injunction. The Natives appealed. Guided by the new principle of legal rights enunciated by the Supreme Court of Canada, the province's Court of Appeal reversed the lower court decision, and ordered that logging be halted pending progress in resolving the Nuu-chah-nulth land claim.[19] Mr. Justice Peter Seaton wrote that 'The Indians have pressed their land claims in various ways for generations. The claims have not been dealt with and found invalid. They have not been dealt with at all ... There is a problem about tenure that has not been attended to in the past. We are being asked to ignore the problem as others have done. I am not willing to do this.'[20] Mr. Justice Alan Macfarlane added the following: 'The fact that there is an issue between the Indians and the province based upon aboriginal claims should not come as a surprise to anyone ... I think it fair to say that, in the end, the public anticipates that the claims will be resolved by negotiations and settlement. This judicial proceeding is but a small part of the whole process which will ultimately find its solution in a reasonable exchange between government and the Indian nations.'[21]

The Court of Appeal injunction had the effect of suspending the province's authority to authorize resource development on provincial crown land that had not been subject to treaty. Over the next few years, some half-dozen similar injunctions were granted, each following a well-publicized protest blockade by a First Nation or a tribal nation. Each injunction created further economic uncertainty in the resource sector and marked a further loss of political face for the province.

Responsibility for meeting the unprecedented circumstances imposed by the Natives, their blockades, and the courts fell to the Social Credit government of Premier Bill Vander Zalm, which took office in 1986. While reiterating the province's refusal either to recognize aboriginal title or to negotiate treaties with the Natives, the new government acknowledged the political salience of aboriginal concerns by creating the Ministry of Native Affairs in 1988. Under successive ministers Bruce Strachan and Jack Weisgerber and deputy minister Eric Denhoff, the new ministry made giant strides in opening communications with Native political leaders. Within this ministry, as well as within the Ministry of the Attorney General, the conviction grew that refusing to negotiate was becoming increasingly untenable.

After 1987 there was another potential legal threat: in the *Delgamuukw* case, the Gitksan and Wet'suwet'en tribal nations had combined to bring forward their claims not only for land 'ownership' but also for exclusive jurisdiction in their traditional territories. Most provincial officials and other observers assumed that any resulting court decision would continue the trend of previous cases in advancing the concept of aboriginal title, thus putting further pressure on the province to negotiate. Weisgerber and Denhoff took on the task of persuading the cabinet that negotiations might be the best option. In 1989, as a major first step, they had the premier appoint a Native Affairs Advisory Council, which included several Natives. During late 1989 and early 1990, the premier and the council toured the province, meeting publicly first with the Nisga'a and then with other major tribal nations.

The summer of 1990 in Canada was dominated by the Oka crisis, in which armed Mohawk warriors confronted the Quebec police and Canadian army in a dispute over land ownership. In BC a number of aboriginal communities (some twenty-four altogether, although not more than twelve at one time) erected rail or road blockades – in part to demonstrate support for the Mohawks, but more directly to press the BC government to agree to enter negotiations. The blockades generated massive news media coverage for weeks and focused intense political and economic pressure upon the provincial government. Quite unlike the premier of Quebec, Vander Zalm visited some of the blockades and spoke with the protesters. In the early autumn, following a recommendation from his advisory council, the premier announced that the province would enter negotiations, but that it still declined to acknowledge the validity of aboriginal title. Soon the province did enter the Nisga'a negotiations.

The BC Treaty Process: The Beginnings, 1990-1

The First Nations Congress (FNC), chaired by Bill Wilson, quickly seized the political initiative[22] by organizing two meetings, one with Prime Minister Mulroney and one with Premier Vander Zalm and his entire cabinet. The FNC invited representatives from communities and tribal nations to the meetings, which were held in public in the Hotel Vancouver in October. In order to facilitate participation by those who had not previously supported the FNC, and also to mark its new role in dealing with the two governments on behalf of aboriginal peoples, the FNC adopted the additional name of First Nations Summit (FNS).[23]

The two meetings, which were cordial, allowed both governments to demonstrate their willingness to undertake new approaches, while the broad Native representation (the only notable absentees were the leaders of the UBCIC) allowed the FNS to demonstrate that a majority of aboriginal communities and tribal nations were in support of its approach. In the meetings both sides proclaimed the values of cooperation as opposed to confrontation. The prime minister indicated a willingness to revise federal policy in order to allow more than one claim to be negotiated at the same time within a province. The premier and his cabinet were more guarded; clearly they had not yet had the opportunity to develop specific policy proposals. In their case it was their presence and their cordiality that provided the main political message.

The FNS leaders' essential fear was that proceeding immediately into treaty negotiations would allow the two governments, either separately or in collusion, to out-prepare and outmanoeuvre the tribal nations, none of whom (excepting the Nisga'a) had had any prior experience in such negotiations. For this reason the leaders proposed that a tripartite task force be established to recommend both the principles and the procedures that should be followed in negotiations. The two governments agreed, and the BC Claims Task Force was established, in December 1990, with seven members: two appointed by the federal government, two by the province, and three by the FNC (the UBCIC was offered one further position but declined). As it turned out, the task force played the key role in establishing the treaty process.

The three Native members were each leaders of their tribal nations – Miles Richardson of the Haida, Joe Mathias of the Squamish, and Ed John of the Carrier-Sekani – and they were chosen to represent the north coast, south coast, and interior, respectively. One of the federal members, Audrey Stewart, was an official with the Department of Indian Affairs; the other, Murray Coolican, was a consultant and expert on treaties. The Native and federal appointees could be expected to agree that treaties should cover a wide range of matters, and that the process should be one in which the Natives and governments should, in principle, be regarded as equal participants.

From this perspective, the outlook of the two provincial appointees was critical, since a majority report opposed by them would be given little credibility by the province, and their opposition would signal a continuing provincial recalcitrance even if negotiations were to proceed. Native Affairs Minister Weisgerber nominated Tony Sheridan, a senior official in the ministry, and Allan Williams, who had been a member of the Bill Bennett cabinet. Sheridan already had a good reputation among FNS leaders, while Williams was perhaps the only past or present Social Credit cabinet minister who was both well known and respected among politically active Natives.

The task force worked harmoniously, producing a unanimous report. It modelled its recommendations upon previous treaty-making in Canada, especially upon the modern round of negotiations in northern Canada that had followed the *Calder* decision. It sought as well to address the particular difficulties that would arise from the unprecedented number of separate negotiations that would be needed; it estimated that there would be some thirty separate treaties, a figure in accord with the number of tribal nations. The task force's recommendations[24] may be summarized as follows:

(1) *Purpose and Scope*. Treaties would serve to 'establish a new relationship based on mutual trust, respect, and understanding,' through voluntary negotiations between First Nations, BC, and Canada. Treaties could deal with any issue that any one of the three principals 'views as significant to the new relationship.' In general, negotiation of the various treaties in the province would proceed simultaneously.

(2) *Participation*. Any aboriginal community or combination of communities (i.e., tribal councils) would be able to initiate separate negotiations relating to its traditional territory; thus, First Nations could decide whether and when to initiate negotiations, and those who had signed Douglas treaties or Treaty No. 8 could use the new process to revise or add to the old treaties. 'Third party interests' (e.g., those of municipalities, resource industries, unions, etc.) would not be direct participants, but would be represented by the two governments.

(3) *Good-Faith Negotiation and Dispute Resolution*. To ensure that each of the negotiating participants was adequately prepared and negotiating in good faith, and also to help resolve disagreements that might arise, there would be a 'British Columbia Treaty Commission' to oversee negotiations (but not itself be a party to them). It would be composed of five members – one federal, one provincial, two aboriginal, and a chief commissioner to be agreed upon by the First Nations Summit and the two governments.

(4) *Standard, Defined Stages in Negotiation*. Each negotiation would consist of six stages:
   (a) submission of a statement of intent by the First Nation or Nations
   (b) assessment and certification by the treaty commission of each party's readiness
   (c) negotiation by the three principals of a 'framework agreement' (i.e., subject matter outline of the treaty)
   (d) negotiation of the 'agreement in principle' (i.e., draft treaty document)
   (e) negotiation of any final details, followed by formal ratification by the three principals
   (f) implementation.

(5) *Public Education*. The three principals would be jointly responsible for 'public education and information programs,' both generally and relating to each negotiation.

(6) *Level Playing Field*. Rather than have the governments set the conditions and provide the loans needed by the aboriginal participants, the treaty commission would receive funding from the two governments and then set the amount, timing, and conditions of the loans.

(7) *Interim Measures.* In order to head off actions that would effectively preclude matters of First Nation interest from negotiation (e.g., authorizing clearcutting of areas containing Native trap lines), the principals would negotiate interim agreements on such matters separately from, and normally prior to, the treaty process.

Two recommendations are worthy of extra comment. First, in recommending the widest possible scope for negotiations, the task force was assuming that the BC treaties would, with one major addition, be broadly similar to those being concluded in Canada's north. The treaties would thus identify some crown lands as aboriginal (in the Yukon, lands amounting to 8 percent of the territory had been so identified) and provide for compensation for other lands. The treaties would also deal with such matters as land management, resource development, protection of language and culture, and taxation.

At the same time, however, the task force was leaving the way open for aboriginal self-government to be provided for in the treaties. This was the major addition. No previous treaty in Canada had explicitly provided for self-government. Self-government had been very much an issue during the negotiation of the northern treaties, but the federal government had insisted that it be provided for through separate, ordinary, parliamentary statute, not through the treaties themselves. With Section 35 of the new Canadian constitution of 1982 guaranteeing treaty rights, the inclusion of self-government in the BC treaties would give it full constitutional protection – that is, place self-government provisions beyond the ability of the BC legislature or Parliament to modify without the consent of the aboriginal community or tribal nation affected. Equally significant, however, was the fact that creating self-government through treaty negotiations would give the province and Canada the ability to influence the nature of self-government and, indeed, to veto any specific proposal put forward for inclusion in a treaty.

Second, in the text of its report, although not as a specific recommendation, the task force rejected the principle of 'blanket extinguishment of First Nations rights, title, and privileges' that had been intended in all previous Canadian treaties.[25] Instead, the task force believed that the principle should be that 'those aboriginal rights not specifically dealt with in treaty should not be considered extinguished or impaired.'[26]

The task force proved to be of crucial importance; its report was endorsed by the First Nations Summit and the two governments, and its recommendations were fully implemented over the next several years. Indeed, among those involved in the actual setting up of the treaty process, the report was commonly referred to as 'the bible.'

Meanwhile, in Court: The *Delgamuukw* Case, 1991 and 1993

By late 1990, the politicians (aboriginal, federal, and provincial) in BC, and the political process they had got under way, were, for the first time, ahead of the courts and the legal process in responding to aboriginal concerns. This new circumstance was demonstrated in March 1991, when Mr. Justice Allan McEachern ruled decisively against the Gitksan and Wet'suwet'en tribal nations in the *Delgamuukw* case in the BC Supreme Court. He

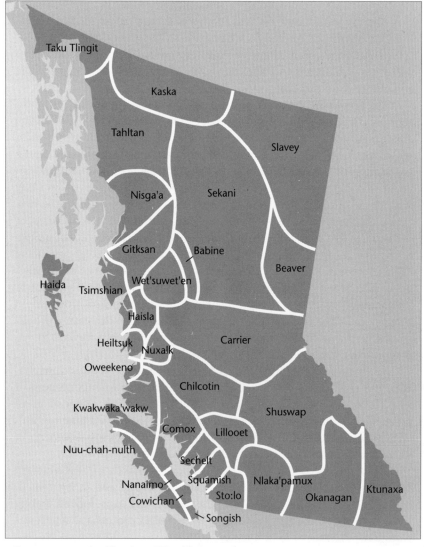

Contemporary classification of First Nations

rejected both aboriginal jurisdiction and aboriginal title: 'In my judgment the plaintiffs' aboriginal interests in the territory were lawfully extinguished by the Crown during the colonial period. It follows that non-reserve Crown lands ... are unencumbered by any claim to aboriginal interests.'[27] As noteworthy as his seeming denial of the conclusion of the Supreme Court of Canada in the *Guerin* case was Mr. Justice McEachern's own explicitly expressed view that Native social, political, and governmental structures had been 'primitive' prior to contact. In substance and conclusion, his views were similar to those exemplified more than a century earlier by Joseph Trutch.

In legal terms the ruling meant simply that the governments were not obligated to respond to the Gitksan-Wet'suwet'en assertions of title, but it did not, and could not, prevent governments from proceeding, as a matter of policy, with the negotiation process – that is, from proceeding as the Court of Appeal had previously suggested the governments ought to. Had the ruling come a year or more earlier, however, it would almost certainly have delayed, if not scuttled, the province's willingness to negotiate; but, coming when it did, it had no direct effect. Still, seeking a ruling that would obligate the governments, the Natives appealed.

In June 1993, a five-member Court of Appeal panel partly reversed the McEachern judgment. Supported by two other judges, Mr. Justice Alan Macfarlane agreed with the trial judge in rejecting the claim 'to an exclusive right to use, occupy and control the lands and resources' (that is, the Natives did not have outright ownership of the land), but ruled that 'the plaintiff's aboriginal rights were not all extinguished'[28] in the colonial period or subsequently. The two other judges agreed that aboriginal land rights continued to exist, but went further than the majority in recognizing the extent of those rights, and disagreed with the majority's rejection of the right to self-government.

As far as aboriginal land rights were concerned, then, the five judges were unanimous in ruling that they continued to exist in non-treaty areas. To this major extent the Natives had been successful, for, unless overturned by the Supreme Court of Canada, the ruling compelled the province and the federal government to respond positively to assertions of continuing aboriginal land rights. The court, however, left it to those involved to work out the details, through the sort of negotiation process that was in fact then being established for BC. Reiterating sentiments he had expressed earlier in the Meares Island injunction case, Mr. Justice Macfarlane observed that

The Gitksan and Wet'suwet'en people have aboriginal rights in a large area of land ... These rights, along with land already in reserves, may provide a foundation for the preservation and development of an Indian community.

Self-regulation ... may be secured in many ways yet to be negotiated ... The parties have expressed willingness to negotiate their differences. I would encourage such consultation and reconciliation, a process which may provide the only real hope of an early and satisfactory agreement which not only gives effect to the aspirations of the aboriginal peoples but recognizes there are many diverse cultures, communities and interests which must co-exist in Canada. A proper balancing of those interests is a delicate and crucial matter.[29]

The BC Treaty Process

Following acceptance of the task force's report, the federal and provincial governments and the First Nations Summit worked harmoniously together over a three-year period (1992-4) in establishing the institutions and procedures of the new treaty process. Several factors explain the continuing harmony that allowed the institution-building to proceed unimpeded during the period. First, treaties and the negotiation process had not become controversial public issues following Vander Zalm's agreement to negotiate or during the 1991 provincial election campaign. As both the Social Credit and New Democratic Parties were in favour of negotiations, and as opinion polls showed little public concern over aboriginal issues, neither party sought to criticize the policy of the other during the campaign.

Second, the NDP, which took office under Premier Mike Harcourt after the election, was much more committed to resolving the full range of aboriginal issues than the previous government had been. For the first time, BC had a government that was more responsive than the federal government in dealing with aboriginal concerns. The NDP expanded the role and importance of the renamed Ministry of Aboriginal Affairs, and later recognized both aboriginal title and an aboriginal right to self-government.

Third, the fact that an impartial but representative treaty commission would oversee the process allowed each of the three principals to proceed through the setting-up stage with some confidence that there was no need to anticipate every potential future difficulty. Fourth, the task force device had allowed the aboriginal side to participate, for the first time ever in Canada, in designing a treaty process, thus minimizing the likelihood of aboriginal opposition as the process was established.

Even though the appearance of harmony on the aboriginal side was somewhat deceptive, given the refusal of the Union of BC Indian Chiefs to participate, it remained the case that no significant Native protest action took place during the summers of 1992, 1993, or 1994. Nor was there, during this same period, any sign of major hostility on the part of non-Natives toward either the treaty process or aboriginal demands. Thus, the BC treaty process was established during a time of abnormal, even artificial, political calm in the sphere of aboriginal public policy in the province.

The steps in establishing the process may be quickly summarized. In September 1992, the two governments and the First Nations Summit signed the 'British Columbia Treaty Commission Agreement,' which marked the formal acceptance of the task force recommendations. Subsequently, the two governments agreed on a cost-sharing formula for treaty settlements; in general, the federal government would provide cash while the province would provide land. In April 1993, the treaty commission was constituted, and in December of that year it began accepting 'statements of intent to negotiate' from aboriginal communities and tribal nations. Actual negotiations began in 1994.

Of the province's 198 aboriginal communities, 130 of them, containing about 70 percent of the registered Natives, had entered the treaty process by October 1995. The number of separate negotiations required, however, was only 47, as 16 tribal councils were acting for 99 communities, while the other 31 communities were acting individually.[30]

Two major patterns were evident in the aboriginal participation. First, to a greater extent than had been assumed by the task force, communities were presenting their claims individually rather than through tribal councils, thus increasing the number of negotiations required and making the process more complicated for the two governments. Second, and much more significantly, a major political and geographic division remained evident within the aboriginal population. Politically, it was the communities and tribal nations supporting the First Nations Summit that had entered the treaty process; those supporting the Union of BC Indian Chiefs were holding back. In the UBCIC view, the province had no legitimate part in the process, because to accept a role for the province would be to accept the de facto displacement of aboriginal governments and their jurisdictions that had occurred when the colony and province had been created.

Geographically, the southern interior of the province was largely untouched by the treaty process. This area contained the traditional territories of the four Interior Salish tribal nations, who provided most of the UBCIC's political support. Opposition to the treaty process was strongest among the Shuswap, Nlaka'pamux, and Okanagan; of the forty communities composing these three tribal nations, only three had entered the process. The division within the aboriginal population became highly evident during the summer of 1995. The major road blockades (near Penticton and at Douglas Lake and Adams Lake) were mounted by Okanagan and Shuswap communities, while the armed stand-off at Gustafsen Lake was mainly the work of a small number of Shuswap individuals.

The Return to Controversy

By 1995 the period of artificial political calm had come to an end. The gathering momentum of the treaty process itself had served to raise concerns among the non-Native public, and the two provincial opposition parties had found much to criticize in the process.[31] During 1995 the protests in the interior unsettled many observers, and the signing of the Nisga'a agreement-in-principle in March 1996 added to the concerns and gave new force to opposition criticism. Aboriginal issues had reemerged as conspicuous and controversial subjects in news coverage and in political debate within BC.

Further Reading

Alfred, Gerald. *Heeding the Voices of Our Ancestors: Kahnawake Mohawk Politics and the Rise of Native Nationalism*. Toronto: Oxford University Press 1995

British Columbia. *Papers Connected with the Indian Land Question, 1850-1871*, 5-11. 1875. Reprint, Victoria: Government Printer 1987

British Columbia Claims Task Force. *Report*. Vancouver, 1991

Dickason, Olive P. *Canada's First Nations: A History of Founding Peoples from Earliest Times*. Toronto: McClelland and Stewart 1992

Drake-Terry, Joanne. *The Same as Yesterday*. Lilloet: Lillooet Tribal Council 1989

Fisher, Robin. *Contact and Conflict: Indian-European Relations in British Columbia, 1774-1890*. Vancouver: UBC Press 1977

Francis, Daniel. *The Imaginary Indian: The Image of the Indian in Canadian Culture*. Vancouver: Arsenal Pulp Press 1992

Muckle, Robert. *The First Nations of British Columbia: An Anthropological Perspective*. North Vancouver: Brookridge 1995

Smith, Mel. *Our Home or Native Land?* Victoria: Crown Publishing 1995

Tennant, Paul. *Aboriginal Peoples and Politics: The Indian Land Question in British Columbia, 1849-1989*. Vancouver: UBC Press 1990

Part 2: The Political Stage

5
The Politics of Polarization: Parties and Elections in British Columbia
Donald E. Blake

Provincial party competition in British Columbia has a sharper left-right focus than in any other part of English-speaking North America. Decentralized federalism has allowed the province's electoral competition to become detached from the main currents of Canada's national politics. Unlike the national party system, where participants balance a host of competing regional, cultural, and socioeconomic interests, the BC party system is based mainly on the ideological and class divisions of the modern industrial state. Contemporary politics are suffused with the rhetoric of fundamental conflict between left and right. Politicians display and manipulate the powerful symbols of free enterprise and socialism against a backdrop coloured by populism.

The origin of this pattern of politics is a complex story. It is linked to an economy that attracted workers and entrepreneurs eager to compete for shares of resource wealth, each jealous of the claims of the other; to settlement patterns that produced higher rates of population growth than in any other province; and to geography that isolated developing provincial communities from each other, as well as the conflict management styles of politicians forced to choose between the financial power of capital and the numerical superiority of labour. During the late 1950s, the growth of the provincial state added a new dimension to reinforce the old one, and propelled the left into a much stronger electoral position by creating a dramatically larger public sector workforce that turned toward the New Democratic Party in provincial elections.

For most of the period since the Second World War, the principal actors on either side of the basic divide were the Social Credit Party and the Cooperative Commonwealth Federation (CCF), and the latter's successor, the NDP. Social Credit dominance of the centre-right was challenged twice, in the elections of 1972 and 1991. The party recovered from the 1972 defeat to reemerge stronger than ever. However, it never recovered from its defeat in the 1991 election, and it was shut out completely in 1996.

The Pre-Party Period to 1903

Despite BC's reputation as a battleground between free enterprise and socialism, it was not always this way.[1] The first thirty years after Confederation were dominated by national issues, such as the Terms of Union with Canada, and parochial concerns linked to the province's frontier status. Legislative politics revolved around individual and local self-interest, a context in which political principles or even party attachments had little place. The period from 1871, when BC joined Confederation, to 1903 was characterized by official non-partisanship in the provincial legislature. In a very real sense, the business of provincial politics was business. The first cabinets contained only the portfolios of attorney-general, provincial secretary, and public lands.[2] Most members of the assembly had business interests and pursued them unabashedly. Those divisions that appeared in the assembly tended to parallel divisions of interest within the business class: Vancouver Island versus the mainland and (on the question of the routing of the transcontinental railway) interior and Island versus the Lower Mainland.

Provincial self-interest dictated strong support in national elections for the Conservative Party, the party committed to fulfilling the Terms of Union it had negotiated. The strong provincial rights and anti-imperial stance that sustained the Liberal Party in national politics had limited appeal in BC given the province's dependence on a beneficent federal government and the use of the former colonial power as an ally in battles for better terms. In addition, and unlike the situation in the eastern provinces, the overwhelmingly British and Protestant character of the white population virtually eliminated religion and ethnic origin as sources of partisan division. Racism was undeniably a feature of provincial politics, but it pitted the white majority against a non-white minority (mainly immigrants from China) who had few political rights and virtually no champions in Victoria.[3]

Non-partisanship in the provincial legislature was ultimately abandoned in the face of chronic government instability and scandal. In 1903 the lieutenant governor dismissed the ministry of Colonel Edward Prior after an inquiry revealed his assistance in awarding a government contract to a firm in which he was involved.[4] In addition, the replacement of a Conservative dominance in national politics by a Liberal one following the 1896 federal election naturally led to an interest in developing a Liberal Party organization in the province. With Liberals and Conservatives now facing each other in national elections, it was not long before competing federal allegiances affected coalition-building attempts in the provincial legislature. When Richard McBride was asked to form a cabinet following Prior's dismissal, he did so by inviting only avowed Conservatives to join. Shortly thereafter, Liberals and Conservatives confronted each other for the first time in a provincial election.

The Traditional Two-Party System: 1903-33

The Conservatives under McBride, victorious in the 1903 election, proceeded to build a formidable party machine using the instruments of government patronage and preferment pioneered by their national counterparts three decades earlier. Differences between Liberals and Conservatives proved to be based on little more than the distinction between being in or out of office.[5] The Liberals denounced the familiar evils of machine politics, patronage, dishonesty, and inefficiency, only to face the same charges soon after winning office in 1916.

Despite conditions that might have been expected to facilitate support for a left-wing party, especially on the resource frontier, socialist and labour parties remained weak throughout the period. Combined labour and socialist support peaked at 15.2% in 1903, and from then until 1928 the left received, on average, just over 12% of the vote.[6] The explanation, in large part, is attributable to splits within the left, between those who favoured participation in electoral politics in order to use government power to ameliorate deplorable working conditions, and those who believed that such participation would only lead to co-optation of the working class and delay the revolution that would produce socialist utopia. Their favoured instruments were socialist education and the strike.

Organizers on the left also faced anti-union campaigns by employers as well as organizational difficulties associated with seasonality, labour mobility, and decentralization of ownership and production.[7] Moreover, the resource frontier held out the prospect of significant material gain through exercise of the same kind of initiative and risk-taking attributed to capitalist entrepreneurs. In other words, the obstacles to engagement in collective action included a significant individualist streak in the working class.

Both Liberals and Conservatives made appeals to the working person, and made some changes in workplace safety and restrictions on union activity. However, when the crunch came, as it frequently did, particularly in the mining areas of the province, both displayed a willingness to intervene on behalf of employers faced with 'rebellious' workers.

The onset of the Great Depression brought an end to the two-party period and to this pattern of party alignment. Simon Fraser Tolmie, who turned out to be the last Conservative premier of BC, like so many other leaders who had the misfortune to be in office when economic disaster struck, was repudiated by the electorate. After winning thirty-five of forty-seven seats in 1928, in 1933 the Conservatives finished behind the victorious Liberals and a new party, the CCF.[8]

Transition and Party System Separation: 1933-52

The CCF entered the 1933 election campaign promising a 'radical transformation of society including the socialization of the financial machinery of the country ... the socialization of the basic resource industries, the socialization of health services, free education from public school through university, the rapid expansion of social services,' and reallocation of the tax burden.[9] Major newspapers greeted the arrival of the CCF with hostility, as did business interests. However, unlike the case some years later (especially in 1941 and 1972), they did not advocate any special strategies to contain the left. The strong CCF showing (31.5% of the vote) could have been viewed as a fluke given Conservative disarray. The CCF caucus was also soon plagued by internal conflicts that diminished its effectiveness as the official opposition.[10]

Moreover, the Liberals won a majority of seats again in 1937, despite a modest Conservative revival. That was sufficient to relegate the CCF to third place in the legislature. In other words, for a time it appeared that two-party, or perhaps two-party plus, politics had returned, a situation in which one of the old-line parties could win a majority of seats on its own, and opponents of the left need not fear a left-wing victory produced by a split in the non-left vote. Moreover, the Liberal premier, Duff Pattullo, moved his party leftward, undercutting CCF support, by advocating massive public works expenditures to combat unemployment, state health insurance, a permanent advisory council on the economy, and increased government regulation of utilities. Pattullo's moves were more than tactical: they reflected a conviction that government had a moral responsibility for the welfare of the individual and must be prepared to intervene and regulate the economy to that end.[11]

However, the 1941 election and its aftermath eliminated a provincial party system that replicated, at least in name, competition in national elections. A substantial decline in Liberal support produced nearly a dead heat in the race for the popular vote. The CCF actually finished first with 33.4%, compared to the Liberals' 32.9% and the Conservatives' 30.9%. The Liberals remained the largest party in the legislature with twenty-one seats, compared to fourteen for the CCF and twelve for the Conservatives. However, the exigencies of the wartime situation, combined with the normal requirement for reliable legislative allies in a minority government situation, led to the formation of a coalition between the Liberals and the Conservatives. This lasted beyond the end of the war and through two elections before being terminated prior to the 1952 election.

Despite appearances to the contrary, the coalition was not designed as an instrument to contain the left. The CCF was initially invited to participate in an all-party coalition, and the party even offered to guarantee support for a Liberal minority government should the Tories drive too hard a bargain. However, the success of the coalition experience combined with the incentives of the parliamentary system to transform 'the non-left into the

anti-left'[12] and ultimately to redefine the basis of provincial party competition. Cooperation within the coalition reduced Liberal and Conservative
differences in their own eyes, as well as in the eyes of the electorate. The
very existence of the CCF as the official, and only, opposition raised the
salience of the division between free enterprise and socialism, especially
given the doctrinaire stance of the CCF leader, Harold Winch.

The coalition won resounding victories in 1945 and 1949, reducing CCF
representation in the legislature to ten and then to seven seats. However,
strains were produced by an arrangement in which the coalition partners
retained their separate identities, legislative caucuses, and party organizations, and by a system of rewards that seemed to the Conservatives to perpetuate their minority status. Federal Liberals and Conservatives were unhappy with a situation in which prominent provincial politicians were
unwilling to assist in national election battles lest this have negative consequences for the coalition, and they pressed for it to be dissolved. Even
the need to contain the left temporarily lost its urgency as the perennial
battle between moderates and radicals resurfaced in the CCF following the
1949 election, and the Liberal Party became convinced that it could win
on its own.

As insurance against a victory by the CCF based on only a plurality of the
popular vote, the coalition partners introduced the alternative vote system
prior to the 1952 election. The ballot required voters to rank candidates in
order of preference. If a candidate received a majority of first choices in a
given riding, he or she was declared elected. Failing that, the candidate
with the lowest number of first choices would be eliminated from the count,
and the second choices on his or her ballots would be allocated among the
other candidates. The procedure would be repeated until one candidate
received a majority of the combined ballots. Proponents of the ballot change
reasoned, apparently, that the Liberal and Conservative voters would divide their first two choices between those parties, that the CCF would win
only those ridings in which it had a majority on the first count, and that a
coalition could be arranged, if necessary, should neither the Liberals nor
the Conservatives win a legislative majority.[13]

None of these assumptions proved correct. The Liberals and Conservatives finished third and fourth rather than first and second, both in terms
of seats and votes, as the leaderless Social Credit Party eked out a single-
seat victory over the CCF. Shortly thereafter, the Social Credit caucus elected
William Andrew Cecil Bennett as party leader and he became premier.
Bennett, a former Conservative MLA and member of the coalition caucus,
had long been an advocate of a permanent coalition to contain the left.
Moreover, by harnessing Social Credit to this objective, he also achieved his
goal of developing a free-enterprise party unfettered by the entanglements

of federal politics. In 1953 he won his first majority victory, following that with five consecutive victories (1956, 1960, 1963, 1966, and 1969) before going down to defeat in 1972.

The Politics of Polarization: 1952-91

Under Bennett, the 'free enterprise versus socialism' slogan became part of every election campaign as a device to discredit the CCF and discourage support for the Liberal and Conservative Parties. From 1956 until its defeat in 1972, his party never held fewer than 60% of the seats in the legislature. Social Credit vote dropped below 40% only once, to 38.8% in 1960 (see Figure 5.1). The Liberal Party struggled bravely on, continuing to compete in nearly every riding during the first twenty years of Social Credit rule, but it gradually slipped from 23.3% of the vote in 1952 to less than 20% during the 1960s. However, they maintained a presence in the legislature (varying from two to six members), whereas the Conservatives disappeared altogether between 1956 and 1972. After 1952 the Conservatives nominated a full slate only once, in 1960.

Bennett also presided over major transformations in the economy and social structure of the province, which created new political forces and thrust new issues onto the public agenda. The labour force doubled during his twenty years as premier, and changed in character. Employment in the public sector expanded along with new demands in the health, education, and social welfare fields. The service, finance, and real estate sectors rather than primary industry experienced the highest growth rates. Phenomenal population growth occurred in the interior. Kamloops and Prince George, which ranked eleventh and seventeenth, respectively, among BC cities in 1952, became important regional centres, and by 1972 were the fourth and third largest cities in the province.

Changes in the province's political economy are explored in more detail in Chapter 2. Our main interest here is in the effect these had on the balance between left and right in the party system. Unwittingly, they helped to bring about the first Social Credit defeat in 1972, precipitating a major realignment in provincial politics that effectively eliminated the provincial Liberal rump from the legislature, producing an almost pure form of two-party competition that was to last for fifteen years. Their principal effect was to increase the numbers and geographical dispersion of potential NDP supporters. In both private and public employment, increasing numbers of British Columbians found themselves in work settings that encouraged NDP support. Large-scale sawmills and pulp and paper operations, formerly confined to Lower Mainland and Vancouver Island locations, expanded throughout the province. In 1951, 18 of 29 sawmills with a daily capacity over 100,000 board feet were located on the Island or Lower Mainland. In 1971, 57 mills exceeded this capacity, 40 of them outside these regions.[14] An even sharper pattern held for pulp and paper capacity. In 1961, 11 pulp and paper mills operated in the Island/Lower Mainland areas and only 3 outside. By 1975, 2 mills were added to the former areas bringing the total to 13. However, elsewhere the number had increased to 12.[15] As economic activity became geographically more homogeneous, so did union membership – traditionally a source of support for the left.

The geographical dispersion of industrial activity is reflected in a decline in the regional concentration of NDP vote between 1966 and 1975. As the province became geographically much more homogeneous than before, at least in terms of industrial activity, differences between regions in party vote shares became quite similar. As Conservative and Liberal support withered at the provincial level, the NDP and Social Credit came to mirror each other so that the NDP became no more heterogeneous geographically than Social Credit. This also had the effect of reducing the salience of regional cleavages in voting and diffusing left/right polarization throughout the province.

Another factor contributing to the expansion of CCF/NDP support from its traditional one-third of the electorate was growth of public sector employment. Provincial public employment grew more quickly from the mid-1960s to the mid-1970s in BC than anywhere else in Canada. From 1965 to 1975, the number of tax returns from direct employees of the province (but not of provincial crown corporations) increased by 88%. The national average increase was 73%. Even more telling, the number of educational employees increased by 62% in BC, but by only 35% in the country as a whole. 'Institutional' employment (mostly in health care) grew by 107% in BC, and by only 73% elsewhere in Canada. In each of these categories, more than two-thirds of the 1965-75 employment growth took place between 1972 and 1975.[16]

The Social Credit defeat in 1972 is in part attributable to dissatisfaction among occupational groups the government had helped to create and nourish. The election was preceded by major battles with hospital and government employees and with doctors and schoolteachers. The victorious NDP leader, Dave Barrett, had himself been a social worker in the employ of the province before entering the legislature. However, Barrett ultimately proved unable to withstand concerted opposition to his government's program, especially by the business community, and to overcome the impression that his government was disorganized and too free with the public purse. A renewed Social Credit Party led by Bill Bennett swept him from office in 1975.

Nevertheless, NDP support continued to grow even after the 1975 defeat, as Liberal and Conservative support collapsed entirely, completing the realignment and the development of a new relationship between societal groups and the party system. Once the new, two-party equilibrium was established, Social Credit regained its position as the stronger of the two parties.

Analysis of public opinion data suggests that realignment occurred in two stages between 1972 and 1979.[17] The first stage saw the collapse of the Liberal and Conservative vote whose combined effect had helped to defeat Social Credit in 1972. Approximately half of those voting Liberal in 1972 repeated that choice in 1975, with most of the rest switching to Social Credit, now led by Bill Bennett, W.A.C. Bennett's son. Many of them undoubtedly followed the sitting Liberal MLAs who defected to Social Credit prior to the 1975 election.[18] By 1979 most of the remaining Liberal supporters had deserted the party. The Conservatives managed to hold on to more of their 1972 support, but that too all but disappeared, lost to Social Credit in 1979. The principal beneficiary of Liberal and Conservative collapse was Social Credit. However, the NDP attracted a significant number of former Liberal supporters, and the lion's share of new voters, so that it entered the 1980s with vote percentages in the low forties compared to the mid-thirties. However, with only two parties in the system, that was not sufficient to displace Social Credit from power.

The accession of a Bennett to the Social Credit Party leadership and premiership and the return of Social Credit to its familiar position as the governing party give a false impression of continuity. In fact, under Bill Bennett, Social Credit was transformed. The party organization was modernized and centralized in the hands of a new generation of political professionals familiar with the techniques of fundraising, polling, and sophisticated election campaigning. Following his third election victory in 1983, and a significant decline in the provincial economy, Bennett took the party sharply to the right with massive budget cuts and a comprehensive program to reduce the size and scope of government.[19] The resulting battle over the 'restraint program' left the province more polarized than at any time since the Second World War.

Following three successive defeats at the hands of Bill Bennett, Dave Barrett resigned as leader of the NDP in 1984. His replacement, Bob Skelly, emerged as the party's new leader after five ballots in a hotly contested leadership convention. It was a victory in which the trade unionists combined with the party's left to deny the leadership to a candidate (David Vickers) who represented the new professional, urban, middle-class activists that had been swelling the party ranks over the previous decade.[20] Skelly lasted for only one election as party leader, resigning after conducting a lacklustre campaign in the 1986 election. His successor, Mike Harcourt, elected by acclamation in 1987, proceeded to downplay the party's socialist past and woo the business community. With Harcourt's victory, the party's new middle-class wing was firmly in control.

Social Credit also replaced its leader before the 1986 election, following Bennett's retirement. Bill Vander Zalm won the post at the most contested leadership convention (there were twelve candidates) in Canadian history in July 1986. Unlike the case in the NDP, Vander Zalm's victory represented the return to prominence of the party's old guard. The convention divided sharply along populist/non-populist and establishment/non-establishment lines, with the candidate favoured by the party establishment (Brian Smith) defeated on the fourth ballot. The result represented a repudiation of Bill Bennett's leadership style and his attempts to modernize the party organization.[21]

Vander Zalm led Social Credit to victory in 1986 despite a small drop in the party's popular vote. However, he proved unable to reconcile his populist, hands-on leadership style with the demands of modern government and the organizational needs of the party. After six by-election losses, a spate of cabinet resignations, an incipient caucus revolt, and an investigation that showed his personal financial dealings had violated conflict of interest guidelines for cabinet members, he resigned in April 1991.[22] His successor, Rita Johnston, elected as interim party leader by the legislative caucus and victorious by a margin of only forty votes in the subsequent leadership convention, proved unable to mend the divisions in the party or overcome the hostility toward Social Credit in the electorate created by Vander Zalm's leadership. In the 1991 election she led the party to a humiliating third-place finish. Following a series of resignations and defections, the once-dominant party was reduced to a single member in the legislature.

Contemporary Realignment: 1991-?
The 1991 election and its aftermath warrant closer analysis for what they may tell us about the likelihood of a return to a polarized two-party system. As discussed above, the polarized party system began in 1952 following the collapse of the wartime provincial coalition of Liberals and Conservatives. Social Credit emerged as the dominant party on the right but did not initially absorb all the anti-socialist forces. A modest Conservative resurgence in 1972, together with the traditional Liberal vote share of 20%, enabled the NDP to win a majority of seats with less than 40% of the vote, when much of the support of the aging Social Credit government splintered and defected. Reactions to that election led to the renewal of Social Credit leadership, the creation of a more modern party organization, and the reestablishment of a new, more complete Social Credit electoral coalition. In that rebuilding, Social Credit finally managed to absorb most of the Liberal elite that had resisted them for two decades. The 1975 election returned Social Credit to power and completed the creation of the modern bipolar party system.

In October 1991, the stage was set for a possible repeat of this dynamic. Before then, the provincial Liberal Party was poorly placed, both strategically and ideologically, to succeed in the BC party system. The party had traditionally (until 1992) operated as a single unit in both federal and provincial politics, giving it something of an identity crisis because the electoral politics of those two political worlds had revolved around quite different issues.[23] Liberals had continued to be as important federally as they were marginal provincially. As a centrist party, the views of whose activists were closer to the NDP than to Social Credit on many issues, it had considerable difficulty breaking into a system 'where polarized politics is the norm.'[24] Given its history and its orientation in federal politics, it could not outflank Social Credit on the right. Its position between Social Credit and the NDP made it vulnerable to defections by left-Liberals eager to secure the defeat of Social Credit and by right-Liberals just as concerned to prevent that result.

In 1991 BC voters elected an NDP government for the second time, ending a string of four successive Social Credit victories. However, unlike in 1972, Social Credit slipped into third place in popular support and legislative representation as the BC Liberal Party staged a spectacular comeback to provincial politics. Its popular vote soared from 6.7% in 1986 to 33.2% and, with seventeen members elected, it formed the official opposition in the legislature.[25] Liberal resurgence was paralleled by Social Credit's collapse. Their gain in vote share (26.5 percentage points) was nearly identical to the Socred drop (25.3 points). The once-dominant party elected only seven members, only one of whom remained identified as a Socred in the legislature within a few months of the election. Four switched allegiance to the BC Reform Party, ending Social Credit's status as a recognized party in the legislature. Despite the Reform foothold in the legislature, the Liberal Party seems poised to replace the Socreds as the counterweight to the NDP in a return to a two-party, ideologically driven system.

Events leading up to the 1991 election campaign and the campaign itself helped to modify the strategic situation facing the Liberal Party. NDP leader Mike Harcourt, formerly a popular mayor of Vancouver, had a considerably more moderate image than the man he succeeded. Liberal leader Gordon Wilson offered an alternative to Social Credit voters and party activists alienated from the party by Vander Zalm or by the struggle to succeed him. Given the NDP's more benign image, a vote for the Liberals presented only a modest risk in policy terms even if the New Democrats won as a result of a split in the non-left vote. With the Social Credit Party in tatters, its former supporters shifted to the Liberals in droves.

Figure 5.1 clearly illustrates the dominance of Social Credit and the NDP from the late 1970s through the 1980s. The combined support for the Liberals and Progressive Conservatives never exceeded 10% after 1975 until

Figure 5.1

BC election results, 1952-91

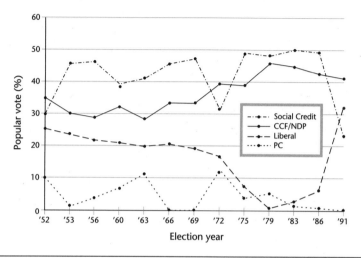

1991. At first glance, in 1991 the Liberal Party seems to have played the spoiler role it shared with the Progressive Conservatives in 1972, siphoning off enough Social Credit votes to give the NDP a majority of seats even though its vote share declined slightly from what it obtained in a losing cause in 1986. Given a very weak party organization[26] and small membership base, Liberal victories depended far more on the peculiar circumstances of the campaign and vote splits in individual constituencies than on any underlying party structure. In fact, most observers were inclined to attribute Liberal resurgence to a single event – the performance of party leader Gordon Wilson in a leaders' debate shortly before election day.

However, as is apparent from Table 5.1, the shift away from Social Credit toward the Liberals was nearly universal. In three out of six regions (accounting for fifty-two of seventy-five ridings), average Liberal gains per riding were within 1 percentage point of Social Credit losses.[27] In fact, across the province, 66% of the variance in Liberal vote increases is statistically explained by Social Credit losses.[28]

Data from public opinion surveys conducted after the election provide evidence of the continuing decline in Social Credit support to the benefit of the Liberal Party until mid-1994. In December 1993, only 41% of those who had voted Social Credit in the 1991 election indicated that they were now prepared to repeat that choice, compared to 32% who would vote Liberal. By March 1994, the figures were 30% and 45%, respectively. The Liberals maintained this level of support (roughly 45%) from former Socreds through the rest of 1994. However, by September 1994 Social

Table 5.1

Average riding level vote swing by party and region, 1986-91 (%)

Region	NDP	Socred	Liberal
Lower Mainland	-1.5	-27.3	+27.1
Vancouver Island	-1.7	-27.9	+27.5
Fraser Valley	-2.4	-28.9	+29.7
Kootenays	-2.5	-15.4	+17.1
Okanagan/Southern Interior	-3.2	-20.6	+26.1
North	+0.2	-15.5	+18.4
Province-wide	-1.6	-24.7	+25.8

Credit support had virtually evaporated with BC Reform picking up most of those who had not already decided to support the Liberal Party.[29]

Gordon Wilson was unable to follow up his party's outstanding electoral performance with organizational renewal. Indeed, he was unable to maintain his own position in the face of severe criticism of his leadership by members of the provincial executive and his own caucus. Significant membership growth did not begin until after his resignation, some eighteen months following the election, and the race to succeed him began. As late as mid-April 1993, the party had just 3,684 members in total, and in over a quarter of the province's seventy-five constituencies the party membership was under two dozen. Once the leadership contest started, that changed very rapidly and by late July membership had grown to 13,446. Virtually all of this growth was the result of efforts by various leadership candidates to recruit support, and a remarkable 29% of the new members were registered in the last week before the membership lists were closed.[30]

The picture of the sources of Liberal Party growth in this realignment, based on movements of the mass electorate, is reinforced by an analysis of party activists. Particularly important in this regard are the views of the thousands of new Liberal Party members, since many of these people were recruited by the victorious Gordon Campbell team. Many of the new members were disaffected Socreds whose addition to the Liberal activist group shifted the Liberal Party's position in the ideological spectrum toward the right. Newcomers are ideologically distinct from veterans. A survey of party activists in 1993 shows that those who joined the party following the 1991 election are significantly more right-wing and populist than those with longer-standing ties to the party. They are also significantly more hostile to increased government spending. As a group to which the new Liberal leader owes his victory, their views must be taken seriously as the party attempts to consolidate and expand its position.[31]

Competing with the Liberals for the allegiance of former Socreds is the Reform Party of BC, which, despite its name, has no official connection with the national Reform Party led by Preston Manning. In fact, the national party has resisted all attempts by those inside and outside the party to contest provincial elections. BC Reform was formed before the federal Reform Party, thus acquiring the right to the name in provincial elections. The party fielded four candidates in the 1991 election who garnered a minuscule 0.18% of the popular vote.

With the collapse of the Social Credit vote in 1991, and the popularity of national Reform in public opinion polls, the provincial Reform Party offered an attractive refuge for dissident Socreds, especially those with more conservative views living in the interior and northern areas of the province. After the election, four of the seven sitting Social Credit MLAs, all representing non-urban ridings, joined the BC Reform Party. Since then, former Socreds have essentially hijacked the party. Its current leader is a former Social Credit cabinet minister, and interim leader of that party, Jack Weisgerber.

A picture of the economic base of party support in the contemporary provincial party system based on public opinion data is provided in Table 5.2.[32] With some important differences, it is similar to the pattern that characterized provincial politics at the height of polarization in the late 1970s and early 1980s.[33] Thus, while the Liberal Party has replaced Social Credit as the party preferred by the more affluent, with a plurality (43.4%) among those with annual family incomes over $55,000, unlike the case in the earlier period, support for the NDP is relatively impervious to differences in income levels. The percentages favouring the NDP in each income category are virtually the same, within sampling error, as the marginal frequency (30.0%). The lack of variation by income in NDP support is in part a result of substantial support for the party among those in professional and managerial occupations, the group whose explosive growth, especially in the public sector, helped launch the party into its competitive position.

The presence of three significant parties following the 1991 election complicates comparisons over time. The NDP is clearly the preferred party among unskilled labour, but their support among skilled labour (31.5%) is within one percentage point of their overall level of support (32.5%) among voters classified by occupation. On the other hand, BC Reform does better among skilled labour (26.9%) than among any other occupational group. In this respect, a significant following among blue collar workers, Reform support resembles that of Social Credit in its heyday. However, they have clearly not captured the former Social Credit constituency among white collar groups. That distinction belongs to the Liberals, who command an overall majority among business executives and those in sales occupations.

Table 5.2

Economic basis of provincial party support

	July 1995 vote intention (%)					
	NDP	Liberal	Reform	Social Credit	Other	Number of cases
All voters						
Annual family income						
< $35,000	30.1	38.6	22.5	2.8	5.9	386
$35-$55,000	30.5	37.4	23.7	2.5	5.9	321
> $55,000	33.2	43.4	19.9	1.4	2.0	346
Union household						
Yes	38.6	35.2	19.4	1.6	5.2	443
No	24.9	44.2	23.3	2.7	5.0	744
Voters in the labour force						
Occupation						
Professional/managerial	38.5	37.5	15.4	2.9	5.8	208
Business executive	15.6	53.1	21.9	0.0	9.4	32
Sales	14.7	55.9	20.6	0.0	8.8	34
Clerical	30.9	38.2	21.8	0.0	9.1	55
Skilled labour	31.5	33.1	26.9	3.8	4.6	130
Unskilled labour	44.4	33.3	18.5	0.0	3.7	27
Employment sector						
Private sector	26.3	40.4	25.7	2.2	5.4	498
Public sector	42.3	36.2	13.1	1.9	6.6	213
Approximate total	30.0	39.9	21.8	2.3	5.1	

Note: Total frequencies differ slightly among the four parts of the table. The figures shown in the last row of the table are based on the distribution of vote intention by employment sector.

As in the past, links between income and occupation and party support are mediated by institutional structures affecting employment. Union membership and employment in the public sector increase the probability of a vote for the NDP. The reverse is true for the Liberals and BC Reform.

Political ideology provides a further link between the electorate and the party system (see Table 5.3). Populism is clearly connected to the choice between the NDP and BC Reform. The most populist quarter of British Columbians (those most likely to believe in grassroots solutions to political problems and most hostile to bureaucracy and 'red tape') are nearly three times as likely (32.7% versus 11.4%) as those in the least populist group to favour Reform. Conversely, the most populist group is only about half as likely (22.3% versus 42.0%) to express a preference for the NDP.

Table 5.3

Ideological basis of provincial party support

	July 1995 vote intention (%)					
	NDP	Liberal	Reform	Social Credit	Other	Number of cases
Populism						
Lowest quartile	42.0	41.6	11.4	0.8	4.1	245
Highest quartile	22.3	37.9	32.7	3.0	4.1	269
Postmaterialism						
Lowest quartile	19.9	49.5	24.8	3.0	2.7	331
Highest quartile	45.8	20.2	13.6	1.0	9.3	301
Neoconservatism						
Lowest quartile	45.5	32.9	13.5	2.1	6.0	334
Highest quartile	13.1	48.2	30.2	3.3	5.2	305
Total sample	31.2	38.6	22.7	2.3	5.3	1,015

Note: See Chapter 1 for details on ideological measures.

Liberal support is virtually unaffected by differences on this ideological dimension.

Neoconservative attitudes have an even more striking effect on party support, affecting preferences for all three significant players in the contemporary party system, but especially for the NDP and Reform. The most conservative voters (those who oppose environmental protection if it leads to higher taxes, government interference with private land use, or more extensive regulation of business) are 3.5 times less likely (13.1% versus 45.5%) to vote for the NDP than the least conservative group. On the other hand, they are more than twice as likely to express a preference for Reform. The Liberals enjoy nearly majority support among ideological conservatives, but the gap between them and the least conservative is not as marked.

The analysis of BC political culture in Chapter 1 showed that a significant number of British Columbians place a higher value on postmaterialist values such as personal empowerment, protection of the environment, and development of a less impersonal and more humane society than on materialist values such as law and order and economic growth. Postmaterialism has the largest impact on the choice between the NDP and the Liberals. The support for the NDP among postmaterialists compared to materialists (45.8% versus 19.9%) is almost the mirror image of the pattern for the Liberal Party (20.2% versus 49.5%). Although the differences are not as dramatic in the case of Reform, that party is almost more attractive to those on the materialist end of the spectrum.[34]

The public opinion survey results confirm the story told by the analysis of vote shifts between the 1986 and 1991 elections and the examination of the views of Liberal Party activists. For the time being, the Liberals have replaced Social Credit as the anchor of non-left politics in the province. However, many of the most populist and most conservative voters have resisted the Liberal pull and, for now at least, have lodged their support with BC Reform. Reform also has a foothold in the working class, undoubtedly linked to that group's greater populism, which has prevented the formation of a clear-cut class division between the two larger parties.

The revival of the provincial Liberal Party and the success of BC Reform have drawn the national and provincial party systems closer together. In the June/July 1995 survey, most provincial Liberals (77.4%) had the same vote intention in federal elections. A similar proportion of provincial Reform voters (73.8%) favoured Reform at the federal level as well. This linkage exists despite the fact that neither party has formal ties with national parties bearing the same name.

On the other hand, while anyone joining the BC New Democrats is automatically a member of the national party, for most of the period from 1972 to 1991, among voters the support for the NDP in national elections was roughly 10% less than in provincial elections. The NDP continues to do better provincially than federally. If anything the gap has increased. In the June/July 1995 survey, only 43.4% of those with an NDP vote intention provincially expressed the same preference for the federal level. Slightly more (44.7%) would have voted Liberal. A surprisingly large number (9.6%) actually favoured the Reform Party at the national level.

Conclusion

With the disintegration of its electoral base, especially the defection of so many leaders and activists, Social Credit has virtually disappeared. With a miniscule percentage of the vote in 1996, a repeat of its post-1972 resurrection is exceedingly unlikely. However, whether the Liberals will simply replace Social Credit in a return to a polarized two-party system will depend, in part, on the fate of the BC Reform Party.

Support for BC Reform hovered at around 20% in public opinion polls throughout 1994-5, with support found mainly in the Fraser Valley and the interior and north of the province. These areas were also the heartland of the Social Credit Party. On the other hand, Reform remains weak on Vancouver Island and in the major urban areas of the province where most voters are located.[35] The history of provincial politics since the early 1950s has shown how difficult it is to mount an electoral challenge from a third place position. Unless the party's popularity increases dramatically, intending Reform voters, among the most conservative and populist in the province, will have to decide whether their interests are better served by voting for the Liberal Party in order to keep the NDP from power. Reform's poor showing in 1996 – less than 10% of the popular vote – undoubtedly reflects this strategic situation.

For itself, the Liberal Party has staked out a policy position on the centre-right of the political spectrum. In speeches following his election as party leader and during the 1996 election campaign, Gordon Campbell gave a clear account of where the party stands under his leadership, emphasizing the need to cut taxes, reduce the size and cost of government, and promising to introduce a balanced-budget law. He pledged to sell dozens of crown corporations and use the proceeds to pay down the public debt, and, perhaps mindful of the much more populist following he helped to attract in his bid for the party leadership, he promised to eliminate subsidies to business and reduce both the number of MLAs (and their pension entitlements) and the number of government ministries. On the other hand, he steered clear of social spending cuts, pledging instead to reorganize delivery of health and social programs so that more of the funding winds up addressing the needs of those it is designed to help, instead of in the pockets of health and social welfare workers.

The Liberal Party continued to grow dramatically during 1994 and 1995. The party had just over 13,000 members when Gordon Campbell was elected leader. By April 1995, membership had reached 40,400, making the Liberals the largest party in the province.[36] With membership growing by 1,200 per week, it had over 50,000 members by mid-summer 1995. The party's vote share increased by roughly 9 percentage points between 1991 and 1996.

In contrast, Reform had under 8,000 members in June 1995, more than half of them from the interior and the north, areas represented by the party's four MLAs. They are exceptionally thin on the ground in the Lower Mainland (2,000) and Vancouver Island (1,000), areas with the largest number of seats in the legislature.[37] Not all their recruitment efforts in the former Social Credit heartland are necessarily beneficial – former premier Bill Vander Zalm joined the party in May 1995, much to the consternation of Reform's leader. In any event, only two Reform MLAs were elected in 1996, both in northern districts.

At least since the early 1950s, Social Credit leaders – most notably W.A.C. Bennett – argued strongly for a provincial alternative to the left that had no institutional affiliation with a major national party. This gave those federal Liberal and Progressive Conservative supporters who were fearful of the left the opportunity to support their parties in national elections, where the possibility of the NDP winning was exceedingly unlikely, and to coalesce behind Social Credit in provincial elections to prevent an NDP victory. The take-over of BC Reform by former Socreds, most of whom support the national Reform Party, has effectively made this strategy obsolete, despite the lack of organizational links between the Reform parties at the two levels. While less overt, the transfer of allegiance of the bulk of Social Credit voters and a substantial number of activists to the provincial Liberals has contributed to that obsolescence.

The 1991 election set the stage for the repetition of the pattern that has characterized the provincial party system since the coalitions in the 1940s. Given a first-past-the-post electoral system in a polarized political setting, protagonists at the extremes of the ideological divide, especially those on the right, are forced to think strategically. This situation leads inexorably to a two-party solution. The NDP remains the strongest player on the left and centre-left. According to one study, roughly 34% of BC voters say that they would 'never' support the NDP, compared to 27% similarly disposed toward Social Credit, 20% toward BC Reform, and only 8% toward the Liberals.[38] As the dominant and 'least unacceptable' player on the right and centre-right, following the 1991 election the Liberals were the best placed of all the NDP's opponents to assume the role once played by Social Credit in the dynamic relationship that has structured the provincial party system for half a century.

The Liberals were almost confirmed in that role during the 1996 election. However, a residual of Reform support, coupled with an unexpectedly strong showing by the Progressive Democratic Alliance, left the party in second place in terms of seats despite a first place finish in the popular vote. However, the two-party polarization will undoubtedly return to the legislature and help to structure voter decisions next time around.

Further Reading

Blake, Donald E. *Two Political Worlds: Parties and Voting in British Columbia*. Vancouver: UBC Press 1985

Blake, Donald E., R.K. Carty, and L. Erickson. *Grassroots Politicians: Party Activists in British Columbia*. Vancouver: UBC Press 1991

Dyck, Rand. *Provincial Politics in Canada*. 2nd. ed. Toronto: Prentice Hall 1991

Elections British Columbia. *Electoral History of British Columbia, 1871-1986*. Victoria: Chief Electoral Officer, 1988

Elkins, David. 'Politics Makes Strange Bedfellows: The BC Party System in the 1952 and 1953 Provincial Elections.' *BC Studies* 30 (1976): 3-26

Wilson, Jeremy. 'Geography, Politics and Culture: Electoral Insularity in British Columbia,' *Canadian Journal of Political Science* 13, 4 (1980): 751-74

6
The British Columbia Legislature and Parliamentary Framework

Norman Ruff

An afternoon's visit to a sitting of the British Columbia Legislative Assembly quickly provides an observer with a sense of much of what this political institution is all about. A reading of the province's Constitution Act and the legislature's own Standing Orders will define the formal institutional framework and specific parliamentary procedures.[1] A sense of the Westminster model will help you understand their application and the larger political and spatial context. Nevertheless, you don't need to know all of the history or details of the rule book to understand the parliamentary game as played in Victoria. Spending an hour as a visitor to the 'Leg' may be like walking on the surface of an iceberg, but what remains submerged is made of the same substance.

In the first forty minutes, after the arrival of the Speaker shortly before 2 p.m., there is a delay while many members are still taking their seats. Those to the right of the Speaker, occupied by the premier and cabinet, are ordinarily the last to fill – particularly after Wednesday cabinet meetings. Then follows up to fifteen minutes of personal welcomes to selected visitors in the gallery, including a melange of friends and relatives of the members, groups of school children, visiting ambassadors or other foreign dignitaries, and parliamentarians, party workers, or others recognized by an MLA.[2] More significantly, some are visiting municipal, school board, or other elected officials from communities within the province, or representatives of organized economic or public group interests. Their presence in the gallery alerts one to the lobbying activities and network of policy processes associated with the working of the legislature, but outside the formal proceedings on the floor of the house.

The formal introduction of government bills and/or ministerial statements by a minister then establish the priority given the business of the governing majority party. Opposition members appear to gain some control in the fifteen-minute oral question period that follows. This is an opportunity to ensure some answerability in the conduct of the cabinet ministers on at least the first rung of government accountability. Government control of the agenda is then resumed with the calling of orders of the day and the government house leader's designation of the next items of house business, such as debate on a bill or consideration of estimates of expenditure. The shift in control that this signals is directly acknowledged by the small proportion of the members who will ordinarily remain on the floor. Similarly, the seats occupied immediately above the Speaker's chair are vacated by the members of the press gallery, the main interpreters of the proceedings to the general public. Although question-period exchanges are far from being parliamentary debates, they have become the primary focus of attention in the relaying of what is perceived as noteworthy legislative business. Televising of the proceedings and the electronic media's thirst for dramatic visuals and pithy, twenty-second sound bites further encourage this focus.

Each afternoon from Monday to Thursday during a legislative session, there is thus an exhibition of the reality of responsible parliamentary government in the Westminster mode. Despite some 'virtual' accountability at the level of answerability, the government's control of the majority of seats and accompanying party discipline and cabinet solidarity ensure that the two levels of effective legislative accountability – substantial censorship or a more final dismissal – have never been reached in the BC legislature. Our parliamentary system is dominated by an all-powerful political executive.

All this will be evident to most observers, but their level of consciousness in large part depends on their political origins. Much of what transpires, including the roles of premier and cabinet, opposition leaders and backbenchers, the daily schedule and proceedings, and even the legislature's physical configuration and seating arrangements, will be familiar to visitors from elsewhere in Canada, the United Kingdom, Australia or New Zealand, and other former British colonies. They all share the same Westminster parliamentary model. Though they all have some distinctive patterns of evolution and have made parliamentary adaptations to their own social and political environment, almost everything will appear familiar and even normal – including the rumbustious behaviour that at times earns a 'zoo' tag. Those from elsewhere, particularly the United States, will be more confused, both in the political culture shock of unfamiliar provincial party labels and in the institutional gap between Westminster and American notions of what a legislature is and does.

Like their fellow Canadians, British Columbians are probably sensitive to the realities of party discipline and the related aspects of parliamentary behaviour that colour current concerns about the effectiveness of their provincial as well as federal political institutions. Few, however, also reflect on the reminders of the contemporary consequences of the colonial heritage that are the source of comfort or confusion in their visitors. These two dimensions form the principal concerns of this exploration of the BC legislature, which examines the BC historical parliamentary tradition, its contemporary functioning, and attempts at procedural and democratic reform.

The Westminster Model: BC Style

To assert that the provincial legislature is by far the most important institution in BC's political system may seem like a simple paraphrase of Ralph Miliband's assessment of the British House of Commons[3] that flies against BC's historical experience. A political tradition of executive dominance pre-dates its entry into the Canadian Confederation, back to its early mercantilist history under the governance of the chief factor of the Hudson's Bay Company. Two decades of unbroken one-party dominance by W.A.C. Bennett and the Social Credit Party perpetuated that tradition, as did his son's own subsequent neglect of parliamentary 'niceties' in piloting his 1983 restraint policies through the legislature. The legislature is fundamentally important, however, in the sense that the legitimacy for the entire framework of provincial government is derived from the status of the legislature as an instrument of representative democracy. The election of Members of the Legislative Assembly (MLAs) to represent various districts of the province, and the formation of a political executive from the majority party within that legislature, legitimates all provincial law-making and the authority of cabinet government. There are moments, such as in the 1963-4 Columbia River power debates or the 1983 restraint legislation, when extraparliamentary organizations seem to become the primary source of effective opposition to an all-powerful cabinet. The immediate political mobilization of such forces, however, also relies on parliamentary debate, and any expectations of long-term success rest on subsequent electoral consequences.

The concept of the Westminster parliamentary model is freely applied to the BC Legislative Assembly in much the same way that it is associated with other parliaments shaped after the so-called Mother of Parliament in Britain. Its specific components are rarely spelt out with any precision, and the concept too easily becomes a vehicle to assert some idealized institutional norm that is deemed sacrosanct. But as the grandfather of all analysts of that model, Walter Bagehot, observed in 1867, 'Language is the tradition of nations; each generation describes what it sees, but it uses words transmitted from the past. When a great entity like the British constitution has continued in connected outward sameness, but hidden inner change, for many ages, every generation inherits a series of inapt words – of maxims once true, but of which the truth is ceasing or has ceased.'[4] There is a tendency to select whatever historical components suit our immediate needs, and, at times, to invent a glorious past of previous parliamentary control over the executive or ignore the modern innovations of the current parliament at Westminster.

The Westminster model has been used to denote one or more of the following traits: first, the Parliament of a former British colony, or adaptation of a British parliamentary framework; second, a framework that, as a minimum, embodies two things: a doctrine of parliamentary sovereignty where law-making power resides in a legislative assembly of elected territorial representatives, and responsible government through a fusion (rather than a division) of legislative and political executive functions in cabinet government whose members are drawn from the majority party within the legislature; and, third, a historic association with certain other features, such as a separation between the formal 'dignified' executive (i.e., the Crown and the provincial lieutenant governor) and the constitutionally 'efficient' institution of the political executive in the cabinet. Other elements, such as cabinet dominance supported by adversarial competition between two highly disciplined political parties, are also often presumed to be necessary requirements or consequences of the model. This adversarial relationship is in turn tempered by the designation of a single official opposition party to institutionalize and legitimize government criticism – a device that reassuringly implies an underlying set of shared political values.

The legitimacy of a provincial government under this model stems from its control of the majority of elected representatives. It also entails respect for parliamentary procedures that provide for the discussion and approval of government initiatives, while also offering opportunities for the scrutiny of government activities. Although individual members may be constrained by party discipline, they are also active ombudsmen for their constituents within and outside the legislature. Since few British Columbians directly witness its work, the legislature has also become outwardly directed with an eye to the communication of events within the chamber beyond its floor and galleries. The Hansard official record of debate and, more notably, coverage by the Victoria press gallery and electronic media are now substantial elements of the parliamentary process. Much of what happens on a daily basis in the legislature and in debates over parliamentary reform is a competition over the use of time, but it is how these daily events are reported that has the most political consequence.

All of the elements in the Westminster model identified above are open to change. Canada's 1867 blend of federalism and parliamentary government, and the 1982 Canadian Charter of Rights and Freedoms limit the sovereignty of the central and provincial Parliaments. In some important respects, the British Parliament has moved away from the idealized Westminster model. In its internal proceedings, for example, British government defeats on non-confidence votes have become accepted at Westminster to a degree generally held unthinkable by most Canadian governments. The device of public consultation through referenda has also become more firmly established as an acceptable political instrument within the UK. Two-party competition and majority government are also less assured. Despite these living Westminster realities, BC has hesitated to rethink its parliamentary framework, and has only recently begun to reshape its parliamentary practices. Externally oriented reform has come still more slowly, while its opponents remain fixated with the 'non-Westminster' origins of such innovations as direct democracy.[5]

Constitutional Evolution

The evolution of political institutions in BC was similar to that of other former British colonies. Evolution of our Westminster model begin with an extension of the British imperial frontier and its mercantile interests in the fur trade. Those interests had initially led to a concentration of economic and political power in the Hudson's Bay Company, followed by a period of state formation in which separate political institutions evolved for Vancouver Island (out of a struggle between independent settlers and the company) and, after 1858, the mainland crown colony of BC. The two colonies joined in November 1866 and five years later became a Canadian province. The full trappings of parliamentary government were slowly extended to this small colony in step with the decline in company-imposed paternalism and the spread of a more individualistic liberal value system.[6]

As it gradually escaped from the tutelage of James Douglas and the Hudson's Bay Company, the 1849 colony of Vancouver Island seemed likely to follow the same path as Nova Scotia in the growth of an elected legislative House of Assembly, alongside the council appointed by Douglas. The new mainland colony of BC, formed in 1858 to meet the political challenge of the Fraser gold rush, was slower to enjoy the principles of a fully representative government. When the two colonies were combined to enhance their financial and economic resources, the mainland's partially elected legislative council model continued for both colonies.[7] As it prepared to enter Confederation, the Terms of Union stated that there would be representative government, and the expectation that the Canadian government would consent to responsible government 'when desired by the inhabitants of British Columbia.'[8] The colony perpetuated its unicameralism by reshaping its legislature under the Constitution Act of 1871 to one composed of twenty-five elected members. Much of BC's provincial constitutional framework continues to rest on that statute. The resignation of Premier McCreight after defeat on a motion of non-confidence in December 1872 signalled the arrival of responsible government. Despite the transformations of society brought about by wave upon wave of immigrants and migrants since 1871, BC's colonial heritage has become institutionalized. That heritage preselected the Westminster model and closed off any other options that union to the United States, for example, would have brought.

The office of lieutenant governor as the federally appointed, provincial representative of the Crown is perhaps the most conspicuous reminder of the historic connections of our parliamentary institutions to a British-style constitutional monarchy. The lieutenant governor's law-making role, statutory powers to make executive appointments, and power to summon, prorogue, and dissolve a legislative assembly are exercised today only on the specific advice of the premier. Modern political parties and majority governments have removed any discretion BC's lieutenant governor might have had in the appointment of a premier.[9] Royal assent to statutes is taken for granted, and the power of reserving assent, together with the unique BC constitutional power to return a bill back to the legislature,[10] are assumed to be spent. Any direct political authority possessed by today's lieutenant governors rests on their own personal stature and standing rather than their dignified constitutional power. In some cases, such as with David Lam (who held the office from 1988 to 1995), the lieutenant governor's authority can become quite considerable, but for many others the office has been purely ceremonial and educative.

As Campbell Sharman has shown in his analysis of the evolution of the province's own Constitution Act, the underlying bias of our parliamentary framework reinforces executive dominance by the premier and cabinet over the legislature.[11] The growth and then removal of limitations on the size of cabinet, the increased recognition given the office of premier, the loss of the preamble references to responsible government, and the removal of any necessity for ministerial by-elections all support the same trend. To his list we can add the lengthening of the maximum life of the legislature from four to five years in 1913, and the pre-1984 government freedom to gerrymander electoral boundaries as further examples of executive dominance.

BC Parliamentary Procedure
The procedures, rules, and timetabling defined in the Standing Orders of the BC Legislative Assembly mirror those in Westminster. Standing Order No. 1 specifically provides a general rule for procedure that unprovided cases shall follow 'the usages, customs and precedents, firstly of this House and, secondly, of the House of Commons of the United Kingdom of Great Britain and Northern Ireland ... as far as they may be applicable to this House.' The rules regulate how the Legislative Assembly's time is spent each sitting day, and establish occasions for that time to be utilized by government and the opposition in their mutual pursuit of the 'business of the House.' Much of what happens is 99 percent predictable. Laws are made

in the Legislative Assembly in the sense that this is where they receive approval by our elected representatives, but their content has already been determined elsewhere in cabinet and in discussions between the bureaucracy and its policy networks. The legitimacy of provincial law-making, however, rests on parliamentary approval of ministerial legislative initiatives, and the procedure that this entails ensures a degree of government accountability within the limits of party discipline. No BC government has resigned following a defeat in the legislature since 1953. The governing party maintains control of the majority in each vote, and most government bills become statutes by making their way through the three readings and committee stage to royal assent by the lieutenant governor without significant change. Few fail to become law by being allowed to die in the face of opposition either within or mobilized outside the assembly.[12]

Though every vote is a foregone conclusion, the debates that precede them are opportunities for opposition parties to present their policy alternatives and mobilize public opinion in their favour. Those opportunities were considerably enhanced with the introduction of the daily fifteen-minute oral question period in 1973, and the introduction of the 'electronic Hansard' televised throughout the province via satellite in 1989.[13] Figure 6.1 summarizes the major procedural opportunities for the scrutiny of the cabinet and opposition debate, and the means for control at the disposal of BC governments. The adversarial relationship that characterizes all that transpires between government and the opposition parties is also found in their competition for the use of the legislature's time. That time is ultimately controlled by the governing party through its majority of seats, by the underlying tilt in the rules of procedure and such tactics as legislation by exhaustion, or, in its more recent version, by inundation. Nevertheless, a legislative session provides one of the most significant opportunities for the opposition to communicate their positions and mobilize their audiences outside the legislature. Despite their dominance, few BC governments relish long spring sessions, and, although filibusters are rare, it is the opposition members who are typically more inclined to prolong debate once the session moves into late June.[14] It should also be noted that the rules of the game offer more to experienced players. The turnover in elected members means that they are not always exploited to full advantage, and, as the seventeen members of the new 1991 Liberal opposition caucus discovered, the learning curve can be steep.

Accountability in government and for all members of the legislature has also found powerful institutional protection in the growth in the number of officers of the house, including the auditor general, ombudsman, conflict of interest and information and privacy commissioners, chief electoral officer, and child, youth, and family advocate. These officers are appointed

Figure 6.1

BC parliamentary procedures and relationships

General opportunities for scrutiny of political executive
- Annual sittings of Legislative Assembly
- Verbatim Hansard (Standing Order (SO) 120)
- TV broadcasting of proceedings (electronic Hansard)
- Oral questions (SO 47a, 47b)
- Select standing committees (SO 68-72)
- Special committees (SO 69)
- Written questions (SO 47, 48)
- Legislative Assembly Management Committee

Opportunities for major debates
- Address in Reply to the Speech from the Throne (SO 45a, 50)
- Budget debate (SO 45a - Schedule 2)
- Estimates, Committee of Supply (SO 60a)
- Consideration of bills

Other opportunities for debate/scrutiny
- Adjournment on Matter of Urgent Public Importance (SO 35, 45)
- Private members statements (SO 25a)
- Public Accounts Committee
- Reports of house officers: auditor general; ombudsman; conflict of interest commissioner; information and privacy commissioner; child, youth and family advocate; chief electoral officer
- Private members' days (SO 75A (1))
- Petitions (SO 73)

Techniques for governmental control of the House
- Money bills require message from lieutenant governor (SO 66, 67)
- Time limits (SO 45a) and notice requirements
- Closure (SO 46) and time allocation
- Government's use of omnibus bills
- Timetabling of house business by government (SO 27)
- Legislation by exhaustion
- Party discipline

---

on unanimous recommendations of house committees and remain directly responsible to the legislature. Together, they have become some of the most influential custodians of the provincial public interest.

Two waves of parliamentary reform and other piecemeal changes have made the proceedings resemble their provincial and federal cousins. But BC's clinging to consideration of Supply within a committee of the whole house and the on-off utilization of standing or special committees both testify to a lingering preoccupation with business being seen to be done on the floor of the chamber. The contemporary predominance of budgetary deficit and public debt concerns, and the accompanying return to a government restructuring agenda may also be about to direct more attention to the Supply process, and increase rather than diminish the potential importance of Estimates exposure. Any new wave of reform is more likely to come from parliamentary customs such as the acceptance of more free, non-party-dictated votes, or as a consequence of modifications of representative democracy, than from the standing orders.

By the 1990s, the legislature settled into an annual mid-March opening (save for electoral or other disruptions, as in 1983 and 1991 – see Table 6.1), and can ordinarily expect to be in session for between 66 and 115 days. The relative degree of legislative activism determines the length of any session and its number of sittings (see column listing government bills passed in Table 6.1 as a simple indicator of quantity, if not scope). Consideration of ministry estimates of expenditure of the Supply process continues to account for the largest number of sittings. The contentious nature of the 1983 restraint legislation is shown in the remarkably high number of vote divisions that were taken in the house during that session, when, for that year at least, attention was focused less on estimates and more on actual legislative debate.

Since 1972, being an MLA in BC has become more of a full-time job with remuneration to match. Where a member received an indemnity of $5,000 plus an expense allowance of $2,500 in 1970, increases in 1973 and in 1974 raised them to $16,000 plus $8,000. Subsequent increases based on

Table 6.1

BC Legislative Assembly session summary: duration, sittings, and bills (33rd to 35th legislatures, 1983-93)

Session (opened)	Sitting days	Sittings total	Sittings estimates	Government bills passed	No. of divisions
1983-4 (June 23)	84	116	29	29	317
1984-5 (Feb 13)	66	93	38	45	52
1985 (March 4)	75	103	68	66	52
1986 (March 11)	53	74	57	23	33
1987 (March 9)	115	158	31	65	57
1988 (March 15)	69	95	69	57	18
1989 (March 16)	85	117	94	83	29
1990 (April 5)	84	114	68	80	39
1991 (May 7)	35	48	24	12	28
1992 (March 17)	112	155	85	81	129
1993 (March 18)	91	124	112	73	122

Source: British Columbia, Legislative Assembly, *Journals*, vols. CXVI-CXXVI.

BC wage rates saw the indemnity steadily rise, by 1990, to $32,812 and the tax-free expense allowance to $16,406. A capital city per diem allowance ($45 for Capital Region members, $100 for outside members) is also paid for the first sixty days of each sitting. While the legislature is in session, it is estimated that about twenty hours a week are spent on the floor of the house or in party caucus, plus time for administrative work, preparation for house business, and social functions. During the other seven or eight months of the year, urban members are said to work about fifty hours a week, with approximately half of that time spent in constituency case work. Rural members add another ten hours in travel time.[15] As with legislators elsewhere, the pay, allowances,[16] and pensions of the members have come under critical public scrutiny. While a 1992 study that attempted a fair comparison with comparable jobs within the province found the 1990 level of remuneration to be fair and adequate,[17] continued political pressures will keep pension reform high on the public agenda.[18]

The Legislature and Parliamentary Reform: Procedure
Eighty years of provincial law-making elapsed in the BC legislature before any attempts were made at major internal parliamentary reform.[19] If Premier Theodore Davie or any of his successors could have walked into the house at any time up until the 1970s, they would have found little had changed save for a more pervasive party discipline. The inherent tilt in the balance of power in favour of the executive was reinforced in BC by the lack of financial and physical resources available to the opposition parties, and by the absence of such parliamentary devices as an oral question period and written official Hansard record of debates. This undoubtedly suited the interests of successive premiers and cabinets.[20] Since there were few compelling reasons for any government to contemplate parliamentary reform, the standing orders of the house thus went unchanged.

In the penultimate year of W.A.C. Bennett's twenty-year Social Credit regime, a limited Hansard was introduced, but excluded coverage of much of a sitting by ignoring the lengthy time spent in consideration of budget estimates in the committee of the Whole House on Supply. The New Democratic government under Dave Barrett brought the first wave of parliamentary reform to the fore under the aegis of a series of studies under a Legislative Procedure and Practice Inquiry Act, which they made one of their first items of business in October 1972.[21] Largely driven by a democratic commitment to remedy the disadvantages they had experienced in forty years of opposition, the new government also sought improved procedural efficiency needed by a democratic socialist government bent on proactive governance. They attempted, for example, to preset the time allocated to consideration of expenditure estimates, but this proved unenforceable in the face of a histrionic opposition and was revoked in June 1977 after the return of a Social Credit government under Bill Bennett.[22] The province thus retained an extremely time-consuming Supply process, and, while there was some discussion of activating the legislature's under-utilized committee system,[23] parliamentary reform was given low priority until 1985.

The increased confidence engendered by Bill Bennett's third successive electoral victory and the deepening impact of the 1982 economic recession led the Social Credit government to embark on a series of legislative measures in the twenty-six bills packaged as a 'New Reality' restraint program. This new level of neoconservative legislative activism revived a drama in the sittings of the legislature not seen since the early 1970s. The opposition sought to exploit all the parliamentary devices at their disposal, and fifty appeals were made against the rulings of the Speaker or chair of the Committee of the Whole. Closure had been rarely used in the history of the BC legislature, but was evoked twenty times during the first session of the legislature in 1983. Though an unwieldy mechanism, it became an addictive supplement to BC's traditional recourse to legislation by exhaustion through all-night sittings (see Figure 6.2).

Once again the needs exposed by a shift in the governing policy paradigm triggered a review of the workings of the legislature, and a second wave of parliamentary reform was implemented in February 1985. Based on a unanimous report from the Select Standing Committee on Standing Orders and Private Bills, chaired by Austin Pelton, MLA for Dewdney, emphasis was more closely focused on efficiencies in the use of time,

Figure 6.2

BC legislature sittings after midnight, 1957-95

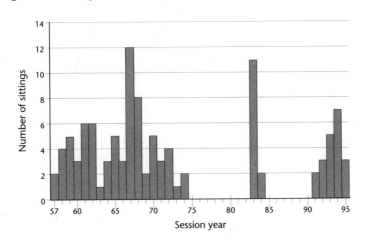

Source: British Columbia, Legislative Assembly, *Journals*, vols. LXXXVII-CXXVII.

including enhanced authority for the Speaker,[24] but the report only gingerly tackled the question of consideration of estimates in Supply. It simplified the Supply motions and allowed the government house leader to refer the votes within the departmental expenditure estimates to a select standing committee rather than the Committee of the Whole House on the floor of the house. The latter reform had been long awaited but was not implemented until 1992 when a newly elected NDP government became the first to take detailed consideration of the estimates off the floor of the assembly chamber. But, though standing and special legislative committees had been allowed to be more active participants in the law-shaping process from 1989 onwards, they were not brought into the estimates review.

In March 1992 the Manitoba model was adopted (with some modifications in succeeding budgets),[25] and the Committee of Supply was divided into two sections for consideration of ministerial estimates. Section A comprises an all-party committee (twenty-four members in 1995) sitting in the Douglas Fir committee room, and Section B is composed of all the members meeting in the assembly chamber. The general rule is that unless they are referred to Section B by the government house leader, all estimates now stand referred to Section A (in practice, seven to eight of the nineteen ministry estimates are considered in B). The official opposition house leader and house leader of the third party may specify three ministerial estimates for consideration in Section B to maintain public exposure. Since the legislature had previously spent up to 40 percent of its time on Supply, this has freed time for debate on legislation and other house business. It has not as yet, however, shortened the length of the legislative session. The innovation was regarded warily by both government and the two main opposition parties – particularly by the latter, who since June 1991 have come to relish the exposure brought by the introduction of province-wide public televising of the house proceedings. Since they had difficulty in attending both committees, it was also unpopular with the growing number of independent members in the 35th legislature. Section B is also deemed a committee of the whole and used for the committee stage of bills after their second reading. Since 1993, the Section A reform has increased bureaucratic accountability by allowing deputy ministers to directly answer certain questions in Section A estimate reviews in the Douglas Fir committee room.[26] An earlier attempt in the fall of 1988 to open the budget process successfully enlisted government backbenchers in the pre-budget review of ministry estimates, but proved to be only a short-lived concession to Premier Vander Zalm's restless caucus.

The same kind of ambivalence and uneasy balance between government interests and those of the members at large is shown in the NDP's introduction of a secret vote for the office of Speaker in March 1994.[27] Like BC's earlier reforms, it can be seen as an adaptation of mechanisms introduced in Ottawa and elsewhere. In principle it was designed to enhance independence in the office of the Speaker. Its implementation midway through the life of the provincial legislature, and the accompanying turnover[28] in the Speakership from Joan Sawicki to Emery Barnes were also open reminders that governments get to set the rules and their beneficiaries. The 1991 NDP government's championing of open government has, however, also shifted some of the balance through the Freedom of Information and Protection of Privacy Act (1992), which has enhanced the research resources at the disposal of the opposition in its preparation for question period, and reduced its dependence on answers to written questions in the house.

External Parliamentary Reform I: Effective Representation
Like every legislature, the existence of the BC legislature is rooted in the evolution of our system of representative democracy. Party discipline may be the foremost influence on their behaviour, but members of the Legislative Assembly are first of all elected representatives of their electoral districts. As with internal reform, conservatism and government dominance has also marked the evolution of BC's framework of representation. Between 1871 and 1983, the number of members grew from twenty-five to fifty-seven under sporadic redistributions of seats and the drawing of new boundaries.[29] In 1991 BC was the last province, except Prince Edward Island, to abandon multiple-member districts. Triggered by Canada's first test of the 1982 Charter of Rights and Freedoms' 'right to vote' and a reform-minded Social Credit leader, Bill Vander Zalm, the 1990-1 redistribution of seats and new electoral boundaries act signalled a new era in political representation within the province.[30]

In 1986 BC's electoral map harboured districts ranging in population from 5,511 in Atlin (86.84 percent below the provincial average of 41,873) to 68,347 in Surrey Newton (63.22 percent above the average). It was thus an easy target for a Charter challenge and became the first electoral map ever to be struck down by the judiciary. Chief Justice Beverley McLaughlin of the BC Supreme Court found 'grossly disproportionate riding populations,' and observed that 'no good end seems to be served by existing population inequalities.'[31] She left it to the BC legislature to take remedial action. Her discussion of representative principles, which would admit only those deviations 'which can be justified on the grounds that they contribute to the better government of the populace as whole,' foreshadowed the 'effective representation' and 'relative parity of voting power' criteria applied in the Supreme Court of Canada's 1991 review of Saskatchewan's provincial electoral boundaries.[32] The redistribution commissioner, provincial court judge Thomas Fisher, appointed by Premier Vander Zalm, had already submitted a preliminary report at the time of Justice McLaughlin's decision. Fisher's final report became the blueprint for a new electoral map that reduced the deviation from the provincial average to a -24.1 to +17.4 percent range.[33] Although the subsequent 1991 census data showed a far higher range at the time of the 1991 general election (-23 to +46 percent, with four districts at +25 percent), the new map represented a significant advance toward the principle of 'effective representation.' Under 1989 legislation, an independent, three-member electoral boundaries commission will in the future carry out redistributions after every second general election.[34] Though deviations of more than 25 percent from a provincial quota will be permitted in very special circumstances, BC had progressed toward political representation reflecting a prevailing national conception of one vote, one value.

Table 6.2

Careers and social backgrounds of BC MLAs

Characteristics	General election			
	1979	1983	1986	1991
Number of MLAs	57	57	69	75
Average age	48	51	49	44
Average years of service		6.5	8.1	4.2
Years of service:				
New MLAs			52%	67%
1-5 years			20%	29%
6+ years			28%	4%
Other elected office:				
Municipal	19%	30%	33%	43%
Number of former MPs	3	3	2	0
Number of women	6	6	7	19
Number of visible minorities:				
Indo-Canadian			1	4
Black			1	1
Occupations:				
Business	23%	23%	49%	25%
Farming	2%		3%	4%
Law	18%	14%	9%	8%
Education	12%	12%	9%	19%
Government			0%	16%
Other/NA	46%	51%	30%	28%
Highest level of education:				
Secondary	44%	46%	26%	21%
Postsecondary	30%	32%	45%	36%
Postgraduate	26%	23%	29%	27%
Professional			0%	11%
No information	0%	0%	0%	5%

Source: Robert J. Fleming, *Canadian Legislatures* (Agincourt: Global Press [annual]).

If the representative nature of BC's legislature is examined in the context of the social origins and characteristics of its members, like other legislatures it fails the social microcosm test. Table 6.2 shows a moderately high turnover among MLAs and their increasing recruitment from municipal government. It also supports the impression that the legislature has become more socially representative over the past decade, but remains a haven primarily for white males.

External Parliamentary Reform II: Direct Democracy

Where parliamentary reform in the 1970s and 1980s was primarily driven by the concerns of the governing party, the reforms of the 1990s address the concerns of BC's voters. It is no coincidence that the Member's Conflict of Interest Commissioner was instituted in 1990 following a succession of political scandals, and was strengthened by the NDP government in 1992 after the controversy surrounding former premier Vander Zalm's sale of Fantasy Gardens.[35] The public's concerns are also evident in the introduction of the instruments of direct democracy such as referenda, recall of members, and citizen's initiatives into the province's political framework.

It may be argued that BC's populist political culture has made it receptive to the language of direct democracy. W.A.C. Bennett's twenty-year maintenance of Social Credit as the governing party, and the 1993 federal successes of the Reform Party both provide ready evidence of this. Populism is, however, a greatly overworked term in BC politics, and what passes for it is often less an assertion of power by the grassroots and more a manipulation of the symbols of that power in a top-down-control politician's brand of populism.[36] The current welding of direct democracy to the province's parliamentary institutions originated in Vander Zalm's own personal predisposition, and was shaped by Social Credit's electoral manoeuvring against the possibility of the Reform Party's entry into the provincial scene. His successor, Rita Johnston, took the 1990 Referendum Act in hand and used it to gauge electoral support for recall and initiative. In the 1991 referendum, these devices received the support of 73 percent of votes cast in the general election – or 81 percent of valid referendum votes for recall and 83 percent for initiatives, as the count is more generally made.[37] Since they had been proposed by the outgoing government, the incoming NDP was not required to implement either measure, but had already agreed to accept that overwhelming verdict. The subsequent history of the legislature's select standing committee's study (chaired by Ujjal Dosanjh) of these devices and the resultant legislation – Bill 36, Recall and Initiative Act (1994) – showed a nervousness at the mix with an idealized Westminster model.[38] This is in part due to long-standing institutional conservatism; it also stems from the personal fears typical of most legislators when faced with the prospect of either weakened control of the political agenda or less job security. The result is evident in the Recall and Initiative Act's highly constrained compromises.

The 1990 Referendum Act gave the cabinet complete control of any consultation with the electorate through the power to set the question, its wording, the date, and area where a referendum would be held. A government asking a question is bound 'as soon as practical' to take steps 'it considers necessary or advisable' to implement the results through 'changes in programs or policy or legislation,' making the referendum more an experiment in semi-people's democracy than direct democracy. In 1994 BC went beyond this in allowing citizens to initiate legislative proposals or the recall of an MLA, but the government also constructed some relatively difficult barriers when compared with the thresholds in place elsewhere.

A recall may begin no sooner than eighteen months after a member's election, by an application for a recall petition stating in up to 200 words why it is warranted. The petition must be returned within sixty days and be signed by more than 40 percent of the registered voters in the district at the last election. If the chief electoral officer determines that the petition meets the requirements, the member would cease to hold office and a by-election would ensue. Unlike the legislative committee's original recommendations, a recall by-election is allowed only once in any one seat between general elections.

A citizen's initiative is permitted on any matter within provincial jurisdiction, and begins with an application for the issue of a petition including a draft bill. Repeat petitions are only permitted after 132 days have elapsed. The initiative petition must be submitted within ninety days, and be signed by at least 10 percent of registered voters in each electoral district. After certification by the chief electoral officer, the petition is referred to a select standing committee of the legislature, which in turn must begin its consideration within thirty days. Within ninety days of its first meeting, that committee must either report with a recommendation for the introduction of legislation or refer it to a general vote. Initiative voting is staged for the last Saturday in September every three years, commencing 28 September 1996. To carry the initiative – that is, to require the government to introduce a bill, or a recommendation by the lieutenant governor (if an appropriation or tax matter) – the initiative must receive more than 50 percent of the total vote in at least two-thirds of the districts.

There are other requirements concerning canvassing of signatures, such as the prohibition of any paid canvassing and regulations governing spending limits, advertising, and disclosure. The signature and vote thresholds that have to be crossed make a flood of initiatives or recalls unlikely. Despite all the talk of empowerment, this legislation will require a good deal of energizing to make it an effective instrument of direct democracy. In this case, it isn't a question of how long the rabbit keeps beating the drum but rather how quickly it can do it to collect the required signatures within the time limits. An initiative would require even greater organizational skills as it requires 10 percent of the eligible signatures in every constituency within ninety days. That will mean 190,000 to 200,000 signatures at the rate of 2,100 to 2,200 per day. It would be a mistake, however, to under-estimate what can happen when an electorate becomes mobilized. As BC's political elites learned in the 1992 Charlottetown Accord constitutional referendum, much depends on the mood of the electorate and the extent to which networks can be formed to mobilize it. In the short run at least, it would seem that the most predictable initiatives will come from the agendas of budget balancers, tax restrainers, right-to-lifers, and aboriginal land-claim constrainers. But those concerned with gambling, environmental protection, sustainable development, and others from both ends of the political spectrum are also possible participants. No one group has a monopoly on direct democracy. The organizational networking that will be required excludes individual, anomic, or spontaneous and locally scattered grassroots initiatives. Those public interest groups and other organizations that already have a province-wide network or overlapping memberships will be the most well placed to take advantage of this new opportunity to set items on the governmental agenda. The most immediate consequence of the high signature thresholds is to favour only the existing large battalions of well-tuned, province-wide organizational networks.

Conclusion

In common with most legislatures around the world, BC's legislature is at a critical stage in its history. Decades of conservative institutionalism and adherence to an idealized Westminster model have given way to two decades of important internal and external reform. The two waves of internal parliamentary procedural reform in the 1970s and 1980s were essentially government driven, and followed a path formed by others who share the traditions of the Westminster model. In contrast, the reforms of the 1990s were externally driven and externally oriented. The reform of the representative nature of the legislature was justified in terms of effective representation and good government. The direct democracy reforms attempted to address rising public alienation from the parliamentary system, and to introduce greater participation and more accountability to the system. They are likely, however, to have only limited impact. The initiative provisions are not *direct* democracy in the sense of direct law-making by people but are appendages to the existing legislative processes. Recall along with the conflict of interest commissioner may similarly be seen as supplementary tools to try to force the accountability of individual members otherwise able to gain shelter under their party's protective umbrella. As was shown in the 1990-1 Fantasy Gardens controversy, party discipline and loyalty typically mean that the parliamentary system continues to operate at a minimal level of accountability, and becomes responsive only under outside compulsion.

Changing perspectives toward elected politicians and politicians' own shifting policy agendas are likely to continue to exert demands for further reform of the parliamentary state embodied in the BC legislature. Continuing parliamentary adaptation and change will be required to ensure that the best of the Westminster tradition can survive in BC, and maintain its political legitimacy in the face of decreasing levels of public esteem and confidence.

Further Reading

British Columbia. Legislative Assembly. Select Standing Committee on Parliamentary Reform. *Report on Recall and Initiative*. Victoria: November 1993

Connaghan, C.J. *Official Report and Recommendations: 1992 Review of MLA Remuneration, The British Columbia Legislative Assembly*. Vancouver: Connaghan and Associates 1992

MacMinn, E. George. *Parliamentary Practice in British Columbia*. 2nd ed. Victoria: Queen's Printer 1987

Ruff, Norman J. 'The Right to Vote and Inequality of Voting Power in British Columbia: The Jurisprudence and Politics of the Dixon Case.' In *Drawing Boundaries*, edited by John Courtney, P. MacKinnon, and David Smith, 128-47. Saskatoon: Fifth House 1992

Sharman, Campbell. 'The Strange Case of a Provincial Constitution: The BC Constitution Act.' *Canadian Journal of Political Science* 17 (1984): 87-108

Wilson, Jeremy. 'British Columbia: A Unique Blend of the Traditional and Modern.' In *Provincial and Territorial Legislatures in Canada*, edited by Gary Levy and Graham White, 126-38. Toronto: University of Toronto Press 1989

See also the BC legislature World Wide Web site at http://www.legis.gov.bc.ca.

7
Women and Political Representation in British Columbia
Lynda Erickson

On 2 April 1991, in the wake of a scandal that had forced her predecessor, William Vander Zalm, from office, Rita Johnston became the twenty-eighth premier of British Columbia and the first woman in Canada to lead a provincial government. As the first woman premier in the country, Johnston was following in the pioneering footsteps of three other BC women who had made important symbolic breakthroughs in Canadian political life. One, Mary Ellen Smith, had become the first woman cabinet minister in Canada (and the British Empire) when she was appointed a minister without portfolio in the BC cabinet in 1921. Another, Nancy Hodges, became the first woman Speaker in the British Commonwealth when she was elected to that position in 1950. The third, Tilly Ralston, was the first woman cabinet minister in Canada to assume a portfolio when she became the minister of education in 1952. In keeping with this pattern of symbolic breakthroughs, when Johnston's government was defeated in a provincial election in October 1991, the newly elected legislature included proportionately more women members than any other legislature in the country. Twenty-five percent of the MLAs were female.

BC's role as a leader in the representation of women in Canadian politics is perhaps not surprising given the post-suffrage organizational strength of the province's social feminists,[1] its reputation for lacking ties to tradition, and its history of socialist and social democratic parties preaching equality. Yet, although BC has been conditioned to change in other domains and experienced in the political rhetoric of equality, its pioneering role for women in the representative institutions of politics has been a limited one. As will be demonstrated below, until 1991 the province's overall record for electing women was modest. The change in 1991 thus raises the question of what accounts for the dramatic increase of women in the legislature and, further, whether it has, in the short term, had any implications for the representation of women's interests. This chapter will explore the record of women's representation in the legislature of BC, with a particular focus on the factors and processes that contributed to the recent gains women have made. It will then explore whether these gains have been followed by a feminization of other dimensions of the provincial state. The chapter will conclude with a brief attempt to assess the impact of the changes in symbolic representation for other dimensions of women's representation.

The Socioeconomic Context of Women's Representation

Politics in BC and the issue of women's representation have been set in the context of a rapidly developing society, a changing population base, and an economy driven by primary industries and their exports. The population has changed in both size and composition, reflecting the diversity of the migrants who have come to BC from the rest of Canada and the immigrants who have come from abroad. Since 1931, when BC was only the sixth largest province, its population has increased proportionately more than any other, growing more than fourfold from 700,000 to 3.3 million. In the process, the provincial population has been transformed from a predominantly British society to one of ethnic and racial diversity. Thus, in the 1931 census, 71 percent of the population were said to be of British extraction, whereas just 35 percent were classified in the 1991 census as of 'British only' lineage. The rest were of mixed British/non-British ancestry (23 percent) or of non-British origin (42 percent).[2]

The continual migration and immigration into BC is said to have created a culture in which calls to tradition have less resonance than elsewhere.[3] As Daphne Marlatt has pointed out, however, the frontier roots of the society have still had an important impact. The non-Native settlers who took over the land from BC's indigenous inhabitants were, in her words, 'less homesteaders than bushwhackers, goldpanners, brothel-keepers, drovers, [and] drifters' and they left in their wake a 'macho culture of frontier heroism' in which women 'have never figured as cultural heroes.'[4] This culture that rendered women less visible was reinforced, historically, by the population imbalance between women and men. Until the end of the First World War, adult males outnumbered adult women in the non-Native population by more than two to one, and it was not until mid-century that the number of women came to approximate that of men.[5]

The resource economy, based first on furs, then on gold, and subsequently on forestry, fishing, and the mining of a variety of minerals, may also have served to reinforce the macho elements in the culture. The quintessential image of resource extraction in these sectors is male, reflecting the employment patterns in them – over 90 percent of the jobs are occupied by men[6] – and the nature of the work undertaken. With women so eclipsed in the economic sectors that have traditionally characterized BC life, a critical element of the provincial identity has had a very masculine flavour.

Notwithstanding the importance of the primary sector as a source of wealth and export income, services have long been the dominant employment sector, and, as a result, urbanization has been a significant feature of social life. By 1911 approximately half the population of BC lived in urban centres, and by mid-century this figure had reached 69 percent.[7] In addition, this largely urban society has lived under conditions of comparative affluence. The annual per capita income in the province has consistently been above the national average, and more recently has been the highest in the country.

The pattern of women's lives has reflected the greater options available in this more affluent, urban society. In this century, the birth rate in BC dropped earlier than it did in other provinces,[8] and remained substantially lower than in the rest of the country until the 1970s when birth rates in all provinces dropped to similar levels. In the 1960s and 1970s, when women across the country were gaining increased access to institutions of higher education, those in BC led the way in terms of their levels of educational attainment.[9] To the degree that lower birth rates, higher incomes, and higher levels of education contribute to more women entering political life, women in BC had become well-placed for entry into politics compared to those in other provinces.

The Political Context of Women's Representation
Socioeconomic conditions are, however, only part of the context for women's entry into the political elite. Political variables are also important. As the only effective vehicles for representation in provincial legislatures, the dominant parties in a system must be willing to nominate women candidates for office and to do so in competitive ridings if women are to increase their representation. Given their commitment to issues of equality, compared to parties of the centre and right, socialist and social democratic parties appear to be more ideologically disposed to increasing the representation of women within the ranks of their competitive candidates. Moreover, cross-cultural research has demonstrated that this ideological disposition has had practical effects. Parties of the left have tended to give more women the opportunity to win office than have parties of the centre or right.[10]

There are, however, substantial differences in levels of female recruitment among parties of the left in different countries, suggesting that an important aspect in the political context is the competitive relationship between the parties in a political system. One factor in this relationship is the overall strength of parties of the left and right.[11] In Scandinavia, for example, where parties of the left have been dominant in postwar parliaments, the proportion of women MPs in parties across the spectrum

increased substantially throughout the 1970s and 1980s, and in most centre and right parties in Scandinavia, women compose a larger proportion
of elected legislators than they do among parties of the left in many other
democracies.[12] The Scandinavian example suggests that where parties of
the left that champion equality have assumed a dominant position
electorally, other parties in the system feel competitive pressure to provide
opportunities for women in their parties as well.[13] Conversely, in systems
where parties of the right and centre-right have dominated politics, few
women have gained access to legislatures even as representatives of the
left.

Another dimension of party competition that may be relevant to gains
for women is electoral volatility and the rise of new parties or the surge in
popular support for an established party.[14] New parties may provide more
opportunities for women to gain party nominations because there are no
incumbents seeking reelection. Incumbents, who are usually male, are rarely
rejected in their efforts to be reselected as candidates. Similarly, parties
experiencing a surge in support may have more room for women candidates in their competitive ridings because not all such ridings are occupied
by incumbents.

In BC the political variables that appear to help the recruitment of women
were, until 1991, not very prevalent. Although the social democratic left
has been a competitive force in provincial politics since 1933, first with the
Co-operative Commonwealth Federation (CCF) and then with its successor, the New Democratic Party (NDP), the right and centre-right dominated the legislative benches. Prior to its recent electoral successes, the
NDP formed the government only once, in 1972. Moreover, in the years
from the late 1960s, when the issue of women's representation was placed
on the political agenda with the rise of the second-wave feminist movement, the party system was relatively stable. With the 1991 election, this
context changed, as the NDP defeated the governing Social Credit Party,
and the Liberals, a very minor player in provincial politics from 1975 until
1991, experienced an unexpectedly strong showing.

Although contextual and systemic conditions are important in helping
to facilitate or hinder the entrance of women into the political elite, our
understanding of change in this arena also needs to take into account questions of agency and strategy. As Diane Sainsbury has argued with respect to
Sweden, the increased representation of women in parliament did not 'just
happen' but was the result of actions undertaken by women within the
parties and the strategies women used in their particular structural contexts.[15] In BC the activities and strategies of women within the NDP in
particular have been important for the recruitment of female politicians,
and the feminist sector in the party appears to have provided an important

source of support and pressure for the inclusion of women's issues on the government agenda.

Women in the Legislative Assembly and Cabinets: 1918-91

In BC, as in the rest of Canada, much of the fight for women's suffrage was predicated on the notion that women had a special contribution to make to politics. Thus, many suffragists sought votes for women not just to extend political equality to women but also to bring women's special perspective to bear on legislation and governing.[16] However, the extension of the franchise in 1917 to include most adult females in the province[17] did not herald an influx of women into the provincial legislature. This was despite continued political activism in the post-enfranchisement era on the part of a number of BC suffragists who worked in support of issues of social reform.[18] Indeed, from 1917 until 1941, only four women sat in the Legislative Assembly as elected members.

The first woman MLA, Mary Ellen Smith, was elected in 1918 in a by-election held to replace her late husband, who had been minister of finance in the Liberal government. Campaigning on a platform of rights for women and children,[19] Smith first won the seat as an independent but in subsequent elections ran on a Liberal ticket. An activist in the women's movement, she had been a founding member of the Women's Liberal Association. This association was created in 1915 after the Liberal Party had distinguished itself from its Conservative rival in supporting female suffrage, first in the 1912 election and subsequently at its 1913 convention.[20]

Smith was appointed minister without portfolio in 1921 but she resigned her cabinet post a mere nine months later, indicating in her letter of resignation that she was not happy at being required to 'assume responsibility of acts of the government without being in a position to criticize or advise.'[21] In a press interview a year later, she also attributed her resignation to the government's failure to meet its promise to create a portfolio for her to deal with women's issues.[22] She sat for ten years as the only woman in the provincial legislature. When she was defeated in the 1928 election, the house was left with no female representatives. In the next provincial election, in 1933, Helen Douglas Smith, who had also been an activist in the women's movement and a supporter of social reform, was elected as a Liberal.

The year 1933 also saw the entrance of the newly formed socialist party, the CCF, into provincial politics. With 32 percent of the votes and seven seats in the legislature, this new party, committed to principles of equality, represented an important challenge to traditional political forces. The party's focus was, however, primarily economic, and feminist issues and the woman question gained scant attention in debates or discussion within its ranks.[23] Yet, given that a statement in support of equal pay and benefits for women employees was part of the party's manifesto, there was some indication that compared to other parties, the CCF might be more tolerant, if not supportive, of women seeking public office.

The party's record in its early years was mixed. None of its first seven MLAs were women. However, by 1941, two women, Dorothy Steeves and Laura Jamieson, were sitting in the legislature as CCF members. Both first won their seats through by-elections. Steeves, who had first been attracted to a socialist party in her youth in the Netherlands because of its endorsement of female suffrage,[24] was first elected in a by-election in 1934 and was reelected in the 1937 provincial election. Jamieson, who had been a leading Vancouver activist in the pre-suffrage women's movement and was a social reformer and juvenile court judge, was elected in a by-election in 1939.[25]

For all parties, the few women who gained seats in the legislature in the interwar period reflected the small proportion of candidates who were female. Just 4 percent of the more than 800 candidates who ran for seats in the five provincial elections from 1920 to 1937 were women, and most of these ran mainly as fringe candidates.[26] Nor did the entrance of the CCF substantially change this pattern. Of the ninety-two candidates the party ran in the 1933 and 1937 elections, only five were women. The predominant view that politics is a man's game and women need not apply clearly had effects in all the parties.

In the 1941 election, although the percentage of women candidates did not improve from 1937, more of them were successful and the percentage of females in the legislature increased to ten. This included three from the CCF and one each from the Liberal and Conservative Parties. However, after the 1945 election, with the poor showing of the CCF and the defeat of its three women MLAs, the number of women in the house returned to prewar levels. It was not until 1972 that the percentage of women in the legislature reached the level of the wartime session (see Table 7.1).

From 1945 until 1969, the average proportion of women in the house was 5 percent, and at the cabinet level just four women received appointments. Of these four, only Tilly Ralston held a portfolio: she served as minister of education for fifteen months. The pattern of female candidacies was also similar to earlier years: of the more than 1,700 candidates who ran in the nine elections that were held, only 7 percent were female and almost half of these ran for minor or fringe parties. Among the major opponents in the party system, differences in the number of women who ran for each party were small. Of the CCF/NDP candidates, 8.4 percent were women, compared to the 5 percent of those nominated by their major rivals, first the coalition and later Social Credit.[27]

Table 7.1

Women elected in BC general elections, 1945-96

Year	CCF/NDP	Social Credit	Liberal[a]	Other	Total women	Total MLAs (%)
1945	0			2[b]	2	4.2
1949	0			2[b]	2	4.2
1952	1	1	1	0	3	6.2
1953	0	1	0	0	1	2.1
1956	1	1	0	0	2	3.8
1960	3	1	0	0	4	7.7
1963	1	0	0	0	1	1.9
1966	1	3	0	0	4	7.7
1969	1	4	0	0	5	9.0
1972	5	1	0	0	6	10.9
1975	4	2	0	0	6	10.9
1979	4	2	0	0	6	10.5
1983	4	2	0	0	6	10.5
1986	5	4	0	0	9	13.0
1991	16	0	3	0	19	25.3
1996	12	0	8	0	20	26.7

[a] The Liberal Party contested the 1945 and 1949 elections as part of the coalition.
[b] Coalition members.
Source: Elections British Columbia, *Electoral History of British Columbia: 1871-1986*; Elections British Columbia *Report of the Chief Electoral Officer: 1991.*

With wartime levels reached in 1972, it took another two decades for further change to occur in the legislative arena. Even in the 1986 election, when, as a result of a redistribution exercise, the legislature grew by more than 20 percent, the proportion of women in the chamber only increased from 10.5 to 13 percent. At the cabinet level, there was some improvement as the practice of assigning women as ministers without portfolio disappeared after 1973, and women who were appointed to ministerial posts were given more high-profile assignments, including that of deputy premier. However, the number who were included in any one cabinet remained very small – no more than two women ever sat at the cabinet table. Even Canada's first woman premier had only one other woman in her cabinet.[28]

Although little change with respect to the representation of women was evident among elected members of the Legislative Assembly during the period from 1972 to 1986, changes relevant to gender issues were being made at the party level, in particular within the NDP. These changes in the NDP began in the early 1970s as a number of women activists started to pressure their party in support of the women's rights issues that the second-wave feminist movement was beginning to articulate. The first success of this group came in 1971 with the resurrection of a Women's Committee in the party.

Earlier, in 1962, the NDP had established a Women's Committee to 'stimulate interest among women, to develop their capabilities in the field of organization and education by providing opportunities to improve their skills and qualifications so they will be more effective as people, as supporters, members, active party officers, or as potential representatives.'[29]

By the mid-1960s, however, this committee had assumed some of the aura of a 'Ladies Auxiliary,'[30] and by the end of the decade had become inactive. After the publication of the Report of the Royal Commission on the Status of Women in 1970, and a lack of initiative on the part of their party on the issues raised by the report, a group of feminists in the BC NDP became convinced of the need for a special party committee that they could use to press matters of women's rights. In 1971, at the urging of these women, the provincial executive reconstituted the 1962 committee as a standing committee within the party. The committee's terms of reference included those of the earlier committee as well as a directive to 'study and work toward implementing the recommendations of the Royal Commission.'[31]

This Women's Rights Committee (WRC) soon became an important forum for the discussion of women's issues, as it initiated conferences, held workshops, produced its own magazine, and developed comprehensive policies for women's rights. At party conventions, an active Women's Caucus gave support and direction to the committee's executive and lobbied in favour of its policy resolutions on the convention floor.[32] The committee also encouraged the formation of women's rights groups at the local constituency level and, in 1974, pressed successfully for the appointment of a women's organizer to help in organizing these local groups and in educating the party on women's rights.

On issues of women's representation, the WRC and the Women's Caucus had a double agenda. One concerned placing women who held a feminist perspective on party committees and in elected party office; the other was to elect feminist party women to public office. Yet, although electing women to office was one of the objectives of the WRC, in the early years of the committee's work, struggles with respect to party structures and policy agendas consumed more of the energies of its members. However, the committee did challenge the party to take seriously the concept of gender parity in elected offices.

As the WRC and the Women's Caucus kept feminist analyses and issues of gender on the party agenda, the number of women candidates nominated for provincial office by the local NDP associations began to increase (see Table 7.2). The proportion of party candidates who were women grew from 14 percent in the 1972 election to 23 percent in the 1983 election.

Table 7.2

Percent of women candidates in BC general elections, 1972-96

	NDP	Social Credit	Liberal	Other*	Total women
1972	14.5	7.2	9.4	15.9	11.9
1975	18.2	3.6	16.3	11.3	12.2
1979	21.1	5.3	0	18.6	14.6
1983	22.8	8.8	19.2	5.2	13.8
1986	30.4	7.2	23.6	11.4	19.0
1991	33.3	24.3	21.1	26.8	26.5

* Includes independents.
Source: Elections British Columbia, *Electoral History of British Columbia: 1871-1986;* Elections British Columbia, *Report of the Chief Electoral Officer: 1991.*

By the mid-1980s, the WRC shifted more of its efforts to the issue of electing women and providing encouragement for women to run for nominations. In 1985, for example, the committee successfully lobbied for the establishment of the Dorothy Steeves Fund to help NDP women candidates in their campaigns. By the 1986 election, the number of women candidates nominated by the party reached 30 percent. Although only five won office, with subsequent by-elections two more were added to the party's caucus. Thus, by the legislature's dissolution in 1991, 28 percent of the NDP legislative contingent were women.

In the meantime, in the interelection period, the WRC had expanded its network designed to encourage women to run by forming a Nomination Support Committee in 1988. This committee then published a booklet for women on winning nominations, and, in 1990, sponsored a workshop for women who had successfully or unsuccessfully run for nominations for the upcoming provincial election. This workshop provided feedback to the committee on the candidate selection process and helped the committee in its work on the nominations that remained to be filled. The target was not just increased nominations for women but nominations that were competitive. By voting time, one-third of the party's candidates were women. Although this was only an increase of three from the previous election, the new nominees were somewhat better placed to win their seats than in the past. Sixty-four percent of the NDP's women candidates won their seats in the 1991 election, compared to 70 percent of the men. In the 1986 election, 24 percent of NDP women won their seats, compared to 35 percent of the men.

As part of the 1991 campaign to elect women, the WRC focused it efforts on the election process as well as candidate selection. The committee sponsored a special workshop for the party's women candidates in the summer before the election, and organized special sessions for women candidates at various candidate gatherings held in the pre-election period. Along with the women's organizer and the party's critic for women's issues, the WRC was also successful in convincing the party's election planning committee to mount a special 'Equality Campaign' to be conducted throughout the province. This campaign emphasized issues of women's equality and focused attention on the women candidates nominated by the party.[33]

Begun in 1990, when the election was first expected, this campaign continued throughout the pre-election and election period. Rallies and other public events emphasizing the equality campaign were held, media advertising that targeted equality themes was mounted, and special campaign materials emphasizing women's issues were distributed. By the time the election was held, the 'Campaign to Women Voters' (as it was also called) had become an integral part of the party's overall election campaign.

When the votes were counted, sixteen NDP women were elected, producing a caucus in which 31 percent of the members were female.[34] Seven members (37 percent) of the new cabinet appointed after the election were also women, a fact that the new premier, Mike Harcourt, emphasized in his cabinet announcements. Stating in a news release in 1991 that 'BC women will have a strong voice at the cabinet table to ensure their priorities are at the top of the political agenda,' Harcourt clearly reiterated an election theme to which his party had committed itself.

While the NDP responded to a changing gender climate within its organization and nominated increasing numbers of women candidates over the course of the 1970s and 1980s, its main rival, the Social Credit Party was much slower to change. In its organizational arrangements for women, Social Credit had retained a Women's Auxiliary. This organization was largely a remnant of traditional politics when women were seen as providing important support networks for parties but were not viewed as an independent political force or potential material for elected office.

That the auxiliary was primarily developed to perpetuate an ethic of party service among its members and was not a forum designed to promote women within the party is evident in the Social Credit constitution. There, the objectives of the auxiliary are stated as follows:

(a) To subscribe to the four principles of Social Credit ...
(b) To support and become informed about:
  (i) the principles and objectives of Social Credit.
  (ii) The program of the Social Credit Government of the Province of British Columbia.
(c) To support the British Columbia Social Credit Party.
(d) To provide assistance to the official Social Credit Candidate of the Constituency during an election.[35]

Although this organization became increasingly irrelevant to party life, even for Social Credit women activists,[36] to many observers its continued existence symbolized a party that found traditional notions of women and politics difficult to shed.

The candidate profile of the party tended to reinforce the view that Social Credit was slow to modernize its approach to women. Only 6.5 percent of those nominated by the party in the five elections prior to 1991 were female. Moreover, from the 1972 election to the one in 1986, there was no growth in its percentage of women candidates. In 1991, however, there was a substantial increase in this figure: 23 percent of those who carried the Social Credit label in that election were women.

What explains this sudden increase? One factor may have been the selection by the party of a new *woman* leader. In July of 1991, the party had held a leadership convention to replace William Vander Zalm. In that convention, Rita Johnston, whose first appointment had been as interim premier for the period between Vander Zalm's resignation and the convention, emerged successful. She defeated another woman, Grace McCarthy, in the final ballot.[37] With a woman at the helm, and one who had been the first woman premier in the country, the party may have appeared more welcoming to women politicians and, as a result, more women interested in elected office decided to seek party candidacies.

Another factor that apparently contributed to the increased number of Social Credit women candidates was the high rate of retirement among incumbents. Only twenty-eight of the forty-one Social Credit MLAs indicated their intention to run again.[38] The party's ratings in the polls were low and many long-time MLAs had taken the opportunity of an election to retire. These retirements, in addition to deaths and resignations earlier in the legislative session, opened up a number of candidacies to new challengers.

Yet having open candidacies would not have been sufficient if party members were reluctant to put forward women candidates. However, given that support for the party among women voters had been declining even more than it had among men, Social Credit members may have become more receptive to female candidates. They may have seen that nominating women candidates was a way of demonstrating the party's openness to women, and thus a means of attracting more women voters.

In the end, however, with the party's fortunes having plummeted as a result of scandals that embroiled the cabinet and, especially, the premier during the administration of Vander Zalm, none of the women candidates were among the seven Social Credit members who won their seats.

The dismal showing of the Social Credit Party in the election was in contrast to the fortunes of the Liberal Party. The Liberals experienced a remarkable resurrection in 1991. After the 1972 election, the provincial

wing of the party had virtually self-destructed as a number of its prominent activists and most of its MLAs moved to the Social Credit Party in
response to the success of the NDP.[39] In the 1975 election, unable to mount
a full slate of candidates, the party won only 7.2 percent of the popular
vote and just one seat. By the 1979 election, it had reached its lowest point
and was reduced to running only five candidates. Liberal fortunes grew
provincially in the 1980s, but only slowly, so that even in the 1991 campaign it was not able to fill all its candidate slots, and many of those who
did run for the party were doing so merely to show the partisan flag on the
ballot. However, after having been also-rans for so long in provincial politics, the Liberals' popularity dramatically shifted midway through the 1991
election campaign, giving them an unexpected seventeen seats in the final
election results and placing them in the role of the official opposition in
the new legislature.

Also in contrast to the Social Credit Party, the provincial Liberals had
modernized with respect to their women members. The party's traditional
women's auxiliary had been replaced by the BC Women's Liberal Commission, an organization whose aims include increasing the role of women in
politics and training women to develop their political skills. However, given
that the party's activists tended to be focused primarily on federal politics[40]
and that the provincial wing was a very marginal player in provincial politics before the 1991 election, the level of activity directed to women's issues and organizing around women's representation at the provincial level
was not very substantial.

With respect to candidacies, once the Liberals began again in the 1980s
to nominate candidates in most ridings, approximately one in five of those
who put their names forward under the party label were women. Given
the party's minority status in the 1980s, its better record for nominating
women compared to Social Credit may not have been very remarkable.
Still, in the 1991 election, when fifteen of the seventy-one candidates nominated by the party were female, three of the seventeen successful Liberal
candidates (18 percent of the caucus) were women.

In summary, the history of women's representation in the BC legislature
was, until 1991, unremarkable in terms of the number of women elected.
Then, in 1991, increased electoral volatility, the growth in popularity of
the NDP, and the presence in that party of a strong feminist wing whose
activities had contributed to the nomination of women candidates in a
number of competitive ridings, produced a substantial increase of women
in the BC legislature. The question to which this chapter will now turn is
whether, since 1991, there have been other changes in government in BC.
Has government moved in a direction that could be called feminization of
the state?

Toward a Feminization of the State?

The feminization of the state would entail a wide range of activities beyond the electoral project, including the appointment of women to important decision-making positions in the government and changing the way institutions function to a manner consistent with feminism. The range of the project is, clearly, considerable, involving the whole of the state apparatus. A full appraisal of the extent to which a provincial government has moved toward a more feminized state is itself also a major venture and one that is, given the limited evidence available, premature insofar as BC is concerned. What is offered here is preliminary and of more limited scope.

Three different aspects of state activity are examined for indications of change. The first is the appointment of women to senior positions at the political level in the cabinet and the legislature. The second involves the functioning of the legislature and the way it works for the women in it. The third concerns the contributions of the new Ministry of Women's Equality.

Women in the Cabinet and Legislative Assembly

If one aspect of feminization of the state requires the appointment of women to senior positions in the governing structures, at the political level it clearly demands that women be assigned highly visible and politically important cabinet positions. As indicated earlier, there were real changes at the cabinet level after the 1991 election. The first cabinet appointed by the new premier had seven women, including the new ministers of health, education, and social services, whose portfolios collectively accounted for the largest expenditures of the provincial government, plus the ministers of energy, mines and petroleum resources, tourism and culture, government services, and women's equality. In addition, on the committees of cabinet, to which much of cabinet decision-making is delegated, women composed half or more of the members in six of the eight committees. Again, in the news releases outlining the cabinet structure, the government emphasized the gender structure of these committees.[41]

In the cabinet shuffle that occurred two years later, the number (and proportion) of women remained the same. Moreover, although women no longer held the important portfolios of education or health, Elizabeth Cull was appointed minister of finance. On the other hand, in cabinet committees women were not as evident. They became a minority in all but the more administratively oriented Regulations and Orders-In-Council Committee.[42] The government made no comment nor did the media note that the gender structure of these committees had been altered.

In the legislature, feminization requires that women be assigned highly visible positions and that they be well represented on legislative committees.

In terms of house assignments orchestrated by the governing party, the most prominent position, that of Speaker, went first to a woman, who remained there until 1994, albeit as a focus of some controversy because of her lack of experience in the house (she was a novice MLA). She was replaced when the government opted for a Speaker elected in a manner similar to that used in the House of Commons: by secret ballot. In the other high-profile legislative positions, those of house leaders, women have been less visible, although not absent. One woman briefly held the position of opposition house leader,[43] and for the government, a woman has occupied the role of deputy leader.

For committee assignments, the NDP initiated the practice of requiring gender parity among its committee members and for the chair and co-chair of each committee. This guarantees some formal presence of women on every committee, but places more demands on women backbenchers than on many of their male colleagues. Without more female members, attempts to provide visibility for women can place a double burden on those available to take on the task, and may thus compromise their capacity to represent effectively.

Overall, however, with respect to appointments in the cabinet and legislature, the evidence suggests that although some of the gains recorded early in the parliament fell back somewhat, the arena of official politics has moved in the directions required of a feminized state. This is not to suggest that goals of parity with respect to the presence of women have been achieved but it is to say that substantial changes in this direction have been made.

Organization and Processes of Legislative Politics

In the organization and processes of the legislature, however, the story is different. There is little evidence that the house and its politics have been substantially altered to reflect the needs or styles of women. As Mueller found in his study of the BC legislature, for many female MLAs, the Legislative Assembly is not woman-friendly.[44] The hours the house sits and the lack of a fixed schedule for the days it will meet or when holidays will be taken make the integration of work and family life difficult. Contacts with friends and neighbours, who provide important social grounding for women as politicians, are all but impossible to maintain during parliamentary sessions. When the assembly is in session, most MLAs must travel from their homes to be in Victoria every week, in addition to doing their constituency work in their local area.

These aspects of house organization, which are modelled on a traditional paradigm of the male politician whose family life is cared for by a wife at home, make the job difficult for contemporary MLAs of both genders. They are, however, particularly problematic for women politicians who have young children or who are single parents. These difficulties were demonstrated in a child-custody case involving an opposition MLA, Judi Tyabji. Her estranged husband's lawyer argued that because Tyabji's career as a provincial politician was too time-consuming, the children's father should be given their custody. The court granted him custody.[45]

In terms of style, the legislative chamber is also modelled on a traditional paradigm, and one that women in the house sometimes find difficult and hostile.[46] The adversarial structure of the institution, with its emphasis on aggressive probing by the opposition and equally aggressive responses from the government, is more compatible with a style our culture characterizes as male. As one woman MLA observed, 'if you look at how the legislature functions, it functions on anger, pure and simple, and the ability to control, manipulate, use, display anger, and of course along with anger goes a big, loud voice, being tall, being imposing, all of those things which obviously play to male experience, male strengths, male conditioning.'[47] While the increased number of women in the legislature may have altered the atmosphere of the legislative chamber to some degree,[48] the essential character of partisan interaction in the house seems unchanged.

This is not to say that women members see partisanship itself as the culprit that compromises women's participation. Most do not.[49] Indeed, the disciplined party system of Canadian legislatures may provide more space and protection for the contributions of women legislators than a system with weaker party discipline and loyalty. Greater competition for *individual* advantage is to be expected in a system less structured by party loyalty, and in situations of individual competition, women's less aggressive style may leave them more marginalized, even as their numbers increase.[50] Thus, evidence from a study of Colorado state legislative committees (where individual power and influence are much greater than that found in Canadian legislatures or legislative committees) found that verbal aggression among male state legislators vis-à-vis their female counterparts increased as the proportion of women committee members grew.[51] While partisanship may create suspicion and mistrust among women across the party divide, within-party solidarity can provide group support in the house.

The Ministry of Women's Equality

In addition to changes in political personnel and legislative politics, feminization of the state clearly requires changes in the bureaucratic and policy processes of the government. These would include the establishment of structures and networks that encourage policy-makers to take women into account as they analyze policies and develop proposals. After the 1991 election in BC, one arena through which changes in this direction have been attempted is the new Ministry of Women's Equality.

For the new governing party, the notion of a special ministry for women had a long history. The WRC of the BC NDP was, from its beginnings, committed to the creation of a separate Ministry of Women's Rights as a structure through which women's interests could be pursued within government. The committee was quickly successful in gaining support from the party's grassroots for the idea of a special ministry for women. As early as 1972, the party's provincial convention passed a resolution in favour of the creation of such a department at the provincial level. However, the NDP government that was in power at that time rejected the proposal. The premier, Dave Barrett, indicated his opposition just hours after the resolution had passed[52] and remained opposed to the idea of such a department throughout his time in office. The committee and many of the women in the party continued, however, to support the notion of the women's ministry. Moreover, support for such a ministry remained on the NDP policy books throughout the Barrett administration and subsequent to it.

Social Credit governments that followed the NDP were, typically, no more favourable to the notion of a special ministry. Even the idea of establishing a cabinet position of minister responsible for women's issues was resisted. Although all the other governments across the country had appointed such ministers, BC withstood pressure to do so until the fall of 1989. Then, with his administration having become increasingly unpopular among women, Premier Vander Zalm appointed Carol Gran as minister of government services and responsible for women's programs. This finally created a formal advocacy position for women within the cabinet. A sub-ministry for women was then established within Government Services, replacing the Women's Secretariat that was at that point a unit in the Ministry of Advanced Education. This new sub-ministry was to play primarily a coordinating role with respect to the various programs throughout government that were relevant to women. Except for dispensing grants to community and provincial organizations for women's projects, its direct program responsibilities were minimal. The new minister did appoint a provincial advisory council to assist her in examining programs, and also undertook two task force investigations as part of her mandate for women's advocacy.[53]

By 1991, with encouragement from women's groups within the party, the NDP commitment with respect to a women's ministry was elaborated. The NDP promised to expand the responsibilities of such a ministry, to improve its status within government, and to increase its input into government policies beyond that of the existing sub-ministry. In the election of that year, the party campaigned on a platform that promised a separate, free-standing Ministry of Women's Equality that had program responsibility and a minister who had a voice in central cabinet committees.

The creation of a free-standing Ministry of Women's Equality (MWE), Canada's first, was proclaimed with the announcement of the first cabinet of the new government. The new ministry was given both program and policy advisory responsibilities, and the minister was given a seat in the two most important cabinet committees – the Treasury and Planning boards – as well as membership in four of the other six cabinet committees. While the appointment of the minister to six of the eight cabinet committees was perhaps an attempt to signal the centrality of the women's agenda for the government, in practical terms it would be virtually impossible for one minister to be an effective member of so many committees. In the 1993 cabinet changes, the minister retained her seat on Treasury Board, but was not appointed to the Planning Board and was left with a position on only two of the five committees in the new cabinet structure.

The program responsibilities of the MWE are seen within the ministry to be critical because they entail a substantial budget and hence give the department some status on budgetary grounds, and because they give the ministry access to various forums of decision-making that are important for women's issues. These program responsibilities have included child care, pay and employment equity, reproductive choice for women, and violence against women, as well as the provision of grants to community and provincial organizations. Currently, the major areas of responsibility for program delivery are for transition houses, as part of the ministry's mandate to stop violence against women, in the funding and development of child care and child care facilities, and the allocation of grants.

Independent estimates have yet to be made of the funding and policy changes that have been implemented in the various policy areas addressed by the MWE. However, some aspects of the new regime deserve comment. With respect to child care and child care facilities, the allocation of overall responsibility for child care to one ministry that has made it a priority issue has raised the visibility of child care issues and should contribute to better overall policy coordination in this area. On transition houses, sexual assault issues, and women's centres, the new ministry has allocated more funds to this arena and added eleven new government-funded assault centres. As well, it has provided stable core funding for other centres that previously had no such provincial funding.

In the ministry's policy advisory role, an important part of the mandate given to its policy division was to look at government decision-making in terms of its impact on women. In this respect the ministry was to function as a central agency working to ensure that 'issues relating to women's equality are reflected in policy, legislation, services and programs throughout [the] government.'[54]

As part of this mandate, the MWE developed an approach to gender analysis it has called the 'Gender Lense Framework.' This framework lays out ways in which policies can be reviewed and analyzed to see if they discriminate against women or support full participation and equality for women. It suggests that in examining policy proposals, analysts should consider four things: the perspectives they bring to their analysis; the nature of the data and information used – for example, 'do the data include information based on both women's and men's experiences';[55] whether policy consultations have included women's groups; and if the policy takes into account differences and diversity among women.

The cabinet in the meantime has agreed that ministries introducing policy changes must address the gender impacts of their changes. In other words, the gender implications of policies should be made explicit. Further, it has recommended the Gender Lense Framework as a useful tool. This has been formalized in the *New Cabinet Submissions Format and Guidelines* directive as follows.

> The impact of a policy option on women must be analyzed. The analysis should focus on the differential impact of various policy options on women and, where appropriate, on specific groups of women (such as older women or women of colour or women living in rural areas). Furthermore, the analysis should consider whether the policy choice supports equality for women. The Ministry of Women's Equality has developed an analytical framework tool that may be of assistance to Ministries.[56]

Ministries have also been encouraged to undertake training from the MWE on how to use the Gender Lense Framework.

As a model of institution-building in the interests of women, the Gender Lense Framework strategy is unique in Canada. Its success will be judged by the degree to which the ministry itself no longer needs to play the role of central agency. In the meantime, however, it must face the criticism from opposition parties that it is too bureaucratic and caters too much to a 'special interest.'

As explored here, the evidence does suggest that, since 1991, BC has taken some steps toward a more feminized state. Within the cabinet there are more women than ever before and the positions they hold continue to be politically significant. In the legislature, although the assembly itself still functions in a manner more consistent with a traditionally male paradigm, women have gained some prominence and political importance. In terms of public policy, with the Gender Lense policy of the MWE and the cabinet's commitment to gender impact analyses, it is more likely that women's interests and concerns will brought into the decision-making process.

Conclusions

With the 1991 election in BC, the proportion of women in the provincial legislature increased to 25 percent, the highest of any in Canada. Following this election there were a number of changes in the composition of the cabinet, in the roles and visibility of women in the Legislative Assembly, and, through the new Ministry of Women's Equality, some shifts in policies and procedures. All of these suggest a greater influence of women and feminist perspectives in government. Some of these developments are at least partly attributable to gains in the representation of women among the province's MLAs. But also important has been the NDP's commitment to a women's program. A strong feminist constituency within the party has contributed to both the recruitment of more women into office and the NDP's adoption of an equality agenda. The result has been pressure from within the caucus on behalf of women's issues and for the integration of feminist values into governing.

In the contemporary partisan context, however, this has been a constituency under siege. The NDP has faced a revitalized and increasingly popular Liberal opposition, whose priorities are fiscal restraint and government downsizing and whose agenda with respect to women is not apparent. There is also a provincial Reform Party to which five of the six former Social Credit MLAs affiliated after the 1992 election,[57] and Reform's opposition to the politics of difference articulated by feminists is well established. While the pressure from feminists for programs and policy input will likely continue, their success may flounder on the lack of a sizeable, distinct women's constituency within the larger electorate.

Epilogue: Results of the 1996 Election

On 28 May 1996 in an election held late in its term, the NDP government managed, just barely, to retain power, winning a slim majority of seats but a marginally smaller percentage of the popular vote than its main rival, the Liberal Party. For women, however, the number of seats held by females, of whatever party, grew by one, to a total of twenty, increasing the proportion of women MLAs to 27 percent. With twelve of its women candidates elected, the NDP retained the same proportion of females in its caucus (31 percent) as after the 1991 election. Eight women were elected from the Liberal Party, and the percentage of females in the Liberal caucus increased from eighteen to twenty-four. Both of the two Reform Party members elected were men.

The NDP election campaign in 1996 was less focused on women's issues than in 1991 and, although new women candidates were selected in a few ridings, overall the proportion of its candidates who were women declined from 33 percent in 1991 to 29 percent. Still, the party pledged to retain the Ministry of Women's Equality, something both opposition parties rejected. Moreover, at points in the campaign, the NDP did stress its commitment to programs that targeted women and argued that the Liberals' budgetary agenda would require cutbacks in these programs. Evidence from public opinion polls taken during the election indicated that the NDP did have an advantage among women voters, suggesting that, for its continued success, the party cannot discount the importance of a women's constituency.[58]

For their part, the Liberals were aware of the importance of women's votes in the 1996 election and prior to the election call were interested in increasing the proportion of their candidates who were women. In at least a few instances this strategy ran up against local resistance as some aspiring male candidates won out over their female competitors in nomination contests. In the end, however, the party did register an increase in its percentage of women candidates, going from the 21 percent recorded in 1991 to 27 percent in 1996. The Liberals' attention to this issue and the degree to which they approximated the NDP record with respect to women candidates tends to confirm the relevance of the Scandinavian lesson. When parties that champion gender equality become electorally successful, other parties in the system feel competitive pressure to recruit more women for their own caucuses.

Further Reading

Arscott, Jane, and Linda Trimble, eds. *In the Presence of Women: Representation in Canadian Governments*. Toronto: Harcourt Brace 1996

Bashevkin, Sylvia. *Toeing the Lines: Women and Party Politics in English Canada*. 2nd ed. Toronto: Oxford University Press 1993

Creese, Gillian, and Veronica Strong-Boag, eds. *British Columbia Reconsidered: Essays on Women*. Vancouver: Press Gang 1992

Latham, Barbara, and Cathy Kess, eds. *In Her Own Right*. Victoria: Camosun College 1980

Lovenduski, Joni, and Pippa Norris, eds. *Gender and Party Politics*. London: Sage Publications 1993

Sangster, Joan. *Dreams of Equality: Women on the Canadian Left, 1920-1950*. Toronto: McClelland and Stewart 1989

8
The Media and
British Columbia Politics
Barbara McLintock and Gerry Kristianson

It is obvious that newspapers, radio, and television all play an important role in provincial politics. The mass media are the filter through which most British Columbians receive their information about the political process. As David Taras notes, 'News permeates Canadian life; information, images, fast-breaking stories flow steadily through the country's bloodstream.'[1] The success and failure of the contenders for political office depend in large part on their ability to court positive news coverage, while a variety of interest groups attempt to create a climate within which their particular issues are high on the public and political agenda.

The Historical Context
The link between journalism and politics was established early in the province's political history. One of BC's most colourful early politicians, Amor de Cosmos, founded the *British Colonist* newspaper in 1860, in part to provide a vehicle with which to oppose what he saw as efforts by Governor Sir James Douglas 'to concentrate power in his own hand.'[2] He then went on to become an active participant in electoral politics, championing such important issues of the day as union of the island and mainland colonies, and confederation with Canada. He served a thirteen-month term as the new province's second premier, as well as a stint as a federal member of parliament.

In the context of the day, de Cosmos's mixing of journalism and politics was unexceptional. One of his early colleagues at the *British Colonist*, David Williams Higgins, struck out on his own with the rival *Victoria Daily Chronicle* in 1862, rejoined de Cosmos by merging the two papers in 1866, and then sold his interest and entered provincial politics in 1866 as the MLA for Esquimalt. Higgins became Speaker of the legislature in 1890, serving in that capacity until 1898 when he resigned because of policy differences with the government.

While his former paper had applauded his election as Speaker by saying that he was 'a man of far more than average ability and of high intelligence,'[3] it took a much less charitable view of his decision to break with the government of Premier Turner. It predicted, with great accuracy, the outcome of the next election. 'Esquimalt has been outraged and no doubt when the time arrives Esquimalt will visit its erring representative with their just displeasure.'[4]

Not only were journalists prominent in our early politics but most of the province's major newspapers took an openly partisan stand. For example, until the late 1940s, *McKim's Directory of Canadian Publications* listed the *Victoria Times* and the *Vancouver Sun* as Liberal newspapers and the *Colonist* and the *Province* as Conservative.

This partisanship also was reflected in the behaviour of each paper's reporters in the provincial capital. In his book *Politicians of a Pioneering Province*, former journalist Russell Walker describes how, in 1920, on his first trip to the provincial capital on behalf of the Vancouver *Province*, he met with Conservative leader William Bowser to offer him a favourable story as a lead-in to an expected general election. He describes the *Province* as 'strongly Conservative,'[5] and says that 'With the instructions of my boss ... I had offered the paper's front page to a political leader who sadly needed a favourable press.'[6] When he was assigned permanently to the press gallery a few months later for the *Province*, 'openly a Conservative Party organ,' he went back to Bowser and 'laid before him a business plan. If he would provide from party funds $250 a month, I would plaster BC with Party propaganda that might help him turn the trick.' He also describes how the *Victoria Times* 'was a strong Liberal paper'[7] and the *Colonist* supported the Conservatives. 'When Opposition Leader Bowser scored a point against the government, Joe McDougall of the Tory *Colonist* could easily fill a column.'[8]

While openly partisan at both the editorial and reporting level, the newspapers of early BC acted as the primary recorders of legislative activity. BC did not begin producing an official verbatim account of legislative debates until 1971. Prior to that time, the legislative library regularly clipped and pasted newspaper reports into red binders that became the official 'memory' of legislative proceedings. MLAs who wished to refer to the results of previous sessions could often be seen in the library, taking notes from these volumes for use in subsequent legislative debates. To this day, these binders reside in the area immediately behind the library's main desk, because of the frequency with which they are consulted.

The advent of Hansard and, more recently, the direct broadcast of legislative debates on province-wide cable television have to some extent changed the role of the media. Reporters no longer are expected to produce a detailed record of what happens in the legislature. What is said is being recorded for posterity, regardless of whether or not a reporter is present in the gallery reserved for the media above and behind the Speaker's chair. Reporters can be elsewhere in pursuit of a story, confident that they can quickly scan the day's proceedings for any relevant debate.

The Contemporary Press Gallery

Despite the development of direct broadcasts and Hansard, the basic responsibility for political reporting in BC today continues to rest with the legislative press gallery. The term 'press gallery' is used to describe three separate things: the physical location in the legislative building where political reporters do their work and socialize; the reporters themselves as a collective group; and the self-perpetuating organization of the reporters.

The physical location has always had at least two parts: a row of seats above and behind the Speaker in the legislative chamber and nearby office space. More recently, public funds have supported specialized studios for radio and television reporting. The location out of the Speaker's line of sight reflects the British parliamentary tradition that since reporters cannot be seen, they need not be included among the 'strangers' who can, on occasion, be excluded from the public galleries. A residual effect of this tradition is found in the fact that, unlike other observers, reporters do not rise to acknowledge the arrival at the legislative chamber of the Speaker or lieutenant governor. They do not rise since, technically at least, they are not there.

The current press gallery includes twenty-four full-time and eleven 'associate' members. Full-time members normally have permanently assigned desks and cubicles in the gallery space, and devote a large part, if not all, of their working time to covering the day-to-day machinations of BC's politicians. Some may be allowed, encouraged, or required by their employers to cover other major news stories breaking in the provincial capital; others rarely step outside the corridors of the legislative buildings.

'Associate' members, on the other hand, normally work full-time elsewhere, most often in the main offices of their newspaper or radio or television station. They come to the legislature to augment their employers' coverage of major legislative stories, such as throne speech days, budget days, or days of cabinet resignations or shuffles. Some, especially those from Victoria-area media outlets, may also come for announcements of more local interest, such as the future of Royal Roads Military College or funding for local highways.

The press gallery organization remains something of an anomaly. It charges membership dues, operates under a constitution and bylaws, has a duly-elected executive, and in many ways can exercise substantial power over the lives of its members. Yet it does not legally exist. When, on various occasions throughout its history, the gallery has considered incorporating itself as a non-profit society, no one (including some top legal minds) has ever been able to figure out a way in which it could enjoy the benefits of incorporation and still maintain the unique position it currently holds in terms of its totally independent relations with government. Formally incorporated societies are, of necessity, circumscribed by various legal obligations; government, likewise, is bound by numerous legislative and regulatory requirements in its dealings with any incorporated company or society.

Hence, the press gallery organization for its authority continues to rely on the goodwill of the members, their employers, and the government of the day. All three groups act on the basis that the gallery organization is 'real,' even though it has no actual legal existence.

Unquestionably, however, the strange gallery structure has led in the recent past to internal problems when individual members are concerned about a gallery decision. Among the most controversial problems are those of gallery membership and of media ethics. The gallery itself normally decides whether applications for membership should be accepted; those applications normally come not from individuals but from news organizations. Gallery bylaws state that membership is restricted to those in the actual news business, as opposed to those producing publications for political parties, the government itself, or lobbying organizations – a rule designed to guard against allegations of conflict of interest on the part of gallery members.

The rule seems simple, yet in recent times members have found there are many grey areas to be considered. An application from the NDP's house organ was easy to turn down, but what about people who put out newsletters devoted to certain areas of government-business relations, such as forestry? The question of freelancers has also raised concerns. Many freelancers also, from time to time, undertake contract work for the government. Should this make them ineligible for gallery membership even though they're also writing pieces for bona fide news organizations? Does it make a difference if the person involved is a writer or a photographer? Few of these questions have ever received black or white answers from the gallery. After hours of lengthy debate, most of these issues are still dealt with on a case-by-case basis.

Gallery Ethics

The questions surrounding media ethics have raised even more controversy, and fewer answers, among gallery members. On a few occasions, one or more members of the gallery have done something of which their fellow journalists disapproved on ethical grounds. The question has then arisen as to whether the gallery as an organization has any right to impose discipline on such a member, or whether it ought to even consider the issue in the first place.

One example in which passions ran high among gallery members is the case of the Bud Smith tapes in 1990. The original 'Bud Smith tapes' were tabled in the legislature by opposition MLA Moe Sihota in an effort to show that Attorney General Bud Smith had been misusing his office for political purposes in a private prosecution fraught with political overtones. A few days later, however, a source told gallery members to look under a car parked in the gallery parking lot to find more tapes of Smith's carphone conversations. The sole purpose of the second set of tapes seemed to be to show that Smith was having a relationship with a female television reporter that went far beyond the normal relationship of a reporter and a source. Talk of late-night meetings, visits to each other's homes, and the bringing of bottles of wine appeared to show that, at the least, the two had a significant personal friendship outside the legislative halls – a relationship that Smith appeared willing to exploit to try to promote his side of a political story.

Gallery members found themselves at a loss as to how to deal with the issue, particularly with television crews from rival stations regularly asking gallery executive members what they thought of the situation and what, if anything, the gallery planned to do about it. Some members of the gallery suggested setting up an ethics committee, the members of which might issue guidelines for reporters' behaviour and might also have the power to recommend expulsion from the gallery for ethical breaches. Others argued, however, that to expel some members from the gallery would be in effect to take away their livelihood or to force them to relocate to a different city. That, they realized, would almost certainly bring legal repercussions, and would bring the argument full circle back to the gallery's lack of legal existence. In the end, the majority view held that such ethical questions were best left as a matter between individual members and their employers, the latter having the legal authority to discipline workers for improper conduct.

Another example occurred in 1995 when a gallery radio reporter, with the full backing of his station, filed a complaint with Conflict of Interest Commissioner Ted Hughes alleging that the premier himself could be in a conflict over his relationship with a public relations firm whose principals had also worked on NDP election campaigns. While Hughes later ruled that no conflict existed, some politicians and other members of the media questioned whether the reporter and his radio station had stepped over the line separating observers of the political scene from the players on the field. The radio station and its supporters argued against this. They compared it to seeking information under the Freedom of Information Act to bring a situation fully into the public light.

Not surprisingly, the premier and government took a different view, as did many other gallery members and reporters. They felt that asking Hughes for what amounts to a quasi-judicial ruling, with the reporter and radio station making the allegation that a conflict *did* exist, was much closer to participating in the process than using a freedom of information law. The gallery membership, however, had much less trouble deciding what to do than in the Smith tapes case. Harking back to that event, gallery members agreed again that it should be a question between reporter and employer, and if the employer was prepared to back the reporter and take the consequent political heat, so be it.

The questions fought about by gallery members range from the sublime to the ridiculous. One fight has involved the question of whether radio reporters should be allowed to have 'flashers' (plastic attachments with their station call letters) attached to their microphones in legislative news conferences. In 1989 gallery members passed a rule banning 'flashers' on the grounds that a raft of them from competing stations were distracting to television viewers when shots were being taken of scrums with ministers. When an 'associate' gallery member declined to remove station flashers during occasional trips to the legislature, full-time radio reporters for competing stations suggested cancelling the renegade station's privileges. Again, some members of the gallery feared that such a step could lead to legal repercussions; they also found it somewhat ridiculous that the gallery could decline to expel someone for what other reporters saw as a major breach of ethical rules, but do so for sticking an inch-square piece of plastic on a microphone.

Aside from the obvious legal problems that could arise from the gallery disciplining one of its members, many reporters realize that to start investigating media ethics within the BC political process might be to open grey areas best left undiscussed. Media ethics, like political ethics, are a subjective matter, and the question of where the line should be drawn is often not an easy one to answer.

The Relationship with Politicians

One question that is periodically asked about the press gallery is whether the social relationship between its members and the politicians they cover is too close. In earlier days, the relationship was so close that it would now be called an unquestioned conflict of interest. Up to the early 1970s, members of the gallery received pay 'on the side' for everything from doing government public relations work to writing blatantly-partisan columns and speeches for MLAs. The practice ended only with the coming of a New Democrat government in 1972, and no one has ever been sure whether that was because reporters and/or politicians began to see the ethical problems, or simply because there weren't any NDP newspapers for the new government to turn to.

In the 1990s, the relationships are more subtle. Some members of the gallery regularly spend their social hours with politicians and aides from one party or another, often playing tennis, golf, or squash. The closeness is more obvious than in many other galleries across the country because of the physical isolation of Victoria. Reporters sent to the capital to cover politics for a short period of time often have no chance to make friends elsewhere in the community. The same goes for politicians who travel from their constituencies on the mainland to Victoria only during the legislative session. For them the loneliness is often worse, because they have left family as well as friends home in their riding.

No money or valuable consideration normally changes hands during these encounters. Yet some analysts wonder if it is psychologically possible to play tennis with someone at 9 a.m. and write an entirely unbiased news story – or worse, analysis – about that person at 3 p.m. They also wonder whether politicians can use reporters with whom they socialize without the reporters ever realizing what is happening. For instance, a politician may float a suggestion about something the government is thinking of doing, or drop a few hints about a hidden opposition scandal. The reporter will almost certainly go chasing after the lead without the politician or aide ever having to be held accountable for having made it public.

It is often difficult to differentiate between a social relationship between politicians and reporters and a symbiotic professional one, especially when it comes to members of the opposition. Although governments enjoy 'good news' stories about what they're doing and hope the major media will write about their initiatives, they always have alternative ways of getting their message out. The most obvious of these is government-paid advertising, which can be used either to tell the public the facts about a new program, or to put political spin on the announcement. Government initiatives that affect any number of people are also almost sure to receive at least some news coverage, simply because any change that affects the readers' or listeners' lives is, by definition, newsworthy.

Opposition members, though, must rely on the media far more to ensure that their criticisms of government reach the ears and eyes of the voting public. Thus, is it not surprising that opposition MLAs and their staffs are always sure to have copies of all necessary documents, and often advise reporters in advance about stories they may be breaking in question period.

Reporters may also use opposition MLAs to further a good story by having them raise it in question period, sometimes even before it's been printed or aired. The reason for this is a simple reflection of the legislative privileges that MLAs hold in the house. A reporter writing or broadcasting a story is governed by the laws of libel and slander. Although these are somewhat less strict with regard to politicians, they prevent any publication of material that directly accuses someone of wrongdoing unless the reporter can offer proof that will stand up in a court of law. MLAs, however, are not bound by any such strictures when speaking within the confines of the legislative chamber (although they are if they repeat exactly the same remarks in the hallway afterwards). Thus, a reporter who is convinced of the correctness of an allegation, but doesn't have the standard of legal proof required, might feed the material to an opposition MLA, knowing that once the question is asked in the house the story can be made public, although to escape legal liability the media must give proper prominence to the government denials of wrongdoing as well as the allegations. These incidents are, however, less common than they used to be since the coming of freedom of information legislation, which makes it much easier for reporters themselves to find the information they need to back up a claim.

The Issue of 'Pack Journalism'

Another complaint frequently made about press coverage of BC politics is that it rarely amounts to more than 'pack journalism,' especially during legislative sessions. In pack journalism, every reporter chases the same story, interviews the same politicians (usually in great moving packs known as scrums – the name not taken from the game of rugby for nothing), and writes basically the same story. The phenomenon is most clearly seen at the end of question period each day when a herd of reporters streams down the stairs from the gallery into the members' corridor to surround whatever minister has been on the hot seat that day. Opposition MLAs who have had interesting questions to ask line up patiently for their chance to face the scrum.

However, a look back at political and governmental reporting during the past decade or so in BC shows clearly that coverage is not restricted to the pack. Various media outlets have regularly broken and worked on stories of their own involving government waste, inefficiency, and wrongdoing, many of which have had major political, and even legal, consequences. Some of those have included the Knight Street pub scandal (BCTV), Bill Reid's giving of government funds to friends (*Vancouver Sun*), and coverups of sexual abuse at Jericho Hill School for the Deaf (*Province*).

On a day-to-day basis, the bulk of BC's political reporting comes from the legislative press gallery. Sometimes the government of the day makes major announcements in Vancouver, or ones of regional importance in the region involved, but most ministers appear to prefer releasing information in Victoria, perhaps on the basis of 'better the devil you know than the devil you don't.' As well, in recent years governments have been criticized for organizing expensive 'photo ops' when a short announcement in Victoria would have sufficed.

This attitude, though, seems to ebb and flow. Occasionally a government will become so convinced that the press gallery is impossibly biased against it that it will start taking almost all its major announcements to Vancouver where it will not have to face the press gallery members. This was the case in the last days of the Bill Vander Zalm government, when Vander Zalm hated to go before the press gallery members because reporters there insisted on distracting the discussion away from the new government initiative with questions instead about Fantasy Gardens or other Socred scandals.

Election Coverage

The exception comes during the twenty-eight days every four to five years when an election campaign is on. Suddenly politics is the top news of the day, day in and day out, and reporters who have rarely touched a political story are 'on the bus' with the leaders. From a purely logistical point of view, the one or two reporters most media outlets have in the press gallery cannot be expected to cover an election by themselves. Two, three, or sometimes more leaders need reporters with them at all times as they criss-cross the province. As well, there are always numerous stories to be covered about contentious nomination meetings, close-fought ridings, reactions to policy announcements, and infinite amounts of election trivia.

The key parts of covering any election in the 1990s, however, seem to have boiled down to two: the leaders' tours and the leaders' debates. Both have become events staged almost entirely for the media, most particularly the television media.

It is the leaders' tours that have produced the phenomenon known not just in BC but across North America as 'the boys on the bus.' As they travel about the province, the party leaders take with them a 'media bus,' leased solely to ensure that the reporters, photographers, and TV camera operators are at the leaders' next appearance so they can cover him or her donning a hardhat, playing with kindergarten kiddies, or whatever the day's best 'opportunity' may be. The most sophisticated leaders' media buses come supplied with fax machines, computer power outlets, and even a cooler of beer. Less sophisticated ones may provide nothing more than seats, a driver, and a few sandwiches left over from the last stop.

Not only the bus but the leaders' schedules normally are set up almost entirely for the benefit of TV and its deadlines. The aides accompanying any leader ensure that the day's photo opportunity occurs in the morning to serve television deadlines – and no major announcement is made without some type of backdrop that can be used for visuals for the TV cameras.

Observers and analysts identify a couple of problems common with this type of coverage. Ironically, too much closeness between politicians and reporters is *not* one of them. Spending virtually twenty-four hours a day with the same politicians, hearing the same speeches and jokes until you can mouth the punch lines, usually seems to turn reporters off politicians rather than make them better friends. And during a campaign, reporters are so attuned to the possibility of being used for electioneering purposes that they look cynically upon any efforts to float trial balloons or drop hints of scandal.

One difficulty is that reporters tend to have no one to talk to but each other while on the bus in the hinterlands. The group often decides among itself, almost unconsciously, whether a leader's speech went well or poorly, whether a crowd was expected to be bigger or smaller, or whether an issue raised is going to become a major feature of the campaign or just a one-day wonder. After such discussions on the bus, reporters too often end up covering the day's story from exactly the same perspective, failing to give voters a wider breadth of views. The problem is often most intense if novice political reporters are on the bus with some seasoned press gallery members – even if they view an event differently, they're unlikely to challenge the veterans publicly.

The second problem is that the bus schedule is most often arranged so that the reporters see only what the politicians and aides want them to see. There is barely enough time to file copy before moving on to the next stop, let alone time to walk around town to talk to the citizenry about their views on the election, their local candidates, or issues. Aides have been known to organize the media bus so well that even if there's a major demonstration outside, the media bus will be mysteriously delayed in leaving the previous stop so that the reporters have almost no time to cover the protest if they want to hear the leader's speech – which, in such cases, they have invariably been promised will contain an important new announcement.

In recent campaigns, some media outlets have made an effort to have their reporters escape the bus, at least for short times. They have had reporters rent cars, make their own hotel reservations, and try to give themselves time to look at the trip with a different focus. There is no question, however, that covering the leaders' tours without the bus is infinitely more inconvenient and often more expensive for outlets, meaning most reporters eventually find themselves back on the bus again.

One of the greatest difficulties in covering a leader's tour during a campaign, especially from the bus, is the need to find something different to say every day. Leaders usually make virtually the same speech, or at best the same two speeches, at every stop on the campaign tour for a week or more at a time, but the media, especially television outlets, can't run the same quotes and clips day after day, with only a different backdrop behind. That means that reporters are often forced to scramble wildly to come up with something that looks and sounds new.

The result of the daily need for newness is that stories may assume an importance far out of proportion to their substantive value. Sometimes, for instance, newness may be found by asking the leaders about comments made, or policies advanced, by the other parties – giving those policies or remarks an importance they don't deserve. A throwaway remark, or even a slip of the tongue by one leader, may suddenly become the lead item on the news if reporters start asking other leaders about it – and if the other leaders are smart enough to take advantage of the gaffe.

On worse days, when no leaders have produced new policies, the media may be forced to focus on the tiniest bizarre incident, simply to find something different. In that way, a few hecklers or protesters with artistic signs may find themselves the top item on the nightly news when, in any other circumstances, they'd have been ignored by the media.

A constant, and oftentimes valid, complaint made by the politicians about this sort of election coverage is that it provides little or no time for any reasoned or detailed analysis of issues, but instead tends to focus almost entirely on the personalities involved. Probably the most glaring example occurred during the 1986 election campaign between Social Credit leader Bill Vander Zalm and NDP leader Bob Skelly. The tour of Vander Zalm, the charismatic charmer, on many days resembled a coronation tour by royalty than a normal election campaign – and the media were frequently front and centre promoting it as such. Like the public, few reporters or analysts seemed inclined to challenge Vander Zalm's statements that he was going to adopt a policy of inclusiveness, consultation, and cooperation – even though during his time as cabinet minister in charge of education, welfare, and municipal affairs, his attitude had been one of almost constant confrontation with practically everyone he dealt with, including fellow cabinet ministers.

By contrast, Skelly, a shy and somewhat reticent man, never at home with the television cameras, got a consistently rough ride from the media, little of it having to do with his actual policies. Skelly got off to a rough start when, at the first news conference after the election was called, he stumbled badly in his opening speech and asked the media plaintively, 'Can we start again?' The frequent repetition of that clip served to portray Skelly as an indecisive bumbler, regardless of his actual performance during the campaign.

The Question of Bias

Another common complaint by politicians and other partisans during election campaigns, and sometimes on other occasions as well, is that the media are biased. Curiously, politicians almost never seem to believe that any media outlets are biased in their favour, only against them. Politicians with grander conspiracy theories may convince themselves that virtually all of the 'mainstream media' are acting in concert to defeat their aims. Others may attribute the plot to only a single major media outlet, such as BCTV or the *Vancouver Sun*. Just how the conspiracy works is most often decided on the basis of which party is complaining. New Democrat believers in the 'conspiracy of bias' argue that since most major media outlets represent big business interests, the owners and senior managers manipulate news coverage to make the NDP look bad. Parties with a free-enterprise bent tend to think that the street-level reporters, most of whom belong to trade unions, all have a liberal, left-leaning bias and are putting that into the news coverage.

In fact, this complaint seems to have far less validity than many of the others made about the media. The days when some newspapers held a blatantly pro-Liberal bias and others were pro-Conservative are long over in BC. There may be the odd occasion when a single manager of a single news outlet encourages staff to go after a particular party, but this is the rarest of exceptions. As for a plot among a number of outlets to bring down a party, this is impossible both for philosophical and logistical reasons. Philosophically, the managers of various news outlets don't talk to each other on a regular basis, and they see the relationship between them as one of rivalry, not cooperation. Indeed, if it were found out that one outlet was determined to go after a particular party, another would probably start looking for ways to support that party, simply to show how different it is from its rivals.

From a logistical point of view, the incredibly tight timing involved in putting out each day's newspaper and TV newscast, and each hour's radio newscast, makes any interagency cooperation virtually impossible, even if it were deemed desirable. Reporters are out in the field all day, and it is not until they phone in or return to the office that the day-to-day editors have much idea of what their stories will be. At daily newspapers and for major TV newscasts, news meetings to determine the day's final lineup are held only a couple of hours before deadline, which is not nearly enough time to orchestrate any plot. As well, decisions on what will be a page-one story or a top item on a TV newscast are normally made by a team of people, often as many as a dozen, making it very difficult for any one person to orchestrate any conspiracy.

Media outlets are more likely to see themselves not as questioning any one political party but as questioning the government of the day, no matter which party is in power. It is true that many reporters and editors seem to develop a natural affinity for the underdog, which, these days, is likely to mean those who are challenging governments or feeling oppressed by them. Many reporters and editors also possess a large dose of scepticism in their makeup – sometimes healthy, sometimes perhaps more extreme than that – and see making an effort to keep government honest and accountable as one of their jobs.

This attitude often comes as a severe shock to politicians when they first form a new government, particularly if they have sat in opposition previously. From the opposition benches, they became accustomed to a relatively easy relationship with the media, with little confrontation and often a good-sized component of cooperation in attacking those in power. The politicians cannot be blamed for coming to believe, as many of them do, that this friendly relationship means that the reporters with whom they deal agree with their policies and philosophies. Therefore, it comes as a rude shock when the same reporters begin cooperating with the new opposition to put the same kind of pressure on their former 'friends.' Many of the reporters who in the early 1990s attacked the NDP government of Mike Harcourt most severely are the same ones who launched exactly the same kind of assault on the Social Credit government of Bill Vander Zalm, although the philosophies and policies of the two administrations could hardly be more different.

Whether these perceptions of bias are justified or not, it is easy to understand the reasons for the politicians' fear when one reviews the audience figures for large BC news outlets. The two major daily papers in the Lower Mainland have a combined weekend circulation of more than 450,000, while Victoria's Saturday *Times-Colonist* is sold to 80,000 households, and presumably read by many more individuals. Radio stations such as Vancouver's CKNW reach 700,000 listeners a week, while 635,000 people tune in each night to BCTV's 6 o'clock news broadcast.

'News' versus 'Opinion'

While government complaints about media bias most frequently relate to the quality of coverage, opposition politicians often bemoan the quantity of space devoted to their side of the political story. There is some objective evidence to support this concern. One study found that during legislative sessions, 'the newspaper references to government and opposition were fairly equal,' but that 'the cabinet had a big edge between sessions, receiving four or five times as much ink.'[9] The same study also found that the volume differences between coverage of opposition and government began to decline after 1972 as legislative salaries increased and more MLAs began viewing their elected role as a full-time job.

One aspect of political journalism in BC that makes it perhaps easier than it should be for politicians to claim bias is the too-frequent mingling of fact with analysis and opinion, especially in the broadcast media. In newspapers, the distinctions between straight news stories, columns, and editorials are usually made quite clear by labelling, placement in the paper, and page design. Straight news stories produce strictly the facts on both sides, hopefully as even-handedly as possible, and invite the readers to draw their own conclusions as to who might be right or wrong in any particular controversy. A typical straight news story might state that the government introduced new legislation, describe the key facets of the legislation, quote the minister involved as to why the bill was seen to be necessary, quote opposition members on the problems they see with the legislation, and quote those affected by it, whether they support or oppose it.

Newspaper reporters who write straight news stories will sometimes also write analysis pieces, describing, for example, what effect a controversial bill or scandal is likely to have on the political fortunes of the government of the day. Those pieces, though, are normally labelled 'Analysis' or 'News Focus' or something similar, so the reader can clearly tell the difference.

Political columnists often produce some of the most fascinating writing about the government of the day. Good columnists will often use their columns to break major news stories, but they nearly always write in such a way that their own opinion and analysis are clear. Columns by the *Vancouver Sun*'s Marjorie Nichols in the 1970s, and Vaughn Palmer in the 1980s and 1990s made no pretence of giving an impartial view of the facts. The same was true of *Province* contemporaries such as Brian Kieran. Similarly, newspaper editorials – the corporate voice of a newspaper – run on a separate page, delineated in such a way that any reader knows immediately that he or she is reading opinion, not fact.

In the broadcast media, the lines tend to be less clear. Many radio stations with a large news and public affairs component do produce daily editorials, clearly announced as such on air, but television does not even have these ninety-second or two-minute labelled spots. Instead, the facts, analysis, and opinion sometimes blend into a single package talking about one particular topic. Thus, when a television reporter says, 'this is the worst crisis to befall this government in the past year,' it's difficult for the viewer to know whether this is an objective fact, the opinion of the individual reporter, or the collective opinion of the TV station's management.

In radio, a similar type of problem often pops up on the ever-popular open-line shows. Many, though not all, open-line hosts have extremely strong political views that shine through many of the conversations they have, both with guests and with listeners. That's not a problem if the host consistently makes it clear that he or she is giving an individual opinion, but in the heat of debate, the opinion often suddenly turns into indisputable fact, a fact repeated many times during the show. 'Absolutely the only people to benefit from this legislation will be the government's friends in Big Labour,' (or Big Business, if a free-enterprise government is in power), the open-line host will intone. That's a statement that sounds on the surface very much like a fact, but is, at rock bottom, nothing more than the host's opinion.

The role of open-line radio also deserves mention because this aspect of media activity has enjoyed an enduring popularity not found elsewhere in Canada. Radio hosts such as Jack Webster and Bill Good have become household names. Others have moved between the media and legislative environments. Barrie Clark (Liberal), Jim Neilson (Social Credit), Rafe Mair (Social Credit), Dave Barrett (NDP), John Reynolds (Social Credit), and Judi Tyabji (Progressive Democratic Alliance) are examples of MLAs who also enjoyed runs as open-line radio hosts.

Another cross-over between the media and politics is found in a growing business aimed at helping politicians and the representatives of various interest groups deal with the media. When live television coverage came to the legislature, many MLAs sought professional advice on both dress and delivery style. Some current and former journalists make regular appearances at workshops and seminars designed to help people improve their ability to deal with media questions.

Reforming the System

As a result of government and public discontent with the media, efforts have been made in BC and elsewhere to place greater controls on the media. In the 1990s, steps the BC government has taken – or tried to take – in this regard include the Freedom of Information and Protection of Privacy Act, changes to the Human Rights Act, and proposed changes to the Elections Act.

The Freedom of Information and Protection of Privacy Act is very much a two-edged sword for the media. There is no question that it gives reporters more access to government documents than they had before. Indeed, in the years after they effected this change, many New Democrat politicians voiced doubts about the wisdom of the step they had taken. The freedom of information law has enabled the media to break stories ranging from the details of the suicide of a twelve-year-old girl at a government treatment centre to the details of payments made to friends and insiders in various patronage appointments.

In other areas, though, the same act reduced the amount of information that public sector employees can legally give to the media, including information that previously was provided. Police and fire departments, for instance, can no longer routinely give out the names of victims of murders or even the addresses of residential fires (the latter being one of the silliest restrictions since the average residential fire is easily located by the presence of smoke, flames, and large numbers of fire trucks). More seriously, though, the act can often also restrict information about government activities as much as it can enhance it. In the case of jail-escaper and rapist Danny Perrault, for instance, the government's own 1994 inquiry report came with whole pages blanked out to protect the privacy of individuals, most of whom were working in the corrections system.

Changes by the NDP government of Mike Harcourt to the province's Human Rights Code prohibit the media from printing anything that might seem to encourage discrimination, racism, sexism, and the like. Some media representatives and lawyers predicted that these amendments would be used to restrict debate on such issues as gay rights or immigration, and to silence the voices of those with more extreme views on these subjects such as controversial columnist Doug Collins, and they promised challenges under the Canadian Charter of Rights and Freedoms.

Media members also became outraged when the NDP government of Mike Harcourt introduced changes to the Elections Act that would restrict some reporting during election campaigns. One of the controversial sections would see limits on election advertising other than by legitimate political parties reduced to $2,000 per group per election. That is seen as a restriction of freedom of expression since normally during election campaigns all sorts of groups with axes to grind (everyone from teachers to abortion activists) are likely to take out advertisements, perhaps supporting a particular party but more likely merely encouraging voters to think about the issues of education, taxation, abortion, health care, or whatever before casting their ballots.

Even more frustrating to the media are the restrictions imposed on the reporting of polls. Polling has long been a contentious issue in BC politics; it was not until the 1970s that the law allowed polling results to be reported at all during a BC election campaign. In the last few campaigns, however, polls have played a prominent role, whether commissioned directly by media outlets or by other interest groups, or taken – and leaked – by the contestants themselves. Politicians are fearful that publication of poll results can be used or abused to unfairly influence voters. That was the reasoning behind the 1995 rules requiring anyone who published or broadcast a poll during a campaign to include in the report the sample size, margin of error, and exact questions. In addition, an attempt was made to require that poll results could be published only with the official permission of those who had commissioned them.

Curiously, despite new and inventive efforts by government to try to control the media, few politicians take advantage of the legal ways, long in place, to ensure abuses don't take place. Chief among these are the laws of libel and slander, which prohibit anyone from disseminating anything defamatory and untrue about anyone else, including a politician. (The exception, as noted above, is printing what was said in the house, in a court of law, or, in some cases, in other public forums.) In expressing their opinions about politicians, journalists have a wider latitude, but any opinion expressed must be honestly held (not said just to make mischief) and must be based on fact. One of BC's more interesting libel cases involving a politician occurred in the late 1970s when Vander Zalm, then social services minister, sued *Victoria Times* cartoonist Bob Bierman over a cartoon that showed him picking the wings off flies. Vander Zalm complained that the cartoon depicted him as a cruel and vindictive person, and couldn't be supported by fact. The newspaper argued that this was normal cartoon exaggeration relating to his treatment of welfare recipients, such as telling them to 'pick up a shovel' and get a job, and suggesting they should be forced to move to parts of the province where jobs were more common. Vander Zalm won at trial, but a five-member panel of the BC Court of Appeal overturned the ruling, agreeing that cartooning was allowed such exaggeration as part of the cartoonist's expression of opinion.

Politicians often threaten to sue media outlets for defamation. Many launch lawsuits, which often has the effect of taking the issue off the table because of the principle that something before the courts might not be a proper subject for public debate. Few, however, follow through on the suits. Neither do politicians frequently follow through on threats to complain to the bodies involved with ethics for the media – the Canadian Radio-Television and Telecommunications Commission (CRTC) for broadcast media, and the BC Press Council for print media.

The CRTC has much more control over its members than does the Press Council; in extreme cases, the CRTC could revoke the licence of a radio or television station if its ethical behaviour had been too far or too repeatedly beyond the pale. All managers at radio and television stations take CRTC complaints very seriously. The Press Council, on the other hand, is a voluntary body, but one to which most major newspapers in BC belong. And though it can't force its members to do anything, they have all signed a contract saying they will publish in full any decision of the Press Council that involves them, be it favourable or unfavourable. The result is that a bad Press Council ruling can cause a newspaper considerable public embarrassment, something most of them would rather avoid.

Yet politicians rarely take advantage of these opportunities when they feel aggrieved. There have been few complaints to either body. At the end of the day, most elected officials seem to conclude that they need the media more than the media needs them.

Part 3: Governing the Province

9
The Government of the Day: The Premier and Cabinet in British Columbia

Terence Morley

We are accustomed to thinking of the government of British Columbia as a permanent and highly complex organization that employs tens of thousands of people whose activities permeate almost every aspect of our lives. Yet the government of BC is also a small assemblage of sixteen or so politicians invited by one person to gather for a time – often a limited time – in one room to talk about how the complex organization might change its pattern of activities so as to consequently transform our lives. The small assemblage is the provincial cabinet and the person who sends the invitations is the premier of the province. The premier and the cabinet are, for a time, the government of the day.

In 1983 Walter Young observed that 'provincial government is premier's government ... the extent of his authority is significantly greater than that of his federal counterpart.'[1] It is the premier who appoints and disappoints cabinet members and who, for the most part, proposes and disposes significant governmental action.

Premiers also appoint deputy ministers, heads of crown corporations, and other key public sector officials, exercise a veto over the appointment of other significant public sector employees, set the cabinet agenda, determine the makeup of cabinet committees, dominate (if they so wish) the party apparatus, and influence the party nomination process. Moreover, the scale of provincial government allows premiers to employ a hand-picked staff endowed with the authority to oversee the public administration and the broad range of public policies. The premier's own deputy minister is the head of the civil service. The Premier's Office monitors the policy initiatives of cabinet ministers and coordinates the whole of the legislative and law-making process. As the leader of his or her party and the government, it is the premier who must appeal directly to the people of BC to seek their support by moulding their opinions.

Premiers have different styles and use their power in different ways. W.A.C. Bennett, premier for twenty years, saw himself as the proprietor of a flourishing business that could only continue to thrive if he, as the hands-on operator, was able to master all the critical details of the enterprise. His successor, Dave Barrett, the first NDP premier, had little patience with detail, preferring to use his charismatic speaking ability to garner support for the broad brush of social change. Bill Bennett, son and political heir of W.A.C., believed the business had grown too large for him to know all the details, but he could, as the chief executive officer, establish a structure that would ensure that the details would be reviewed by people reporting directly to him or to those closest to him on the Premier's Office organizational chart. Mike Harcourt, the second NDP premier, used the powers of his office to force antagonists to a bargaining table, where, he hoped, consensus would be reached – as it sometimes was. Glen Clark, who succeeded Harcourt as premier and then led the NDP in 1996 to a second consecutive term, consciously set out to provide a forceful and determinative approach to governing that was very different from the consensus seeking of his predecessor.

Yet for all their undoubted power, exercised in whatever way, BC's premiers have, from the beginning, been unable to protect themselves from the fickle nature of public sentiment and from the constant hostility of political rivals, mostly, as it happens, rivals in their own parties and governments. Duff Pattullo, who led a Liberal government at the outset of the Second World War, was betrayed by his close friend John Hart, and forced out of the premiership by cabinet colleagues determined to forge a wartime coalition that would inevitably lessen the influence of the more state-interventionist members of their own party, the most prominent of whom was Pattullo. John Hart, who became his successor, wearying of the tensions inherent in a two-party coalition and lured by the promise of a seat in the Canadian Senate, resigned for 'reasons of health.' The Liberal Prime Minister of Canada, Mackenzie King, declined to offer the Senate sinecure (as he had previously declined to offer it to Pattullo), and Hart was forced to recover sufficient health to serve as the Speaker of the Legislative Assembly. Hart's successor as premier, Byron 'Boss' Johnson, after a near-fatal car accident, had his Conservative coalition partners walk out on him, and in the subsequent election the Liberals were reduced to six seats (out of forty-eight) and Johnson was personally defeated in New Westminster.

W.A.C. Bennett, as leader of the upstart Social Credit Party that 'won' the 1952 election with nineteen seats to eighteen for the CCF (the forerunner of the NDP), enjoyed a remarkable twenty years in office. He stayed too long. In the 1972 election, Social Credit won just 31 percent of the vote and held only ten of the fifty-five seats in the assembly. Bennett's last campaign featured a remarkably personal attack from none other than the inimitable Phil Gaglardi, a long-time cabinet colleague whom Bennett had several times saved from the effects of political self-mutilation. Gaglardi declared that Bennett was 'an old man who doesn't understand what is happening with the young people of this province.' The old man cried on election night.[2]

Dave Barrett, the winner in August 1972, was hurled from office by the voters before the end of 1975. He lost his own seat in the assembly and had to accept the departure of Robert Williams, who had served as his most powerful minister, in order to be able to be returned to the assembly as leader of the opposition from Williams's safe Vancouver East seat. Barrett stayed as NDP leader until 1984, losing two more elections. Bill Bennett, who won those elections, decided that ten years as premier was sufficiently trying and gratifying for him. His announced retirement was followed by a Social Credit leadership convention boasting twelve leadership candidates, including four of Bennett's ministers and two proteges – Bud Smith and Kim Campbell – who served him in the Premier's Office. They all lost. The winning candidate, Bill Vander Zalm, had served in Bennett's cabinet from 1975 until 1983, had never really played by Bennett's rules, had called his cabinet colleagues (including Bennett) 'gutless wonders,' and had refused to run in 1983 when it looked as though Bennett would lose the election. Vander Zalm's victory was a symbolic repudiation of Bill Bennett's governing style and his attempts to modernize the Social Credit Party. After suffering this humiliation, Bill Bennett was further aggravated by serious charges that he, along with his brother R.J. Bennett and Herb Doman, the proprietor of one of BC's large forest companies, had illegally sold shares in Doman Industries using inside information and had consequently cheated the share buyers of millions of dollars. Bennett's defence against these charges was costly and seemingly interminable.

Bill Vander Zalm handily won the 1986 election. His reward was to be in the lead car of an out-of-control political demolition derby. His attorney general, Brian Smith, who placed second in the 1986 leadership contest, publicly accused him of plotting to subvert the administration of justice. Another minister, Grace McCarthy, who placed third in the leadership race and who had almost single-handedly rebuilt the Social Credit Party after the 1972 defeat, believed that he had used his influence to help line the pocket of his friend, and putative business partner, Peter Toigo. The police investigated him over his relationship with Toigo. His business, known as Fantasy Gardens, was failing, and following the sale of the Fantasy Gardens property to a Taiwanese speculator, it was determined by Ted Hughes, the former deputy attorney general and a former superior court judge in Saskatchewan, that he had used his office to help complete the land transaction and to obtain money (provided in US bills) in return for a promise to help the speculator acquire adjacent properties from a federally owned oil company. Vander Zalm was forced to fire his closest confidant and, ultimately, to resign in disgrace.

Rita Johnston, who succeeded Vander Zalm, was premier for only six months. Forced by law to call a 1991 election, she endured a disastrous campaign that ended in a humiliating defeat for Social Credit. Only seven Socreds were returned to the seventy-five-seat assembly and Premier Johnston lost her own seat.

The NDP, under Mike Harcourt, were returned to power in 1991. Harcourt, reacting in part to the scandals of the Vander Zalm years, proudly announced that his government would legislate the toughest conflict of interest standards in Canada. Harcourt was determined that his regime would be seen to be cleaner than clean. It is consequently ironic that Harcourt was forced to retire early from the leadership of the NDP and as premier of BC in the aftermath of findings by a forensic auditor (appointed by Harcourt) that party officials, during the 1980s, had concocted a scheme to divert funds, legally destined for charity, to NDP coffers. In 1993 the party paid back these funds to the Nanaimo Commonwealth Holding Society (NCHS). That society, described by David Stupich, its controlling personality and some-time NDP cabinet minister in the Barrett government, as an 'arm of the NDP,' had itself been convicted of criminally converting trust monies belonging to various charities. The party should, therefore, have paid back funds, not to the NCHS, but to the province's director of charities.

Although Harcourt himself was not implicated in any wrongdoing, the fact that the NDP had been engaged in a cover-up, combined with the perception that the whole affair had been mismanaged by key figures in the Premier's Office (and combined with a low standing in public opinion polls), led Harcourt to conclude that many of his party colleagues no longer had real confidence in his leadership and so he quit. It was not a happy ending to a twenty-five-year career in public life.

Harcourt was succeeded by Glen Clark who, the day before being sworn in as premier, was plunged into a new scandal concerning the ownership of shares in a BC Hydro subsidiary. Clark had been the minister responsible for the government-owned utility. As the premier designate, Clark had the two top Hydro officials immediately dismissed and followed this with the appointment of the former Social Credit attorney general Brian Smith to investigate the matter. In the end, Clark survived this political bombshell and proceeded to win a narrow victory at the polls, taking thirty-nine seats to claim a majority of two over the other parties. The Liberals, with thirty-three seats, obtained 3 percent more of the popular vote than the NDP, thus providing Glen Clark with much to consider.

There is a fairy-tale quality to 'climbing to the top of the greasy pole' (to use Benjamin Disraeli's evocative phrasing) and finding oneself on a pinnacle of political power provided with the authority once bequeathed to puissant monarchs. It is noteworthy, therefore, that all the endings, but one, of these made-in-BC stories seem to be rather sad.

King Cabinet

Perhaps these sad endings reflect the underlying reality that the premier is not the sovereign. The premier possesses very little independent authority; the premier requires colleagues and, although he or she appoints the most important of these and although the lieutenant governor will undoubtedly dismiss a minister or deputy minister who displeases the premier, the authority to govern remains vested in a congregation styled the Lieutenant Governor in Council, and the council, designated as the executive council, is in fact the provincial cabinet.

Cabinet Selection

The premier chooses the cabinet. He or she is not free, however, to choose simply anyone. In constitutional theory and practice the premier must choose from among those persons who have been elected to the legislative assembly (MLAs) or who will, within a reasonably short period of time, seek such election. In 1952 W.A.C. Bennett decided that there was no one among his eighteen followers in the assembly suited to fill the two key posts of attorney general and minister of finance. He appointed a Vancouver lawyer, Robert Bonner, as attorney general and a Vancouver chartered accountant, Einer Gunderson, as minister of finance. Bennett persuaded two Social Credit MLAs to step down, and Bonner and Gunderson were elected in the subsequent by-elections. However, when Gunderson was unable to gain a seat in the 1953 election and later in a by-election, Bennett had no choice but to accept his resignation as a cabinet minister.

Premiers need to recognize and measure other constraints on their choice of cabinet colleagues. BC is a vast territory composed of quite distinct regions, and voters living in these regions seem to expect some 'representation' at the cabinet table. A premier who only selected MLAs from the Lower Mainland could expect a considerable political fallout in the rest of the province. A premier would be foolish to neglect to appoint two or more MLAs from Vancouver to the cabinet – unless, of course, Vancouver voters had neglected to provide the premier's party with the necessary MLAs to ensure cabinet representation. There is an expectation that certain places – if they have elected MLAs on the government side – are entitled to a seat or two in the cabinet. When Premier Harcourt decided to drop Prince George MLA Lois Boone from his cabinet, he was careful to promote the other NDP MLA from Prince George, Paul Ramsay, to the inner circle. Some regions may be safely over-represented for a time – Vancouver Island, particularly the lower Island, was over-represented in cabinet during the Harcourt years – but no region can be safely ignored by a premier intent on reelection.

Premiers are first and foremost party leaders. A lieutenant governor, in contemplating the formal offer to make one man or woman premier, is obliged to make the assumption that the leader of the political party boasting a majority of seats in the assembly is best able to persuade the assembly to levy the necessary taxes, and vote to provide the appropriate funds, to ensure that the government of the province continues to function. The lieutenant governor is required by our constitutional understanding to assume that any person other than the leader of the majority party would fail to obtain the needed funds, and could not, therefore, govern the province and must not, consequently, hold office. Of course, if no party leader commands a majority following in the assembly, the lieutenant governor is obliged to choose the person, invariably the leader of one of the parties in the assembly, who will have the best chance of persuading the assembly to vote the necessary funds to sustain the operation of the government. In 1952, when no party had a majority, the lieutenant governor allowed himself to be persuaded by W.A.C. Bennett that he, Bennett, was that person. Bennett was subsequently able to persuade the assembly to support him, and, with the exception of a few months in 1941, the 1952-3 session has been the only time since the advent of party government in 1903 that no party, or formal coalition of parties, has had a majority in the BC Legislative Assembly.

It follows, however, that since premiers are first and foremost party leaders, they must make certain that their party followers do not desert them. In choosing a cabinet they need to recognize the claims of certain members of their party who have influence and even independent followings within the party. A party leader who refused to include such individuals in his or her administration risks losing the party's majority in the assembly and, in parties with a mechanism for removing a leader – and all significant parties in BC now have such mechanisms – even risks a revolt of sufficient party members that could lead to the selection of a new leader. Premier Vander Zalm, caught in the midst of rumours about financial improprieties, was openly opposed by several leading members of the Social Credit Party. The party caucus in the assembly was sufficiently divided to the point that newspapers and other media speculated that a majority of the Social Credit caucus wanted Vander Zalm removed as leader and premier.

The central constitutional rule in the parliamentary system is that if a majority in the assembly vote to express an explicit lack of confidence in the government – that is, in the premier and the cabinet – the premier must offer his or her own resignation and that of the government to the lieutenant governor. This act of resignation is almost always followed by a general election. In practical terms, an election that follows a split in a premier's own party and caucus is most likely to result in severe losses for the government party. In other words, if government party MLAs vote against the government in sufficient numbers when combined with opposition votes to pass the motion of non-confidence, then many, if not all, of those government MLAs can expect to lose their seats in the subsequent election. This is an obvious deterrent to pursuing such a course of action, and, obviously, these systemic rules make it extremely difficult – some would argue impossible – for unhappy caucus members to remove their leader by taking this route.

In the instance of significant and substantial unhappiness over Premier Vander Zalm's leadership, the argument was put forward that a majority of the caucus might choose an alternative leader, inform the lieutenant governor of their choice, and then the lieutenant governor would be obliged to dismiss Vander Zalm and appoint the caucus choice as premier. However, since Vander Zalm continued to have a significant number of Social Credit MLAs, certainly almost all the members of the cabinet, pledge loyalty to him, the reality was that any alternative leader selected by the caucus would be unable to persuade the lieutenant governor that he or she could command a majority in the assembly as a whole.

No doubt David Lam, then the lieutenant governor, made himself familiar with the constitutional rules. And no doubt the suspicion within the Social Credit caucus that the dissidents would need to persuade sufficient Social Credit MLAs constituting a majority of the assembly – in practice an impossible task – to avoid an election meant that the revolt against Vander Zalm was bound to fail. And yet following Ted Hughes's judgment, Vander Zalm, given caucus sentiment, had no choice other than resignation. Mike Harcourt, facing less intense and less well-organized opposition, decided that resignation was the best course for him in the face of substantial unease in the NDP caucus over his handling of the Nanaimo Commonwealth Holding scandal. For all their powers of appointment and disappointment, premiers need to pay attention to the feelings of party activists, and particularly to the feelings of those chosen by the electorate to be legislative colleagues.

Premiers are constrained in their cabinet choices in other ways. The talent pool in a caucus of approximately forty elected members is sometimes, though not always, a little shallow. Certain ministries (finance, attorney general, labour, social services, and environment) and certain posts (house leader) require talented individuals in them. A graceless minister of labour or even of finance will not always prove fatal for a government, but certainly the political fates are tempted, and a premier who cannot rely on key ministers is handicapped. Moreover, premiers, as with other heads of complex organizations, benefit from matching the different kinds of talent available to them with the different kinds of tasks that need be accomplished.

Cabinet Authority

The cabinet exercises a wide authority. It invokes the law and thereby commands obedience of all those living in BC who are subject to the law. The laws themselves, at least those laws that flow from the Canadian constitution's grant of authority to the provinces, are made by the legislature. Yet most of those laws are deliberately set down in general terms using imprecise, even vague language. The cabinet supplies the details by means of regulations and orders that have the force of law and that, in many instances, are far-reaching elaborations of the general principles set out in the legislation itself.

These regulations are a form of 'subordinate' legislation. Of course, the original legislation only becomes law when it is signed by the lieutenant governor after passage through the assembly. The lieutenant governor will only provide his or her signature when told to do so by the cabinet. Moreover, cabinet ministers, although a minority in the assembly, almost always dominate that body. The cabinet directs the assembly agenda. As well, only ministers may introduce bills and resolutions to raise and spend money. Perhaps most important, the cabinet, by controlling the flow of information to the public, including to government MLAs not in cabinet, is able to extract support for its proposals from the whole government caucus because those not in cabinet are never well-informed enough to effectively combat ministers in argument.

Cabinets and premiers have forced government caucuses to accept startling shifts in public policy. W.A.C. Bennett and his cabinet, after warning voters during the 1960 election campaign that their NDP rivals would 'nationalize' the BC Telephone Company and the BC Electric Company – and the sky would fall – required the caucus to accept and vote for a government take-over of the BC Electric Company and the creation of BC Hydro. Mike Harcourt and his cabinet forced a very reluctant caucus to support continued logging in the sensitive Clayoquot Sound watershed on Vancouver Island.

The cabinet is the central directorate of government. Cabinet priorities are government priorities. As the *Guide to the Cabinet Committee System* notes, 'Cabinet is the final decision making forum within government. A decision has not been made on individual policy items until it has been made by cabinet.'[3] This means that a resolute cabinet can dominate the whole policy process, including the flow of documents, the range of groups and personalities who will give a policy preliminary consideration, and the timing of announcements and legislative or regulatory action. In addition, the cabinet structures, manages, and directs the activities of the whole of the public service. The cabinet also influences the activities undertaken in the whole of the public sector and in those parts of the private sector dependent on government policy. Tax policies, as it happens, have a major impact throughout all sectors of the economy. Indeed, cabinet influence is often, though not always, determinative of policy and economic outcomes.

Most key public sector appointments are made by cabinet. These include senior civil servants, members of boards, commissions, and regulatory agencies, directors of crown corporations, including the chairs and other officers of those boards, the chief executive officers of crown corporations, provincial court judges, governors of universities, members of police boards, members of regional hospital boards, commissioners of inquiry, and, until recently, public representatives on the governing bodies of self-regulating professions including the Law Society and the College of Physicians and Surgeons. These latter appointments are now made by individual ministers. Indeed, when key public sector positions are not appointed by the collective direction of cabinet, they are appointed at the direction of individual cabinet members. Although most government employees and public sector employees are still hired as the result of a public job competition, over 6,000 key positions are filled by order-in-council (OIC or cabinet order) or by ministerial order. Moreover, in recent years the Public Service Commission (PSC) has been stripped of its authority to oversee civil service hirings, and the resultant dispersal of that authority to ministries and other agencies has meant that the cabinet and cabinet minister are able to have a determinative influence on hirings throughout the government service.

In summary, the provincial cabinet as the central directorate of government dominates the executive actions of government, or, put another way, it controls the executive branch of government. It also dominates the legislative branch of government by being able, except in rare and extraordinary circumstances, to direct the votes of a majority of MLAs, to shape the public policy-making process, and to fill in legislative details by passing subordinate legislation as orders-in-council. Until the early 1990s the cabinet even acted as a kind of court, hearing appeals on land use and transportation matters. Cabinet still remains closely associated with the administration of justice in the province by appointing provincial court judges and commissioners of inquiry, and by virtue of the fact that one cabinet minister, the attorney general, is the senior law officer of the Crown in the province.

King Cabinet – Checked and Balanced

All this authority and power – and even glory – has conspired to make witnesses (including scholars) to Canadian constitutional dramas conclude that cabinets are the dominatrixes of Canadian governance. This theme of executive control and popular submission has long been a mainstay of treatises, ancient and modern, on government in Canada. As David Smith notes in discussing the impact of judicial decisions on provincial power:

It needs to be emphasized, however, that it was the governments of the provinces and not their legislatures who reaped the harvest; for within the expanded provincial universe the executive faced no rivals. Unlike their state counterparts in Australia ... Canada's provincial second chambers were weak or non-existent ... [The] executive was exclusively a party body whose members almost invariably came from the same party ... The Crown endowed the provinces [and their executives residing in cabinets] with unlimited potential for action ... The legitimacy of the federal state is tested by its capacity to mediate internal cleavages; the provincial states have never had to face comparable challenges.[4]

The idea of *checks and balances* designed to curb executive power is seen as peculiarly American (though imitated in post-colonial climes not blessed with British parliamentary traditions), and, it is argued, the Canadian provinces, with small legislatures and relatively large cabinets, are saved from even the modest curbs on executive power found in Ottawa. Yet provincial premiers, at least as observed in BC, end their political days in sorrow. Their cabinet ministers often toil in obscurity and end their political days in sudden dismissal, sometimes by premiers, sometimes by voters, and occasionally by both. If provincial cabinets enjoy dominance, they seem remarkably unfulfilled by the experience. Perhaps they are not so dominant as has been thought.

Certainly British cabinets and prime ministers are no longer, if they ever were, monarchs of all they survey. British MPs on the government side regularly vote to defeat government measures, the House of Lords is perfectly pleased to hoist government bills onto a six-month holding shelf, and the cabinet must pay attention to directives issued by the Council of Europe. Members of the European Parliament are increasingly inclined to criticize the parties that sent them there. Even Margaret Thatcher, graphically described as the 'Iron Lady,' and before whom various men in politics were observed to cower, was summarily deposed as prime minister by disenchanted members of her own party caucus.

The government of Canada is also subject to checks on its powers, and its authority is necessarily balanced against the claims of others, notably the provinces. Although the interdependencies inherent in late-twentieth-century economies have meant that provincial and federal governments increasingly share jurisdiction over critical public policies such as the regulation of commercial undertakings, environmental standards, and social programs, it is still true that provinces may claim 'exclusive' jurisdiction to legislate on a range of subjects, and, in practice, they exercise substantial control over many important areas of government activities. Federal power is often checked by provincial authority.

The courts, as interpreters of the law, also check and balance federal government desires. The advent of the Charter of Rights and Freedoms has inspired many judges to interpret, modify, and even strike down laws passed by Parliament and policies pursued by the federal administration. Prime ministers have always felt a political need to pay attention to the wishes of certain ministers, notably those who have independent followings in the different regions of the country.[5] Cabinet ministers, including the prime minister, even if they are not fans of the BBC's *Yes Minister* series, are often captivated by senior civil servants. These mandarins check not only cabinet ministers but also one another. All of them seem anxious to ensure that no one department, crown corporation, central agency, or even the Prime Minister's Office (PMO) or the Privy Council Office (PCO), seizes control of public policy development and public administration management.

No government or cabinet can ignore the media. Opposition parties, even in weakened conditions, are often able to use the media to alter the government agenda. Some parliamentary committees make an impact that is different than the impact envisaged by cabinet planners. The Senate, particularly if an opposition party has a majority in that *other place*, occasionally wakes from political slumber and votes down a key government measure. Governors general may only speak in governor generalities, but prime ministers, out of both politeness and duty, need to listen to their warnings and, rarely to be sure, listen carefully to their concerns about constitutional propriety. And, most of all, prime ministers and cabinets must listen to the electorate for fear that failing to do so will lead to the torments of losing office after the next election. The reality of the next election is a potent check on cabinet power.

There are similar checks on the BC government. Provincial authority is clearly circumscribed by federal authority – and by the power and prestige of the government of Canada. In 1871 BC joined a federation in which the central government was manifestly the senior government. The wording of the law seemed to relegate provinces to an inferior, even colonial status. The central government appointed lieutenant governors and could, and did, instruct them to dismiss provincial premiers and cabinets; the judges in the important courts were all appointed by Ottawa; the federal cabinet and Parliament were empowered to override the province's 'exclusive' authority over education in order to protect denominational schools; Parliament could relieve provincial legislatures of their jurisdiction over works and undertakings; and the federal cabinet could even set aside or disallow a law duly passed by the provincial legislature.

Echoes of imperial Ottawa are still heard in the land. The federal government may no longer even dream about using the power of disallowance (though that power is still a part of the fundamental law of the Canadian constitution), but it does not hesitate to use the power of the purse to constrain provincial governments. Certainly since the Second World War, the federal government has occupied the major portion of the most lucrative tax fields, justifying their tenancy in the postwar years by arguing that they spend the money across the whole country to ensure common standards for health, education, welfare, and other social programs. That argument proved successful with most Canadians and most British Columbians until recently. In the 1990s the federal government continues to occupy the most lucrative tax fields, but spends an increasing proportion of its revenues on paying the interest on debt and now spends less and less money on social programs.

The consequence of this for the BC government has been a need to raise its own taxes and cut its own social expenditures. The BC government is thereby constrained and checked. In 1995 the BC cabinet, alarmed by rising welfare costs and the growing proportion of single employable persons collecting welfare, decided to impose a three-month waiting period on newcomers to the province before they could collect welfare. The federal government, seeing this as a fundamental attack on the principle of national standards, decided to punish the provincial government by withholding certain transfer payments still owed to the province. The province retaliated by suing the federal government for the return of these funds.

And, of course, the courts are not only a check on federal power but also act as a substantial check on provincial power and on the activities of the premier and the cabinet. The courts interpret and thereby make the law, and the law, in part, determines the jurisdictional reach of governments. The courts also determine whether or not cabinets, and officials directed by cabinets, are carrying out their duties and responsibilities in conformance with the law. They can, therefore, order cabinets and officials to modify or even abandon a particular course of action.

Of course, the cabinet could ask the legislature to change the law to get around the order of the court. However, if the order of the court were based upon an interpretation of the Charter of Rights and Freedoms, then the legislature could only override the Charter (and only certain sections of the Charter) by a deliberate and formal declaration of its intent to override. Such a declaration is likely to provoke significant public opposition, and, certainly, public opinion checks and balances the power of provincial cabinets.

Public opinion and political reality have always constrained governments. The constraints may become more obvious – and more exuberant – in an era when people have access to the devices of popular sovereignty: the initiative, the referendum, and the recall. BC already allows citizens to petition to place a public policy proposition on a ballot, already requires a referendum to be held before the Legislative Assembly gives its consent to changes to the Constitution Act, and already provides a mechanism, between elections, for removing individual MLAs from their place by means of a popular vote. It is true that initially the use of these devices requires enormous expenditures of political energy; however, once the rules are relaxed, the prospect of a popular vote is bound to check the power of the premier and the cabinet.

The opposition parties, dedicated as they are to removing the government from office, are often able to provide a balance to government proposals. In combination with a cynical media, the forces in the province opposed to the government can sometimes place it in check. The opposition parties, certainly, have been made more effective by legislation that gives them access to what had been confidential documents and transcripts of conversations. The lieutenant governor's constitutional powers, as Vander Zalm discovered, must be given consideration. Public servants sometimes thwart the will of cabinets, often with rational arguments but sometimes by placing confidential documents in brown envelopes or on fax machines, which then gives the documents a wider circulation than even Freedom of Information legislation provides.

The government of the day does not always speak with one voice; it is institutionally, and often emotionally, divided. The people in the Premier's Office are eager to oversee the activities of those in the offices of the ministers. Ministerial assistants try to use the predispositions of the different people in the Premier's Office to obtain leverage in putting forward their own ministers' proposals. Ministers are rivals as well as colleagues. Central agencies have very different agendas than do ministries. Ministries are often powerless in their own public policy enclaves because they are constrained by the activities of crown corporations, whose chief executive officers sometimes have better access to the premier than do cabinet ministers.

And, as it happens, governments have deliberately added to this policy-making complexity, and to the checks on themselves, by creating new agencies and new structures, most notably by providing certain officials with a hierarchical autonomy. Some government employees have always had a statutory obligation to carry on at least some of their functions without reference to cabinet directives. The deputy attorney general, the chief forester, and the superintendent of child welfare have all been given statutory obligations that allow those officials, on occasion, to act independently.

When the Office of Ombudsman was created in order to investigate and make recommendations about government policies and actions, it was deliberately constructed so that the ombudsman would report only to the assembly itself. The ombudsman is not beholden to cabinet and, to ensure this autonomy from the government of the day, is effectively chosen by an all-party committee of the assembly that makes a unanimous recommendation to the assembly as a whole. In recent years other officials have been chosen in this way and are completely independent of government. The auditor general reports to the assembly on the province's finances and often, in the report, is critical of government procedures. The information and privacy commissioner decides what government documents the press (and public) can see. Those decisions can have grave political consequences, and ministers are bound to be constrained in their actions by the mere knowledge than they cannot control the flow of information. The chief electoral officer has recently joined the ranks of these 'officers of the legislature,' and makes independent decisions about party financing and campaign practices that could well determine the outcome of an election campaign. King cabinet – even the premier member of that cabinet – is today as beset by powerful external forces as is any American president, and cabinets and premiers cannot compensate for the checks and balances of outrageous fortune, as can a US president, by dreaming of naval flotillas and army manoeuvres or by taking cosy journeys on their own (for a time) private 747.

The Labyrinth of Decision-Making

The multiplicity of checks and balances are reflected in the elaborate and labyrinthine workings of cabinet decision-making. The process has developed over many years. The recent Harcourt government constructed an intricate structure for cabinet decision-making. That structure continues to be shaped and changed by the personal style of Harcourt's successor, Glen Clark.

Cabinet may make final decisions; however, except when there is a political crisis (a not infrequent condition of BC politics), the cabinet as a whole does not consider submissions outlining alternative courses of action until these have been reviewed by ministry or central agency officials, by designated task forces including the Deputy Ministers' Council, by the staff assigned to cabinet committees, by the members of those cabinet committees, and by senior members of the Premier's Office. Since the premier establishes the cabinet committee structure and appoints the members of the committees and their staffs (except for Treasury Board), there is a certain overlap in responsibilities and some ambiguity about who reports to whom on which issues. The premier, of course, may intervene and put an end to any ambiguity, and yet the premier cannot always intervene because he or she cannot always know when an intervention is necessary.

Figure 9.1 outlines the formal structure utilized by the Harcourt government. Ministries, in this scheme, are at the bottom of the chart; they are, if you will, the grassroots of policy-making. When ministers or their ministries have an idea that they wish to turn into a cabinet directive, they prepare a formal submission. This submission goes to the Cabinet Committee Coordinating Group (CCCG), which makes recommendations about

Figure 9.1

Guide to the cabinet committee system

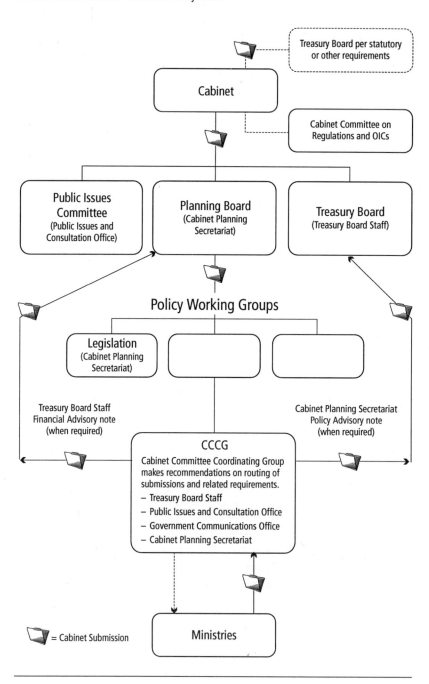

which committee or agency should examine the issue and further prepare the submission for cabinet consideration. This is mostly an informal
process involving interaction between key people working in the central
agencies. The CCCG is composed of representatives of these agencies, specifically of Treasury Board, the Public Issues and Consultation Office (PIC)
which became the Government Priorities Committee (GPC), the Government Communications Office (GCO), and the Cabinet Planning Secretariat,
the operating arm of the Planning Board. In cases of disagreement, the
'routing' issue is decided by the deputy minister to the premier, who will
generally consult the premier's chief of staff (who also holds deputy minister rank) and the premier.

Issues primarily financial in nature are dealt with by Treasury Board.
Indeed, the Financial Administration Act requires that certain financial
issues be considered by Treasury Board. Treasury Board is chaired by the
minister of finance, and its staff work closely with finance ministry staff.
Most other important issues are considered by the Planning Board. However, in part because considering all these issues would overwhelm the
Planning Board agenda, various working groups of ministers would be established to consider issues such as land use planning and aboriginal treaty
mandates, and staff would be assigned from the central agencies to assist
these working groups. The GCO is supposed to contribute advice on the
public relations impact of the various issues as they develop. PIC was the
agency designated to ensure that those issues that were central to the government's long-term plan for reelection were given priority in this delib-
erative process.

In the first two years of the Harcourt mandate, there was a concern that
this process created a kind of 'inner cabinet' of ministers who were on both
the Planning Board and Treasury Board. Ministers who were not members
of either board often felt that by the time the full cabinet dealt with an
issue, the decision about what to do had in fact been taken earlier by this
'inner' group, and that cabinet was merely a rubber stamp. When Harcourt
shuffled his cabinet and changed the key people in the Premier's Office in
September 1993, he dealt with this concern by significantly reducing the
overlapping memberships on both boards, and by directing that when critical issues were being considered by the boards or by working groups, the
process of consideration would be directed by PIC. John Heaney, the director of the PIC operation, reported directly to Chris Chilton, Harcourt's new
chief of staff. The boards and the working groups were also instructed to
take advice from the GCO headed by Evan Lloyd, who had served as the
NDP caucus media director during the NDP's opposition days.

This elaborate web of consultation and deliberation, augmented by the
Deputy Ministers' Council (chaired by the deputy minister to the premier),
by the Cabinet Office (directed by the deputy minister to the premier), by

the Cabinet Planning Secretariat, and by the Cabinet Committee on Regulations and Orders-in-Council, was not seen as user-friendly by elected MLAs (including many cabinet ministers) and was often viewed as impenetrable by those outside government who, nonetheless, needed to deal with government. A series of political setbacks forced the premier once again to change his chief of staff (appointing John Walsh, who had initially seemed destined for the position but lost out in a byzantine power struggle and had to content himself with being a deputy minister, first of tourism, then of aboriginal affairs) and to placate the most powerful critics of the system by appointing them to a committee to oversee the PIC operation.

Harcourt named the six ministers most likely to take a run at the leadership (no doubt on the theory that if they were all in the same room together they could keep an eye on one another for him), and, as it happened, they soon came to be seen as a new kind of 'inner cabinet' minus the premier. In fact, the PIC office, serving two masters (the Government Priorities Committee and the premier's chief of staff and his deputy minister), became somewhat immobilized and this elaborate process became unhappily constipated. Harcourt's resignation and Clark's accession to the premier's chair purged the system and concentrated power again in the premier's hands.

Following the 1996 election, Clark appointed Dr. Tom Gunton as a deputy minister in the Premier's Office with a mandate to coordinate and control both the policy-making and communications functions of the labyrinthine process. Harcourt's deputy minister, Doug McArthur, continued to serve as deputy minister to the premier, with responsibility for overseeing the activities of other deputy ministers and of the public service generally. Dr. Gunton, once Clark's graduate school supervisor, is responsible for ensuring that the policy development system is efficient and coherent. No doubt a future premier will further change the system and structures to reflect his or her own style of personal governance.

Personal Governance

In the end, the government of BC is personal – it is indeed 'premier's government.' But premiers are not medieval kings, nor are they twentieth-century dictators or even populist firebrands free to shape public opinion to their liking. They are often in check and they always require balance.

W.A.C. Bennett, premier of BC for two decades, is widely believed to have been a 'one man band' and a bit of a demagogue. In fact, Bennett gave considerable latitude to his most trusted ministers – including Robert Bonner, Ray Williston, and Wes Black – and he was constantly and vigorously opposed by opposition parties, by the media (particularly the Vancouver dailies), and by a wide assortment of important groups including large corporations (whose senior executives voted for and helped elect 'high-priced waterfront' Liberals and Conservatives), labour unions, teachers, and university students.[6] Bennett, as his own minister of finance, mastered the details of government, but although he was always confident of reelection it was never certain, and although he was always certain of his purpose in governing he was not always confident that he could achieve it against the wishes of the federal government, the media, and all the other forces who tried to keep him in check.

Dave Barrett, a compelling orator, was not shy about making up public policy as his speech of the moment gathered emotional momentum. He found, however, that it was one thing to promise $25-a-year automobile insurance and quite another to actually deliver on the promise. The Barrett government did deliver a multitude of new policies – the Agricultural Land Reserve, legal aid, public automobile insurance, municipal voting rights for tenants, a more robust labour relations dispute-settlement process, new moneys from resource royalties, and so on – yet once the economy began to falter after the 1973 oil shock, the government found itself surrounded by a crowd of hostile forces that first checked its progress and then managed its defeat. Throughout almost the whole of his term, Barrett careened from initiative to initiative, seemingly unable to establish a process for distinguishing between the important and unimportant, between the necessary and the desirable, and between the doable and not doable. In just thirty-nine months he was undone.[7]

Bill Bennett, who succeeded to his father's job after the Barrett interregnum, did not inherit his father's personality, nor did he adopt his father's governing style. The younger Bennett could not cope with making decisions on the fly on the basis of cacophonous advice, and he set about constructing a more formal decision-making structure designed to bring peace and quiet to the policy process and to the Premier's Office. Relying on advice from political operatives with experience in managing the Ontario Conservative government for the so-called 'Big Blue Machine,' Bennett established a cabinet committee structure designed to ensure that all proposals before the full cabinet were examined in detail and vetted by staff in the Premier's Office for both administrative and political workability.

Bennett set up three types of cabinet committees. Standing committees, chaired by senior ministers, examined proposals on environment, land use, and social services. Special committees were established from time to time to consider such matters as Canadian constitutional reform and urban transit. There were also three coordinating committees: one for legislation to examine the work of the lawyers drafting the new laws; Treasury Board; and a Planning and Priorities Committee that, like its counterparts in Ottawa and Toronto, often acted, with the premier's permission, as a kind of 'inner cabinet.' The Premier's Office, responsible for coordinating the coordinators, had two heads: a principal secretary, reporting to the premier on political matters; and a deputy minister, ostensibly in charge of policy and administration but necessarily concerned with the political implications of these matters.

Bill Bennett often seemed remote from his government (he spent much of his time outside Victoria and when in the capital city lived in a hotel), and his reliance on his key staff irked certain ministers who felt that he did not pay enough attention to his elected colleagues. Bennett, nonetheless, had enormous confidence in his staff – and in the corporate model of administration that he adopted – and the staff, in turn, established a mastery over the policy-making process.[8]

Bill Vander Zalm did not like, and was not like, Bill Bennett and he concocted a very different style of governing. Vander Zalm restructured his cabinet and the policy-making process by naming regional ministers, with the intention of bringing government closer to the people. In fact, however, he concentrated all significant political and administrative power in his own hands and then let it be used by only one other person. Vander Zalm abandoned the two-headed Premier's Office and appointed David Poole as the sole member of his staff with ready access to the premier. Poole was constantly at Vander Zalm's side, he issued political directives to the party organization, hired and fired all the other members of the premier's entourage (except for the premier's driver), hired and fired deputy ministers, helped the premier select new ministers and gave the bad news to departing ministers, involved himself with all significant policy developments (and with some insignificant ones as well), attended all cabinet meetings, and on one famous occasion in the premier's absence actually called the cabinet to order. Poole, not surprisingly, made many enemies, and Vander Zalm, after losses in key by-elections and investigations of his own financial affairs, was forced to let Poole go in hopes that this sacrifice would placate his own multitude of critics inside and outside the Social Credit Party.

After Poole's departure Vander Zalm seemed to lose heart and control of events. The formal cabinet committee structure was revived, the premier no longer opposed any consensus that emerged from that process, Frank Rhodes, a respected career civil servant who had no personal ties to Vander Zalm, was brought in as the premier's deputy minister, and later Jerry Lampert, who had been Bill Bennett's last principal secretary, returned to that position to work for Vander Zalm. Vander Zalm's power and authority was now effectively in check – handed to others – and he was ultimately forced from office. His successor, Rita Johnston, a long-time Vander Zalm loyalist, made no substantial changes to the administration of the government in the few months she served as premier, and her focus on political survival brought nothing better than a humiliating electoral defeat.

The NDP, with Mike Harcourt as party leader, anticipated victory and well before the election designed an elaborate plan to take over and run the government.[9] Harcourt, as the leader of a party that many British Columbians openly expressed fears about concerning its ability to govern, was well aware of hostile forces to check and balance NDP proposals. Perhaps because of this recognition that political power is necessarily constrained (a recognition in part forced on New Democrats by the recollection that Dave Barrett's disdain for constraints had only led to defeat), those closest to Harcourt felt it important to construct an impenetrable policy-making process and a palace guard to filter the bad news and stare down the hostile forces. The consequence was an administrative style that seemed closed to all but a few party and labour movement initiates conversant with the secret signs of the social democratic faith. Harcourt, a naturally gregarious person, seemed to tire of his isolated office – and was considerably happier away from Victoria, preferably in some agreeable foreign clime on a trade mission – and, in the end, he quit politics.

The NDP, just before Glen Clark became party leader and premier, anticipated defeat and feared decimation. Clark took advantage of this 'what-have-we-got-to-lose' mood by taking a series of relatively bold actions, unimpeded by any real consultative process. This strategy, dictated both by events and by Clark's personality, proved successful in gaining the NDP a victory in the 1996 election, albeit a victory of thin proportions. Clark continues to pursue his province-building goals by means of frequent personal interventions and an administrative style that emphasizes clear lines of control and command. Clark is bound to obtain personal credit for what goes right – and probably fated to be visited by personal opprobrium for whatever goes wrong.

Conclusion

The premier and the cabinet are the government of the day. Sometimes for many days, sometimes for only a few. To a large degree, the premier's personality shapes the government. The government and, in particular, the cabinet, and more recently the Premier's Office, confine the premier. The premier – confined – and the cabinet and other key players – confining – are thereby constrained to consider their situation and consider the play of forces that allows them to do one thing and not another. Things can be done – the premier holds power and the cabinet exercises its authority. Yet some things cannot be done with the best will in the world. In BC, as in Ottawa and other places, the power of office is tempered, and checked and even corrupted, by the power of place.

Further Reading

Archer, Keith, Roger Gibbins, Rainer Knopff, and Leslie A. Pal. 'The Political Executive.' Chapter 6 in *Parameters of Power: Canada's Political Institutions*. Toronto: Nelson 1995

Mason, Gary, and Keith Baldrey. *Fantasyland: Inside the Reign of Bill Vander Zalm*. Toronto: McGraw-Hill Ryerson 1989

Mitchell, David. *W.A.C. Bennett and the Rise of British Columbia*. Vancouver: Douglas and McIntyre 1983

–. *Succession*. Vancouver: Douglas and McIntyre 1986

Morley, Terence. 'From Bill Vander Zalm to Mike Harcourt: Government Transition in British Columbia.' In *Taking Power: Managing Government Transitions*, edited by Donald J. Savoie, 187-212. Toronto: Institute of Public Administration of Canada 1993

Smith, David. *The Invisible Crown: The First Principle of Canadian Government*. Toronto: University of Toronto Press 1995

Tennant, Paul. 'The NDP Government of British Columbia: Unaided Politicians in an Unaided Cabinet.' *Canadian Public Policy* 3, 4 (1977): 489-503

Young, Walter D., and J. Terence Morley. 'The Premier and the Cabinet.' In *The Reins of Power: Governing British Columbia*, edited by J. Terence Morley, Norman J. Ruff, Neil A. Swainson, R. Jeremy Wilson, and Walter D. Young. Vancouver: Douglas and McIntyre 1983

10
Provincial Governance and the Public Service: Bureaucratic Transitions and Change
Norman Ruff

Bureaucracy has long been held synonymous with perverse self-serving rigidities and resistance to change. Yet few social or political institutions can match the amount of innovation and change experienced by the British Columbia public service over the past twenty-five years. Some of that change represents catching up with, or drawing lessons from, other jurisdictions, and some has been driven by changes in the governing parties, their leadership, policy priorities, and approaches to governance. The aftershocks of profound changes in the main institutional characteristics and administrative styles of the provincial public service continue to have unsettling effects – with more to come.

Shifting degrees of administrative and policy-making decentralization and accompanying departmental and ministerial reorganizations, government restraint, retrenchment, privatization, and the contracting out of professional and other services, and democratization of the workplace through public sector collective bargaining rights have all reshaped the government's bureaucratic culture. Recognition of the proactive policy roles of senior bureaucrats from deputy ministers and directors on down, and more open and accessible government through the acknowledgment of the legitimacy of outside policy networks of groups in providing policy advice and the progressive application of the 1993 Freedom of Information and Protection of Privacy legislation, have also changed the bureaucracy's external face. Though thus far immune to any direct manifestation of the 1990s preoccupation with 'reinventing government,'[1] the exits and entrances into the ranks of senior officials have contributed to a high level of turbulence within the BC public service, and have left little organizational memory.

Scope of the Public Service
Contemporary debates over the size of government and of public employment have made most British Columbians aware that there is more to the

provincial public service than the senior managers and clerical staff located in government ministries or departments in Victoria or in the regional offices around the province. The stereotype of a bureaucrat is built around the images of office paper-clip benders, but policy debates during the last two decades have increased our awareness of the wide scope of public employment beyond the departments directly managed under a government minister. Autonomous crown corporations and agencies such as BC Hydro, BC Ferries, and others, teachers, university and college instructors, nurses, and other hospital and social service agency employees together make up the full spread of provincial public service employment. With some 30,000 municipal employees, the entire provincial public sector is estimated to be 327,000 (see Table 10.1).

Such numbers have been used alongside financial reporting on the size of the annual budget deficit and total provincial public debt as indicators of the burdensome growth of government. They are, however, subject to even more uncertainty and political manipulation than the financial accounts. Differing ministry, agency, and crown corporation sources, changes in hiring practices, and movements back and forth in the use of personal service consulting contracts and 'privatized' employees rather than regular staff employment, plus exclusions from the full-time equivalent (FTE) control counts, can distort the numbers reported for government ministries.[2] In 1983 the Social Credit government of Bill Bennett successfully reduced the authorized number of full-time equivalent employees (calculated as one FTE for each 1,827 hours worked per year) by a quarter, from 46,806

Table 10.1

Number of BC public employees (estimated 1992)

Area/sector	Number
Direct government public service	40,000
Crown corporations and agencies	25,000
Public schools (education K-12)	60,000
Hospital and health institutions	100,000
Social service agencies	40,000
Universities and colleges	32,000
Municipalities	30,000
Total	327,000

Source: Judi Korbin, *Final Report: The Public Sector in British Columbia*, vol. 2 of *Report of the Commission of Inquiry into the Public Service and Public Sector* (Victoria: Crown Publications 1993).

FTEs (1982-3) to 35,410 (1984-5). This reduction was achieved through privatization, shifting employees from salaries to individual contracts, attrition, and, to a lesser extent, termination. Privatization of road and bridge maintenance, for example, led to a reduction of transportation and highways FTE employees from 9,245 to 6,998. In some instances the decline was accompanied by savings in personnel wage and benefit costs but increased expenditure in the case of several professional classifications, such as those within education where contracts were estimated at 58 percent above employee costs.[3]

Privatization through the sale or transfer of government operations from the public to the private sector began under Bill Bennett in 1979 with the transfer of the assets of the three forest resource companies and shares in WestCoast Transmission, which were acquired by the previous NDP government. Every British Columbian was eligible for five free shares in the new private company, BC Resource Investment Company. Privatization of actual government operations began in a limited fashion after 1983, but was made a priority in the second year of the 1986-91 Vander Zalm government. In October 1987 two crown corporation divisions (BC Hydro Mainland Gas and BC Hydro Rail) and the BC Enterprise Corporation Expo Lands holding at False Creek, together with eleven other government operations (including road and bridge maintenance and forest nurseries), were sold for $1,012 million. This first phase, overseen by the Privatization Implementation Committee, affected some 7,240 crown and government employees.[4] This policy direction, however, lost much of its steam by 1989, after the BC Steamship Company, which operated the *Princess Marguerite* ferry between Victoria and Seattle, was sold to BC Stena, which then promptly cancelled the service.[5] Privatizations planned for the BC Systems Corporation, Queen's Printer printing, and small government liquor retail stores were abandoned. In 1994 a new crown corporation, the Victoria Line, restored the Victoria-Seattle connection, but the NDP, who had strenuously opposed privatization, made little effort during its 1991-6 term as government to turn the clock back. In fact, it was NDP Premier Clark who finally disbanded the BC Systems Corporation in 1996 – a twelve-year-old target for privatization – along with the BC Trade and Development Corporation.

By 1995 the number of direct government FTEs had grown to 38,996. As shown in Table 10.2, however, after adjustments are made to give comparable basis for reporting actual employment, the increase was from 35,753, or 9.1 percent over the past five years rather than the 41.1 percent derived from the *Estimates* blue book. If one restates this growth in proportion to the 11+ percent population growth, then the rate of increase per capita appears still less, and political debaters are free to choose whichever incarnation suits their purpose.

Table 10.2

Full-time equivalent direct government employees (fiscal year ending 31 March 1986-96)

Year	Budget estimates approved FTEs	Adjusted for 1996 FTE comparability
1986	34,008	37,598
1987	34,314	36,522
1988	34,077	38,372
1989	30,653	37,577
1990	27,335	35,267
1991	27,635	35,753
1992	27,993	36,774
1993	29,541	38,322
1994	30,256	39,037
1995	39,419	38,500
1996	38,996	38,996

Source: British Columbia, Ministry of Finance, *Estimates*, Schedule E/D and Public Service Employee Relations Commission.

The Public Service and Equity

As elsewhere in Canada, recruitment and promotion to the provincial government public service has been protected for over fifty years by the Public Service Act's assertion of the 'merit principle' in recruitment and promotions. This act is now administered by the BC Public Service Employee Relations Commission (PSERC) as heir to the old watchdog functions of the original Civil/Public Service Commission.[6] Larger social systemic factors have, however, hindered the public service in being a representative bureaucracy in the sense of itself directly embodying the full diversity of BC's population. The results of a 1994 workplace profile survey are summarized in Table 10.3.

Women make up 90 percent of clerical classifications and just 21 percent of the upper managerial level. Of the seventeen deputy ministers in March 1996, four were women – one less than the number of women cabinet ministers. Occupational ghettos also produce different ministry workplace profiles, and women made up just about a third of the Ministry of Transportation and Highways and Office of the Auditor General, but 80 percent of the Ministries of Health and Social Services.

Restructuring and Management Coordination

The structures of provincial ministries and processes of interministry coordination appear to reflect long-established approaches to the structuring of

Table 10.3

BC Public Service Employee Relations Commission
employment equity workforce profile, 1994

Social group (self-identification)	Government employees (%)	Population (%)
Aboriginal people	1.6	5.3
Visible minorities	5.2	14.2
Persons with disabilities	6.4	8.0
Women	57.5	50.3

Source: BC Public Service Employee Relations Commission (Victoria, July 1994).

ministerial responsibilities for policy-making and implementation. Most ministries follow along primarily functional criteria (Agriculture, Education, Skills and Training, Employment and Investment, Environment, Lands and Parks, Forests, Health), or process (Attorney General, Finance), or clientele (Women's Equality, Labour, Municipal Affairs, Social Services). Despite a short-lived flirtation with the idea of regional ministers in 1987, there has been little experimentation in 'super' ministry structures to facilitate policy coordination beyond interministry, secretariat-style bodies such as the Land Use Coordination Office. The recommendations of the 1995 Gove Report into Child Protection for a clientele-based Ministry for Youth and Children illustrate many of the difficulties in achieving integrated policy approaches by existing ministry and secretariat structures.[7]

Continuity in ministry names, however, can be misleading. Shifts in policy paradigms and the fine-tuning of the financial and public personnel management/collective bargaining processes, effected through the 1983 restraint program downsizing, 1987-8 restructuring and privatization, and implementation of the reforms proposed by the 1992-3 Commission of Inquiry into the Public Service and Public Sector, have fundamentally reshaped the nature of the public service. In 1991 there was an awareness that the government was lacking in effective coordination of policy development, planning, and overall financial control. Management reports by KPMG consultants, for example, suggested that the Treasury Board, as the cabinet's Financial Management Committee, required a single integrated staff agency, and that support staff were required for the cabinet's legislative and strategic policy committee, the Planning Board. The proliferation of at least 176 crown agencies with sixteen different types of relationships to government also led to insufficient coordination between them and government. Responsibility for the latter was given to a Crown Corporations Secretariat housed within a Ministry of Employment and Investment. The new ministry assumed responsibility for coordinating all government investment activity under a long-term investment program, with its various undertakings grouped under the umbrella of BC 21.[8]

In 1973 the Higgins Commission on employer-employee relations in the public service had introduced a modified private sector model of collective bargaining into the BC government.[9] Twenty years later, the 1993 Korbin Commission proposed a set of new government values in its reform of public sector human resource management, as well as an integrated co-management approach for the various public sectors to achieve comparability in employment standards and potentially contain costs and address the anomalies from previous contracting out and privatizations.[10] The resultant 1993 Public Service Act redefined the role of the former Government Personnel Services Division to create a centralized corporate personnel agency. The Public Service Employee Relations Commission (PSERC) was constituted with five branches: Management Services; Labour Relations, to conduct collective bargaining; Employee Development and Staffing, with responsibility for new selection standards under a competency-based (Knowledge, Skills and Abilities [KSA] model) hiring system and the Employee Development Centre; Compensation and Benefits; and the Equity and Diversity Branch to monitor equal opportunities for advancement and provide training programs on harassment and discrimination. In addition PSERC was to collaborate with the BC Government and Service Employees' Union in a joint Partnership Council to improve public service.[11] The parallel Public Sector Employers' Act, 1993, put a new integrated co-management structure in place for all public sector employers. Made up of councils for each sector of the public service, a central Public Sector Employers' Council is composed of the minister of finance as chair of Treasury Board, the PSE Council commissioner, nominees from each of the non-government public service sector employers' groups, and seven ministers and/or their deputy ministers. This framework treads a fine line between centralized control and effective co-management, but its accompanying rationalization of bargaining units was a long overdue reform to help bring wage and salary costs for the whole provincial public sector under control. It is premature, however, to judge the impact of restructuring of collective bargaining and the consequences for managerial coordination, accountability, and employer-employee relationships.

Politicalizing the Government Senior Bureaucracy
Over the past twenty years, the senior ranks of the government public service have shed an earlier passive administrative culture that understated the policy-shaping contributions of the government's senior bureaucracy. The twenty-year W.A.C. Bennett government, for example, stressed a politics/policy-administration/implementation dichotomy in which premier and cabinet alone were the policymakers and shapers. While contemporary

public service reforms in the United Kingdom and New Zealand are being built around a reassertion of ministers' roles in setting policy objectives, and the responsibilities of senior government managers as managers, this earlier form emphasized a passive non-proactive public service. It undermined the sense of managerial responsibility and encouraged insularity. Departmental management was built around a BC civil service careerism that rewarded long and patient employment within its own ranks. This crumbled with the advent of the first NDP government in 1972-5, which parachuted several new program-oriented deputy ministers into the senior levels. The 1983 paradigm policy shift of the succeeding Social Credit government further pummelled the old model with demands that its senior management be 'on side' in the implementation of restraint, downsizing, and privatization. Between 1986 and 1991, there followed an unprecedented number of turnovers in the ranks of the deputies and shuffles among ministries to emphasize their status as general managers.[12] The subsequent formation of a Deputy Ministers' Council, chaired by the deputy to the premier, further reinforces a sense of their corporate management responsibilities within government.

From this point on, BC seems to have pushed at the boundary line between a program-oriented senior bureaucracy and one whose commitments and sense of accountability extend beyond programs, the legislature, or public to their authors – the governing party. At the top two ranks of the public service, deputy ministers have always been appointed by cabinet order-in-council, as have, since 1976, all associate and assistant deputy ministers. A post-1991 influx of senior 'outsiders' with Saskatchewan, Manitoba, and Yukon government backgrounds produced the epithet 'Saskmanyuk,' a symbol for what some saw as signs of a political network and a related politicization of the BC bureaucracy.[13] No doubt some of these fears stemmed from the unaccustomed experience of a government turnover and the wide range of appointments in a variety of agencies that are at the disposal of any new government, but proactive governments everywhere are prone to challenge the old bureaucratic order. The question is whether the participants are clear on the distinction between accountable and proactive management to meet the needs of a modern $20 billion provincial government enterprise, and old-style political patronage.

Public Service Morale

The much-touted distrust of things political and declining confidence in government, which is said to be a mark of our times, targets not only elected politicians but government employees. Such scapegoating is not a new phenomenon, particularly for government bureaucracy, which has been a target throughout history. Add to these criticisms the uncertainties of an unstable working environment rocked by top-down continuous reorganizations, impending transfers, budget cuts, or prospects of layoff or privatization, and one has a recipe for low morale. 'Reinvention' may provide its own new kinds of positive challenges and rewards for government managers who are given responsibility for performance,[14] but 'doing more with less and less' and the uncertainties of the next decade will make government employment vulnerable to the debilitating consequences of declining morale. Where recruitment continues, the entry of non-BC public service managers also erodes the potential for advancement through traditional public sector careerism, and all segments of mid-management may find themselves bumping against glass ceilings.

It is often difficult to come by more than anecdotal evidence for declining morale, but it was readily evident in an organizational health inventory for the BC Ministry of Education reported in the 1995 Ministry as Employer Survey. Despite strengths in areas such as levels of workplace acceptance, support, and security, work challenges, and training opportunities, problem areas included: a sense of separation from management; a lack of open dialogue on performance development, career opportunities, and both current and future ministry plans; an inability to effect their work environment and work processes; heavy workloads with unrealistic expectations and internal ministry inconsistencies; and to a lesser extent a familiar concern with 'excessive levels of bureaucracy' and harassment. In this instance the ministry responded with a review of such concerns as part of a restructuring process, but it would be a delusion to pretend such feelings are not shared elsewhere.

New Approaches, Performance, and Accountability

Although not packaged as a major political initiative in a 'reinventing government' vein, the BC public service has moved a long way to address concerns for efficiency and effectiveness in the delivery of public programs. Against a backdrop of cutbacks in federal government transfers and other shrinking fiscal resources, government and opposition parties are all committed to downsize the numbers of public employees and ministries. The February 1996 Clark government, for example, named as two of its first initiatives the elimination of 452 management and supervisory positions (following the streamlining recommendations of the Organizational Review Initiative[15]), and the elimination of another 1,023 ministry positions through a reduction in the number of ministries by three to a total of fifteen. The mid-1990s have also seen still more significant attempts at a longer-term strategic rethinking of provincial programs, and at assessment of whether programs should continue within the public sector, be replaced by new public initiatives, or continue with substantial redesign or new modes of delivery.

Privatization and the de-institutionalizing of certain social services after 1982 produced a growth in contracted community services to both commercial and voluntary agencies.[16] In 1992 a still more dramatic organizational change was attempted in the restructuring and decentralization of the health care delivery system precipitated by the report of the 1991 Seaton Commission, *Closer to Home*.[17] Tagged 'New Directions,' this program shifted responsibilities from the central Ministry of Health to twenty regional boards working in conjunction with local community health councils.[18] Difficulties in implementing the new regional-local structures, however, seem to indicate that the usual difficulties of achieving effective local autonomy have come into play. The 1993 three-year health care accord with the Hospital Employees' Union, however, successfully – and controversially – smoothed a reduction in the number of acute-care patient days with a package of wage increases and relocation, retraining, and early retirement provisions for hospital employees.

The Ministry of Skills, Training and Labour's labour market programs and the 1994 Forest Renewal Plan under the crown corporation Forest Renewal BC[19] provide examples of newly emerging public-private partnerships as a way to meet policy objectives. New, non-adversarial or consensus-building structural approaches to public decision-making are also reflected in both the 1992-5 regional land use plans of the Commission on Resources and the Environment (CORE), and the BC Treaty Commission process as the 'keeper' of the current aboriginal treaty negotiations.[20]

Long-term trends in BC's governance are best gauged in the shift from the old-style compliance and control orientation regime – 'value for money' – to a 'managing for results' performance management. A joint 1995 report from the provincial auditor general and the departmental Deputy Ministers' Council, *Enhancing Accountability for Performance in the British Columbia Public Sector*, launched discussion of a new accountability and management framework to improve measurement of program effectiveness and increase public accountability. Informed by reforms underway elsewhere, it is argued that while both financial accountability reporting and spending authority compliance continue to be important, program choices also include consideration of such issues such as fairness and equity. The report held that citizens want to know 'that government is actually achieving what it intended to; that money is being spent wisely; that they are getting value for money for their tax dollars; and that government is conducting its business in a fair, legal and ethical way.'[21]

The goal is to provide effective performance management through a mix of clear objectives, effective implementation strategies and aligned management systems, performance measurement, and reporting with real consequences. In the process, traditional management focus on inputs and outputs is to be replaced by thinking about outcomes. This is potent stuff for a public service that was sheltered from the 1960s and 1970s preoccupations with the similarly motivated Planning-Programming-Budgeting systems, and that abandoned a belated attempt at zero-based budgeting in 1983 in the face of a recession-driven collapse in government revenue. This time the legislators are themselves being co-opted into making a commitment to accountability standards through the Legislative Assembly's Public Accounts Committee. It remains to be seen what any new accountability framework can contribute to future restructurings of the size and scope of provincial government in BC.

Further Reading

British Columbia. Auditor General and Deputy Ministers' Council. *Enhancing Accountability for Performance in the BC Public Sector*. Victoria: Queen's Printer for British Columbia 1995

Korbin, Judi. *Report of the Commission of Inquiry into the Public Service and Public Sector*. 2 vols. June 1993

–. *Interim Report*. December 1992

Peat Marwick Stevenson and Kellogg. Project Reports, BC Financial Review. *The Issue of Crown Agency Accountability*. Victoria, 1992

–. *The Issue of the Structure and Process of Financial and Policy Management*. Victoria, 1992

Rekart, Josephine. *Public Funds, Private Provision: The Role of the Voluntary Sector*. Vancouver: UBC Press 1993

11
Administering Justice
Terence Morley

Justice and the Constitution

Laws concerning the administration of justice in British Columbia are to be made by the legislature of the province. The Canadian constitution, by means of the words of the Constitution Act of 1867, grants this jurisdiction 'exclusively' to the legislature 'in each Province.' And so on 8 July 1871, when the union between Canada and BC was consummated, by Imperial order, it was understood that justice would henceforth be seen to be done – or undone – by those set in local authority as the government of the province of BC. A daunting responsibility for new office holders chosen from among the 12,000 or so white residents of the newest Canadian province.

The idea that justice should prevail was a habit of the Victorian mind and, consequently, a settled belief in the later nineteenth century in BC. Justice was not automatically confused with law – there were too many readers of Charles Dickens's *Bleak House* for such a conflation. At the same time, those gentlemen eligible for office in the new province, having the smatterings of a classical education, would very likely agree with Cicero that 'the origin of Justice is to be found in Law.' That hard sentiment was no doubt complicated by their mothers and their sisters and their aunts and their wives who, echoing Portia's exhortation to Shylock, sought to persuade gentlemen that 'in the course of justice, none of us should see salvation: we do pray for mercy.' The nineteenth-century mind, raised up by Shakespeare and Milton and mindful of sin and damnation along with crime and punishment, believed that the justice found in the law was properly tempered by some mercy.

This was no simple matter. The rough justice of the frontier was often harsh. Colonial law-making was usually remote and always austere. British settlement on the west coast of North America was never inevitable and was often precarious. The responsibility for justice could not have been entirely welcome.

And so, perhaps in wisdom, the responsibility for justice and for the law in Canada and in British Columbia was in fact, if not in the plain words of constitutional law, divided. The provincial government was granted authority over 'the administration of justice ... including the Constitution, Maintenance and Organization of Provincial Courts, both of Civil and of Criminal Jurisdiction and including Procedure in Civil Matters in those Courts.'[1] At the same time, those who constructed the fundamental document of the Canadian constitution, ever mindful, in the immediate aftermath of civil war, of what they believed to be the excesses and mistakes of the American constitution, decided that criminal law must be determined by the central government. Parliament was granted 'Legislative Authority' to 'make Laws' on the subject of 'The Criminal Law, except the Constitution of the Courts of Criminal Jurisdiction, but including the Procedure in Criminal Cases.'[2]

The effect of this constitutional scheme in the years following the union between BC and Canada was to confirm the legal subordination of the province to federal authority. In this constitutional instance, those laws most closely associated with prevailing conceptions of justice – criminal laws – were to be written and pronounced by Ottawa and merely administered in Victoria. And for greater certainty, the laws written in Victoria by the legislature could be vetoed or 'disallowed' by the central government; the superior courts established by the legislature operated with judges appointed by the central government; and the legislature itself was composed of an assembly and a representative of the Queen (the lieutenant governor) who, in the first years following 1871, was obedient to instructions provided by that central government.

It is a commonplace observation that the 1867 constitutional scheme, in the words of K.C. Wheare, 'contradicts the federal principle' that central and regional governments should be 'coordinate and independent.' Wheare describes Canada as a 'quasi-federal system' in which the provincial governments were legally placed in a circumstance of colonial subordination to the national government in Ottawa. As Peter Russell observes, 'the process whereby the prevailing constitutional ethic in Canada came to be something very close to Wheare's conception of classical federalism is one of the central themes of Canadian history.'[3]

The struggle to emancipate the administration of justice from the mandated shackles of federal domination continues to irritate federal-provincial relationships today. Indeed, the advent of the Charter of Rights and Freedoms in 1982 seems to further constrict provincial authority over the administration of justice. Consequently the Charter has the potential effect of sharpening federal-provincial conflict over issues of law and order and justice. Certainly, the Charter sets out conditions for the administration of justice that invite judges to make binding administrative rules to significantly alter administrative processes hitherto sanctioned by attorneys general on behalf of provincial governments. The Legal Rights sections of the Charter set forth principles of liberty, due process, and limits on punishment, in terms unmistakably similar to those in the United States Bill of Rights, with the result that patterns of administering justice in Canada have changed to more closely resemble patterns in the American justice system.

So, for example, the Charter proclaims that 'any person charged with an offence has the right to be tried within a reasonable time.'[4] In the *Askov* case, the Supreme Court of Canada announced in 1990 that a delay 'in the range of some six to eight months between committal and trial might be deemed to be the outside limit of what is reasonable.' What followed in Ontario over the next year, as described by Rainer Knopff and Ted Morton, was an astounding failure to proceed with 43,640 charges, including 'one charge of manslaughter, 817 extreme assault charges, 290 sexual assault charges and 11,623 charges of impaired driving.'[5] An even more dramatic change in the pattern of law enforcement has emerged from a series of decisions that reversed a long-standing Canadian practice whereby the courts would generally 'admit improperly obtained evidence that was relevant and reliable.'[6]

Following the introduction of the Charter and American practice, such evidence is very often inadmissible, and consequently some individuals who would have been charged and convicted of offences in the past now escape punishment. As a result the guidelines followed by crown prosecutors in deciding whether or not to lay charges have been significantly altered by the operation of the Charter. Charter antagonists, including Knopff and Morton, persuasively argue that the Charter has had the effect of subordinating governments, including provincial governments, to the courts. These courts have determined that they themselves embody the fundamental law of the constitution. The judges now decide on the validity of legislation and on the rules that guide administration, including, perforce, the administration of justice.

It may be that many judges, and in particular a majority of Supreme Court of Canada judges, are inclined, at least for the time being, to restrain judicial power over lawmaking and public administration. Yet because of their disinclination to renounce the power bestowed by the Charter, and because they need fear no other interpretation of the constitution other than their own, the judges have effectively 'enhanced their own discretionary power at the expense of the discretion of other officials.'[7]

The Justice System

Since the early 1970s, it has been fashionable to imagine a justice system that *processes* offenders from apprehension through to rehabilitation. In this system the police are at the front end to caution and sometimes detain persons who may have transgressed the law. The circumstances of every police action that might result in a significant fine or imprisonment are then reviewed by crown prosecutors, who then decide whether or not to proceed with laying charges. Those charges are dealt with by courts deciding whether the charges have been proved and, if so, what is appropriate penalty under the law. The punishment of offenders is overseen by prison guards and bailiffs empowered to seize assets. Upon release, probation officers and other social workers are imagined to conduct a healing course of rehabilitation. The fit between imagination and reality is best understood by examining in some detail the elements of such a process in light of the constitutional authority surrounding the administration of justice.

The Police
In 1996 there were close to 7,000 police in BC, including almost 300 civilian employees sworn as peace officers and therefore authorized to arrest and caution suspects. More than 70% of police officers are members of the Royal Canadian Mounted Police (RCMP). The presence of the mounties in BC is more pervasive than in any other province for two reasons. First, because Ontario and Quebec have provincial police forces, BC is the largest province to use the RCMP as a provincial force. Second, as in the other seven provinces using the RCMP for provincial policing, the mounties also police smaller municipalities. This has meant in BC that when these relatively new municipalities grew up to become suburban cities – Burnaby, Surrey, and Richmond are examples – the RCMP then found themselves as the municipal force in very large communities with populations of 100,000 and up.

BC disbanded its own provincial force in 1950, in large part because the federal government promised to pay for half the policing costs in those areas of the province using the RCMP. Over the years such generosity has been less and less bountiful. In 1994 the federal government paid 30% of general provincial policing costs, just over 24% in municipalities with populations between 5,000 and 15,000, and just under 8% in municipalities with populations greater than 15,000. The twelve independent municipal forces (most of these have survived in municipalities incorporated before the First World War) receive no federal money but do obtain a little over 3% of their costs from the provincial government. The larger (over 15,000) municipalities with RCMP contracts receive no provincial funding, but those with populations between 5,000 and 15,000 receive just over 2% of their costs from the province.

Formally, and constitutionally, the attorney general, as the chief law officer of the Crown in the province, provides direction to the police. In practice the attorney general's ability to supervise police activities is increasingly limited in BC. This is so for three reasons:

(1) The RCMP necessarily serve two masters. On the one hand, constitutional protocol requires that the force pay attention to the directives of the attorney general. On the other hand, the RCMP continues as a paramilitary structure with a chain of command that moves through the ranks from constable to corporal to senior NCOs (non-commissioned officers) to commissioned officers and to, ultimately, the commissioner of the RCMP in Ottawa. This commanding officer, by law, reports to the solicitor general for Canada and is expected to take direction from this federal cabinet minister acting on behalf of the central government. There have been instances, mostly involving civil disobedience, when the provincial and federal authorities have had very different views on how the matter should be handled. Compromises have invariably been reached. Nonetheless, an attorney general needs to recognize that it would be a brave commissioner who would follow provincial direction in defiance of federal instructions. It would be an even braver RCMP officer stationed in BC who would refuse to obey the commissioner because of an instruction from the attorney general.

(2) Attorneys general have grown increasingly reluctant to exercise authority in situations that are seen to have political overtones. These include almost all forms of civil disobedience, such as blocking logging roads by environmental activists or occupations of either public or private lands by aboriginal groups in pursuit of a land claim. Attorneys general, acutely aware that they are both law officers of the Crown and politicians, seem to prefer to leave critical decision to the discretion of the police. Certainly this was a stated policy during the 1995 standoff involving armed and militant aboriginals at Gustafsen Lake.

(3) The police, and in particular the RCMP, are increasingly reluctant to take action that might be publicly controversial simply at the direction of a government official. As the cultural impact of the Charter becomes entrenched, the police have increasingly come to expect judicial direction by means of a court order before acting. This expectation is only partly reduced by means of a formal policy, such as the directive to police to always lay charges in cases of spousal violence or to be more vigorous in the pursuit of fathers who have failed to make court-ordered maintenance payments.

The Oppal Report

The central issues of police governance were canvassed in 1993 by Mr. Justice Wally Oppal of the BC Supreme Court, acting as a one-person commission of inquiry into police governance and discipline. Commissioner Oppal focused on the problems associated with the police investigating complaints about themselves and on an appropriate civilian monitor for police activity, and in particular for disciplinary proceedings concerning those activities. The government decided not to shut down the Police Commission in existence but instead to negotiate with the police and other groups a protocol for monitoring the police. The experience of the NDP government in Ontario using a civilian 'watchdog,' which came to be despised by all the police forces in that province, made the NDP government in BC more cautious about setting up a similar body.

The Ministry of the Attorney General

The office of attorney general is unique – as attorneys general themselves do fondly testify. The attorney general is a cabinet minister appointed by the premier of the province. The attorney general is also the chief law officer of the Crown in the province – that is, he or she acts as the 'Queen's Attorney' (the government's chief lawyer) and, in that capacity, is responsible for criminal prosecutions, for directing the police, and for taking civil suits on behalf of the government against private citizens and against other governments. The attorney general is also responsible for advising the government as a whole on all legislation, especially on the legal and constitutional implications of legislative change. As the chief law officer of the Crown, he or she is expected to make independent determinations and, more particularly, to act in accordance with the law and not at the behest of the premier or cabinet colleagues.

For many years the federal cabinet has included two law officers of the Crown: the minister of justice and attorney general for Canada and the solicitor general of Canada. Some provinces have adopted this model. In BC, in 1988, Premier William Vander Zalm divided the responsibilities of the attorney general's ministry and gave control over policing, corrections (the provincial prisons), and motor vehicles to a new Ministry of Solicitor General. Vander Zalm took this step following a resignation statement in the legislative assembly by then Attorney General Brian Smith in which Smith accused the premier of planning to split his ministry in order to weaken the independence of the attorney general's office. In 1991 the new NDP premier, Mike Harcourt, reamalgamated the two law officer ministries under Attorney General Colin Gabelmann.

Gabelmann soon came to believe that the amalgamated ministry was unwieldy, boasting more employees than any other ministry except health. It was responsible for 'administering the justice system' and also 'charged with managing liquor distribution and licensing, provincial elections, emergency preparedness and a large number of boards and commissions.'[8] The government responded by providing the ministry with a second deputy minister position. The deputy attorney general, who has certain statutory obligations to provide independent legal advice to government, continued to oversee the criminal justice branch, the legal services branch, the land titles office, and the Coordinated Law Enforcement Unit (CLEU), whimsically known as 'clue.' The new deputy minister, a prominent NDP activist and University of Victoria law professor, came to direct the operations of the largest part of the ministry including responsibility for police services, corrections, liquor control and licensing, management services, policy and legislation, and court services.

The deputy attorney general, a career public servant, was somewhat underemployed. His major remaining responsibility was to oversee the work of the 'government law firm,' which, through the legal services branch, was headed by two half-time assistant deputy attorneys general. The branch-placed solicitors in other ministries employed barristers, including members of the private bar hired on contract, to argue the government's case before courts and other tribunals, and, in addition, vetted legislation including order-in-council regulations.

Of course, the deputy attorney general also had the assistant deputy attorney general for criminal justice (ADAG) report to him. However, following the passage of the Crown Counsel Act in 1991, the individual holding this position was effectively free from the deputy attorney general's direction. The Crown Counsel Act unanimously passed by the legislature, in the session before the NDP won power, was inspired by a public perception that the prosecutorial process was vulnerable to political interference. The Vander Zalm government had been plagued by scandals involving several cabinet ministers and the premier himself. Some of these scandals raised suspicions of criminal activity – Vander Zalm was the subject of an active RCMP investigation over his relationship with a friend suspected of influence peddling – and there were a number of voices raised, in the media and more privately, questioning a system where ultimate responsibility for prosecutions lay with an attorney general and a deputy attorney general both appointed to their offices by the premier and both continuously involved with cabinet ministers and other key government officials.

The government asked Stephen Owen, the provincial ombudsman, to conduct a commission of inquiry on prosecutorial discretion. In his report, Owen argued that 'The challenge of the fair and effective administration of criminal justice is to achieve the proper balance between *independence* from political interference and *accountability* to the political process for the investigation and prosecution of crime.'[9] Owen made two recommendations that were embodied in the Crown Counsel Act. Gabelmann summarizes the first:

> The Act is designed ... to ensure individual prosecution decisions are made free from partisan considerations. It does so by clearly defining how the Attorney General and the Deputy Attorney General may intervene in the running of the Branch. If either one of us issues an instruction affecting a specific prosecution the directive must be in writing and must be published

in the *BC Gazette*. If we issue a directive concerning the Criminal Justice Branch's policy on the approval or conduct of prosecutions, we must put any such directive in writing to the ADAG. If we send out a directive respecting the Branch's administration, the ADAG can require us to put it in writing. In the latter two instances, the ADAG also has the discretion to require publication in *The Gazette*.[10]

The second recommendation was to have special prosecutors appointed in cases 'involving the investigation and prosecution of crimes involving persons of particular influence,' including 'cabinet ministers, senior public officials, and police officers, or persons in close relationships to them.' The NDP government used special prosecutors on several occasions, most notably in the prosecutions of the Nanaimo Commonwealth Holding Society and its controlling personality, David Stupich, a long-time NDP MLA and MP and sometime minister of finance in Dave Barrett's NDP regime. The special prosecutors are effectively appointed by the ADAG and drawn from a list of prominent members of the private bar.

When Stephen Owen was appointed deputy attorney general by Premier Harcourt in 1995, the responsibility for Court Services was transferred from Deputy Minister Maloney to him and, as well, he was centrally involved in providing advice to the attorney general on framing appropriate relationships between the ministry and the minister and the police, particularly in high-profile incidents such as the stand off at Gustafsen Lake. The deputy minister continued to be burdened by justice policy particularly in two areas – corrections and legal aid – which provided much of the focus for justice system policy-making during the NDP years in office.

Corrections
The catalyst for the examination and review of the corrections branch of the ministry was a young man named Danny Perrault. In 1991 Perrault, in an advanced state of intoxication, beat an elderly hotel employee to death and, after a guilty plea to a manslaughter charge, was, as a young offender, sentenced to three years in custody. He served that sentence at the Willingdon Youth Detention Centre, a secure facility, where he received temporary absence passes up until 1993 when he failed to return from the authorized absence. After ten days he turned himself in and was sentenced, this time as an adult, to an additional forty-five days in prison at Willingdon. After completing the escape sentence, he was then transferred to an open custody correctional centre to complete his manslaughter sentence. Perrault walked away from the open facility and, after being at large for almost a month, broke into an apartment and terrorized and sexually assaulted a twenty-eight-year-old woman. He was arrested two days later and subsequently sentenced to fourteen years imprisonment.

When these facts became known public outrage ensued. The government, through the attorney general, responded by appointing Madam Justice Jo-Ann Prowse of the BC Court of Appeal as a sole commissioner to inquire into the transfer of Perrault to the open facility. Commissioner Prowse found that several ministry employees did not follow corrections branch policy, and that two employees in particular made wrong judgments that led to his escape and to the subsequent assault. Employees were disciplined for their failures and the procedures for classifying offenders and assessing those at risk of escape were tightened.

The long-standing problem of assigning prisoners to appropriate facilities and programs, despite the change in procedure and policies inspired by this unhappy incident, is a central problem for all systems of incarceration that operate in democratic societies. The problem is further complicated in BC because a diproportionate number of prisoners are aboriginal persons. There is an apprehension that this imbalance not only produces racial tensions inside the prisons but also makes it very difficult to design a corrections system that has a positive impact in aboriginal communities with different traditions and perceptions of crime and punishment. The government now encourages alternative sentences more in keeping with aboriginal practices – in particular, healing programs designed to modify behaviour that has led to alcohol, drug, and sexual abuse – rather than traditional forms of incarcerated punishment.

Legal Aid
At the same time as the government was dealing with these controversial issues of sentencing, inmate classification, and corrections policy generally, it was also forced to wrestle with deep differences of opinion about appropriate models for the delivery of legal services to individuals unable to afford needed legal assistance. The struggle over legal aid proved bitter and unfruitful.

Some lawyers have always acted for clients who could not afford to pay any or all of a fee by substantially reducing or even eliminating it. By the 1960s this personal charity was transformed into a system of collective obligation organized in BC by the Law Society. Lawyers were not required to take such cases, yet a sense of professional obligation, combined with peer pressure, encouraged many lawyers, primarily those with some experience in criminal law and often senior practitioners, to agree to take a few cases every year on this basis. By the 1970s the idea of using public funds to subsidize this charitable impulse had gained widespread acceptance throughout most of North America, and in BC the Barrett NDP government established a Legal Services Commission to oversee the development of a program to deliver legal services to people who could not afford them.

The Law Society was unhappy with this arrangement, arguing that the government-appointed commission compromised the independence of the lawyers working in this system, who, by this time, were mostly junior practitioners attracted to legal aid work by the promise of a secure, through greatly reduced, fee for their services. Most lawyers were also unhappy with the NDP government's plan to open legal aid offices staffed by lawyers not in private practice. They argued that a California-style 'public defender' system would inevitably mean that many criminal defendants would be inadequately represented by beginning lawyers content with routine work and a career with little room for significant income growth. After the NDP was defeated, the Law Society prevailed on the Bill Bennett Social Credit government to abolish the commission and place the legal aid program under the direction of a newly created Legal Services Society (LSS).

Funding for legal aid was mostly provided by the provincial government and by the Law Foundation of BC. The Law Foundation receives its income from a portion of the interest generated by the pooled trust funds of all law firms and practitioners operating in BC.[11] Following government cutbacks in the early 1980s, the governors of the Law Foundation became increasingly concerned that the growing legal aid budget would soon claim all the Foundation income. They took steps to limit the percentage of their revenues that must flow to legal aid, eventually utilizing a capped three-year grant to force the government to make up the inevitable shortfalls in the LSS budget.

The crisis in legal aid funding became acute in the early 1990s. It was precipitated only in part by the Law Foundation's reluctance to continue to provide significant funding to the burgeoning program at the expense of other Foundation projects. More important were Supreme Court of Canada decisions requiring governments to ensure that certain classes of persons, in particular those charged with offences that would on conviction likely lead to incarceration, be provided with legal counsel. This Charter-driven course, in combination with a 1991 Social Credit government decision to allow the LSS to double the tariff paid to lawyers from the private bar, led to a dramatic increase in legal aid costs in BC. In 1988/89 the LSS spent just over $27 million. Just three years later in 1991/92, following the introduction of the higher tariff, the LSS spent just over $65 million. In 1992/93, with the Harcourt government now in the second year of its mandate, those costs jumped to just over $88 million, and then to just over $100 million in 1993/94.

The Harcourt government was quickly persuaded that legal aid costs were out of control and that the system needed an overhaul. The first step was a study commissioned by Attorney General Gabelmann and conducted by Tim Agg, who in his report favoured hiring staff lawyers to undertake at least half of the legal aid work. Agg argued that this would not only help control the burgeoning expenditures but would also mean that the LSS could ensure that more legal aid practitioners would have an interest and training that would allow the provision of a broader mix of services, particularly family law services, than had been the current practice.[12] The current legal aid practice was dominated by private bar lawyers undertaking criminal defence work.

With the Agg report in hand, the ministry persuaded the LSS board to adopt a series of reforms to the legal aid scheme. In February 1994 the LSS board approved a 'mixed model' that would have the LSS hire 160 new staff lawyers and 78 paralegals, so that instead of 85 to 90 percent of legal aid services being delivered by the private bar being paid tariff rates, the caseload would be split evenly between the private bar and staff lawyers. In addition, during 1994 the LSS restricted the use of legal aid, which previously had been granted to anyone charged with an indictable offence who met the financial eligibility criteria, to those charged who had a 'reasonable' chance of being jailed upon conviction. The LSS also required staff to seek out alternative services for non-emergency family matters, and held back a significant portion of tariff fees payable to private bar lawyers.

Not surprisingly, the legal aid lawyers, organized as the Association of Legal Aid Lawyers (ALL), were extremely upset with these reforms. In July 1994 they began to withdraw their services in an attempt to change the government's mind. The ALL members were also angry that the Law Society appointees on the LSS board had not united to halt the changes, and were concerned that the Law Society itself, dominated by benchers who did not practice criminal law or receive income from the legal aid plan, was not appropriately supportive. Fortunately for ALL, the benchers became more supportive following the passage of Bill 55, which changed the structure of the LSS board from seven members appointed by the government and seven by the Law Society to a tripartite arrangement with five members appointed by the government, five by the Law Society, and five by the Association of Community Law Offices and the Association of Native Community Law Offices. Bill 55 also prohibited the LSS from operating a deficit.

Three of the Law Society appointees to the LSS board resigned on the passage of Bill 55 and the other two also tendered resignations to come into effect when the bill was proclaimed into law. The ALL 'strike' continued until late September 1994, when the attorney general agreed to hire no more than ninety staff lawyers in order to produce a seventy/thirty split between private bar and staff delivery of services. This compromise did not, however, reduce expenditures, which exceeded $101 million for the fiscal year ending 31 March 1995, resulting in an illegal deficit position of some $6.2 million.

Although the government permitted the LSS board to 'carry-over' the deficit into 1995/96, and although further cuts have been made to service provision (by the end of 1995 almost forty of the staff lawyer positions remained unfilled), the LSS continued to be trapped by cuts in federal transfer payments, provincial government attempts to eliminate the operating deficit in the 1996 budget, the higher tariff, rising costs of administration, and raised expectations for the provision of adequate legal services in the age of the Charter. By the middle of 1996 the LSS directors, no doubt inspired by a prospect that they might have some personal liability for overruns, had essentially abandoned the program of creating a large number of staff lawyer positions.

The Legal Profession

Lawyers occupy a middle ground, which they often proclaim to be the high ground from which they make themselves heard as loud advocates. Lawyers stand between contesting partisans and go between distinct interests. In the criminal justice system, lawyers provide the interface between clients, including governments, and the courts. In private disputes, lawyers mediate as well as advocate. The courts and other tribunals in turn dispense solutions, however imperfect, to particular problems. Lawyers grease the wheels and make the system function.

The legal profession, under the Legal Profession Act, governs itself, as do certain other professionals including physicians and surgeons, dentists, engineers, and chartered accountants. Unlike other professionals, however, lawyers are also able to claim the privilege of self-government because the judges, all once-upon-a-time lawyers, retain vestiges of the original authority that allowed them to determine who they would hear plead before them. The historic relationship between the legal profession and the courts gives lawyers public duties and also public privileges. Lawyers necessarily claim their independence from the state and from governments because they are inextricably associated with the laws that organize the state and emanate from its governments.

The Legal Profession Act provides that all practicing lawyers must be members of the Law Society of BC and that the society itself shall be 'governed by the benchers.' This imposing congregation consists of the attorney general, whose status as a bencher is visible manifestation of the intersection between the legal profession and the provincial state, twenty-five members of the Law Society elected by lawyers from eight judicial counties, and three persons appointed by the cabinet as lay benchers. The head of the society is styled, under the law, as 'treasurer.' No doubt this partly reflects the historic focus of the legal profession on financial well-being.[13]

The treasurer normally assumes office after serving several years as an elected bencher and after being subsequently elected as the assistant deputy treasurer.[14] He or she serves a year as assistant deputy treasurer, moves on for another year to act as deputy treasurer, finally completing the three-year cycle in the top job.[15] The chief administrative officer of the society is called the 'secretary,' partly reflecting this person's duty to correspond with members about fidelity to the society's rules.

The main purpose of the society is to determine the rules governing the practice of law and to decide who is fit to undertake and continue in the practice. In pursuit of this, the benchers set requirements for admission; mandate programs to sustain competent practice including continuing legal education courses, practice assistance, and personal assistance; require all practitioners to carry liability insurance; administer a special compensation fund to pay victims of lawyer misappropriation of funds; act on complaints about unauthorized practice by non-lawyers such as debt collection agencies; and deal with complaints about lawyers and, if so disposed, discipline lawyers found guilty of professional misconduct.[16]

There are over 8,000 practicing lawyers in BC. Almost 30 percent are women, a dramatic increase over the past twenty years. Almost 75 percent of lawyers in BC are in private practice, with most of the remaining lawyers working for government and for public and private corporations. In contrast to the English tradition, in Canada a lawyer can be both a barrister – who argues cases before courts and other tribunals – and a solicitor – who drafts documents and gives advice on the law. According to the society's 1994 annual report, 'it is interesting to note that time in the profession appears evenly split between what are barrister's and solicitor's practice areas.'[17]

There are now more than 500 new lawyers admitted to the profession in BC each year. Less than half of these are recent graduates of the two BC law schools, and over one-quarter have recently come to the province from other jurisdictions. Of course, lawyers also leave the practice of law. A handful are appointed as judges every year, a few more than a handful retire, and some never retire although they do cease to practice at death. Recently a significant number of members, mostly women and mostly recent calls to the bar, opt for non-practicing status. A few lawyers leave the profession after being found guilty of professional misconduct.

The Law Society oversees a fairly elaborate complaints and discipline program. In 1994 there were 1,559 complaints and inquires from the public about the conduct of individual members of the society – up 2.6 percent from 1993. A majority of the complaints were determined by Law Society staff to be unfounded or unprovable, with an additional 15 percent classified as outside the society's jurisdiction. Of the remaining 30 percent, less than half were deemed serious enough to be referred to either the discipline committee or the competency committee. Most of these were handled without citing the lawyer for professional misconduct. In 1994 only 2.1 percent of the complaints led to a citation. Over three-quarters of the citations led to a penalty being imposed, ranging from reprimands or fines to temporary withdrawals from practice or disbarment. In 1994 only two lawyers were disbarred.

The supervisory and remedial powers granted the Law Society are extensive. The benchers establish the terms and conditions for membership in the society, and they decide on the conditions for being enrolled as an articled student and set out the terms that frame the relationship between these articled students and their principals. The benchers may prevent certain lawyers from acting as principals and may provide for examinations and other tests governing admission to the profession. Once admitted, members may be required to submit to an audit of all personal financial and other records. Members may also be suspended from practice without notice by three benchers, their property relating to their practice may be seized and managed by a custodian, and, after a hearing, they may be disbarred and prevented from ever again practicing law in BC. In certain respects, the benchers, as the guardians of the society, have the same authority as a judge of the Supreme Court of BC, and, consequently, an appeal by a member of the society regarding supervisory and disciplinary decisions is made directly to the Court of Appeal.

Lawyers in BC are also members of the BC branch of the Canadian Bar Association (CBA). The CBA, in its provincial and regional emanations, strives to act as an advocacy body for the interests of lawyers generally. It has regularly been referred to, often with self-conscious sarcasm,[18] as the trade union for lawyers. The CBA provides a multitude of services to its members by endorsing service suppliers for insurance needs, investment advice, law office supplies and equipment, professional and law firm development, vehicle purchases, and travel discounts. And, no doubt mindful of the profession's advocacy traditions, the CBA regularly presents the views of its activists on a range of public policy issues, especially constitutional reform, to governments.

The practice of law is diverse. In BC lawyers are forbidden by the Law Society to hold themselves out to be 'specialists' in an area of law (unlike physicians and surgeons). In reality, however, almost all lawyers develop specialized practices. Lawyers are permitted to advertise their 'preferred areas of practice' as a genteel means of indicating to the public their areas of expertise. The profession also is divided into highly distinct organizational cultures. The pattern of practice, and of living, is very different for those associated with the criminal bar than it is for solicitors working in downtown Vancouver office towers, different again for litigators in Victoria than for real estate lawyers acting for Kamloops developers, and different again for a small firm of general practitioners in Fort St. John than for labour law specialists in Burnaby 'boutiques' composed of three or four politically active union advocates.

Judges

Judges, as high officials of the Canadian state, in both its federal and provincial processions, preside over courts of law. Judges are seen to embody the law – certainly they make law and proclaim equity.

The judicial branch of government, to use Peter Russell's phrasing,[19] has emerged since 1982 and the passage of the Charter of Rights and Freedoms as a force to be celebrated and feared, to be reckoned with and analyzed, and to be understood. Judges are now seen to be political actors who often direct public policy, if sometimes reluctantly, and who often are able to have the last important word in a political controversy, even though they are expected to have shed the partisan associations they enjoyed before their appointment to the bench.

In BC the last important word is spoken by judges who, by law, reside in Ottawa and are justices of the Supreme Court of Canada (SCC). The SCC is a court of last resort – there is no appeal from its decisions. These are final. This, however, is not to say that the decisions can never be altered. The court may reverse itself, although it prefers to do so by making the most of the different facts that are inevitably part and parcel of a new case under consideration. These new facts allow the Supreme Court justices to apply the principles of judicial reasoning in a creative manner so as to yield a new, and sometimes opposite, interpretation of the law. Moreover, the judges sitting in lower courts, though formally bound by SCC decisions, are also able to make use of new facts and judicial reasoning and careful judgments to effect alterations to the last important word and thereby to the law itself.

Before 1949 the court of last resort for British Columbians was effectively dominated by a British cabinet minister (the Lord Chancellor)[20] and mostly composed of judges who, by necessity, resided in London, England. This court, styled the Judicial Committee of the Privy Council (JCPC), particularly in the years when it was commanded by two Lords Chancellor (Lords Watson and Haldane), revealed the legal foundation for provincial autonomy in a federal Canada. Most provinces, including BC, were dismayed when the JCPC, led by a Lord Chancellor who saw himself as a political ally of Canada's most centralist party (the social democratic CCF), declared that the Parliament of Canada, acting without provincial consent, could nonetheless obtain from the British Parliament an amendment to the Canadian constitution that would make the SCC (whose justices are appointed solely by the prime minister of Canada) the court of last resort.[21]

Since 1975, when the SCC won the power to decide which cases it would hear, only a tiny fraction of cases decided by BC courts wend their way to the Supreme Court in Ottawa. Almost all cases involve criminal laws (made by Parliament) or have a public and constitutional law aspect, leaving the

BC Court of Appeal as the effective court of last resort for most litigants and for judicial elaboration of the laws made by the legislature.

The Court of Appeal consists of a chief justice, twelve justices of appeal, and up to thirteen supernumerary justices of appeal. The court is established by an act of the legislature entitled the Court of Appeal Act. The chief justice and the justices of appeal are appointed to the court under provisions of the Judges Act, an act of Parliament passed as an elaboration of Section 96 of the Constitution Act, 1867. Consequently, although the province's highest court is created by a provincial law, the offices of chief justice and justices of appeal are filled by the federal government according to the provisions of a national law. Nonetheless the federal government may only appoint justices to a vacancy established under the provincial law. A vacancy is created in one of three ways: the resignation of a sitting justice; the death of a sitting justice; or the decision of a sitting justice, over the age of sixty-five and with fifteen years service as a superior court judge, to accept supernumerary status. A supernumerary justice continues to have all the powers of an ordinary justice of appeal and continues to collect the same salary as before, but has a substantially reduced workload and less attractive and spacious office accommodation.

As an appellate tribunal, the court is divided into panels, selected by the chief justice, of not less than three justices, to hear cases. The act states that 'the judgment of a majority of a division is the judgment of the court.' Since the individual justices are known to bring differing perspectives on legal principles and social practices and structure, the composition of the panels would seem to be important to case outcomes. The chief justice undoubtedly knows well the predispositions of his or her colleagues on the court, and, consequently, the power to name the panels combined with administrative authority over the operation of the court and control over who on the court may attend conferences or other meetings 'relating to the administration of justice' make the chief justice a considerable force in shaping the law and other public policies in BC.

The Court of Appeal is a superior court. That is, the justices of the court claim an inherent jurisdiction in supplement of the jurisdiction granted by statute to apply the law and dispense justice as though they directly exercised certain prerogative powers, such as the ultimate guardianship of all children, associated with the sovereign power of a head of state, in this case, the Queen as Queen of Canada. The other superior court in BC is a trial court inaccurately styled as the Supreme Court of BC (SCBC). This court is certainly not supreme as its decisions, rendered in judgments of individual judges, may be overturned by the Court of Appeal and by the Supreme Court of Canada. The SCBC consists of a chief justice, an associate chief justice, eighty-two other judges, and up to eighty-four supernumerary judges.[22] The SCBC is also created by a provincial law – the

Supreme Court Act – with the judges appointed as Section 96 judges by the federal government. Until 1989 all SCBC judges resided in Vancouver, and justice in the other parts of the province was dispensed by a third tier of Section 96 judges appointed to county courts. The legislature then abolished the county courts and caused the county court judges to be transmogrified into superior court judges who, in their larger numbers and greater dignity, continued to live and work outside the judicial county of Vancouver.

The SCBC, as a superior court, is granted the widest possible jurisdiction to hear 'all cases, civil and criminal, arising in the Province.'[23] In practice they deal with the most significant cases. On the civil side, they must deal with any case where there is a claim for more than $10,000. The Criminal Code requires that superior court judges preside over trials of those indicted for the most serious offences, such as murder, treason, and, the favourite of law students across Canada, 'astonishing the Queen.'[24] For indictable offences deemed less serious, the code permits the person charged to elect to have the case heard in either the superior court or in a provincial court with judges appointed by the provincial government. The code provides[25] that for indictable offences deemed even less serious, the person charged is not able to elect and these cases are invariably heard in the provincial court. Summary offences, where the code requires, or the prosecution decides, that there be no preliminary hearing before a provincial court judge to ascertain whether or not the Crown has sufficient evidence to justify a trial, are heard directly by provincial court judges. When the Crown proceeds on a summary basis, there is the expectation that the penalties will be less severe on conviction than if the offence is indictable.

Most trials in BC are before a judge acting alone without a jury. The judge performs the task of a jury by deciding on what to believe about the facts as presented. Of course, the judge also provides an interpretation of the law. However, in BC and the rest of Canada, any person charged with an offence 'where the maximum punishment for the offence is five years imprisonment or a more severe punishment'[26] has the right to demand a jury trial. The jury, members of which must not be lawyers or connected to the justice system, decides the facts and makes a determination to convict or acquit. The judge presides over the trial and summarizes the evidence and the law for the jury before they deliberate. The verdict must be unanimous. Litigants may also obtain the benefits of a jury trial in certain civil cases, though juries are used far less in BC and Canada than in either the United States or the United Kingdom. Civil case juries are composed of six to eight persons and a verdict only requires the agreement of 75 percent of the jurors listening to a civil trial.

SCBC judges also act as appellate judges for cases on appeal from the Provincial Court of BC. The dignity of all superior court judges with appellate jurisdiction is secured by their being called Honourable Mr. and Madam

Justices of the court and by the ancient habit of addressing them in court as Your Lordship and Your Ladyship.

Although the SCBC judges must deal with the most significant trials, it is the provincial court judges who cope with the largest caseload. The Provincial Court of BC is also created by provincial law, and for this court the judges are formally appointed by the lieutenant governor in council – that is, by the provincial cabinet on the recommendation of the attorney general. The Provincial Court is the largest court (with 140 judges in 1995), and its judges reside throughout the province in more than forty communities. In the largest centres, the judges may be assigned to the criminal law division, the small claims division, or the family law division. Most provincial court judges deal with all these matters. As 'inferior court' judges – called magistrates until the early 1970s – they all live with restrictions on their authority. For the most serious criminal offences, they are restricted to conducting a preliminary or committal inquiry; in many instances those charged with an offence are able to choose to be tried in the SCBC; the $10,000 small claims ceiling deprives them of most of the significant civil litigation cases. Even in family matters, and even following initiatives by both federal and provincial governments to permit provincial court judges to play a central role in adjudicating disputes arising from marital breakdowns, they are unable to order property divisions (although they can dispose of children with custody orders) or grant divorces.

Provincial court judges are supervised by a chief judge with extensive powers to assign judges to particular cases or kinds of cases, and to determine where they will hear these cases and the extent of their other duties. The chief judge also conducts investigations to determine whether other judges are fit to be judges. As with chief justices, there is now some concern that the executive and administrative powers given these officials constitute a new threat to the independence of individual judges.[27] Many provincial court judges across Canada, mindful in part of the substantial salary differential between themselves and superior court judges, have claimed that the ability of provincial governments to control their incomes constitutes an infringement on their independence and is a violation, therefore, of the Charter.[28] Perhaps as a means of soothing the ruffled feelings consequent on a fairly rigid judicial hierarchy, provincial court judges are now entitled to be called the Honourable Judge and in court continue to be addressed as Your Honour.

Judicial Appointments and Disappointments
No job is more highly prized than that of judge. Other careers may be seen as more glamorous – movie star and hockey player come to mind – and more lucrative – baseball players usually make more money and, more to the point, so do lawyers in large downtown Vancouver law firms – and

occasionally more prestigious – scientists working on discoveries that might lead to a Nobel Prize or best-selling authors are likely in this category – but no regular job, certainly not one in the public sector, has as many sought-after conditions of employment.

Judicial salaries in BC are not huge when compared to senior corporate executive compensation packages or to the top quintile of professional incomes, and yet superior court salaries and benefits are larger than all but a handful of other public sector salaries and benefits, and even perennially dissatisfied provincial court judges are paid more than most deputy ministers. In addition, most judges can look forward to handsome pensions (some might argue that superior court judges who become supernumeraries enjoy a form of retirement to the age of seventy-five on a 'pension' the same as their full salary). Superior court judges also have a security of tenure that far exceeds that granted the most distinguished of university professors.[29] Although provincial court judges do not have the same constitutional guarantees securing their tenure in office, they can only be removed before retirement age by a process set out in the Provincial Court Act.

It is no little wonder that the process of appointment to these desirable positions has been, since the beginning, a matter of some public controversy, the more so because it is widely believed that judicial decisions should be made by disinterested persons, and yet judicial office is in the gift of partisan politicians and often given to aspirants with partisan connections.

By law, appointments to superior courts are made by the governor general. The governor general, of course, does not provide a commission without the consent of the federal cabinet. The cabinet is led in matters of judicial appointment by the minister of justice and the prime minister. The minister of justice makes recommendations on most superior court appointments. The prime minister recommends the appointments of chief justices and associate chief justices. There is no formal ratification process.

The minister of justice and the prime minister no longer make their recommendations solely on the basis of political calculation. For many years they sought opinions from the Canadian Bar Association on whether a lawyer (only practicing lawyers are eligible for appointments to the superior courts) was qualified to be a judge. This informal 'old boy' process was significantly altered in 1988 with the creation of the office of Commissioner for Federal Judicial Affairs. Currently, lawyers who wish to be considered for appointment to the BC superior courts make their desire known to the commissioner and fill out a 'personal history' form.

The names and personal histories are then provided to the BC Advisory Committee, which consists of a nominee of the Law Society; a nominee of the BC Branch of the Canadian Bar Association; a superior court judge named by the chief justice of the Appeal Court (who consults with the chief justice of the SCBC); a nominee of the attorney general; and three persons named by the federal minister of justice. The Advisory Committee then assesses the applicants as either 'recommended,' 'highly recommended,' or 'unable to recommend.' Not all those 'recommended' or even 'highly recommended' will be appointed. The committee is made aware that 'ultimate responsibility and accountability for appointments rest with the Minister of Justice.'[30] The minister does, certainly, continue to consult with some judges and lawyers not on the Advisory Committee (some of whom are, or have been, activists in his or her own party) and with the attorney general, who, since 1988, has not been a supporter of the party in power in Ottawa.

Peter Russell and Jacob Ziegel, the two leading Canadian academics interested in the judicial appointment process, concluded in a recent study that something close to half of the judicial appointments made by the Mulroney government 'had a known political association with the Conservative party.'[31] In BC this is not surprising since during the Mulroney years the minister of justice circulated the names of possible appointees – after they had been vetted by the Advisory Committee – to an informal task force of Conservative Party lawyer activists for comment.

Even so, there were many appointments to the BC superior courts given to individuals not associated in any way with the Conservatives. When Pierre Trudeau and John Turner, as successive ministers of justice in the Liberal governments of the late 1960s and early 1970s, appointed a handful of Conservatives and New Democrats to the SCBC, this was seen as a startling departure from the venerable tradition that parties in power only gave judicial appointments to their own supporters. The Mulroney Conservatives, by contrast, worked closely with the province's chief justices (who all had had Liberal connections before their appointments to the bench) and the result was that a majority of new appointments and promotions were not handed out to those with Conservative affiliations. The Mulroney government did not get much public credit for this change of direction, possibly because some appointments, including one to the Court of Appeal, seemed to have been made at the behest of then Attorney General Brian Smith, who himself boasted strong ties to the federal Conservatives. The Chrétien government has not been criticized for making partisan appointments and has, indeed, generally appointed individuals without strong partisan connections, although they have invariably been associated with law firms that themselves have strong Liberal associations.[32]

By law, appointments to the Provincial Court of BC are made by the lieutenant governor in council. The lieutenant governor must await cabinet direction before signing the commission, and the cabinet is led in matters of judicial appointment by the attorney general. The appointment process is structured to make it seem that the attorney general makes a recommendation to cabinet based on advice from others.

Lawyers who wish to become provincial court judges must fill out a formal application form and submit to an interview. The application is considered, and the interview conducted by the Judicial Council of the Court. This council, first established in 1969, is composed of the chief judge, who presides; one of the associate chief judges as determined by the cabinet; the treasurer of the Law Society or an appointee; the president of the CBA (BC Branch) or an appointee; and up to four other persons appointed by the cabinet.

Following the interview, the council makes a recommendation to the attorney general. Those favourably recommended are placed on a list, and when it is determined that there is a vacancy the attorney general recommends a name to cabinet from the list. This does not mean that the attorney general cannot play a central role in choosing provincial court judges. The attorney general and his or her advisers, including political advisers, can and do encourage applications from people they would like to see appointed to the provincial bench. Chief justices and their senior colleagues, acting on their behalf, do the same for those who they would like to see appointed to the superior court bench.

However, the more limited number of consultations required of attorneys general makes it possible for them to act swiftly in placing an individual on the bench. If no place can be found on the SCBC for a deputy attorney general who feels out of favour in government, then a consolation can be provided immediately on the provincial bench. If a law firm that the attorney general appreciates, politically or otherwise, is disappearing because of other appointments, then the remaining partner can be placed on the court even after the bureaucracy has been informed that someone else was to be chosen. Attorneys general, of all parties, if given a wide latitude by a premier and the cabinet, are well placed to use their authority to shape the court more to their partisan, ideological, multicultural, and personal liking – and they do so.

Tribunals and Commissions

Judges are not the only public officials armed with the power to make determinations on the basis of their finding of facts. The most significant 'quasi-judicial' bodies in BC that exercise powers of general application[33] are the Human Rights Commission and the Human Rights Tribunal, the Office of the Ombudsman, and various commissions of inquiry. All of them, in imitation of the courts, have the power to compel witnesses and to make judgments, although not all the judgments are binding on the parties concerned.

The Human Rights Commission, established by legislation passed in 1995, replaces the Human Rights Council established in 1984, which itself was a new structure replacing the Human Rights Branch, a semi-autonomous public service entity established by the Barrett NDP government. The branch was dismantled by the Social Credit government and the new commission was an attempt by the Harcourt NDP government to transform the Social Credit scheme.

The commission is composed of three full-time officials: a commissioner, a deputy commissioner given powers to initiate investigations, and a commissioner of investigation and mediation to conduct investigations. The commission is enjoined to take advice from a Human Rights Advisory Council appointed by the cabinet but can, legally, reject the advice. The commission may refer complaints to a newly created Human Rights Tribunal. The tribunal is composed of three full-time members and not more than six part-time members. A complaint may be heard by a single member of the tribunal designated by the chair of the tribunal, or by three members, also designated by the chair. The deputy chief commissioner can order that he or she be made a party before the tribunal to any complaint.

The tribunal, like a court, can issue cease and desist orders similar to injunctions, can order compensation for individuals based not only on moneys lost as a consequence of the discrimination but also to 'compensate for injury to dignity, feelings and self-respect.' There is no limit on the amount of a compensation award, and the tribunal may also order a party to pay costs of the hearing. The orders are enforceable under the law as though they were orders of the SCBC.

The ombudsman, in contrast, cannot compel anyone to do anything or to pay any fine. The ombudsman is empowered to conduct investigations of decisions, recommendations, acts, or omissions of public bodies, including government ministries, municipalities, universities, crown corporations, and governing bodies of the professions including the legal profession. The ombudsman cannot, however, hold an investigation if there is a right of appeal to a court or tribunal from decisions, recommendations, acts, or omissions. The ombudsman is restricted to making recommendations, in the first instance, to the 'authority' concerned and, if she or he feels that the response has been inadequate, to the cabinet and the Legislative Assembly. The ombudsman does have the power to compel witnesses – who could be convicted of perjury if it is subsequently shown that they have not told the truth under oath – and to require the production of documents from the authority under investigation. The ombudsman is appointed by the legislature after an all-party committee has made a unanimous recommendation for a term of six years, which may be renewed once by the assembly following a second unanimous committee recommendation. The salary is set by law as the equivalent of the salary of the chief judge of the Provincial Court.

Commissions of inquiry also make recommendations. Governments have traditionally used these commissions (sometimes styled as royal commissions) to help them cope with problems that have stirred a public response that cannot be handled by the usual political processes – at least not without risking a major political catastrophe. Governments generally hope that by appointing an inquiry commissioner the problem will be moved off the front pages and television newscasts for a useful period of time. Governments sometimes hope that the commissioner will provide a solution to the problem. The Harcourt government over four years appointed eleven commissioners to investigate such matters as policing (the Oppal Inquiry); public sector collective bargaining (the Korbin Commission); BC Ferries loading procedures (the Nemetz Inquiry); the government's purchase of MacMillan Bloedel shares (the Seaton Inquiry); the operation of the Vancouver stock exchange (the Matkin Inquiry); and the death of a small child at the hands of his mother (the Gove Inquiry). Most commissioners are judges granted leave from their judicial duties to conduct these inquires. Those who are not judges usually have a special knowledge of the subject.

Commissioners are appointed by the cabinet under an order-in-council authorized by the Inquiries Act in circumstances when there is a general perception that an independent investigation of a matter needs to be conducted. Judges are most often chosen as commissioners because of the general perception that they are bound to be independent of the government of the day. The commissioner has the power to obtain records, compel witnesses, and determine who has standing in the matter being investigated and who is entitled to legal counsel. The commissioner is required to report the findings to the cabinet, usually by a certain date, which is usually extended because inquiry commissioners often decide that they need more time in order to conduct a more exhaustive inquiry. Thomas Gove, the provincial court judge appointed as a commissioner to investigate the circumstances surrounding the death of one child at the hands of his mother, decided to turn his inquiry into a year-long investigation of all aspects of child protection provided by the provincial Ministry of Social Services. The government had intended that Judge Gove conduct a focused and speedy investigation into Matthew Vaudreuil's death. Yet the cabinet found it politically impossible to restrict Judge Gove's activities, and in the end his determination prevailed and the government was unable to control Commission spending.

Conclusion

The system for administering justice in BC is elaborate and complex. Moreover, even though the system is created by the words of the Constitution Act, it always faces new challenges and is subject to continual change. The justice system bequeathed by law and by precedent to BC is said to be adversarial. Certainly it is controversial. In recent years concerns have been raised, and occasionally controversies have raged, over access to the system for those unable to pay high legal fees and costs; over plea bargains where the prosecutors agree to ask the judge for a lesser penalty in return for a more efficient guilty plea; over the uses of juries; over the length of time it takes to have a matter come to trial; over who, in particular trials, has the right to be present and make arguments (known as 'standing'); and over the role of the public, including victims of crime, in helping shape the system.

Perhaps the most controversial changes now emerging are those associated with the creation of an aboriginal justice system. The Harcourt government, in response to the fact that almost 18 percent of the inmates of BC prisons are aboriginal persons even though they make up less than 5 percent of the general BC population, appointed Provincial Court Judge Anthony Sarich as a commissioner of inquiry to investigate the impact of the justice system on aboriginal persons living in the Coast-Chilcotin region. Judge Sarich argued that the distinctive cultural perceptions of aboriginals has meant that a system designed by white Europeans has ill-served those aboriginal persons caught in its logic and mores. This argument led the government to expand the RCMP aboriginal constable program to make it possible for some aboriginal communities to have their own police, and to encourage judges to substitute traditional 'healing' processes for the forms of punishment prescribed by the Criminal Code. These initiatives are inevitably criticized and opposed by those in the province who believe that the law should apply equally to all and that there should be no 'special status,' neither for Quebec and Quebeckers nor for aboriginals.

In an age of uncertainty, a country of fragility, and a province of promise, justice continues, as it began, to be elusive and the law continues to change.

Further Reading

Knopff, Rainer, and F.L. Morton. *Charter Politics*. Scarborough: Nelson Canada 1992

Macleod, R.C., and David Schneiderman, eds. *Police Powers in Canada: The Evolution and Practice of Authority*. Toronto: University of Toronto Press 1994

McCormick, Peter, and Ian Greene. *Judges and Judging*. Toronto: James Lormier 1990

Morley, J. Terence. 'Courts and Cops.' In *Reins of Power: Governing British Columbia*, edited J. Terence Morley, Norman J. Ruff, Neil A. Swainson, R. Jeremy Wilson, and Walter D. Young. Vancouver: Douglas and McIntyre 1983

Russell, Peter H. *The Judiciary in Canada: The Third Branch of Government*. Toronto: McGraw-Hill Ryerson 1987

Part 4: The Patterns of Public Policy

12
Lobbying and Private Interests in British Columbia Politics
Gerry Kristianson

After a brief visit to the British Columbia legislature some years ago, a reporter for the *Seattle Post-Intelligencer* told his readers that one of the most telling differences between politics in Olympia and Victoria was that BC legislators were 'unsupervised by lobbyists.' In Olympia, he said, the ratio of lobbyists to legislators was ten to one, while in Victoria there was only a single lobbyist for every ten politicians.[1]

This comment reflected a common misunderstanding about the nature of both the BC and Canadian political systems, and the role played by pressure groups and the lobbyists who work for them. As he sat in the area reserved for journalists above our legislative chamber, the reporter had asked a member of the Victoria press corps where the lobbyists were to be found. His local colleague had pointed to the west side of the back row in the public gallery at the opposite end of the house, and identified the handful of people sitting there as Victoria's lobbyists. The visitor had then compared this group with the hundreds of registered lobbyists in his own state.

His mistake was in not realizing that the half-dozen or so people who are to be found around the legislative buildings on a daily basis while the house is in session are only the advance guard of a host of individuals and groups who attempt to influence provincial government decisions on behalf of an endless variety of private interests.

There is no evidence that the actual level of pressure group activity is any different in Victoria than it is in Washington State or any other American jurisdiction. What is different is the way in which the two political systems make decisions. US politics, with its separation of powers between the legislature and executive, does not require the cabinet and caucus solidarity that is essential to maintaining a legislative majority in the BC version of cabinet government. Furthermore, a high level of secrecy has been assumed to be essential to maintaining the appearance of solidarity. As a result, most of the activity of pressure groups in BC politics takes place behind closed doors in the offices of public servants or cabinet ministers. Relatively little takes place in US-style legislative committees or other public forums.

This does not mean that active lobbying by a host of private interests is not taking place at all levels of the provincial political process. It simply means that this activity tends to take place away from the glare of public attention and media scrutiny. However, before describing the political environment that surrounds the relationship between private interests and government in BC, it is necessary to discuss briefly some of the terms that will be used and to flag some basic questions.

While some writers in this field use the terms 'interest group' and 'pressure group' as synonyms,[2] it seems more precise and more useful to use the term 'interest group' in the more general sense of a group sharing a common interest, and 'pressure group' to describe an interest group that has chosen to embark upon political activity. Lobbying, in turn, refers to one form of the activity of pressure groups, activity 'aimed at securing favourable policy decisions or the appointment of specific government personnel.'[3] The origins of the term 'lobbying' are British, not American. It first came into common usage in eighteenth-century England as the representatives of various groups found that the best places to contact politicians were the lobbies outside the House of Commons.

When considering the present role of pressure groups in BC, it also is important to keep a number of basic questions in mind. It is worth asking whether there is adequate transparency to this aspect of the political process; whether there are unfair inequities in the amount of access that different groups have to government and in the lobbying resources available to them; whether partisanship plays a positive or negative role when groups approach the government process; and whether the quasi-official status of some organizations gives them an undue advantage over competitors.

BC's Plural Society

British Columbians, like their neighbours to the south, live in a plural society that recognizes as both legitimate and necessary the right of individuals and groups to pursue their interests, political and otherwise. A quick look under the heading 'Associations' in the Yellow Pages of the Vancouver telephone directory gives an immediate indication of the number and variety of groups, and these are simply the ones who can afford a phone listing. More than 500 are listed, along with fifteen or so additional headings under which to search.

Unfortunately, however, while our constitution recognizes the rights of individuals and groups to be involved in the governmental process, our political institutions, with their basis in nineteenth-century Britain, do not do much to facilitate such activity. To use current computer jargon, government is not user-friendly if you are a trade or professional association, an environmental or recreational group, or an ad hoc collection of tax payers concerned about the escalating costs of government.

The Lobbying Tradition in BC

Pressure group activity and its most direct manifestation, lobbying, have a long and active tradition in BC. There have been lobbyists around the corridors of power in Victoria since the first governmental institutions were established in the middle of the nineteenth century. Various private interests have been trying to influence decisions by both politicians and public servants since Governor James Douglas's legislative council grappled with the province's first law and established a licensing system for taverns and a tax on liquor sales. Dr. Helmcken, the province's first physician, recalled that the proposal was opposed by 'the whole body of publicans and other bloodsuckers ... preying upon the vitals of the colony.'[4] Cabinet records in the provincial archives show that our early politicians were the frequent recipients of lobbying activity. During the last decade of the nineteenth century, for example, the Women's Christian Temperance Union (WCTU) was writing to the executive council to demand prohibition of all liquor sales, while the Independent Order of Good Templers was calling for a 'control' system of liquor distribution. On a different social issue, the Loyal Orange Order was complaining about changes in the method of religious instruction in public schools.

On the economic side, railroad promoters were asking for land grants, financial concessions, and other forms of support, as were an association of Sea Island Farmers, the BC Fruitgrowers Association, and numerous local governments. The Vancouver Board of Trade, in 1891, was asking the government to pass legislation giving additional powers for business creditors to garnishee funds due to them. Labour groups such as the Victoria Trades and Labour Council, the Rossland Miners Union, and the Miners and Mine Labourers Protective Association were agitating for such changes to working conditions as adoption of the eight-hour day.

While these representations were being made to the executive council, other groups were approaching the Legislative Assembly directly. On a typical day in March during the 1892 session, the province's MLAs received petitions seeking legislative action from the Municipality of Surrey, the Law Society of Vancouver, the Coquitlam Electric Company, and a group wanting changes to the Game Protection Act. A private bill was introduced to incorporate the Kootenay Power Company, and the City of Victoria sought changes to the act governing its incorporation. In addition, the MLA for West Kootenay (Mr. Kellie) rose on a question of privilege to complain that after agreeing to sponsor a private bill to incorporate the Consumers' Waterworks Company of Nelson, he had been attacked in the corridor outside the chamber and called a 'liar, a stinker and a traitor' by a federal politician, Mr. Frank Barnard, MP for Cariboo, who was acting as a lobbyist for the company in question. Barnard had objected to Kellie's announcement that his support was conditional on a provision being added to the legislation that would allow the City of Nelson to purchase the new utility once it had been incorporated. The offending MP eventually apologized both to Kellie and the legislature, but not before a future premier, Charles Semlin, had suggested that he 'did not think it was right for the promoters of private bills to be all the time lobbying while the House was in session, and more especially when their particular bills were up before the House for discussion.'[5]

Active lobbying for economic benefits does not seem to have been deterred for any period of time by concerns of this sort. During one period in 1912, six major railway bills sped through the legislature in four days, and this period of frenetic lobbying by business promoters was followed almost immediately by the extensive pressure group campaign that led to the province's brief flirtation with prohibition. Active participants were organizations as disparate as the WCTU, the Merchant's Protective Association, the Vancouver Trades and Labour Council, and the Workers' Equal Rights Association.

The newspapers of the 1920s provide frequent testimony to the activity of interest groups. The decade opened with medical doctors and chiropractors squaring off against each other in Victoria, and with the optometrists and opticians also seeking to carve professional territory away from the more established physicians and surgeons. The Victoria *Daily Times* reported the story under the headline 'Active "Lobbies" Prepare to Descend on Members of House.'[6]

Later the same year, 300 unemployed men invaded the corridors around the legislative chamber in a successful effort to persuade Premier John Oliver and his colleagues to embark upon some public works projects as a way of putting ex-servicemen back to work.[7] Later in the decade, delegations representing the Timber Industries Council, the Lumber and Shingle Manufacturers Association, the Victoria Chamber of Commerce, the Vancouver Board of Trade, the Retail Merchants Association, the Canadian Manufacturers Association, the Mining Institute, and the Chilliwack Board of Trade joined forces in Victoria to oppose a new minimum-wage law.[8]

The extensive newspaper coverage of this protest reflects the extent to which the newspapers of the day and some of their employees became direct participants in the political process. Russell Walker, a member of the legislative press gallery in the 1920s and 1930s, tells in his autobiography how he accepted fees from various interest groups to lobby for legislative changes in Victoria. He takes personal credit for having defeated government efforts in 1923 to transfer property taxation powers to local governments,[9] as well as boasting that he earned $900 a couple of years later for persuading the politicians to back down from new proposals on hours of work.

While seeing nothing exceptional in his own behaviour, Walker is critical of 'Lawyers on $50 and $100 per day retainers ... lobbying all over the
place.'[10] Indeed, the pervasive nature of lobbying during this period
prompted efforts in 1927 to bar lobbyists from the corridors of power in
Victoria. George Walkem, the Conservative MLA for Richmond-Point Grey,
claimed that the activity of lobbyists was 'disgraceful.' He asked Speaker
Buckham what he intended to do about the 'disgraceful lobbying' that had
gone on during recent sessions. It was most objectionable, he said, to have
the corridors of the legislature 'forever crowded with lobbyists.' According
to the next day's Vancouver *Province*, Premier Maclean 'expressed keen sympathy with the protests,' but explained that the remedy lay with the members and not the government, since, in this era, 'no one could enter the
lobbies of the House without a card signed by a member.'[11]

The following Sunday, *Province* columnist F.W. Luce, a colleague of Russell
Walker, provided a tongue-in-cheek description of the typical Victoria lobbyist as 'sleek, well fed, exquisitely groomed,' and with a bankroll 'of generous proportions,' but predicted that in the end, 'The suggestion that the
lobbyist should be given the order of the boot ... is not likely to be carried
out. The lobbyist wouldn't stand for that at all. He would lobby against it
night and day, and in the end he would win out.'[12]

This cynicism was well justified. In the end nothing was done, prompt-
ing the Reverend Robert Connell, sometime leader of the CCF, to campaign for office in the mid-1930s on a promise to abolish lobbying. These
efforts also came to nought, but the perception that a problem existed
didn't disappear. In the late 1970s, a Social Credit cabinet minister successfully insisted that a system of corridor passes for lobbyists should be rein-
stituted in Victoria, and in 1992 newly appointed NDP Speaker Joan Sawicki
stopped issuing these passes, thereby finally succeeding in doing what MLA
Walkem had been trying to do in 1927: ban lobbyists from the corridors
immediately outside the legislative chamber.

The lobbyists, however, also managed to bear out columnist Luce's pre-
diction that 'in the end' they would win. They managed to avoid the ban
when they discovered that possession of a pass to the legislative library
provided them with de facto access to the legislative lobbies. Given the
geography of the Parliament Buildings, one can't get to the library without
passing through the members' lobby!

Cabinet records in the provincial archives show an interesting trend in
the relationship between the W.A.C. Bennett government and interest
groups. In 1952 the newly elected cabinet met with twenty-five delegations and accepted briefs from seven others without meeting them. In 1953
the number of delegations remained the same, and fourteen additional
briefs were sent to the cabinet, although some requests to meet with the

government were turned down. Early in the year, the BC division of the Canadian Manufacturers Association (CMA) asked to meet with the cabinet before it implemented its plans to cut the provincial labour board to part-time status as an economy measure. The CMA then sent its brief to the presidents of local chapters of the Social Credit League, asking them to help lobby the government. This prompted Premier Bennett to fire what the Vancouver *Province* called a 'verbal blast.' Brandishing a copy of the brief, the premier said that his government 'does not yield to power lobbying.'[13]

Despite this anger with one group, the pace of consultation began to grow, and by 1959 the number of annual delegations had increased to eighty, in part stimulated by a 1958 decision to begin taking the cabinet on tour. In 1959 the cabinet received interest group delegations in regional centres such as Salmon Arm, Kitimat, Prince George, Vancouver, Courtenay, Penticton, and New Westminster, as part of a run-up to the 1960 election.

A further innovation was made in 1962 when the government began to give groups the option of meeting with a cabinet committee rather than with the full executive council. This practice continued throughout the remainder of the W.A.C. Bennett years, although its interest in actually meeting such delegations seems to have declined steadily with the total number falling to seventeen in 1971. In the final year of Bennett's rule, the cabinet did not agree to meet a single interest group delegation, and went down to defeat in the August general election.

While one needs to keep in mind that the available records show only formal representations to the full cabinet or a cabinet committee, and do not include other forms of contact between individual cabinet ministers and various pressure groups, the Socred's defeat does suggest a possible relationship between a government's enthusiasm for consultation and its degree of political success.

The arrival of a New Democratic Party government in 1972 prompted some important changes in the relationship between pressure groups and government. Since many of the province's unions were directly affiliated with the NDP, these organizations expected to be able to take advantage of this relationship once their party had taken over the reins of government. While they were given a major role to play in the drafting of the province's new labour code in 1973, they were extremely disappointed with some of the Barrett government's later actions, especially the legislated end to labour disputes involving police and fire-fighters in 1974, and forest workers and supermarket employees in 1975.

The return of the Socreds, and the increasing polarization of the provincial political environment as the Liberals and Conservatives disappeared from the legislature, had an obvious impact on pressure groups with openly partisan NDP connections. Their attempts to approach government were often rebuffed with the advice that they ought to be talking instead to their 'friends' on the other side of the legislature.

The polarized environment of the late 1970s and early 1980s also was characterized by Socred attempts to discourage non-partisan pressure groups from consorting with the 'socialists' in the legislature. It was not unusual for the leaders of such groups to be told that the government would consider any business or social meeting with the NDP caucus to be an unfriendly act. Those who chose to ignore this advice had to keep in mind that in any case it simply was not wise to schedule a social event in Victoria to which both government and opposition MLAs were invited. Not only did some influential Socreds resent the fact that pressure groups insisted on fraternizing with the socialist 'enemy,' but many of the MLAs on both sides of the legislature simply didn't like each other. A bipartisan event could quickly become living proof of the extent to which the forces of 'socialism' and 'free enterprise' were at odds with one another.

The early days after Bill Vander Zalm became premier often consisted of a contest in which various pressure groups competed with one another to see who could be the last one to have the premier's ear before he made a public statement. The decision during the 1986 general election to promise a $1 cut in the price of a case of beer is a vivid example. An off-hand suggestion by a beer distributor while driving the premier between campaign stops became party policy during the next public appearance.

As the Socreds encountered increasing political problems, in part because of the premier's idiosyncratic approach to policy-making, a number of attempts were made to formalize the lines of communication between pressure groups and the government. For example, in the contentious area of liquor policy, the government established two committees, the Substance Abuse Advisory Committee and the Liquor Licensing Advisory Committee, which gave the manufacturers and vendors of beverage alcohol, as well as groups concerned with the social problems caused by alcohol abuse, an opportunity to meet regularly with senior political and public service officials to discuss important policy issues.

The Socreds also established a system that facilitated ready access to key decisionmakers on the two key cabinet committees, social policy and economic development. Groups would be placed on the agenda of the relevant committee, their brief circulated as part of the agenda, and then given the opportunity to speak to ministers at their weekly meeting. This practice ended with the return of the New Democrats to office in 1991. While, as indicated in one of the case studies that follow, some of the groups affiliated with the NDP found their access to government greatly improved, the NDP abolished the Socred practice of access to cabinet committees.

The New Democrats did experiment with some other innovations designed to enhance communication between government and various interest groups, especially in efforts to find consensus on contentious issues of natural resource development. Formal consultative processes involving competing interests were an interesting departure from past practice. These developments are discussed in more detail in the chapters by Kathryn Harrison and George Hoberg.

The Current Situation: The Array of Interests in Contemporary BC

Since BC has no requirement for registration of lobbyists, it is not possible to provide a comprehensive list of the groups that attempt to influence the governmental process in Victoria or the people who work for them. This said, it is possible to list a number of prominent groups according to some obvious categories such as major economic interests, professional and occupational associations, environmental organizations, and those whose members are distinguished by racial or ethnic background.

A number of organizations have long represented the interests of key sectors of the provincial economy. These include the Council of Forest Industries (COFI), the Mining Association, the Federation of Agriculture, the Fisheries Council, the Chamber of Mines, the Hotels Association, the Manufacturers Association, and the BC Federation of Labour. More recent additions to this list include organizations representing various segments of the brewing, winemaking, and distilling industries. Most of these groups are based in Vancouver, sending representatives to Victoria as needed. A few, including the farmers and the brewers, maintain permanent offices in the provincial capital.

Representatives of a number of occupational and professional groups are active participants in efforts to influence decisions of the provincial government. Many of the individual unions that belong to the BC Federation of Labour approach government both directly and through the federation. Non-affiliated unions such as those representing teamsters, nurses, and teachers also conduct their own lobbying activities. The BC Teachers Federation is one of the province's long-established and strongest pressure groups, but it was weakened in recent years when school principals and vice-principals formed a separate organization. Other bodies include the Medical Association, the College of Dental Surgeons, the Law Society, groups representing both registered and licensed practical nurses, and professional associations representing the interests of three kinds of accountants.

A number of these organizations are in the rather peculiar position of being, in effect, government-mandated pressure groups, existing by virtue of the statutory powers granted them by the provincial legislature. Questions about possible conflict between their responsibility to protect the public interest and their desire to represent their members' interests to government were raised by a recent royal commission.[14] Other groups, composed of locally elected officials, are also involved in vigorous efforts to lobby the provincial government. Examples are the Health Association (representing the boards of local hospitals), the School Trustees Association (representing local school boards), the Federation of Independent Schools Associations (representing the boards of private schools), and the Union of BC Municipalities (representing local councils).

Recent years have seen the proliferation of a variety of environmental organizations. Groups such as Greenpeace, the Sierra Club, the Western Canada Wilderness Committee, and a host of others have become active players in the political and governmental arena.

Groups whose membership is distinguished by common cultural characteristics include the First Nations organizations discussed in Paul Tennant's chapter, and associations representing Canadians of francophone, Chinese, Japanese, East Indian, and a variety of other racial and ethnic backgrounds.

Most of these organizations are represented by their own members or staff travelling to Victoria, or interacting with government in Vancouver or another location. Some use their lawyers as lobbyists. An increasing number of organizations, such as the School Trustees Association and the Union of BC Municipalities, employ staff with a background in government relations, one of the traditional sources of recruitment being the offices of provincial cabinet ministers or participants in the legislative internship program. Some BC companies have added to their staff 'public affairs' officers specifically charged with managing the firm's relationship with government.

Given the physical isolation of the provincial capital on Vancouver Island, it is not surprising that most of BC's pressure groups have chosen to make their headquarters closer to Vancouver, the province's commercial centre. This has created the opportunity for a modest-sized industry serving the interests of a variety of organizations by providing professional 'public affairs' or 'government relations' services. The first such business was established in Victoria in 1975, and there are now a half-dozen such firms offering their services to a variety of clients.

Tactics and Strategies

As mentioned earlier, this province's political institutions are not very user-friendly for groups that feel the need to influence the direction or actions of government. They almost seem to assume that our politicians, by virtue of getting and staying elected, somehow acquire the wisdom necessary to make informed public decisions. Our system does not contain any political or administrative institutions that provide outside interests with regular or systematic means to come before the provincial decisionmakers to state their case. There has been very little use of legislative committees or similar methods of public consultation. In BC, when the legislature has gone into committee to discuss the details of legislation or ministerial spending estimates, this usually has meant relaxing the rules so that the MLAs can discuss issues more easily and senior public servants can support the minister, but not admitting participation by 'strangers,' as they are referred to in the legislature's rules.

The occasional royal commission or other public inquiry has been the most common type of formal public consultation, although the Commission on Resources and the Environment, established by the NDP government in 1992 under former ombudsman Stephen Owen, attempted to create a continuing process by which a variety of interest groups could participate in the development of resource management proposals for controversial or environmentally sensitive parts of the province. Most of the time, however, groups have had to force themselves into the political and administrative process, often attempting to influence the course of events only after the key decisions have been made and announced.

Some representative examples give an idea of the dynamics of the relationship between private interests and government in BC.

Mass Rallies on the Legislative Lawns
The most conspicuous, although not necessarily the most successful, examples of pressure group efforts to influence the public policy process have been periodic mass rallies at the legislature. Examples are the 1974 rally against Bill 31 (the Mineral Royalties Act), the 1976 Women's Rally for Action, the demonstration by Operation Solidarity against restraint efforts by the Social Credit government of Bill Bennett in 1983, and the 1994 protests for and against the NDP government's forest policy. In each case, the group or coalition brought thousands of people to the lawns in front of the parliament buildings in Victoria in an effort to focus media and public attention on some issue.

In most cases the rallies were failures in the sense that they didn't prompt an immediate change in public policy. Indeed, in the case of the mining rally, 5,000 protesters arrived in front of the legislature the day after the bill had been given final approval. However, while the rally may not have had an immediate effect on the legislative process, it was a major contributor to growing sentiment against the NDP government of Dave Barrett. In a very direct sense it contributed to the government's defeat in 1975 and its replacement by a Social Credit administration that subsequently repealed the legislation. Similar comments can be made about each of the above examples. While they did not result in immediate legislative or executive action, they played a significant role in mobilizing public opinion.

Government Financial Support of Independent Schools

Another example of a major lobbying effort in BC was the lengthy struggle by the Federation of Independent Schools Associations (FISA) to secure government financial support for private schools. In this case, faced with a situation in which all of the province's political parties were opposed to the policy in question, FISA embarked on a program of trying to change party rather than government policy. Its members ensured that policy resolutions on the subject began to appear on the agendas of every party convention, and well-briefed spokespersons were available to plead the FISA case at appropriate moments.

Over a five-year period from 1970 to 1975, FISA managed to ensure that each of the province's active political parties – Social Credit, NDP, Liberal, and Conservative – adopted as policy some version of support for state aid to independent schools. By the time Social Credit returned to office after the 1975 election, the new education minister (a former Liberal) was successful in recommending to his caucus colleagues the introduction of such legislation. The bill ultimately passed unanimously through the legislature, although with the helpful absence of a number of NDP MLAs who disagreed with their own party's policy of benign support, but were not prepared to foment an open breach of party solidarity on the floor of the legislature.

Empty Bottles and Cans

An example of another sort comes from more recent efforts to secure changes in the provincial policy related to the management of empty beverage containers. This issue came to the public agenda in response to efforts by the soft drink industry to persuade government to remove the deposit-refund requirement from pop containers in exchange for industry support of part of the capital costs of setting up a 'blue box' household collection system.

This example demonstrates vividly the complexity of pressure group interaction. When putting forward their proposal, the soft drink producers made the tactical error of including a request that the deposit requirement also be removed from beer cans. Such a step would have had the practical effect of diverting a substantial volume of valuable aluminum into blue boxes. While this was beneficial from the perspective of the proponents, it also meant the permanent diversion of about $3 million a year in scrap revenue from the beer industry to the new collection system.

The cries of outrage from the brewers prompted the minister of environment to form a stakeholder committee representing all the major interest groups involved in this issue. The government charged the committee with trying to find a consensus position. This effort continued for many months, with the discussion eventually outlasting the government. Represented on the committee were producers of all the major beverage streams (beer, wine, spirits, pop, juice, and bottled water), representatives of major grocery retailers who did not want empty containers coming back to their stores, and environmental or other public interest groups such as the Recycling Council of BC, the Environmentally Sound Packaging Coalition, and the Consumers Association.

The new NDP government led by Mike Harcourt came to office just as the stakeholder process delivered up a consultant's report outlining in considerable detail the costs and implications of a comprehensive deposit-based system. The arrival of the new government meant some changes in the players involved in the stakeholder process. Now sitting at the table were both government and private sector unions that had not previously been present, as well as some additional environmental groups – most conspicuously, Greenpeace. This changed the dynamics, with the unions forming an alliance with the environmentalists and arguing that an expanded deposit system ought to be implemented by means of government-run depots employing unionized workers.

The result was a stalemate, with the proponents of expanded deposits squaring off against those who wanted what they saw as a less costly source collection or blue box system. Faced with this situation, the new government, reflecting its basic commitment to consensus decision-making, appointed a senior public servant to meet with the parties and try to work out a system acceptable to all. This process went on for several months but eventually failed.

The process then reverted to separate and competing representations by different players:

- The soft drink industry and its grocery chain allies continued active lobbying of public servants and politicians in favour of the blue box source collection proposal, but also formed a new corporation to implement a deposit-based depot collection system for soft drink containers and thereby provide an alternative to return-to-retail.
- The beer industry pursued separate efforts to preserve its own return-to-retail deposit system and keep it separate from other collection systems.
- The environmental groups invited the minister of environment to their annual meeting and elicited from him a commitment to deliver expanded deposits. The minister had to leave office for unrelated reasons before this promise could be implemented.
- Cabinet made several efforts to move toward expanded deposits but was foiled each time by intervention from the Premier's Office.
- A resolution on expanded deposits appeared on the agenda of the NDP's annual convention in 1995 and was passed.

As the NDP government moved toward the end of its initial mandate, there seemed every chance that the competition between various groups would continue to make it impossible for the province's politicians to develop a widely acceptable policy.

Wine in Grocery Stores

Another interesting case study involves efforts in the early 1980s to persuade the Social Credit government to allow the sale of BC-produced wine in grocery stores. The initiative in this case came from a major supermarket chain that had experience in the United States of the benefits of retailers being allowed to sell wine in grocery stores. With the help of government relations consultants, it put together a coalition of economic interests that would benefit from the change.

The group's first step was to commission the consulting firm of Price Waterhouse to study the results of grocery store sales in other jurisdictions, and prepare a report designed to allay concerns that increased availability would lead to increased consumption. At the same time, a simple questionnaire was distributed to customers in grocery stores across the province. The response to the question 'Would you like to be able to buy wine when you purchase groceries in this store?' was overwhelming. Over 80 percent of some 80,000 respondents said yes, although a substantial portion complicated their answer by adding that they also wanted to be able to purchase beer.

While the presentation of this information to government prompted some indications of political support, it also led to accusations that the sample was biased and unrepresentative since the questionnaire had been presented to all customers, who then decided whether or not to return it. This forced the group to commission a properly structured opinion poll, which confirmed the results of the first questionnaire but also showed that opposition was strongest, by unfortunate coincidence for the proponents of change, in areas of the province then represented by Social Credit politicians, especially the lower Fraser Valley and the Okanagan.

By this time, the questionnaire and other aspects of the campaign had started to provoke some negative reaction, especially from the BC Government Employees' Union, which saw the proposal as threatening the jobs of people working in liquor stores, and from groups opposed to any relaxation of the rules controlling liquor sales.

In the end, despite resolutions in favour of the sale of both wine and beer in grocery stores being passed at the Social Credit Party's annual convention, the government made clear to the proponents that they were wasting their time and money. The reason was a straightforward political equation. The politicians had decided that while there was general support for change, the proponents didn't feel so strongly about the subject that their vote would be determined by the outcome. On the other hand, the opponents would be likely to desert the Social Credit government if the rules were changed. Since the opponents were concentrated in ridings held by the government, the political risk simply was too great.

Issues for the Future

In concluding this review of pressure group politics in BC, it seems useful to raise some questions for further thought and consideration.

Is There Adequate Transparency to This Aspect of the Political Process?

In an essay a number of years ago on pressure group activity at the federal level, a member of the staff of the Research Branch of the Library of Parliament reached the conclusion that there was a need for greater transparency in the relationship between pressure groups and government decisionmakers. 'The importance of pressure groups,' he said, 'undoubtedly warrants the establishment of means to identify them.'[15] It seems obvious that this author was reflecting prevailing sentiment in Ottawa since it wasn't long before Parliament had passed a law requiring the registration of lobbyists.

There is no similar registration requirement in BC, although a private member's bill on the subject was introduced during the 1994 legislative session but died on the Order Paper. In practical terms, registration may seem less necessary to the politicians and bureaucrats in Victoria since the smaller size of the community means that most of the regular lobbyists are well known.

On the other hand, as has been the case at the federal level, agreement with the principle of registration leaves a number of questions to be answered. For example, it raises problems of definition. Who qualifies as a lobbyist? And is simple registration of names, clients, and areas of interest enough, or should the public also be entitled to know the names of all persons lobbied and the fees received by the lobbyists?

In fact, if the object of the exercise is to introduce transparency to the decision-making process, it might be better to reverse the equation. Instead of asking lobbyists to register and even to disclose their specific contacts with public officials, it might be better to require public officials to disclose the sources of the information upon which they base their decisions. Weekly or monthly disclosure of a log of contacts between decisionmakers and the public would shed a great deal more light on the flow of political influence than does the registration of lobbyists. Reducing the level of secrecy in the BC political system would be an effective way of ensuring greater transparency.

Equality of Access

A more fundamental question is whether the present system discriminates against some pressure groups at the expense of others. In the past, concerns in this area have led to such things as the providing of 'adversary funding' during some public enquiries and royal commissions. Groups have been given public money so that they can more effectively represent their interests before a tribunal charged with advising the government on a major public policy issue.

Use of a technique such as adversary funding leads to the question of whether or not more fundamental change is necessary. Has the time come to make our political system more user-friendly. Should we be providing public subsidies to some groups on special occasions, or should we be changing our political institutions and process to make certain that interested parties have an opportunity to make their views known before public officials make important decisions?

As mentioned earlier, cabinet government, with its emphasis on political solidarity, has imbued our political system with a high level of secrecy. In BC, most decision-making takes place behind the closed doors of government offices, with little formal opportunity for representatives of various interests to make their views known. People have to force themselves into the system, giving an obvious advantage to those able to afford professional help with their lobbying.

Recognition of the plural nature of our society, and of the legitimate right of interests to make their views known before government decisions are made, requires reform of both the institutions and process of government to ensure that representatives of various public and private interests have a formal opportunity to put forward their views as policy is being developed. Similarly, at the stage where legislation has been introduced, the process could easily be changed to provide a point where the public has an automatic opportunity to come before the legislators with its views – instead of being forced to carry placards on the lawns in front of the legislature.

The Implications of Partisanship

As mentioned earlier, groups whose partisan affiliation with the party in power grants them preferred access to decisionmakers can face difficult problems when their political friends are consigned to the opposition benches. Given the risk of being on the losing side in an election campaign, and because they realize that the personal views of their membership inevitably cut across partisan lines, most groups try to maintain some measure of neutrality in electoral terms, feeling that this gives them the best opportunity to work with the party that wins. Indeed, many have come to use the period of an election campaign as the prime moment to lobby all contestants for political office by circulating questionnaires to all candidates, while they are in a 'promising' mood.

Disparities in Resources

It is obvious that there are great differences between the resources available to pressure groups, although it is less clear how these differences affect their influence over government. Some attempts have been made to codify these differences, and to suggest that they may be part of a continuum.[16] In practice, however, we lack sufficient comparative data to determine with certainty the relative value of various group assets such as money, membership size, staff resources, and the nature of the cause. In part, this lack of data makes it difficult to reach firm conclusions about the need to level the playing field between various groups. For example, substantial improvements in the accessibility of government might do much more to ensure that contending points of view get a fair hearing than will efforts to try to provide direct assets through such things as adversary funding.

The Impact of Being 'Official'

A related issue prompts discussion of the fact that some groups, as already mentioned, have official or quasi-official status because they have been created by statute. Is this status an undue advantage over competing organizations? Is it a disadvantage in that they must tailor their activities in such a way as to avoid losing this status or having it watered down in some way?

Conclusion

Pressure groups have become an important factor in BC's political environment, despite the fact that the province's formal political institutions do not take much account of their existence. Against this background, it is not surprising that pressure group activity raises a number of important questions for which there are no simple answers.

There have been tentative steps toward institutional change aimed both at meeting demands from a variety of groups that their interests be better reflected in the making of government policy, and at ensuring public scrutiny of the type of pressure they bring to bear. Unfortunately, however, our political system contains substantial impediments to change that might better reflect the increasingly plural nature of BC society.

13
Public Finance and Fiscal Policy in British Columbia

Brian Scarfe

The BC Economic Environment

Although considerable strides have been made toward the diversification of the BC economy over the past decade, it is nevertheless the case that BC remains heavily dependent upon the income-generating capability of its resource-based export industries, and especially the forest products industry. In consequence, the cyclical nature of world market prices for resource-based commodities has a considerable impact upon the performance of BC's economy. The capital intensity of BC's resource-based industries also makes its economy vulnerable to world interest rate movements. International trade disputes, such as the long-standing one involving softwood lumber exports from Canada to the United States, can also threaten BC's prosperity. Indeed, even trade conflicts between third parties, such as the United States and Japan, have potentially significant spill-over effects on Canada's Pacific Rim province.

Despite its vast geography and abundant natural resources, from an economic perspective BC is but one small open island in the total world archipelago, and the only sensible perspective to take on its economic fortunes is a global one. As a small open economy, BC is a price-taker for most of its commodity exports, and for virtually all of the goods and services it imports. It is therefore vulnerable to movements in these prices, and especially to fluctuations in its export prices relative to its import prices, or its terms of trade. An improvement in the terms of trade can often trigger an investment boom, while the cost-price squeeze that results from a collapse in the terms of trade is the primary reason for economic recessions. Market-determined movements in the US-Canadian dollar exchange rate and other Pacific Rim exchange rates can have important effects on the competitiveness of BC's export industries and on the employment prospects they provide, while the lack of an independent monetary and exchange rate policy reduces the scope for dampening the employment and income consequences of instabilities in world commodity markets.

The BC economy last experienced a prolonged recession from 1982 to 1986. During this period, a fall in world market prices for BC's major commodity exports was compounded by high real interest rates and an appreciation of the Canadian dollar in relation to the currencies of BC's offshore trade competitors. This compounding feature reflected the temporary strength of the US dollar in relation to European, Japanese, and other third-country currencies, which itself was driven by high real interest rates in the US. Thus, although the Canadian dollar depreciated in relation to the US dollar, it strengthened with respect to these other currencies. In consequence, the BC economy remained mired in recession until the mid-1980s when both the US and the Canadian dollars began to depreciate relative to offshore currencies. By contrast, as the US economy recovered from the 1982 recession, it quite quickly pulled the manufacturing heartland of central Canada along with it.

The situation in the early 1990s was quite different. Indeed, the prolonged central Canadian recession of 1990 to 1992, which was exacerbated by the tight monetary policy orchestrated by the Bank of Canada, was hardly felt in BC. The main reasons for this were the relative buoyancy of world market prices for BC exports and the substantial inflow of foreign direct investment from Pacific Rim countries that was partly triggered by the relatively low international values of both the US and the Canadian dollar in terms of offshore third-party currencies. The migration of people to BC from other, less prosperous parts of Canada has also buoyed the BC economy. Thus, the course of each of the last two Canadian recessions has had very different impacts on the separate regions of the economy, depending upon relative price movements and exchange market developments.

During the period from July 1994 to July 1995, the momentum of economic activity in BC has been particularly strong. This recent momentum has provided the provincial government with expanded taxation revenues, including higher natural resource rents largely generated by the forest sector, so that a balanced provincial budget is projected for the 1995-6 fiscal year. There are now, however, clear signs that the pace of economic expansion is cooling off. Resource export prices seem to be peaking, while real interest rates remain high by historical standards. Obviously, the economic environment has important implications for fiscal policy in BC, as will be further demonstrated later in this chapter.

The Federal-Provincial Context

Canada has a federal system of government. In consequence, the federal and provincial fiscal systems are intertwined. Transfers from the federal level to the provinces and various cost-sharing programs create interdependencies on the expenditure side, while the existence of shared tax bases and various tax-harmonization initiatives create interdependencies on the revenue side. Deficit control measures and debt management strategies for the two main levels of government are also interconnected in various ways.

Federal fiscal transfers to the provinces have essentially been organized around three program areas: equalization payments to the seven 'have not' provinces (all provinces except Alberta, BC, and Ontario), Established Program Financing (EPF) transfers for health care and postsecondary education, and Canada Assistance Plan (CAP) transfers, which support the social welfare system. Although few changes in the rules governing these intergovernmental transfers are forecast for 1995-6, significant changes are planned for 1996-7. The resulting reductions in transfers will have sizeable impacts on provincial government revenues.

While the equalization system will remain intact, the cost-shared transfers under CAP and the block-funded transfers under EPF will be transformed into a single block-funded transfer system, the Canadian Health and Social Transfer. Total transfers will shrink by $2.8 billion in 1996-7 and by an additional $1.8 billion in 1997-8. Since a combination of tax-point transfers and residual cash transfers will continue to be involved, these reductions in entitlements will inevitably lead to dramatic reductions in the cash transfer component since the tax point component will grow with the overall economy of each province.

Provincial governments are clearly faced with further off-loading of expenditure responsibilities from the federal government, especially from 1996-7 onwards. Indeed, the problem of off-loading has serious implications for the future of fiscal federalism. For example, the impact on the BC provincial budget is illuminating. It is estimated that the combined transfers from the federal government for EPF and CAP now finance only one-third of BC's expenditures for health care, postsecondary education, and social assistance; only a decade ago, the federal share was one-half. Indeed, the cumulative impact of federal off-loading over the past decade appears to have reduced federal transfers to BC by about $2.2 billion in the most recent fiscal years. The corresponding figure for all provinces combined is about $15.6 billion.

In BC's case, roughly one-half of this cumulative reduction relates to a sequence of rule changes that has decreased EPF transfers to the provinces. The other half results from the 'capping' of the supposedly cost-shared CAP transfers for the three 'have' provinces: Alberta, BC, and Ontario. In 1990 the federal government imposed a 5 percent cap on program growth for these three provinces – that is, the provinces that also do not qualify for equalization payments.

The projected impact of the introduction of the Canadian Health and Social Transfer in 1996-7 would further reduce fiscal transfers to BC by an additional one-third of a billion dollars, with the corresponding figure for

Ontario being approximately one billion dollars. As indicated earlier, further reductions are planned for 1997-8, but the distribution of these cutbacks across the provinces will depend upon the nature of the new allocative formula that the federal government intends to negotiate with the provinces for the Canadian Health and Social Transfer. It is, of course, highly likely that entitlements will be based upon provincial population, and will be equalized on a per capita basis. Offsetting variations in tax-point versus cash transfers are therefore likely to be observed across the provinces, as has been the case with the EPF arrangements. How the various provinces will deal with the resulting revenue shortfall remains to be seen.

There is no question that federal-provincial fiscal arrangements require renegotiation. Provincial expenditure responsibilities for health care, postsecondary education, and social assistance seem to suggest that further decentralization of revenue sources is desirable. Unfortunately, the federal fiscal crisis provides no revenue sources to decentralize. Nevertheless, given the significant differences in fiscal capacities among the provinces, the federal government is at least maintaining the constitutionally enshrined equalization program. BC, of course, is not a recipient of transfers from this program.

Although the redistributive goals of a sharing and caring society might seem to require the maintenance of a strong federal presence in the social programs area, the most recent federal budget simply tries to put the best face on the further devolution of social program responsibilities to the provinces. Whether or not support for national standards in the provision of social programs can be maintained under these circumstances remains questionable. Nevertheless, the federal government insists that the fundamental principles underlying the Canada Health Act and the provision of social assistance without the imposition of provincial residency requirements will both be continued under the auspices of the Canadian Health and Social Transfer. How the federal government intends to maintain its leverage in this area as transfers are reduced remains to be seen.

The federal and provincial governments share a number of important tax bases. Most important among these are the personal income tax, corporate income tax, and sales taxes that are applied at the retail level. The personal income tax system is essentially a 'tax on tax' system in which provincial income taxes payable are set as a percentage of federal income taxes payable. Various surcharges and flat tax arrangements have, over time, led to the complication of this system, partly to accommodate different preferences about the progressivity of the personal income tax system that exist across provincial jurisdictions. This has led to some consideration of changing the system to a 'tax on base' arrangement. Nevertheless, there are important grounds for maintaining a common base to the personal income tax system regardless of the taxpayer's province of residence. These grounds include allocative efficiency, tax collection efficiency, and inter-personal equity. All provinces except Quebec use Revenue Canada as the collection agency for the personal income tax.

The corporate income tax system is a 'tax on base' system in which the common base to which both the federal and provincial corporate income tax rates apply is essentially defined by federal tax legislation. Quebec, Ontario, and Alberta, however, administer their own tax collection systems, while the other seven provinces use Revenue Canada as their corporate income tax collection agency. Since larger corporations have some ability to change the jurisdictional location in which their taxable income appears, there are strong pressures for tax harmonization in this area. These pressures are also international in scope.

The tax base for the federal Goods and Services Tax (GST) is essentially 'value added.' Firms that collect the GST on their final sales also receive rebates on their purchases made from other supplier firms. The base for the GST therefore differs from, but overlaps with, the provincial sales taxes (PSTs) that are applied at the retail level, without offsetting rebates, in all provinces except Alberta. Moreover, both the goods and services covered and the rate of PST applied vary across provincial jurisdictions, making for a complicated web of sales taxes across the country that would be difficult to harmonize. Interestingly, the closest degree of harmonization is between Quebec's PST and the federal GST. Nevertheless, it is possible that further attempts will be made to harmonize the bases of PSTs with that of the GST as time goes on. In BC the PST rate of 7% is additive to the GST rate of 7% for many basic goods. However, many services sold at the retail level are exempt from the PST, but not the GST, while most basic foodstuffs that are sold for home consumption are exempt from both.

Since both the revenue and the expenditure sides of the provincial and federal financial accounts are intertwined, it should come as no surprise that overall budget balances, and attempts to control them, are also intertwined. In recent years, all major governments in Canada have struggled with the problem of controlling substantial fiscal deficits and growing debt burdens. This is especially true at the federal level, where debt service charges now account for one-quarter of Ottawa's expenditures and one-third of its tax revenues. The burden of interest payments on public debt has undermined the ability of governments to continue providing the level of public services to which Canadians have become accustomed. Widespread tax resistance has been associated with the increase in the tax-price of government services that inevitably results from a rising wedge of debt-service payments.

In principle, a government's deficit can be separated into two components. The cyclical component is the portion of the deficit that would disappear if the economy were operating at a full capacity utilization or full employment level, because, at such a level, tax receipts would be larger (given existing tax rates) and welfare transfers to individuals would be smaller (particularly at the federal level, including unemployment insurance benefits). This component is supportive of an economy in recession. The structural component of the deficit is the portion that would still exist at full employment. There has been a long-standing need at the federal level for this structural component to move toward zero. At the present time, the underlying federal fiscal deficit of $35 billion could be divided approximately into a cyclical component of 40% and a structural component of 60%, depending upon the estimate made of the degree of slack in the economy.

The fundamental trade-off for fiscal policy is to balance the objectives of fiscal prudence and economic stabilization. Fiscal prudence requires the combined deficits of the federal and provincial governments to be smaller than the current normal growth in gross domestic product (GDP) times the existing ratio of aggregate government sector debt to GDP (a number that is approximately unity at present, with the federal component being about 0.735 and the overall provincial component being about 0.265), thus ensuring that the total government sector debt to GDP ratio begins to fall, rather than increasing further. Technically, if the interest rate on government borrowing exceeds the economy's normal rate of growth, as it ordinarily does, fiscal prudence requires regular primary or operating surpluses of sufficient size to be generated. Several provinces, including BC, now have annual deficits that fall significantly short of their debt service charges and are therefore generating operating surpluses, although this is not yet true of Ontario and Quebec. The federal government will begin to generate substantial operating surpluses with the 1995-6 budget. Given Canada's historically high level of net foreign indebtedness (at 45% of GDP), capital market perceptions about the prudence of our fiscal policies are particularly important.

Economic stabilization requires cyclical deficits to support the economy in times of substantial unemployment, with low or negative economic growth. Years of living with structural deficits at the federal level, or deficits that do not disappear even in buoyant economic times, have generated a debt-service burden that leaves virtually no fiscal room to manoeuvre. From a stabilization perspective, this is an unpleasant fiscal arithmetic. Moreover, the federal government must consider the implications that changes in federal-provincial transfers, and particularly off-loading, may have on the ability of provincial governments to move their budgets toward balance. Similarly, Ottawa must be able to assess the ramifications that changes in provincial fiscal policies, at least for large provinces, may have on the overall state of the Canadian economy. Finally, Ottawa must decide what the appropriate mix of fiscal and monetary policies should be, given the state of the economic environment.

Other fundamental trade-offs occur in the attempt to satisfy three basic fiscal policy objectives: that the taxation and expenditure system be efficient, equitable, and reasonably simple to deal with from a transactions and reporting cost perspective. Generally speaking, equity and efficiency would both currently be served by coupling the broadening of tax bases with offsetting revenue-neutral reductions in the corresponding tax rates. High tax rates may adversely affect the efficiency with which resources are allocated across the production sectors of the economy, while tax bases that are unnecessarily narrow, or tax credits and subsidies that only advantage a privileged few, may not be perceived to be equitable.

Provincial Responsibility for Expenditure Programs

Since Canada has a federal system of government, residents in each of the provinces are affected not only by federal government policies but also by the policies of their respective provincial governments. Provincial governments, however, do not have quite the policy scope open to the federal government. The federal government is able to apply fiscal, monetary, and international commercial policy initiatives to influence the pace and direction of Canadian economic activity. Although federal fiscal policy can be applied regionally, federal monetary and commercial policies are common to all Canadian provinces, though they may have differential impacts across the provinces. It is impossible to provide provincially tailored exchange rates or interest rates. The general universality of monetary policy implies that it is beyond the control of the individual provincial governments. For this reason, from a macroeconomic perspective, provincial policy instruments are essentially limited to fiscal policy instruments such as taxation, subsidization, and expenditure policies.

The ability of a province to engage in fiscal policy initiatives of a stabilization nature depends upon the size of the province and its borrowing capacity, and thus upon its reputation for fiscal prudence. The borrowing capacity of BC cannot really be considered to be a major barrier, at least in the short term, to the application of fiscal policy to stabilization objectives, since BC has the smallest provincial debt to provincial GDP ratio and the highest credit rating among Canada's provinces. However, at current levels of market interest rates, all new borrowing is expensive, so there are strong grounds for maintaining a prudent fiscal stance.

Provincial fiscal policy is subject to larger leakages than federal fiscal policy. In the federal context, fiscal policy has to contend with expenditure leakages arising from the importation of foreign goods. In a provincial context, fiscal policy must also be concerned with interprovincial trade. As

C.L. Barber notes, 'While an increase in provincial spending or a reduction in provincial taxes will lead to some increase in the demand for goods and services produced within the province, a substantial proportion of the increased expenditure may be for goods produced in other provinces or outside Canada entirely.'[1]

A further consideration in the application of provincial fiscal policies to stabilization objectives concerns their potential effectiveness. 'In evaluating the ability of the provinces to pursue an independent counter-cyclical policy much depends on the severity of the cyclical fluctuations which are anticipated.'[2] Given that provincial governments are more constrained by limitations to their borrowing capacity than the federal government, and that provincial fiscal policy is subject to larger leakages, it is not surprising that provincial governments may only be able to respond to moderate cyclical fluctuations. Any discussion of the effectiveness of provincial fiscal policy from a stabilization perspective must recognize this fact.

Table 13.1

Expenditure by function, consolidated revenue fund, 1976-7 to 1995-6 (selected years, $ millions)

	Actual 1976-7	Actual 1981-2	Actual 1986-7	Actual 1991-2	Budget estimate 1995-6
Health	942.8	1,973.5	2,860.6	5,616.7	6,706.7
Social services	507.7	1,087.7	1,614.3	1,993.7	2,879.7
Education	871.7	1,547.6	1,913.9	4,521.5	5,597.7
Protection of persons & property	180.5	356.9	453.3	814.6	1,023.7
Transportation	410.8	755.5	975.4	1,262.1	890.6
Natural resources & economic development	287.0	610.2	614.9	1,404.3	1,252.7
Other expenditures	252.0	591.4	777.1	612.7	623.1
General government	89.5	147.8	195.6	286.0	232.8
Debt servicing	15.6	16.9	393.6	642.8	979.0
Total expenditure	**3,557.6**	**7,087.5**	**9,798.7**	**17,154.4**	**20,186.0**
Gov't expenditure deflator	48.9	76.9	100.0	121.1	125.8
Constant 1986 dollar expenditure	7,275.3	9,216.5	9,798.7	14,165.5	16,046.1
Growth rate		4.8%	1.2%	7.6%	3.1%

Sources: James Cutt, 'British Columbia: Provincial Public Finances,' chap. 10 in *Volume I Provincial Public Finances: Provincial Surveys*, ed. Melville McMillan (Toronto: Canadian Tax Foundation 1991), 295-6; British Columbia, *Budget '95 Reports* (Victoria: Ministry of Finance and Corporate Relations, March 1995), 89; and Bank of Canada Review, Summer 1995, Statistical Table H3, p. S87, for the Government Expenditure Deflator.

Canada's provincial governments have major expenditure responsibilities in the areas of health care, education, and the provision of social services. In BC's case, fully 75 percent of estimated budgetary expenditure for 1995-6 is allocated to these three areas. Much of this expenditure occurs through third-party institutions and agencies in the MUSH sector (municipalities, universities, schools, and hospitals).

Table 13.1 provides the breakdown by function of provincial expenditures in BC for particular years, selected at five-year intervals. These intervals correspond roughly to periods of separate BC governments. The periods 1976-7 to 1981-2 and 1981-2 to 1986-7 correspond to years in which the Social Credit Party under Bill Bennett was in control of the BC legislature. The period 1986-7 to 1991-2 corresponds roughly to Bill Vander Zalm's Social Credit government, while the most recent period corresponds roughly to the New Democratic Party government of Mike Harcourt. In real terms, overall government expenditure grew fastest in the Vander Zalm years and slowest in the second five years of the Bennett regime.

Table 13.2 looks at expenditure by function as a proportion of total expenditure (after adjustments described in the footnote to the table). From this table, it is evident that the provision of health services has absorbed an increasing share of public expenditure dollars over the past two decades.

Table 13.2

Expenditure shares in selected fiscal years (%)*

	1976-7	1981-2	1986-7	1991-2	1995-6
Health	26.6	27.9	30.4	36.1	37.3
Social services	14.3	15.4	17.2	12.8	16.0
Education	24.6	21.9	20.3	22.9	24.2
Protection of persons & property	5.1	5.0	4.8	5.2	5.7
Transportation	11.6	10.7	10.4	8.1	5.0
Natural resources & economic development	8.1	8.6	6.5	9.0	7.0
Other expenditures	7.1	8.4	8.3	3.9	3.5
General government	2.5	2.1	2.1	1.8	1.3
Total	100.0	100.0	100.0	100.0	100.0

* To reduce the distortions in these numbers, expenditures on debt service have been eliminated from the calculations in all years. These expenditures have risen rapidly over time, from less than 1% of unadjusted total expenditures in 1976-7 to almost 5% in 1995-6. In addition, education expenditures in 1991-2 and 1995-6 have been reduced by the property tax receipts of the provincial government for school purposes (as given in Table 13.3). However, the 75% figure given in the text for the combined budgetary allocation of overall expenditures to health, social services, and education in 1995-6 is based upon the unadjusted numbers given in Table 13.1.

Table 13.3

Revenue by source, consolidated revenue fund, 1976-7 to 1995-6 (selected years, $ millions)

	Actual 1976-7	Actual 1981-2	Actual 1986-7	Actual 1991-2	estimate 1995-6
Taxation					
Personal income	810.6	1,848.1	2,248.1	4,013.1	5,040.0
Corporate income	236.9	580.0	280.6	577.4	1,325.0
Social service (retail sales)	663.0	1,129.5	1,540.8	1,990.5	3,034.0
Fuels	179.7	371.4	373.4	538.8	678.0
Property[a]	–	–	–	965.9	1,250.0
Other[b]	156.5	287.7	418.6	908.7	1,426.0
Total taxation revenue	**2,046.7**	**4,216.7**	**4,861.5**	**8,994.4**	**12,753.0**
Natural resources					
Petroleum, natural gas	255.1	356.9	170.3	208.7	311.0
Minerals	60.7	62.4	55.6	41.8	79.0
Forests	81.9	106.7	185.3	583.5	1,522.0
Water and other	18.0	71.6	246.4	267.2	539.0[c]
Total natural resource revenue	**415.7**	**597.6**	**657.6**	**1,101.2**	**2,451.0**
Other revenue[d]	355.2	680.3	589.5	1,626.0	1,783.0
Contributions from government enterprises[e]	162.6	326.5	447.6	700.5	970.0
Contributions from federal government[f]	671.7	1,082.3	1,993.3	2,197.9	2,343.0
TOTAL REVENUE	**3,651.9**	**6,903.4**	**8,549.5**	**14,620.0**	**20,300.0**
Gov't expenditure deflator	48.9	76.9	100.0	121.1	125.8
Constant 1986 dollar revenue	7,468.1	8,977.1	8,549.5	12,072.7	16,136.7
Growth rate		3.7%	-1.0%	7.1%	7.5%

[a] Property tax revenues include residential and business property taxes raised for school purposes only, plus all rural area property taxes. At the beginning of the decade, the provincial government took over full financial responsibility for K-12 education from urban and municipal governments, as well as the property taxes allocated for school purposes.

[b] Other taxation revenue includes that from the taxation of tobacco, property transfers, corporation capital, insurance premiums, hotel rooms, and horse racing.

[c] Water and other revenues include, in 1995-6, a sum of $250 million associated with the downstream benefits from the Columbia River Treaty arrangements with Bonnyville Power Authority, which is unlikely to be received within the fiscal year.

[continued on next page]

Table 13.3 [continued]

ᵈ Other revenue includes medical services plan premiums, motor vehicle licences and permits, other fees and licences, investment earnings, BC endowment fund earnings, and miscellaneous revenue.
ᵉ Contributions from government enterprises include revenues from the Liquor Distribution Branch, BC Hydro and Power Authority, the BC Lottery Corporation, and other enterprises.
ᶠ Contributions from the federal government include EPF transfers for both health care and postsecondary education, CAP transfers, and other transfers.
Sources: James Cutt, 'British Columbia: Provincial Public Finances,' chap. 10 in *Volume I Provincial Public Finances: Provincial Surveys*, ed. Melville McMillan (Toronto: Canadian Tax Foundation 1991), 297-8; British Columbia, *Budget '95 Reports* (Victoria: Ministry of Finance and Corporate Relations, March 1995), 87-8; and Bank of Canada Review, Summer 1995, Statistical Table H3, p. S87, for the Government Expenditure Deflator.

Budgetary data for other provinces would demonstrate a similar trend. Transportation, on the other hand, has absorbed a decreasing share of public expenditure dollars. However, since the NDP government came to power, there has been an increasing tendency to finance transportation expenditures (including expenditures on highway and ferry construction) outside the regular operating budget, shifting them to provincial agencies such as the BC 21 Fund and thereby biasing downwards the most recent expenditure estimates for this area. Off-budget expenditure shifting and other issues related to the debt-financing of infrastructure expenditures will be addressed in a later section of this chapter.

Education expenditures have fluctuated at around 23 percent of adjusted overall expenditures, without any discernible trend. Expenditures financed from school property taxes have, however, been excluded from this figure to ensure consistency over time, as responsibility for school financing has shifted from municipal and urban governments to the provincial government. As a percentage of adjusted total spending, social service expenditures seem to have fluctuated inversely with the state of the economy. Debt service payments have been on a strongly rising trend and now account for almost 5 percent of unadjusted total expenditure, a point that we revisit later in this chapter.

Tax Policy and Revenue Generation
Table 13.3 provides details on BC government revenues by source for selected years, again chosen at five-year intervals. In real terms, revenues have grown considerably more strongly over the past decade than over the decade prior to that. In large part, this difference reflects the effects of changes in the overall pace of economic activity on the tax bases available to the provincial government. However, in recent years, tax rate hikes have led to a higher provincial ratio of government revenues to provincial gross domestic product. This ratio will be approximately 19.6 percent in the 1995-6 budget year. Revenue growth has resulted from tax increases

Table 13.4

Revenue shares in selected fiscal years (%)*

	1976-7	1981-2	1986-7	1991-2	1995-6
Taxation					
Personal income	22.2	26.8	26.3	29.4	26.5
Corporate income	6.5	8.4	3.3	4.2	7.0
Social service (retail sales)	18.2	16.4	18.0	14.6	15.9
Fuels	4.9	5.4	4.4	3.9	3.6
Other	4.3	4.2	4.9	6.7	7.5
Total taxation revenue	**56.0**	**61.1**	**56.9**	**58.8**	**60.4**
Natural resources					
Petroleum, natural gas	7.0	5.2	2.0	1.5	1.6
Minerals	1.7	0.9	0.7	0.3	0.4
Forests	2.2	1.5	2.2	4.3	8.0
Water and other	0.5	1.0	2.9	2.0	2.8
Total natural resources revenue	**11.4**	**8.7**	**7.7**	**8.1**	**12.9**
Other revenue	9.7	9.9	6.9	11.9	9.4
Contributions from government enterprises	4.5	4.7	5.2	5.1	5.1
Contributions from federal government	18.4	15.7	23.3	16.2	12.3
Total Revenue	**100.0**	**100.0**	**100.0**	**100.0**	**100.0**

* To reduce the distortions in these numbers, provincial property tax revenues
have been omitted from the share calculations in 1991-2 and 1995-6.

imposed in the early years of the Harcourt government, as well as from the buoyancy of the provincial economy.

Table 13.4 looks at the same revenue breakdown, but expressed as a percentage of overall provincial government revenues adjusted for the transfer of school property taxes to the provincial government at the beginning of the current decade. This table indicates that the share of personal income tax in total provincial revenues has fluctuated around 26 percent, that the share of corporate income taxes has been strongly pro-cyclical, and that the contribution of cash transfers from the federal government to overall provincial government revenues has declined significantly over the past decade, illustrating the off-loading phenomenon described earlier in this chapter.

The share of provincial government revenues attributable to natural resources has also fluctuated in a pro-cyclical manner. These revenues reflect the Crown's ownership of the natural resources within provincial boundaries. However, the petroleum and natural gas sector provided the lion's share of these revenues in the energy boom years of the late 1970s, whereas the forestry sector is providing a similar share of overall revenues today. The increases in stumpages and royalties imposed in the spring of 1994 and dedicated to financing Forest Renewal BC are not included in the 1995-6 estimates. These dedicated revenues are expected to provide about $400 million per annum to Forest Renewal BC over a five-year period.

The ability of the provincial government to raise these forest revenues is, of course, dependent upon the international market prices for forestry products, particularly softwood lumber. Since target stumpage rates are related to softwood lumber price indices, and not directly to pulp and paper prices, movements in pulp and paper prices only affect stumpage prices to the extent that they are correlated with softwood lumber prices. This correlation is by no means close, largely because cyclical fluctuations in pulp and paper markets normally do not have the same phasing as cyclical fluctuations in softwood lumber markets. However, cyclical movements in pulp and paper prices strongly influence corporate income tax receipts.

For the past decade, the softwood lumber industry has been an ongoing target for countervailing duty activity by the US government. In fact, the softwood lumber dispute has now entered its fourth phase. Canada (and BC) won the first battle within the US international trade tribunals in 1982-3, bought its way out of the second in 1986-7 by imposing a 15 percent export tax on softwood lumber shipments to the United States, which was later rolled into significant stumpage increases by provincial governments, especially in BC, and won the third under the dispute settlement mechanisms of the Free Trade Agreement in 1992-4. Unfortunately, a fourth countervail action could be precipitated by the US-based Coalition for Fair Lumber Imports, despite significant increases in stumpage and royalty charges in BC. Some adjustments to pricing policies for access to crown forest resources, and to the institutional arrangements under which crown timber is sold to forest product companies, could forestall another US countervail action. Alternatively, volumetric border controls could be imposed on shipments of softwood lumber from Canada to the US. Further remarks on natural resource revenues will be made in a later section of this chapter.

Deficits and Debt Management
Table 13.5 provides an overview of budget balances in BC from 1966-7 to the present. After many years of a 'pay as you go' budgeting philosophy, substantial deficits began to appear in BC in the recession years of 1982-6. The fiscal restraints imposed in the later Bennett years can be viewed as an attempt to get the budgetary situation under control. However, the budget did not move substantially toward balance until rapid economic growth

resumed in 1987. Indeed, budget surpluses were realized in 1988-9 and 1989-90. The big spending programs of the later Vander Zalm and early Harcourt years again pushed the budget significantly into deficit. Most recently, the operating budget has again been moving toward balance, partly as a result of a buoyant economy, but also because of the provincial government's debt management plan. Indeed, the main focus of the budget announced on 28 March 1995 was debt management.

As indicated in Table 13.6, the total debt of the provincial government is largely composed of three major categories of debt. The first of these is direct provincial government debt. This is the debt that arises cumulatively as the government experiences deficits on its regular budgetary operations. This debt increases whenever overall government expenditures on programs plus debt servicing charges exceed the direct tax and transfer revenues of government. Surpluses on regular budgetary operations would be required to reduce this debt. Clearly, this debt is taxpayer-supported.

The second category of debt includes that of fiscal agencies that invest in social infrastructure development, including hospitals, schools, highways, ferries, and transit systems, none of which is fully supported by direct revenue receipts from its own operations. The degree to which these infrastructure development expenditures are self-financing clearly varies

Table 13.5

Consolidated budget balances, 1966-7 to 1995-6 (selected years, $ millions)

	Revenues	Expenditures	Balance
1966-7	731.6	660.5	71.1
1971-2	1,480.2	1,396.7	83.5
1976-7	3,651.9	3,557.6	94.3
1981-2	6,903.4	7,087.5	(184.1)
1986-7	8,549.5	9,798.7	(1,249.2)
1987-8	10,087.4	10,135.4	(48.0)
1991-2	14,620.0	17,154.4	(2,534.4)
1992-3	16,243.0	17,935.7	(1,692.7)
1993-4	17,997.8	18,912.9	(915.1)
1994-5[a]	19,244.0	19,614.0	(370.0)
1995-6[b]	20,300.0	20,186.0	114.0

[a] 1994-5 figures are the revised forecast, as opposed to the actual accounting figures for earlier years.
[b] 1995-6 figures are budget estimates.
Sources: James Cutt, 'British Columbia: Provincial Public Finances,' chap. 10 in *Volume I Provincial Public Finances: Provincial Surveys,* ed. Melville McMillan (Toronto: Canadian Tax Foundation 1991), 300; British Columbia, *Budget '95 Reports* (Victoria: Ministry of Finance and Corporate Relations, March 1995), 87-9.

significantly between the BC Ferries Corporation and the public school system. Nevertheless, these investments are all to some degree taxpayer-supported. Unlike these taxpayer-supported agency debts, the commercial debt of crown corporations such as the BC Hydro and Power Authority is supported from the corporation's own operations. This third category of debt, while guaranteed by the provincial government, is not considered to be part of the taxpayer-supported debt.

It is important to consider the nature of the second category of debt – the fiscal agency debt – more closely. Essentially, one must ask whether or not it is legitimate to take major capital expenditures on items such as roads and hospitals out of the government's operating budget and charge them instead to agencies such as the BC 21 Fund. Although commercial crown corporations generate revenue streams that generally provide for the payment of debt interest plus the eventual retirement of outstanding debt, for the most part no such returns are directly available for social infrastructure investments. A plan that sets aside future tax revenues for debt servicing and eventual debt retirement is therefore required. In other words, it is

Table 13.6

Key net debt indicators, 1991-2 to 1995-6 (debt at year end, $ billions)

	1991-2	1992-3	1993-4	1994-5	1995-6
Taxpayer-supported	12.5	15.9	18.0	18.8	19.5
direct debt[a]			10.3	10.2	9.8
fiscal agency debt[b]			6.8	7.7	8.9
other debt[c]			0.9	0.9	0.8
Crown corporation/					
commercial debt[d]	7.5	7.5	7.9	8.1	8.3
Total provincial debt[e]	20.0	23.4	25.9	26.9	27.9
Nominal GDP	81.3	86.3	92.1	98.7	103.7
Ratio of taxpayer-					
supported debt to GDP	15.4	18.4	19.5	19.1	18.8
Debt service cost of					
taxpayer-supported debt					
per dollar of revenue (cents)	6.4	6.9	7.0	7.2	7.4

[a] Direct debt results from the accumulation of operating deficits incurred by the provincial government.
[b] Fiscal agency debt results from infrastructure expenditures in areas (such as hospitals, schools, highways, ferries, and transit systems) that are not self-financing.
[c] Other debt includes loans to other fiscal agencies and provincially guaranteed debts of individuals and private sector firms.
[d] Crown corporation commercial debt refers to the provincially guaranteed debt of crown corporations (such as BC Hydro) that are self-supporting operations.
[e] The unfunded liabilities of public sector pension plans are not included in the figures given for total provincial debt.
Source: British Columbia, *Budget '95 Reports* (Victoria: Ministry of Finance and Corporate Relations, March 1995), 40, 60.

only legitimate to move major capital expenditures on social infrastructure development off-budget if annual charges are made to the provincial government's operating fund in future years in order to amortize the resulting indebtedness as it matures. Thus, for example, the BC 21 Fund only makes sense from an economic perspective if sinking funds are set aside out of annual operating revenues to enable the retirement of BC 21 Fund debt as the investments it has financed wear out over time. New borrowing will be required when these depreciated infrastructure investments must be replaced.

At present the BC government indicates that sinking fund investments totalled $4.9 billion as at 31 March 1995, against a total outstanding debt of $26.9 billion. Its policy apparently is to establish sinking funds only for debts with terms of five or more years. Given the term structure of overall provincial debt, sinking fund coverage is insufficient since no sinking funds are currently established for the substantial portion of debt that is to be rolled over within five years.

The NDP government's debt management plan has four major goals and benchmarks.[3] These are:

- to maintain the highest credit rating of any province in Canada
- to eliminate over a twenty-year period the $10.2 billion in direct operating debt by replacing budget deficits with budget surpluses
- to reduce the ratio of taxpayer-supported debt to provincial GDP from its current level of 19.1 percent to 10.2 percent within twenty years
- to contain the interest cost of taxpayer-supported debt within a limit of 8.5 percent of provincial revenue in each of the next twenty years.

The government believes that these four objectives are achievable provided that the BC economy grows at an annual average rate of at least 2-3 percent per annum in real terms over the next twenty years, and real government expenditure growth is maintained at least 1 percent below real GDP growth. The path taken by real interest rates will, of course, have important implications for the viability of this debt management strategy, as will the degree to which the federal government takes further action to off-load social expenditure responsibilities onto the province.

The goals and benchmarks of the government's debt management plan have important implications for social infrastructure investments. The fiscal agency debt associated with these investments currently bears a ratio of 8.6 percent to provincial GDP. The second and third benchmarks together imply a cap of 10.2 percent for this ratio, assuming that direct operating debt can be reduced to zero over the next twenty years. Accordingly, social infrastructure investments will need to grow at a more prudent rate than has been the case for the last four years.

Fiscal Policy and Intergenerational Equity

A prudent debt management strategy is essential if fiscal policy is to satisfy the requirements of intergenerational equity. It is clearly inequitable to future generations of BC residents if they inherit a large public sector debt in relationship to the ability of the BC economy to service this debt, as measured by the provincial net debt to GDP ratio. The ability of the BC economy to service debt depends, in large part, on its overall net wealth. Large-scale borrowing, especially from non-residents, undermines wealth creation unless this borrowing is undertaken to finance the creation of productive assets. Resource depletion also reduces the economy's overall level of wealth, and therefore its overall production potential.

To some degree, BC has been treating its renewable resource wealth as if it were non-renewable. Mature old-growth forests have been harvested without adequate investment in reforestation, including replanting, thinning, and silviculture treatments. Coastal salmon stocks have also been depleted. Both of these phenomena relate to market failure.

For long-lived renewable natural resources such as BC's forest resources, intertemporal market failure is virtually inevitable. There are no effective futures markets whose prices could provide adequate incentives for sufficient investments to be undertaken in second- and third-growth timber stands to replace BC's old-growth forests. Moreover, even if such markets existed, current market levels of interest rates clearly would deter ecologically sound investments in timber replenishment. In addition to this, even with long-term and renewable acreage-based tenures, such as the tree farm licences that provide exclusive harvesting rights to timber stands on crown lands, property rights to future timber stands are not sufficiently vested in private corporations for them to replenish fully the timber they harvest. But there is certainly no public sentiment toward further alienation of crown timber resources to forest products companies. Accordingly, forest resource depletion remains a major issue in BC. Provincial residents cannot count on the net forest revenues currently flowing to the provincial government through the stumpage system being there in perpetuity.

The West Coast salmon fishery, while heavily regulated, still suffers from the market failure problems common to open access resources. Essentially, these resource stocks become depleted well below their optimal levels because of the 'tragedy of the commons.' Property rights to the fishery resource are so tenuous that overexploitation becomes virtually inevitable. Inefficient regulatory regimes do little to prevent the dissipation of economic rent, and with it the wealth-generating potential, of the fishery. A prudent fiscal policy would recognize these ecological concerns and not impose additional wealth-reducing burdens on future generations by saddling them with large debt burdens on top of depleted natural resource stocks.

The Budgetary Process and Expenditure Control

In this final section, we turn to process concerns, essentially those of the budgetary process and expenditure control. As pointed out by Maslove, Prince, and Doern,[4] each annual budget may be regarded as an important goal-setting and tactical occasion: 'Budgets in the form of the budget speech and/or the tabling of the annual expenditure estimates constitute one of the two major non-election occasions in which a government attempts to communicate to its citizens and to private decisionmakers its view of national or provincial goals and priorities. The other main occasion is the Speech from the Throne.'[5] Obviously, the debt management plan contained the most important goals of the BC provincial budget brought down on 28 March 1995.

The annual budget is prepared by the Department of Finance with specific input from all major spending departments of government and strategic input from the provincial cabinet. The provincial cabinet itself has a special financial management committee – the Treasury Board – that is the central cabinet agency charged with controlling both the allocation of expenditure across program areas and individual departments and the totality of this expenditure. The Treasury Board is ordinarily chaired by the minister of finance, and supported by Department of Finance officials.

The preparation of the annual budget, which is usually brought down just before the commencement of the new budget year that begins on the first of April, takes several months, during which specific budgetary information and line item requests emanating from spending departments are distilled by the Department of Finance within the overall strategic direction set by cabinet through the Treasury Board. A modified zero-base budgeting approach is used in this process. The overall political-economic environment, including specific forecasts of provincial economic performance over the next year or more and the timing of the election cycle, provides important context to the budgetary process. The Department of Finance itself is largely responsible for the revenue side of the budget, though tax structure and tax rate changes ordinarily require Treasury Board approval.

After it is presented, the budget is scrutinized by the legislature through a committee of the whole, or through a legislative committee known as the Committee of Supply. The budget for each department is usually examined and voted upon separately in this time-consuming process, which often takes up to three months from the time of the budget speech. Once approved, expenditure control is largely exercised by the Department of Finance acting in conjunction with the financial administration arms of each of the spending departments. Various tactics, such as carry-over provisions (or the lack of them), guidelines that limit certain categories of expenditure, and (upon occasion) expenditure freezes, are used in this process. Particularly important in this context are the parameters that are sometimes announced with respect to wage and salary determination for public sector employees. For example, in both 1994-5 and 1995-6, public sector wage increases were strictly limited by the BC government.

The legislature's Public Accounts Committee, strongly aided by the provincial auditor, scrutinizes actual expenditure outcomes, by department and program area, by comparing them with the approved budget allocations determined at the beginning of the budget cycle. Ordinarily, for a particular budget year, this process is completed almost twelve months after the end of the budget year, and almost twenty-four months after the budget speech for the year in question. Thus, a budget that is prepared in year zero to be operative in year one is ultimately put to bed toward the end of year two, when the provincial auditor has completed his or her work on the expenditure and revenue outcomes of year one in relation to the original budget that was proposed. The provincial auditor also investigates the tax expenditures of government and comments on the prudence of its debt management plan.

Finally, BC has not yet experimented with a legislated approach to expenditure control, such as the balanced budget amendments that are common to some US state legislatures. Given the cyclical nature of BC's resource export markets, the rigid adherence to a balanced budget rule on an annual basis would exacerbate the cyclical fluctuations that BC experiences, since the ebb and flow of tax revenues and social transfers provide, in a modest way, a built-in stabilizer in the face of these cycles. Nevertheless, a more complicated approach that attempts to balance the budget over business cycles of (admittedly) variable intensities and durations would seem to be a more appropriate approach to fiscal prudence, without completely rejecting the stabilization role that provincial fiscal policy can, in a modest way, be brought to play.

Further Reading

Barber, C.L. *The Theory of Fiscal Policy as Applied to a Province*. Ontario Committee on Taxation. Toronto: Queen's Printer 1966

British Columbia. *Budget '95 Reports*. Victoria: Ministry of Finance and Corporate Relations, March 1995

Cutt, James. 'British Columbia: Provincial Public Finances.' Chap. 10 in *Volume I Provincial Public Finances: Provincial Surveys*, edited by Melville McMillan. Toronto: Canadian Tax Foundation 1991

Maslove, Allan M., Michael J. Prince, and G. Bruce Doern. *Federal and Provincial Budgeting*. Vol. 41 of Royal Commission on the Economic Union and Development Prospects for Canada. Toronto: University of Toronto Press 1986

14
At the Edge of Canada's Welfare State: Social Policy-Making in British Columbia
Michael J. Prince

The edge is a useful metaphor for understanding social policy in British Columbia. Modern social policy is a contested boundary line between the market economy and the democratic political system. The history of the welfare state in industrialized countries has in part been about modifying economic market forces and softening the hard edges of capitalism. Within Canadian federalism, social policy intersects the national and provincial governments, and has been at the leading edge of province-building and much of our intergovernmental relations. Situated on the Pacific Rim, BC is geographically on the periphery of our nation-state, and possesses a multicultural society and a relatively strong economy. Ideologically, the making of social programs in BC has been a place where contending paradigms of social development and competing political parties, interest groups, and professional associations often clash. In terms of government finances, the social policy field represents the largest wedge of the budgetary pie, accounting for about three-quarters of provincial spending in the 1990s.

Many of the beneficiaries of social policy are at the margins of society and the economy, coping with limited resources and opportunities, and living daily with various risks, insecurities, and anxieties. Others are in the mainstream of the community, using education, health care, tax benefits, and other services, perhaps without seeing these as social programs or themselves as users of the welfare state. Accordingly, much of the ethics and politics of social policy-making concerns notions of connections between people, ideas about obligations to strangers in society, and the relations between different groups of people and governments.

This chapter describes and examines the nature of formulating social policy in BC. It focuses on social policy as an aspect of provincial politics and provincial government activity. Some attention is paid to the role of the federal government and other institutions such as municipalities and the voluntary sector, but the spotlight is on the BC government. The provinces

are the primary level of government in Canada – constitutionally, legisla-
tively, and financially – responsible for developing and implementing social policies. A good deal of the authority and visibility of the provincial
government in BC, as elsewhere in Canada, is linked to its social programs.
The emergence of the provincial government as a major policymaker with
complex administrative systems and modern professional-based structures,
a phenomenon dubbed province-building (see Chapter 3), is due largely to
the expanded social policy responsibilities of the province. The intervention of the province in matters of health, education, housing, training,
income support, and other social endeavours has yielded a West Coast welfare state. It has also resulted in a strong and active provincial state within
Canadian federalism, involving federal-provincial arenas, agreements, and
arguments. It is not much of an exaggeration to say that, over the past four
decades or so, provincial social policy-making *was* the process of province-
building.

This chapter is organized into four sections. The first defines some key
concepts, such as the welfare state, social policy, social policy processes,
social policy communities, and the social division of welfare. The second
section addresses the ideology of welfare by outlining the two main contending paradigms of social policy-making evident in the province –
residualism and institutionalism – and notes some key political issues and
policy ideas. The third section surveys the evolution of social policy in BC
over the past 125 years, highlighting major developments and broad trends
but concentrating on the contemporary period. The fourth section provides concluding observations and considers whether, at this juncture, the
welfare state is at the brink of decline or on the verge of renewal. It is
argued that while the federal government's social role is in decline, the
days of province-building and social policy reform in BC are far from over.

Key Concepts

A sometimes-overlooked aspect of politics is the terminology used to define and discuss things. Definitions are choices. They are selections and
assertions of certain ideas and items over others. In examining social policy-
making in BC, it is essential to understand the following concepts: the
welfare state, social policy, social policy processes, social policy communities, and the social division of welfare. Different definitions of social policy
or the welfare state can convey and conceal particular value preferences
and political beliefs. Whenever reading social and public policy literature,
one should develop the habit of noting the definitions offered of key concepts, comparing them to those in other texts, and reflecting on the implications of these differences for citizens, governments, and other institutions in society.

The Welfare State

The welfare state is a twentieth-century phenomenon, especially of the past fifty years, apparent in many nations. Consider some definitions of the welfare state:

- 'the institutionalization of government responsibility for maintaining national minimum standards'[1]
- 'the welfare state means in essence public action to meet basic human needs and offers the guarantee of collective social care to all citizens'[2]
- it is the government's role in the social sphere as rule setter, insurer, or provider. As government's role expanded to that of doer and the manager of all social problems, the welfare state became the 'nanny state.'[3]
- 'the set of programs that provide entitlements to benefits in the form of income and access to health and social services, and the institutions through which those benefits are delivered.'[4]

As a political concept that can mean several things, the welfare state is both ambiguous and contentious. These sample definitions have several shades of differences and reveal fundamental points of debate over the purpose and nature of the welfare state.

Understood narrowly, the welfare state is seen as providing a selective range of benefits and services to certain defined groups, such as the elderly, persons with disabilities, and the 'truly' poor. The basis of eligibility is either through prior contributions into a social insurance scheme such as the Canada Pension Plan, or through income and needs testing as with social welfare and assistance. The level of social provision is held to be at minimum standards sufficient only to meet basic needs, leaving considerable room and onus for personal effort and private responsibility. The welfare state here, then, is a safety net.

Understood more widely, the welfare state is viewed as offering a fairly comprehensive set of services and benefits to multiple client groups covering the whole population. A central principle of eligibility is that many of these services and benefits are guaranteed or institutionalized. That is, they are entitlements offered as a matter of right, such as public education or medical care. Indeed, many writers regard the welfare state as a vital part of contemporary citizenship because it extends notions of rights and duties into the social realm. The level of provision, under this perspective, is deemed to be at socially defined standards of adequacy and quality. An intended impact of the welfare state is to achieve a measure of progressive redistribution of income or wealth from the more advantaged to the less advantaged. The welfare state here is like Robin Hood. In addition, many people see the welfare state, or at least major elements of it, as expressing core values of civility, equity, sharing, and compassion; values that help

define who we are as a political community and that distinguish us somewhat from our American neighbours and their social programs.

If a welfare state exists when social expenditures are the predominant
type of government spending by a jurisdiction, then BC became a welfare
state during the 1960s and early 1970s. As the province's budget has grown
over the years (see Chapter 13), the portion of social expenditures has grown
even more. Social spending has gone from accounting for half of BC's budget
in 1965, to almost two-thirds in 1985, to three-quarters by 1995. In the
main, provincial government spending is social policy spending. The BC
government now spends seventy-five cents of every dollar in the provincial budget on health, education, and social services. Budgets are a form of
quantified political memory on which current and future demands are based.
In broad terms, social and economic interests in the province are aware of
these trends and use them to press their claims that, given this or that
pattern of priorities, their field should now (or continue to) receive high
ranking.

For our purposes, the welfare state refers to the formation of a wide range
of social programs by governments and related public bodies, of which at
least some programs are provided as a right. Across the federal, provincial,
and territorial levels of government in Canada, we effectively have thirteen welfare states. If aboriginal self-governments and major urban municipalities are included, we arguably have even more. There may be some
common features among them, but each is unique to some extent in terms
of context, authority, resources, goals, needs, and issues. The range of welfare state programs covers a large area of public policy activity and employs
every possible governing instrument – cash transfers, tax measures, service
provisions, laws and regulations, symbolic gestures, public ownership, and
privatization. In BC the range of public bodies includes government ministries, boards, and commissions; school districts, colleges, and universities;
the courts and other parts of the justice system; and regional districts,
municipalities, and other local entities such as library and police boards.
As a descriptive idea, the welfare state suggests a significant social role played
by modern governments within the community and economy. This role,
as our survey of the evolution of BC social policy will show, represents a
historically situated set of policy commitments by governments grounded
in various statutes, agencies, personnel, and programs. As a normative ideal,
the concept of the welfare state projects a set of beliefs and expectations of
what the social role of government ought to be, and what the quality of life
might be in society. This normative side to the concept is examined further in the section on the contending paradigms of social policy.

Social Policy

But what is social policy? As an area of public policy-making, social policy is larger in scope and more diverse in substance than most people realize. As a political activity by the state, social policy involves the authoritative expression of values and the allocation of resources, statuses, and opportunities within our society. Rice offers the following description: 'social policy endeavours to affect the nature of the quality of life of Canadians. It creates conditions that are intended to increase the welfare of Canadians, insure just treatment of individuals, provide resources to those who, due to an inability to earn income, are unable to meet their own needs, and reduce or, if possible, eliminate social inequalities through redistribution.'[5]

This portrait of social policy fits with the idea of the BC welfare state in its broader dimensions. Social policy is about much more than welfare and providing relief to those in dire straits. It also entails providing essential services and benefits to the general public; building social infrastructure such as schools and parks; and investing in people through learning and training as a way of both promoting human development and managing the economy. The value base of social policy embraces more than compassion or pity for those in society who are less fortunate than others, although these are traditionally important motivations. It also includes, among others, ideas of economic security, personal safety, social justice, and individual opportunity. Much social policy seeks to meet people's needs and improve their well-being. Yet though the aims of social policies may seem to be on the side of the angels, the devil may well be in the details of their implementation. There are other possible functions of social programs, including the imposition of control, the punishment of certain behaviours, and the reproduction of inequalities.

While health, education, and social services are the main provincial activities in this policy field, social policy in BC is about far more. It also encompasses matters of aboriginal affairs, human rights, justice, corrections and policing, recreation, sports, tourism and leisure, the arts, multiculturalism, consumer protection, income maintenance, immigration, women's equality, employment and the labour market, and housing. In addition, there are usually social edges to economic policies. Examples include activities in industrial programs for promoting the role of women in small business; regional development initiatives that help create or maintain employment in rural areas; and in transportation policy, issues of safety and the accessibility of public transit to help people access jobs and services.

Social Policy Processes

The concept of social policy processes directs attention to certain aspects of politics, governing, and public administration. In thinking about social policy, it is important to recognize that at any given time there are several processes in action in and around governments. There are processes for budgeting, legislation, and consultation; there are procedures for inter-ministerial and intergovernmental relations; and there are systems for developing new policy ideas and for administering old programs. The political basis of social policy-making includes the choosing and ranking of public goals and human values, the organization of activities into authoritative structures, and the selection of policy instruments to secure social acceptance and compliance of goals often in the face of contending interests.

Policy-making involves making decisions. Dobell and Mansbridge describe the social policy process as consisting of 'the complex web of interaction among politicians, public servants, the public and non-governmental organizations, leading to decisions affecting the provision of social programs.'[6] This facet of the policy process is commonly depicted in the literature as a series of stages, such as: problem recognition and the appearance of an issue on the public agenda; problem examination and resultant official definition; determination of the public interest and possible policy objectives; generation of alternatives for tackling the problem and meeting the objectives; and the policy decision of choosing some course of action or inaction. Beyond these steps of policy formation are the stages of implementation for putting policies into practice, evaluation for assessing the results of policies, and, perhaps, the adaptation or termination of a policy.

While this perspective on the process is helpful in noting that policy-making entails a number of actions and procedures, 'it tends to view policy-making as though it were the product of one governing mind, which is clearly not the case. It fails to evoke or suggest the distinctively political aspects of policy-making, its apparent disorder, and the consequent strikingly different ways in which policies emerge.'[7]

Social Policy Communities

Not only do policies emerge in different ways but different areas of social policy have their own dynamics and patterns of development. Each area has a policy community or network of governmental and non-governmental agencies and actors that have a stake in, and knowledge about, the issues in that area. Policy communities are also networks of power relationships and contending interests and preferences. Social policy communities can differ in relation to a number of attributes, including the relative influence and role of professions; the nature of federalism in effect; the kinds of principles, rhetorical language, and values exercising an influence on the policy; the mix of public sector versus private sector activity; the balance of formal and informal care in a given area; and public attitudes toward specific social programs and client groups.

In health policy, for example, the medical profession looms large as the key provider group in the province in terms of authority and influence.

Through the BC Medical Association (BCMA), the profession negotiates directly with the provincial government on fees, payments, and other policy issues in a way like no other profession or occupation associated with the welfare state. Education is probably the main area of social policy in which the province enjoys the greatest autonomy in relation to the federal government. In income support policy, the centuries-old principles of relief and means testing still persist, despite the arrival of social insurance and repeated proposals to replace these ideas with a guaranteed annual income. In housing policy, the main suppliers of shelter in our society are firms in the business sector. Housing is widely treated as a private consumption good and most people are expected to obtain their own living accommodations. In many areas of the social services, such as care of the frail elderly or sick family members, most of the work is done by women as informal and unpaid caregivers. Canadian public opinion ranks social programs and their clientele groups according to degrees of perceived ethical or political legitimacy. The public strongly favours health care, old age pensions, and education; the unemployment insurance program and social assistance (welfare) are less positively ranked. Groups that are seen as highly deserving of more social benefits from government typically include senior citizens, children, and persons with disabilities. Groups that the public has ranked comparatively low in the hierarchy of claims to *additional* social support are the unemployed, immigrants, and unions.[8]

Nonetheless, there are strong elements of commonality across the various areas of social policy in BC. They are all inherently political activities, involving the use of the state for purposes of human and social development. They are all forms of collective action in which public power is exercised and public resources employed. They are all concerned with affecting people's identities, prospects, and social relationships – in short, their well-being. It is not surprising, then, that all areas of social policy can generate public concern, media coverage, and political conflict. Social policies are always, it seems, an issue in provincial politics. There is controversy, real or potential, over what represents an adequate level of benefit, over whether the scope of a program should be expanded or contracted, and over which level of government, if any, should finance and administer particular social programs. In varying degrees but with similar intentions, social policies create minimum standards of benefits and services, rights and duties. Over time, social policy coverage of client needs and of the general population has grown, and this expansion has transformed the size and nature of the provincial state, firmly establishing BC as a primary policy-making institution and public service entity in Canada. The province's social role must be seen within the context of all the institutions that determine the formation and distribution of social resources.

The Social Division of Welfare

The social division of welfare refers to the assemblage of institutions within society, including the state sector, that develop and provide social programs or similar welfare activities. The concept rests on the observation that social policy and human welfare are the subject and product of many social structures. This situation is sometimes called 'welfare pluralism' or 'the mixed economy of welfare.' In BC and elsewhere in Canada, the social division of welfare consists of five conceptually distinct sectors: the state sector; the informal sector; the voluntary sector; the aboriginal sector; and the private sector. In actuality, of course, they are interconnected.

The state sector includes the provincial government, the federal government, municipal governments including the school districts, and public employee associations and unions. This is what is normally thought of as the welfare state or public sector. The informal sector refers to the role of social support networks such as families, households, friends, ethnic communities, and neighbours. Experience tells us that it is misleading to think of this domain as unorganized or marginal compared to the welfare state. In fact, the bulk of health care and family care still occurs in this sector, provided primarily by women. The voluntary sector consists of a wide range of non-profit agencies that offer a broad spectrum of services and benefits to individuals, families, and communities. The sector encompasses charities, foundations, self-help and mutual aid groups, as well as churches and other religious organizations. The aboriginal sector includes self-government structures, First Nations communities themselves, and other bodies such as Native friendship centres located in urban parts of the province. In response to increasing Native demands for self-determination, over the past quarter century some welfare state services and resources have been transferred to aboriginal groups to enable them to design and deliver programs more in line with their own needs and values. The private sector is another realm of social policy activity and power, and it includes individual firms, business associations, banks, insurance companies, professional associations, as well as certain unions and labour federations.

The interrelationships between these sectors and their respective social roles are apparent in both the clash of welfare ideologies and the evolution of BC social policy.

Contending Paradigms of Social Policy

The grand ideological debate over social policy concerns the societal division of welfare between the various sectors. What kind of society do we want to live in? With respect to the promotion and provision of social development, what should be the balance between the five sectors? Usually the debate is framed in terms of a number of related questions. What ought to be the relationship between the state and the other institutional sectors? Should governments do relatively more or about the same or less in the social policy field? What activities constitute public issues and social needs versus private troubles and personal wants? Should the burdens of social care and the costs of economic change be allowed to lie where they fall or is there a place for public action? If there is a call for public action, what should be the extent and form of that response? The macro-politics of social policy involve claims and counterclaims about the benefits and limitations of the sectors, as well as about preferences for expanding or restricting the responsibility and authority of different sectors. Should other sectors be used as instruments of provincial social policy for funding, planning, or delivery purposes? This leads into the micro social politics of deciding the adequacy of particular benefits, the legal meaning of a given right, or the quality of specific services.

The provincial welfare state has refused to be the product of a single ideology. Social policy in BC is not necessarily, or even usually, socialism in action; nor is it simply past Social Credit thinking embedded in administrative practice. In fact, much of the value orientation underlying social programs in Canada, especially outside of Quebec, is rooted in liberalism of one form or another.[9] Present also are elements of other ideologies and their variations across the country: conservatism (New Right and red Tory), socialism (deep red and light pink), and nationalism (maple leaf and fleur-de-lis).

Besides these familiar 'isms' of politics, there are two paradigms or mini-ideologies of social policy: residualism and institutionalism. As paradigms, they are politically based sets of ideas and actions associated with the field of social policy and the welfare state. What Keynesianism and monetarism are to economic and fiscal policy (see Chapter 13), residualism and institutionalism are to social policy and the social role of the state in the economy and society. While other paradigms or models exist in social policy literature, the residual and institutional conceptions represent the dominant ideological edges of social policy in Canada. Our federal and provincial welfare states embody aspects of both paradigms, and the history of social policy in Canada has involved a fairly regular, though rarely equal, push and pull between these two belief systems.

A residual conception of social policy holds that most government social programs should come into play only when the family, local community, and market economy break down or fail to meet exceptional needs and circumstances. There is faith in the superiority of private provision to meet needs and offer supports. Residualists believe that government programs frequently rob individuals of their initiative to work and their commitment to family responsibilities. Social policy is identified with protecting the less fortunate – the 'worthy poor,' the sick, and the elderly. The role of the state, then, is to act as a safety net, stepping in as a last resort when actors or agencies in other sectors experience serious problems. This policy paradigm thus contains a narrow view of what the welfare state is or should be. That the provision of health and social services are the responsibility of local communities, charities, and municipalities was a stance held strongly by provincial governments and the federal government up through the 1930s.

With welfare states now in place in BC and other Canadian jurisdictions, it is tempting to conclude that residualism is a thing of history, that the more collectivist institutionalist paradigm has triumphed, and that no longer is there a grand clash of welfare ideologies but rather just minor skirmishes over program techniques. Though perhaps tempting, such a conclusion is an overly simplistic view of the recent politics of social policy.

From the late 1970s onward, there has been a resurgence in residualist thinking and policy action. Its contemporary political form is neoconservatism or the New Right. Preaching a far more modest approach to public responsibility, calls are made for reducing the size of government, returning certain activities back to the family or community, and replacing the public sector delivery of social programs with voluntary sector or private sector provision. Part of the residualist critique of the modern welfare state is that by becoming so large and intrusive, it has weakened the values and functioning capacities of voluntary groups and community associations. Taxes are viewed as a necessary evil at best, and in recent decades have risen to excessively high levels. Taxation has become the public confiscation of private wealth. In addition, the residual approach holds a particular view of the relationship between social policy and the economy. Social development is dependent upon economic development, and social policy-making is seen as a function of economic growth. Without productive and competitive producers and workers in the private sector, we cannot maintain existing social programs or add new ones.

The institutional view of social policy rests on a distinctive set of beliefs and values. In industrialized countries, government social services and programs are needed to play a regular ongoing role alongside other institutions such as the family, the church, and the economy. The welfare state is thus an *institution* integral to the cohesion and integrity of modern life. Social policy is regarded as a set of actions that provide for basic human needs of all members of society, not just those on the margins. People experience risks and states of dependency at all stages of life, be it injury or illness, childhood or old age, discrimination or violence, learning or training requirements; all are features of the human condition in modern societies. Publicly provided social services to address these needs should therefore be viewed as legitimate services, and their use should not bring any shame. For institutionalists, public sector social programs are not like band-aids responding to particular problems, but are meant to be active measures engaging with societal trends.

Moreover, institutionalists advocate the redistribution of resources, through government expenditure and taxation policies, in order to realize a greater equalization of social well-being. Taxes are an essential tool for funding adequate cash benefits and high-quality services. Thus, income taxes, health care premiums, and school property taxes, among others, are seen to represent private contributions to public wealth. Further, the tax system can be used to deliver income support such as fuel tax rebates for people with disabilities. The welfare state is not a safety net but rather is a provider of essential public services and social rights to all citizens. Social welfare and economic development are treated as interdependent functions of Canadian society. Institutionalism does not accept the view that economic policy can be a substitute for social policy. Even though institutionalists acknowledge that the achievement of many social goals requires economic programs to promote employment, they assert that social programs do not just follow economic programs; these policy fields must go hand in hand. Social justice and economic success are intertwined. Social spending by government is not inherently an unproductive expenditure nor automatically a burden on the economy, but is seen to be an effective investment in people and their communities.

These paradigms represent quite different approaches to social policy-making. Each promotes certain values and certain sectors over others in the social division of welfare. These paradigms are not just theoretical models held by academics. They are also used implicitly and, at times, expressed explicitly by policy advocates, bureaucrats, and politicians. Specific social policy debates on issues such as creating jobs, ensuring fair access to services, or cracking down on welfare fraud are influenced by these sets of ideas.

The residualist view, for instance, was put forward in a 1983 BC government document as a rationale for the government's cutbacks to income assistance and social service programs of the then Ministry of Human Resources: 'The Minister of Human Resources looks to churches to assume the role which was their Christian role over history and that is to care for those who are in distress rather than to become advocacy groups to push governments at all levels to greater expenditures. The Minister believes that the community has also a very great responsibility and should be shouldering that responsibility.'[10] This statement contains a number of powerful messages regarding the social division of welfare and the curtailment of provincial social programs. One is that the churches should not be speaking out on social policy matters, particularly if religious leaders and groups are urging governments to do more. To do so transforms them into special interest advocacy groups. Instead, their welfare role should focus on the traditional charitable activity of taking care of those in distress. A second message is that the community – presumably the informal and voluntary sectors – can and should do more in helping British Columbians in need. A third is that government can then reduce or eliminate certain social benefits and services with little if any adverse impact on clients, because private provision will substitute for public programming.

In contrast, an institutionalist view of social policy is apparent in the BC government's 1994 Speech from the Throne: 'Social programs are a vital part of the BC economy and society. Programs such as medicare, social assistance, unemployment insurance, public education and a minimum wage define who we are as a society and how we take care of each other. They help us to cope with the unpredictable crises of life, such as the loss of a job or ill health.'[11] This statement likewise expresses certain beliefs about social policy and the welfare state. First, government-provided social programs are accorded a central place in the social and economic life of the province. Such programs are both appropriate and essential forms of assistance and security for people facing the risks and contingencies of today's world. Second, a fairly wide view of what constitutes social policy is presented, notably including minimum wage laws. Third, what may be called a cultural conception of social policy is emphasized, one that is highly positive. Social programs are held up as defining elements of our civic selves and democratic community. By reflecting shared values and containing broad assumptions about mutual obligations, social policies are cultural symbols.

In broad terms, the residualist paradigm may be equated with the political centre-right and the institutionalist with the political centre-left. Yet BC's social policy history, in times recent and long past, reveals that all governing political parties in the province have adopted aspects of both paradigms.

The Evolution of Social Policy in British Columbia

The history of the welfare state and social policy in BC can be surveyed as four periods: 1871 to the 1940s, the 1940s to 1982, 1983 to 1991, and 1991 to 1996. While the choice of time periods, like the concept definitions, is somewhat arbitrary, each corresponds to significant political events, key socioeconomic developments, and major policy trends. In brief overview, social policy-making during the first period can be described as outlining some of the rudimentary edges of the welfare state that was to come later. The 1940s to 1982 period in BC was marked by social policy gaining the edge and becoming the provincial government's major field of activity. From 1983 to 1991, various social programs, rights, and agencies faced the cutting edge of restraint measures imposed by the final Bill Bennett Social Credit government. Social policy was then on edge, due to the erratic and doctrinaire leadership style of Bill Vander Zalm. The 1991 to 1996 period, corresponding to Mike Harcourt's New Democratic Party (NDP) government, shows the province's social policy edging along, maintaining most programs and revising others in the face of financial constraints and the continuing retreat of the federal government from its previous role.

Looking at the long-term evolution of social policy assists in better understanding where we have come from, where we are now, and where we may be heading as a political community. More specifically, it serves to identify shifts in ideas regarding the role of the state within the social division of welfare; notes organizational developments in the structure of government; and shows when policy innovation takes place and when policy inertia exists. A historical survey also helps us recognize the legacy of policy and budgetary commitments that a political party inherits when it forms a government.

Outlining the Edges of Social Policy: 1871 to the 1940s

This period witnessed the transformation of BC from a sparse rural society to an urban industrial society. The province entered Confederation in 1871 as a frontier society with a small population of about 36,000 people scattered throughout the province. By the 1930s, the population had grown to over 700,000 people, most of whom were concentrated in the Lower Mainland. With urbanization came the matters of housing, public health and sanitation, public security, and other social issues. With industrialization came not only new technologies but also increased incomes and living standards, altered family ties, and new opportunities and risks associated with major economic transformations. Provincial politics in this phase was dominated by the Liberal and Conservative Parties (see Appendixes A1 and A4). The first provincial cabinet comprised just four departments, of which only one, the Attorney General, can be said to be a social policy department. The next social ministries in the BC government were not established until well into the twentieth century, with the Labour department formed in 1917 and the Education department in 1920. It would be another twenty-six years before a Health and Welfare department would be formed.

During this entire period, a residualist approach to social policy-making generally prevailed. Important exceptions were public health, law and order, and elementary public education, which were recognized early on as important needs of the community in general that required action by government. Not until the 1920s and 1930s did other social services and income support programs, directed at particular groups, appear on federal and provincial policy agendas. Outside the state, families, churches, and paid employment were relied on as the main channels of resources and help for people. A number of charities and voluntary service agencies were set up in BC in this period. These included the YMCA, YWCA, Salvation

Army, CNIB, Victoria Order of Nurses, Red Cross Society, and the predecessors of today's United Way. Within the state, municipalities had the biggest responsibility for dealing with social policy. Health, education, and social welfare were all thought of as essentially private or local in nature. Social programs were responses to individual destitution, economic depression, social disorder, epidemics, and disease.

In the early part of this period, the provincial government's social role consisted of providing grants to municipalities, charities, hospitals, and schools. In addition to this funding role, the province passed legislation and enforced regulations pertaining to education, justice, and liquor, and supervised local authorities charged with public health responsibilities. The province gradually assumed a role in various areas of social security. Minimum wage laws and a worker's compensation scheme were established. In 1920 the province introduced a public assistance program, a mother's pension plan. In 1927 the provincial government entered into a cost-shared program of old age pensions with the federal government. In 1931 BC instituted a program of medical care for the poor, the first province to do so.

The later part of this period was defined by the shattering impact of the Great Depression of the 1930s. Guest has noted some crucial points for the development of social security programs in Canada that resulted from this crisis:

> The depression was so devastating in its effect that it brought home to the average Canadian the interdependence of citizens in an industrial society. Unemployment was seen less as a result of personal inadequacy and more as a common and insurable threat to the livelihood of the average citizen. Secondly, the concept of local responsibility for the relief of the unemployed was replaced first by the assumption of provincial and then of federal responsibility. From this point on, unemployment was seen as a national problem rather than a purely local or regional one.[12]

In response to high levels of unemployment and the limitations of families and municipalities to cope with the financial burden it imposed, the BC government participated, as did other provinces, in federal unemployment relief programs introduced throughout the 1930s. So severe was the depression that by 1933 nearly one in four people in BC was obtaining public assistance in the form of work projects or other measures.[13] In this time of economic crisis, the traditional structures of welfare provision were found seriously wanting. Residualist attitudes toward social care held by the public and the political elites were challenged and partially altered, and the social policy activities of the provincial and federal governments were in transition, moving hesitantly toward new and expanded roles.

Gaining the Edge of the Welfare State: 1940s to 1982

In this period, the BC government and others in Canada crossed the divide from one kind of state to another – the welfare state. A significant transformation in the social fabric and policy structures of the country took place. The provincial population grew from less than a million to over 2.7 million. These years saw the creation of the modern health care system, the postsecondary education system, the income security system, the social services network, and the social housing stock. In retrospect, it seems that it took only a modest length of time to produce a major amount of social policy.

The 1940s to the early 1980s were the heyday of social policy in BC. At the national level, this was evident in federal leadership in key areas of income security and in intergovernmental financial arrangements with the provinces. At the provincial level, this was reflected in a widespread acceptance of the programs associated with a more socially activist government, in social expenditures emerging as the largest part of provincial budgets, and in social services becoming major sources of public employment and professional development for the growing workforce. BC developed a wealthy, resource-based economy, and, with strong revenue growth, the provincial budget was in surplus for all but a handful of years.

An initial wave of key provincial policy developments took place in the 1940s. A comprehensive social assistance act was passed in 1945 and a Department of Health and Welfare was formed the next year. Then in 1948, the provincial hospital insurance plan was adopted, BC being the second province to do so, after Saskatchewan. Reforms such as these led to shifts in responsibilities from municipal governments to the provincial government, and encouraged the professionalization of services and staff.

For over half of this period, the Social Credit Party formed the BC government. In particular, it was during the twenty-year premiership of W.A.C. Bennett, from 1952 to 1972, that most of the provincial welfare state was constructed. Social policy-making under Bennett, like cabinet decision-making generally, was dominated by the premier. Policy processes were effectively centred in the premier's office and the finance department, a portfolio the premier also held for his entire time in power. Social policy also developed in response to the pressures of the baby boom and to initiatives by the federal government. In the 1950s, BC participated in several shared-cost social programs with Ottawa for the elderly, blind, disabled, and needy unemployed, as well as for hospital insurance.

A third wave of policy change occurred from the mid-1960s to the early 1970s, when the federal government launched several major social reforms, including the Canada Pension Plan, medical insurance (also popularly called medicare), a consolidation and expansion of previous welfare schemes under the Canada Assistance Plan, the guaranteed income supplement for low income seniors, the Canada Student Loan program, federal assistance to higher education and employment training, and substantial changes to the Unemployment Insurance program. The institutionalist approach to welfare seemed in full bloom. Expansionary and active provincial governments launched still other social policy initiatives. In BC these included a social housing corporation and set of programs, a human rights commission and code, and the creation of Simon Fraser University, the University of Victoria, and several community colleges. All in all, the Bennett governments created the foundation of much of BC's welfare state.

The 1972 to 1975 NDP government of Dave Barrett gave a high priority to social policy issues and the institutional paradigm. This welfare disposition was rooted in the NDP's ideology and historic image of itself as a progressive movement, and was strengthened by the personal convictions of the premier and the minister of human resources, both of whom were social workers.[14] With respect to social policy-making processes, Barrett, unlike Bennett, did not impose strong control and leadership from the centre. For executive decision-making, the NDP cabinet was essentially unaided in terms of committee structures and support staff. Most social initiatives came from within the departments or from activist ministers, such as Minister of Human Resources Norman Levi, who enjoyed considerable freedom and undertook no fewer than eighteen new programs. The most significant change in welfare policy during the Barrett years, and arguably over the entire postwar period, was the wide-scale reorganization of the province's social service delivery system. Under the 1974 Community Resources Board Act, regional and community resources boards were to be formed. The policy themes here, as with reorganizations in other social departments, were service decentralization, coordination across services, and citizen participation at the local community level. By the end of 1975, when the NDP lost power, about sixty boards were in the process of being established.

Other noteworthy NDP social policy measures included public auto insurance and the Insurance Corporation of BC (ICBC); the prescription drug subsidy plan Pharmacare; an income support program for persons with disabilities and those aged sixty and over; increases in welfare rates of between 20 to 40 percent; consumer protection legislation; the Alcohol and Drug Commission; rent controls for residential premises; and a Legal Services Commission to administer legal aid programs. With these measures also came new government departments for consumer services and housing. In addition to generating fresh programs, numerous existing programs such as day care were modified in content or scope. Though in power for only 1,200 days or so, and dreams of greater changes shattered, the Barrett government did alter social policy in significant ways and left a legacy of reforms, of which most are still in effect.

Under the first two Social Credit governments of Bill Bennett (1976-9 and 1979-83), social policy developments continued. A few NDP initiatives such as the high profile community resources boards were quickly dismantled, but Social Credit retained most social programs introduced by the Barrett government and even expanded some, such as the Pharmacare program and special services for children with disabilities. Another example is the consolidation of the province's income assistance programs in the Guaranteed Available Income for Need (GAIN) policy, for which benefits were adjusted most years. The early Bennett years also offered up some new social programs: a family support worker program, emergency child abuse services, the Shelter Aid for Elderly Renters (SAFER) program, denticare, and the long-term care hospital program. After a narrow election victory in 1979, the Bennett government maintained an emphasis on social policy. Major social capital commitments were made in relation to the construction and refurbishing of courts, schools, colleges, universities, and hospitals. Overall provincial expenditures on social programs steadily grew. Some social measures were intended explicitly as economic management. Increased capital spending and expanded operating expenditures on training programs were aimed at avoiding skill shortages, creating jobs, and stimulating the provincial economy. Also implemented in this period was a 2 percent increase in the social services tax and a personal income tax surcharge levied on higher income earners, both designed to raise revenues for program spending.

Reforms to the cabinet structure of provincial policy-making involved the formation of a Planning and Priorities Committee chaired by the premier, a treasury board secretariat, increased staff assistance for policy advice and management, and a standing committee on social services. Other organizational developments included the establishment of the Ministry of Universities, Science and Technology, and the Office of the Ombudsman, both in 1979, and efforts in various ministries to decentralize or regionalize the provision of services.

From the 1940s to 1982, then, a welfare state was established in BC, a process apparent in the growth of the provincial public service. The number of public service employees jumped from about 7,000 to over 43,000; total provincial government expenditures increased from a few hundred million dollars to about seven billion; and the number of social ministries in the cabinet grew from three in the early 1940s to eight by the early 1980s. Contrary to the belief of some, particularly residualists, that the expanding welfare state would squeeze out community groups, the voluntary sector in BC also expanded in this period. The number of voluntary agencies increased – in response to new social needs, government funding, and social activism – as did the scope of their activities. More groups engaged in identifying public issues, providing services, and advocating reforms. In the later years of this period, provincial funding to the voluntary sector grew significantly for delivering community-based programs. In general, however, a fairly clear distinction still existed between the provincial state and the voluntary sector in the organization and delivery of social services.[15]

While BC is commonly described as an ideologically polarized polity, the province's welfare state is a hybrid of ideologies and the efforts of different provincial governing parties. Liberal and Conservative governments were initially involved in the creation of social policy, but BC's welfare state is primarily the product of Social Credit governments and a short-lived NDP government. There were many resemblances between Social Credit and the NDP.[16] Both parties were suspicious of the merits of using human services professionals in the provision of social care and welfare. Both had links to grassroots movements and had biases toward populist approaches to policy-making. They both appealed to the 'common sense' of ordinary British Columbians and relied little on policy analysis by experts. A good social program was one that the public needed and supported. Both parties as governments generated new social policies and modified existing ones. Both accepted the idea, along with successive federal governments, that governments can provide stimulus to the economy to counter short-term unemployment through an array of economic and social measures. Both favoured, though perhaps for different reasons, a social division of welfare that included the public and private delivery of social services. The outcome of these shared beliefs was a mix of voluntary, private, and public services, a vast increase in the scale of BC's social policy activities, a modest complement of professionally trained social workers in the system, and BC being one of the last provinces to establish even a basic system of cabinet organization and analytical support.

But there were also differences. The ideological heart of Social Credit was always fonder of the residualist approach to social policy-making than the more interventionist institutional paradigm, and the core of their political support was the small-business and anti-socialist constituencies in the province. Social Credit also tended to scapegoat welfare recipients. Ministers responsible for social services often responded to work ethic values and welfare rolls by introducing 'workfare' programs aimed at reducing the number of employable recipients of social assistance. Getting tough on recipients through workfare was viewed as a politically wise thing to do. The government could be seen by the public as taking appropriate action by policing malingerers and improving training opportunities for the unfortunate. A latent benefit could be to deflect attention from other problems in the economy.[17] Unlike the Socreds, the NDP leaned toward institutional welfarism. They were dubious of the claimed successes of workfare programs and saw them as stigmatizing those on welfare. Political support

for the NDP has traditionally come from the labour movement, community activists, and social organizations. The Barrett government was distinctive in the social policy realm by its extremely ambitious reform agenda,
its attention to disadvantaged groups, and a significant over-run in the
welfare budget.

The greatest differences in social policy between Social Credit and the NDP,
though, starkly surfaced in the 1983 to 1991 period. It was then that con-
frontational politics became the norm in BC's social policy community.

Social Programs on the Cutting Edge of Neoconservatism: 1983 to 1991

With respect to social policy, this time period was characterized by the
sense that the provincial public sector was in crisis. Many social programs
and their clientele felt the sharp edge of the sword of restraint. The legislative and budgetary actions of the last Bennett government, from 1983 to
1986, marked a major departure in the tone and trajectory of social policy-
making in Canada since the 1940s. While other administrations in the
country had been trying restraint measures since the mid-1970s, the BC
government's actions were more radical and severe. The province became
the centre of national and international attention because of the swift
and comprehensive restraint program introduced after the 1983 provincial election.

Reelected with a sizeable majority, Social Credit soon unveiled a sweeping restraint package of twenty-six legislative bills and a budget. The ag-
gressiveness of the program was caused by a variety of factors, which con-
gealed in the midst of a deep recession – the worst in Canada since the
1930s – that hit hard the BC population, economy, and public purse. These
factors included the desire of Premier Bill Bennett to put his own decisive
imprint on BC history; a genuine concern that resource markets would be
in a long-term state of decline unless they were made more competitive;
strong business pressures of varying kinds, made more persuasive by the
depth of the recession; and the impact of the growing world-wide
neoconservative critique of modern government, promoted in BC by the
Fraser Institute, a right-wing policy group based in Vancouver.

The provincial government's explanation for its restraint policy, the credibility of those reasons, and the appropriateness of the procedures have
been critically examined in a number of works.[18] Here, the restraint measures taken in relation to social policy will be briefly noted. From an overall
budgetary perspective, BC's social programs appear to have been maintained or to have even grown during these years. As Cutt states: 'With the
exception of the elimination of the new denticare program and a few low-
cost but high-profile programs such as the Office of the Rentalsman, there
was no significant curtailment of public programs in the social area. Only

in the 1984/85 budget was there an absolute reduction in the level of expenditures and in the social area; this ... was effected primarily by wage and salary costs and not by program reductions.'[19] Looking at the welfare state in public finance terms, however, captures only some facets of social policy. When the focus is on the details of individual programs for particular groups, social regulations, or public sector employment, a different picture appears. In these areas, the ideas of neoconservatism and the retreat on social policy provision are much more evident.

In income assistance, for example, GAIN benefit levels were not raised to account for inflationary increases in the cost of living, and thus the purchasing value of benefits declined in real terms. In addition, the benefits of some specific groups were reduced: for young people aged twenty-five or under, for single parents with young children, for individuals with a physical or mental disability, and for persons awaiting unemployment insurance benefits. As Hugh Curtis, the minister of finance, noted in the 1984 provincial budget, 'By limiting payments made to certain types of clients, the government will reduce the chances of creating a permanent group of unemployed persons and of attracting potential recipients from outside the province.' In 1984 one in seven members of the BC labour force was out of work, and the provincial unemployment rate had more than doubled since the early 1980s.

In the social services area, the Bennett government eliminated the Family Support Worker Program, the Provincial Inservice Resource Team, and Mental Retardation Coordinator positions as part of a major downsizing of the staff in the then Ministry of Human Resources. Ironically, the purpose of these programs was to assist families in providing care to children and dependants with special needs, and thereby reduce the need for institutionalization. Similarly, the Community Involvement Program, which offered a modest monthly payment to people with disabilities and those unemployable who performed twenty hours a month of volunteer work for a non-profit agency, was abolished. The irony is that all these programs served to promote values akin to the residual paradigm of social policy – family, community, voluntarism, and work. That they were cut suggests that Social Credit was driven more by 'new right' considerations of rolling back the public service. Furthermore, a number of privatization initiatives took place in the social area. One example was the transfer of most government-operated child care facilities to non-profit societies.

In the realm of social rights and protections, important agencies and activities were eliminated or reduced. The government wished to cut the use of professional staff in support of regulatory processes. The Office of the Rentalsman, the Human Rights Commission, and the Employment Standards Board were all abolished. These were among the most provocative cuts in this period. There were also cutbacks in the Ministry of the

Attorney General, with more priority given to private sector legal advice, and the ministry shrank by 20 percent, losing the equivalent of about 1,100 employees. These restraint moves startled many British Columbians because they suggested a de-emphasis on the goals of bringing about greater equality of treatment, fairness, and civil liberties.

In the education field, reductions in school financing resulted in the elimination of approximately 1,000 jobs and triggered a strike by the province's teachers. After many years of declining, the pupil/teacher ratio rose again. The postsecondary education sector absorbed a cut of nearly 10 percent in real terms (that is, after accounting for inflation) in operating budgets.

Health care, often called the sacred trust of Canadian social policy, was not untouched over this period. It is probably true that the medicare institutions were less vulnerable than income assistance, social services, and education. But, although calling health care their highest priority, the Bennett government did make cuts in health programs. The Ministry of Health as an organization underwent a 27 percent reduction in the number of employees. Under the Medical Services Plan, payments to physicians in BC were capped for two years and then restricted in subsequent years. To reduce the supply of physicians and to encourage their location in rural areas of the province, the government endeavoured to limit access to billing numbers that doctors require to practice and invoice the province for payment. Pressure was put on hospitals to become more efficient, and about 1,200 acute-care beds were closed. Other cuts to locally based health services and preventive programs were consistent with neoconservatism. These included funding reductions to community health clinics in Vancouver and Victoria of nearly 30 percent, and the complete elimination of funding for Planned Parenthood and the Vancouver Women's Health Collective.[20]

The impacts of this severe restraint program were many, including some fiscal savings for the provincial accounts, real costs to public employees and disadvantaged citizens, the rise of food banks, intense political opposition, and the early departure of the premier from power. Barely three years into his mandate, Bennett resigned in 1986.

The Socreds were once again returned to office under Bill Vander Zalm, and another variant of neoconservatism operated from 1986 to 1991. By this time, too, a neoconservative agenda was apparent in Ottawa with the Mulroney government. In BC the economy had recovered from the recession and was growing. Government revenues increased strongly and spending rose as well. Unemployment in the province dropped from 12.5 percent in 1986 to 8.3 percent in 1990, before rising to 9.9 percent in 1991. The population grew by almost half a million people in this period.

Under Vander Zalm, there was a shift in the tone and rhetoric of policy-making, and his leadership style was reminiscent of the populism of W.A.C. Bennett and Dave Barrett. There was an easing of some aspects of restraint, especially on expenditures, and a continuation of others such as privatization. Due to prior cuts, strong revenue growth, and creative accounting practices, the province's budget was virtually balanced by 1987-8, ran surpluses in the next two years, and was then followed by deficits reaching a record $2.4 billion in 1991-2. Broad social policy themes referred to helping those most in need, maintaining cherished values and the quality of life in BC, providing better access and opportunity, and ensuring the continuity of social programs. Social expenditure priorities included providing more assistance for the disadvantaged, preserving the family unit, and controlling the costs of the health care system while maintaining program standards.

In part, the Vander Zalm government responded to the legacy of the restraint program. Basic support allowance rates under GAIN, which had not been raised for five years, were increased for families by 5 percent in mid-1987 and a further 5 percent at the end of 1987. Funding for legal aid, student assistance, and services for persons with disabilities increased significantly. More generous spending on education and training activities also emerged, and the formation of the University of Northern British Columbia was announced. At the same time, pointing to relentless cost pressures in the health care system, the Vander Zalm government introduced user fees for physiotherapy and chiropractic services, increased medical services premiums, and began requiring senior citizens to pay for some of the drug costs under the Pharmacare program. Negotiations with the medical profession sought to bring doctors' fee levels into line with those in other provinces.

BC social programs were on edge because of Vander Zalm's own approach to making policy. This approach has aptly been called 'policy gambling,' with surprise, unpredictability, and uncertainty the norms. Harsher critics have called it chaos without style or substance.[21] The premier's eagerness to take action and to do what he deeply believed in meant that he did not always consult his caucus or the cabinet or use the public service in formulating policy ideas. While not the first premier in BC to do this, Vander Zalm seems to have done it in a number of program areas. Frustration over the perceived centralization of power led to the resignation of key ministers, the creation of a cabinet Planning and Priorities Committee in 1988, and contributed to the eventual downfall of Vander Zalm.

In the social domain, a major example of this policy gambling concerned abortion. The premier's private morality drove much of the public policy on this issue in the province. In 1987-8, funding for family support services was increased for the purposes of providing care to children, preserving the family unit in society, and helping reduce the province's 'high abortion rate.' Additional funding was provided to encourage alternatives to abortion. When, in early 1988, the Supreme Court of Canada struck down Canada's abortion law, the Vander Zalm government responded immediately by withdrawing all provincial funding for abortions. The cabinet amended the regulations to the Medical Services Act so that abortions were not regarded as medically necessary. The province would therefore no longer be required under the Canada Health Act to fund abortions. The premier's action sparked a strong reaction from women's groups, the opposition parties, health organizations, the BC Coalition for Abortion Clinics, and several members of his own government. The BC Civil Liberties Association quickly requested a judicial review of the government's regulatory amendment by the BC Supreme Court. The chief justice found the amended regulation to be invalid because it was not authorized by the Medical Services Act and it was inconsistent with the Supreme Court of Canada's finding that a pregnant woman's right to an abortion may be an expression of her right, under the Canadian Charter of Rights and Freedoms, to liberty and the security of her person. Reluctantly, the premier accepted that abortion services would be funded, but also announced a $2.2 million ad campaign on alternatives to abortion and another family support program of $20 million directed at pregnant women and single mothers.

Vander Zalm's efforts to enact an anti-abortion policy through regulations served to polarize and alienate large segments of the public. One observer has said of this abortion debate in BC: 'The Premier and his cabinet's obvious unwillingness to use consultation to find common ground and possible compromise in developing a reasonable policy on abortion ... resulted in the necessity to use the Court as a last resort to strike down the Premier's draconian attempts to impose his own personal moral views on an entire province.'[22] An acutely sensitive issue, the de-insuring of abortions was a gamble that Vander Zalm lost, causing considerable personal anxiety and political tension among British Columbians in the process.

This episode illustrates another feature of contemporary politics: the judicialization of policy processes. Governmental policies and procedures are increasingly subject to judicial scrutiny and influence, giving rise to a policy style that is more formal and legalistic. Since the inclusion in 1982 of the Charter of Rights and Freedoms in the Canadian constitution, judicial decisions have become more important in political and policy systems. This is discussed further in the chapter by Morley on the justice system (Chapter 11). Interest groups and individuals are taking issues to the courts to seek redress of perceived policy wrongs and to establish claims to perceived rights. Judges at both the federal and provincial levels are reaching decisions that are highly political and social in nature. To the extent that judges give authoritative meaning to laws and regulations in their rulings, the courts are (re)making or unmaking public policies.

The Vander Zalm government, in keeping with an ad hoc populist style, was also notable for a number of policy reviews and consultations it launched using royal commissions and task forces. Many of these reviews' reports landed on the desk of the Harcourt government, and did influence social policy-making. Reviews and consultations included the Royal Commission on Education (1988), the Justice for All study (1989), the healthy schools and healthy communities initiatives (1990), the report of the advisory council on community-based programs for women (1990), and the Royal Commission on Health Care and Costs (1991). With respect to organizational change, a Premier's Advisory Council for Persons with Disabilities was formed, and a Ministry of Native Affairs was established as a structural response to the province's acceptance, finally, of having a responsible role in the negotiation of aboriginal land claims and treaty rights within BC. In early 1991, a Child and Youth Secretariat was created in the provincial bureaucracy to help coordinate interministry policies and programs for youth, along with regional and local committees to consider service-delivery issues. Over this period, the considerable contracting-out of health and social services to non-governmental organizations blurred the boundaries between the provincial state sector and the voluntary sector. Concerns were raised about the autonomy and local responsiveness of community agencies reliant on government service contracts.

Social Policy and Social Reform Edging Along: 1991 to 1996
The main outcome of the 1991 provincial election – Mike Harcourt's NDP forming the government – was not a surprise. What was surprising was the decimation of Social Credit, the return of the Liberals to the legislature as the official opposition, and the appearance of Reform Party members in the assembly. The polarized nature of BC party politics had become pluralized. For the NDP, this meant that they were facing a more diverse and generally inexperienced opposition. Economically, this period began with a deep recession in Canada in general, though relatively not as serious in BC. The rate of unemployment in the province rose to 10.4 percent in 1992, and then declined to 9.7 in 1993 and 8.4 in 1994. Population growth continued, reaching over 3.7 million, and BC enjoyed strong economic growth and job creation.

Social policy-making by the Harcourt government can be depicted as edging along – moving gradually on many issues, disappointing supporters on some, and advancing reforms on still others, all the while making its way through the pressures of global economic change, declining federal commitment to national standards, and the diversity of lifestyles in society. With the NDP in power, the provincial government was no longer espousing the 'new right' ideology but rather a belief in a strong and secure social security system. Their challenge lay in trying to renew the postwar welfare state in a postmodern world.

At a broad level, much of the Harcourt government's policy language sounded similar to its predecessors. In throne speeches, budgets, and other documents, the NDP's policy themes included eliminating the deficit and reducing the provincial debt, protecting the social safety net, maintaining stability in the health care system, and investing in people through education and skills training. If these sound like echoes, they do reflect underlying economic interests in the province, genuine concerns of the public, and the imperatives of running a welfare state. Newer social priorities expressed by the NDP included promoting equality for women through pay equity, child care, personal safety, and assistance to victims of violence; forging new relations with aboriginal peoples; increasing the fairness of BC's tax system by raising the revenues to maintain essential public services on the basis of people's ability to pay; and clearing up the 'backlog' in health care and education services by investing in needed social infrastructure.

Social policy-making must always be viewed in relation to the overall budgetary stance of a government. When provincial politicians talk of putting the government's financial house in order, we must remember that social programs comprise most of the rooms. The Harcourt government earnestly strove to be viewed as a responsible manager of the public purse. This effort was partly motivated by the Harcourt NDP's desire to contrast their government's fiscal responsibility with the apparent profligacy of the Vander Zalm government, and partly to exorcise the image of financial mismanagement by the Barrett NDP government. The Harcourt government's fiscal strategy was to eliminate the provincial deficit by the start of the 1996-7 year. They effectively pursued this goal by slowing the growth in overall program spending; raising taxes in their early budgets before introducing in the 1994 budget a three-year freeze on provincial personal and business income taxes, sales, and other consumer taxes; promoting economic development; and reaping the benefits of strong job growth in BC. At the same time, they increased funding to health care, education, and postsecondary education at rates higher than any other Canadian province in this period.

Upon taking office, the NDP had the recently released report of the Royal Commission on Health Care and Costs to consider. Entitled *Closer to Home,* the report urged the province to move away from a centralized health system with an emphasis on institutional care toward a more decentralized and community-based care approach. The Harcourt government soon established a twenty-four-member team, with representation from both inside and outside the health care system, to advise the government on how to take action on the report's many recommendations. A group of officials within the Ministry of Health played a similar part. The government's published response, 'New Directions in Health Care,' accepted most of the 'closer to home' ethos, and entailed a restructuring of the delivery and governance of health care in the province. A modest though not insignificant portion of health care resources and providers are shifting to community care work. Budget dollars and program responsibilities are being transferred from the health ministry to twenty-one regional health boards. As of the 1996 municipal elections in BC, these health boards will be made up of equal numbers of municipal appointees, provincial appointees, and, most significantly, directly elected members. This composition will add a new democratic dimension and political dynamic to local health authorities. These regional boards will eventually assume responsibility for the management and funding of health services in their respective areas. Under these boards, numerous community health councils are to serve as advisory bodies to enhance citizen participation and responsiveness to diverse local needs. In addition, the government set up a $42 million Closer to Home fund to assist localities in devising community-based health initiatives to compensate for reduced hospital services.

To deal with the workforce adjustments needed to shift priority from institutional care to community care, the Harcourt government negotiated a labour accord with unions in acute- and extended-care facilities and some continuing-care facilities. The accord provides employment tenure for bargaining unit employees in the three big unions in BC hospitals for the term of the accord (fall of 1993 to spring of 1996). The accord was formulated based on the government's goal of removing the equivalent of 10 percent (4,800) of the full-time staff from hospitals in order to direct staff and the savings to community-level health services. This was to be realized through a combination of early retirement, regular attrition, a reduced work week, job sharing, and transfers from acute hospitals to other kinds of facilities. The accord also saw the creation of the Healthcare Labour Adjustment Agency to manage the placement of unionized employees made redundant under the health reforms or for other reasons.

In a related process, the Harcourt government enacted a new Medical and Health Services Act that provides for the co-management of health finances by the government, the BCMA, and the public. Under the act, the Medical Services Commission – which has nine members, three each from the provincial government, the BCMA, and the public – has responsibility for managing the Medical Services Plan (MSP), with the government retaining responsibility to set the overall MSP budget. In 1992 a five-year working agreement between the Medical Services Commission, the BCMA, and the government took effect. There is an annual cap on total MSP payments to physicians for the medical services they provide, and clinical practice guidelines are being developed to avoid unnecessary tests and procedures. Over the term of the agreement, the aim is to manage the growth of the health care system and, by controlling costs, save $383 million.

These initiatives in medical services and in labour adjustment represent a *corporatist* approach to health policy-making. Corporatism is when there are highly organized and influential interest structures in a policy field, which the state recognizes as central partners and with which it negotiates in an attempt at building consensus and directing public and private resources. In the health care field, there are clearly defined and relatively strong interest structures, including that of the welfare state. The labour accord and the working agreement were formulated by the provincial government in close collaboration with union and medical profession elites. These processes of shared decision-making produced policy frameworks for managing changes in public budgeting and program delivery in health care. As a form of intermediation between activist government and other major organizations in society, the corporatist approach is related to the institutional paradigm of social policy.

Links between social policy and economic development were highlighted in this period by the NDP's measures on the labour market and infrastructure investment. In 1993 the government held a Premier's Summit on skills development and training, which brought together representatives from business, labour, education, communities, and government. Here again was an example of the province attempting to forge connections across sectors, include stakeholders in policy discussions, and find areas of agreement on directions for reform. The NDP's major labour market policy initiative, Skills Now, was announced in May 1994. It is a $200 million training plan over 1994-6 to boost the skills level and employability of people in BC. Touted as a new partnership, Skills Now includes a twenty-six-member labour development board with co-chairs from the BC Business Council and BC Federation of Labour. The board's role is to provide advice to the government on job market and training measures. This skills strategy has four themes: linking high school to the workplace; opening more doors, and the right doors, to college and university; retraining workers closer to home; and moving from welfare to the workforce. The overall thrust is to develop 'real skills for the real world.'

The Harcourt government also undertook a major program of capital expenditures on social infrastructure in the province. More than $2 billion was invested in the construction and improvement of public schools, colleges, and universities. Other social investments have been on hospitals and health care, courthouses, non-profit housing units, child care spaces, and recreational and cultural facilities. These investments are responses to population growth and backlogs in needed facilities. They are also ways to stimulate present and future economic activity and support the quality of life in BC. To finance these infrastructure projects, the NDP borrowed money and thus increased the provincial debt. They defended this approach by arguing that today's taxpayers should not be expected to pay for the entire cost of services and facilities that will yield future benefits and be used by other British Columbians for decades to come.

In 1994 a Premier's Forum on New Opportunities for Working and Living was established to provide the government with guidance on renewing BC's social policy. The exercise was supported by a small group of officials within a Social Program Renewal Secretariat. The forum was composed of thirty-three appointees who met from mid-1994 to early 1995. Their task was to consider how social programs could remain relevant, compassionate, and affordable. Their purview was wide and included pensions, health care, income assistance, child care, education, and skills training. The forum published a series of informative background papers and produced a report, *Opportunities for Renewal*, which was released in April 1995.[23] It is worth noting that the government chose to use a low-profile task force device attached to the executive rather than a legislative committee or full-blown royal commission, both of which would be less subject to the government's control and could have a higher political profile.

That the NDP government edged along in social policy reform is perhaps most apparent in the area of income assistance and poverty. Here, their record is a mix of reformist measures, opportunities missed, and, at times, residualist messages. Poverty, in financial terms, is when people with low incomes spend disproportionate amounts of their money on the basic necessities of food, clothing, and shelter. In the early 1990s, poverty rates in BC increased. The portion of the provincial population living in low-income poverty rose from 13.8 percent in 1989 to 17.3 in 1993. While poverty among senior citizens had been dropping for over a decade, poverty among families with children had been rising.[24] In their 1994 throne speech, the NDP said: 'Restoring the integrity of our social safety net is a pressing concern. We must provide for those who are truly in need and help people on welfare back to work, while enforcing strict regulations that curb fraud.' Fighting poverty with major increases in the benefit levels of income security programs, a strategy traditionally favoured by antipoverty activists, was not a high political priority for the Harcourt NDP.

Much of their activity on welfare related to promoting skills training, revising features of the welfare program, and establishing a public image of being tough on welfare abuse. More opportunities and expectations are being put to income assistance recipients to pursue further education, undertake training, and search for work. Under the Skills Now program, $78 million has been allocated from 1994 to 1996 for training of up to 50,000 people on welfare, about one-sixth of the total caseload. On reforming the income assistance program, the NDP removed disincentives to work by raising exemption levels that allow people on welfare to earn more money without losing benefits; expanded working families' eligibility for child care subsidies; and changed the regulations so single parents with young children can choose when to return to work rather than, as previously, being categorized as employable when their child reached the age of six months. These positive changes, among others, are part of the good news for people who are poor in BC. Yet there has also been bad news in the NDP's treatment of the poor. The Harcourt government's attention to welfare abuse rather than to other social issues, and Harcourt's own public comments about welfare cheats, dismayed many of his supporters and discouraged many social service providers and recipients. The ideas of residualism and the language of neoconservatism were still alive, it seemed, even in a social democratic government.

In 1994 the Harcourt government announced seven new income assistance policies that they presented as a means to combat welfare fraud: computer identification of individuals who may be claiming assistance in more than one province; a new rule that cash will no longer be provided in response to repeated reports of lost and stolen cheques; all employable single persons and childless couples are required to complete report cards listing days worked, job search efforts, and any training activities; new procedures to recover security deposits directly from landlords that have been paid by the government on behalf of welfare tenants; all employable single persons and childless couples were required to pick up their March 1994 cheques in person; federal-provincial actions to eliminate duplicate payments of unemployment insurance and income assistance; and a change to the single parent exemption policy in that single parents would now be considered employable when their youngest child is twelve years of age, rather than nineteen. The measures, developed largely by the Ministry of Social Services, were introduced as a pilot project, and the minister predicted that savings would be about $20 million a year.

This group of policies constitutes the most comprehensive and politically visible action on 'welfare fraud' in modern BC social policy. Estimates of fraud over the years have usually been between 3 to 5 percent of caseloads. The main reasons for welfare fraud in BC seem to be the non-disclosure of income from other sources and counterfeit identification produced by organized crime. The NDP's interest in welfare fraud likely came from several sources: media attention on a few cases of proven fraud and leaked internal studies on the matter; financial cutbacks at the federal level on cost-sharing for welfare; high welfare caseloads in BC in the 1990s; continuing residualist values and public concerns of waste and abuse; and the symbolic politics of a left-wing government not wanting to be seen as 'soft' on welfare fraud.

The NDP's mixed record on welfare reform was again apparent with the BC Benefits Program announced by the minister of social services, Joy MacPhail, in November 1995. This program is really a set of measures, phased in over several months, aimed at reducing the province's welfare expenditures and making low-paid work more attractive than welfare benefits. As of January 1996, benefits for 'employable' recipients with no dependents were reduced by $46 a month, a measure affecting about 67,000 recipients. The earnings exemption – the amount of money recipients can earn without losing welfare benefits – was also reduced, effectively amounting to a major tax increase. As of July 1996, two new programs take effect. The Healthy Kids program will provide dental benefits and vision care for children of working families with low and moderate incomes; and a family bonus program will provide a monthly cheque of up to $103 a child for this group of families too. Later in the year, new job-training courses for the unemployed will be introduced. The most controversial measure, however, was also the most immediate one. As of December 1995, the BC government began enforcing a residency requirement to prevent newcomers to the province (all other Canadians and new refugees) from collecting income assistance until they have lived in BC for three months. The then federal minister responsible for welfare transfer payments to the provinces, Lloyd Axworthy, quickly withheld $47 million from BC on the grounds that this residency rule contravened the conditions of the Canada Assistance Plan Act. The issue generated a serious conflict between the two levels of government, and in January 1996 the province launched a lawsuit in the BC Supreme Court to recover the withheld funds. In the current age of restraint, citizens could easily believe that this conflict had more to do with political posturing and fractious federalism than with either government protecting the social safety net.

Another NDP social policy disappointment for the poor and their advocacy organizations is that welfare rates were not increased enough to offset inflation and historically inadequate benefit levels. Welfare incomes in BC, as with all the provinces and territories, still fall below the poverty line. Moreover, the minimum wage, while it increased 20 percent, needed to rise further to significantly reduce poverty.[25]

The social machinery of government in the provincial welfare state underwent some important changes in these years. In addition to those noted above, organizational developments by the NDP include: a new Freedom of Information and Privacy Act and Commissioner; expansion of the Ombudsman Office's jurisdiction to cover municipalities, the education sector, and self-regulating organizations; expansion of the scope of the BC Human Rights Act and Commission to include protection from discrimination on the basis of age, family status, or sexual orientation; and creation of the Ministry of Women's Equality. This new ministry works with other BC ministries to ensure that issues relating to women's equality are reflected in policy, legislation, and services throughout the government. The ministry seeks to eliminate discrimination against women, support equity and equality, and advance the understanding of feminist perspectives. The ministry also has responsibilities for program delivery in child care, transition houses, and grants. Still other structural changes involved the creation of the Office of the Child Advocate; appointment of the Minister's Advisory Council on Income Assistance, to the minister of social services; establishment of the BC Treaty Commission with First Nations' representatives and the federal government; the legal recognition of midwifery as a health service profession; and the replacement of teachers' collective bargaining at the level of school districts with a province-wide process. Following a judicial inquiry into the death of a child who had been under care by provincial social workers, an inquiry that also looked into the overall provincial child welfare system, the Harcourt government responded, in part, by replacing the Child and Youth Secretariat with the Office of the Transition Commissioner for Child and Youth Services. The hope is that this new office, created in early 1996, will have more resources and executive powers to coordinate and work across the several ministries relevant to children and families.

The composition of a cabinet tells us something of the policy priorities of a premier and government as well as of the times in which they govern. By the mid-1990s, the number of social ministries in the BC cabinet had reached nine, representing half of the portfolios. Only thirty years earlier, there were five social ministries in a cabinet of sixteen. This growth in the ministerial administration of social policy has several implications for policy communities and processes. With the formation of ministries headed by executive politicians comes additional bureaucratic sources for policy initiation and protection, and new access points for certain interest groups. Other groups in society may, in turn, be prompted to call for their own ministerial representative. The nature of budgetary bargaining within a cabinet committee and between the Treasury Board and ministries cannot help but be different if there are nine or ten social policy players versus five. With the growth in cabinet portfolios and policy-making in more hands, there is a corresponding need for regular means of coordination at the centre of government. The complexity of structures and processes may limit somewhat the power of a premier today, but they serve to reinforce the central place of the cabinet in the making of social policy.

Mike Harcourt's decision to step down as premier was certainly another political surprise of this period. Early in 1996, at a party convention, he was succeeded as leader and premier by Glen Clark. As a member of Harcourt's cabinet, Clark had first held the important finance portfolio and then another economic portfolio, though not a social ministry. From

these positions, however, and especially the former one with lead responsibility for the provincial budget, Clark played a central role in shaping
both the fiscal decisions and social policy priorities of the NDP.

The Clark NDP and the Winning Edge: 1996 and Beyond

The selection of a new party leader, and particularly one as premier, is a
central means for re-energizing a political party as well as influencing social policy-making. The leadership style and policy objectives of a premier
are chief determinants of the substance and processes of social programs.
Glen Clark is a hands-on leader who is interested in a wide range of public
issues, who gets involved in policy development, and who is more aggressively partisan than his predecessor, Mike Harcourt. Social policy and social spending were key elements in Clark's strategy to resuscitate the NDP,
bringing the governing party quickly back to political life and electoral
success.

Before the May 1996 provincial election, Clark took action in several
social program areas. Along with the premiership, Clark assumed the portfolio of minister responsible for youth and convened a Premier's Youth
Forum to signal the future of youth in BC as a high priority topic. In education, Clark's government announced a freeze on university and college
fees for 1996-7, and increased funding by $64 million for the 10,000 new
students entering the kindergarten to grade 12 system. The NDP also unveiled plans to reduce the number of school districts in BC from 75 to 57,
amalgamating 34 smaller ones into 16 new ones, for a projected savings of
$120 million over four years. At the same time, Clark and his education
minister promised trustee and teacher associations that the province would
slow down the pace of changes in the education system. In April 1996, the
legislature passed the Education and Health Collective Bargaining Assistance Act, which gave the cabinet the power to impose settlements, based
on the recommendations of a mediator, in labour disputes involving education and health care workers. The act was in effect only until 30 June
1996, and effectively prevented any strikes in these sectors during the election campaign. The Clark NDP presented a preelection budget in the legislature that was not debated or passed because of the election call. The budget
was symbolically important, however, in that it forecast a small surplus for
the second year running and promised that the personal income tax rate
would be cut by two percentage points over two years. A number of other
taxes were frozen or reduced, and the homeowner grant threshold for property tax relief was to be raised.

In the campaign itself, social policies were used by both major parties,
the NDP and Liberals, to woo voters, to distinguish their party from the
others, and to try to help win the election. The Liberal leader, Gordon
Campbell, promised to put more money into health care and education

from unspecified savings elsewhere in the provincial budget. He attacked welfare fraud, contending it was far higher than the NDP said, and proposed a new crackdown to rid the income assistance program of abuse. Campbell also promised a tax cut for middle-income people and more targeting of social programs. Glen Clark announced a plan to protect the health care system that included a Medical Charter and Patient's Bill of Rights, a new five-year health funding formula, and bans on extra-billing and on doctors in publicly funded facilities referring patients to private clinics. Clark promised to extend his postsecondary tuition freeze for another year, while adding 11,600 student spaces to BC universities and colleges. On welfare, Clark said little other than that the NDP's three-month residency rule was having the intended impact of reducing the size of the province's welfare rolls. Clark also pledged to tie the province's minimum wage to the rate of inflation.

The 1996 election saw the Liberals edged out by a revitalized NDP. The NDP won thirty-nine of seventy-five seats, forming a small majority government; they received less of the popular vote than the Liberals or than what they themselves had obtained in the 1991 election. In politics, however, there is no time like the present and no place like in government. The NDP remains the actors and the Liberals and other parties the spectators in BC's political drama. Even with a slim majority government, under our parliamentary and federalized form of government, Premier Clark and his cabinet are the lead actors in the social policy process. Yet they confront a more polarized legislature than the previous one, with the NDP and the Liberals accounting for nearly all the seats.

It does matter which party wins an election. For social policy, it makes a difference for the mix of values held and aims pursued by those in authority, the structures and processes employed for taking action, and the relative influence of organized interests in the community. Over time it can have consequences for the social role of the provincial state and the overall division of welfare in BC.

With their first ever back-to-back election wins in BC, the NDP have become the governing party of the 1990s. They have the opportunity to carry on implementing legislative achievements from the Harcourt years such as the Child, Youth and Family Advocacy Act, policy reforms such as 'New Directions in Health Care,' and organizational innovations such as the Ministry of Women's Equality. They will continue, for example, to control health care costs, while seeking to protect the principles underlying medicare and putting more resources into community-based care. Parts of the policy agenda are more or less outside their control. The political salience of the welfare budget and the issue of welfare fraud will not go away, and as the BC population continues to expand, new and upgraded social infrastructure in the form of school, health, and community facilities will be required. Clark's own agenda gives emphasis to educational and employment issues related to young people.

Prospects for Social Policy:
On the Brink of Decline or the Verge of Renewal?

Social policies and provincial politics are inseparable. In many respects, the modern provincial state is a welfare state, and major social programs define our provincial government. Making social policy is the working through of political ideas, human needs, and public interests in a community. Social programs express values and allocate resources. They involve the exercise of public and private power. They affect the life chances and statuses of individuals and groups. Over the past few generations, the scope and content of this West Coast welfare state has changed enormously. It now contains many goals, various organizations and processes, several policy communities, and a multiplicity of laws and programs. The 'socialness' of the provincial government is apparent in the budget, the profile of employees, and the cabinet portfolios. Though the focus in this chapter has been on the provincial government, social policy extends beyond the state to the informal, voluntary, aboriginal, and business sectors. This social division of welfare raises the fundamental question of what the role of the state should be in relation to these other sectors, a question that is always partly open for debate.

Social programs are historical products as well as political creations. The history of social policy is not some great dustheap but a rich record of innumerable biographies and beliefs. In BC this history has involved a struggle, at the level of beliefs, between the residual and institutional paradigms of welfare. The province's welfare state has on it the stamp of both paradigms. This network of social provisions is not the result of a grand plan. An explanation of the adoption of each part of the welfare state requires the telling of many separate stories in federal and provincial policy history. As specific achievements, social programs are frequently the result of intensive political debate and differing conceptions of human nature and federalism. In some social areas in some periods, BC has been a policy leader: old age pensions in the late 1920s, public hospital insurance in the 1940s, and the first provincial housing department in Canada in 1973. In other areas, the province has been a policy laggard: not forming a department of health until 1946 or a provincial ombudsman until 1979 (the second last province to establish the latter), and the late introduction of modern policy analysis and budgeting methods. Even today some of the ideas and practices in social policy are from the Victorian era.

Overall, BC social policy is fairly Canadian in that its pattern of development has been similar to other provinces, having been shaped, in large part, by intergovernmental relations. From the 1870s to the 1940s, basic outlines of pre-welfare state social policy were developed. The 1945 to 1982 period saw the emergence of the provincial welfare state and social programs becoming the primary policy role in government. The years 1983 to 1991 correspond to the last Social Credit governments and the ascendancy of neoconservatism in BC, with social policy feeling the cutting edge of restraint. The 1991 to 1996 period found provincial social policy-making, under the Harcourt NDP, edging along through a political thicket of opportunities and obstacles.

What of the future? The prospects for social policy in BC are connected, in important ways, to the future of social policy at the national level in Canada. The role of the federal government in the social policy field has been diminishing for several years and is on the brink of further serious decline. The BC government estimates that it will lose $477 million in 1996-7 when Ottawa replaces the existing federal transfer payments with the Canada Health and Social Transfer. As the federal role declines, the provincial role almost necessarily advances. After a decade or more of deficit control actions, the federal government still has a sizeable deficit and a large debt, leaving Ottawa with few new resources and the Chrétien Liberals little inclination to launch new social programs. The financial situation of the federal government is considerably worse than that of the provinces. This suggests that social policy-making will shift even more to the provinces, First Nations governments, and the courts, given the momentum of aboriginal self-determination, the Charter, and the new discourse on rights in Canadian political culture. For BC in particular, the days of province-building on the social front are not over. With financially sound public accounts, a strong economy, and a growing and ageing population of diverse peoples, the provincial government has both the capacity and the necessity to exercise its powers. Considerable room exists for the democratic reform of social policy so that successive generations of British Columbians may feel that they too can cope with and shape the world they face.

Further Reading

Baines, Carol, Patricia Evans, and Sheila Neysmith, eds. *Women's Caring: Feminist Perspectives on Social Welfare*. Toronto: McClelland and Stewart 1991

Banting, Keith G. *The Welfare State and Canadian Federalism*. 2nd ed. Montreal: McGill-Queen's University Press 1987

Cairns, Alan C., and Cynthia Williams, eds. *Constitutionalism, Citizenship and Society in Canada*. Toronto: University of Toronto Press 1985

Canada. *Security, Opportunities and Fairness: Canadians Renewing Their Social Programs*. Report of the Standing Committee on Human Resources Development. Ottawa: Queen's Printer 1995

Grady, Patrick, Robert Howse, and Judith Maxwell. *Redefining Social Security*. Kingston: School of Policy Studies, Queen's University 1995

Ismael, Jacqueline S., ed. *The Canadian Welfare State*. Edmonton: University of Alberta Press 1987
Sayeed, Adil, ed. *Workfare: Does It Work? Is It Fair?* Montreal: Institute for Research on Public Policy 1995
Sutherland, Ralph, and Jane Fulton. *Spending Smarter and Spending Less: Policies and Partnerships for Health Care in Canada*. Ottawa: The Health Group 1994

The main periodicals in the social policy field for BC and Canada include *BC Studies, Canadian Journal of Political Science, Canadian Public Administration, Canadian Public Policy, Canadian Review of Social Policy, Canadian Social Trends, Journal of Canadian Studies, Perception,* and *Policy Options*. Individual professional associations associated with the welfare state also have journals, such as the *Canadian Review of Social Work*, which contain articles relevant to social issues and policy processes. Other useful sources are Carleton University's annual review of federal policies and priorities (*How Ottawa Spends*), think tanks such as the Social Planning and Research Council of BC, the C.D. Howe Institute, and the Caledon Institute of Social Policy, as well as the reports of provincial government advisory councils on income assistance, persons with disabilities, and seniors.

15
The Politics of Sustainability: Forest Policy in British Columbia
George Hoberg

Forests are an essential part of the heritage and identity of British Columbians, and forest policy has long been central to BC politics. In the past several decades, forest policy has become increasingly controversial, and in the early 1990s the issue erupted into one of the most dominant concerns of government. This chapter chronicles the evolution of BC forest policy, focusing on the dramatic changes that have occurred during the present decade. While reform efforts began in the 1970s, they accelerated greatly in the 1990s, transforming the traditional policy regime that emphasized rapid timber harvesting and economic development into a modern regime in which environmental values have been brought into greater balance with developmental ones.

After a brief overview of forest policy, this chapter examines a prominent series of policy initiatives during the 1990s that reshaped BC forest policy. Because of its centrality to BC politics, the Clayoquot Sound case will be given particular attention. The next section provides an explanation for these developments by examining the interests and resources of the major actors in BC forest policy, and discussing how changes in resources available to the different actors contributed to the transformation of policy. The conclusion speculates about the durability of the policy change.

Overview

The central dilemma in BC forest policy is how to balance the conflicting uses of forested land. BC forests contain vast tracts of commercially valuable timber, and forest products constitute the largest industry in the province. BC forests also contain spectacular wilderness areas, some of the last extensive tracts of virgin forest on the continent, and an extraordinary diversity of fish and wildlife habitat. These environmental values are in many cases in direct conflict with timber harvesting. Policymakers must determine how to allocate land use among these various competing interests.

This conflict of interest in forest land use is complicated by the spatial distribution of interests. Residents of rural communities across the province depend on extractive activities such as logging for their livelihood. While many people in timber-dependent communities treasure the forests' environmental values, the environmental amenities are also cherished by residents of urban areas who rely on them for recreation. And because virtually all of these forests are owned by the Crown, all British Columbians have some claim over how they are used, not just those who live in adjacent areas. As a result, much of the political conflict over forest policy has been dominated by an urban-rural cleavage.

In Canada, jurisdiction over forests belongs almost exclusively with the provinces. At the provincial level in BC, the government owns virtually all (95 percent) of the forested land, and thus the BC Ministry of Forests is the key regulator and manager. The Chief Forester is an assistant deputy minister of the BC Forest Service, and is responsible for ensuring that all crown (i.e., government) forest lands are managed according to the objectives laid out in the governing statutes.

BC's forest land is managed through a complex system of 'tenures.' The two dominant forms of tenures are the area-based Tree Farm Licences (TFLs) and the volume-based Timber Supply Areas (TSAs). As of April 1991, 75 percent of BC's annual allowable cut was represented within thirty-six TSAs, with the remaining 25 percent represented by thirty-five TFLs.[1] In both forms of tenure, the ministry delegates certain forest management responsibilities to private timber companies in exchange for long-term guarantees of timber supply. Traditionally, holders of TFLs have undertaken considerably more responsibility than companies operating in TSAs, but the differences seem to be lessening somewhat.

This system of tenures has come under persistent attack from a number of sources. Economists have attacked the system on two grounds. First, because stumpage rates – the amount timber companies are charged to get access to crown trees – are set by the government and not the market, there is little confidence that the price accurately reflects the full value of the resource. Among other things, this pricing system has left BC vulnerable to persistent challenges from the US forest industry that its stumpage system provides a subsidy to producers. Second, by limiting the property rights timber companies have in the resource, there is less private incentive to ensure proper long-term stewardship of the forest. These criticisms have been supported by the Forest Resource Commission, appointed by the last Socred government to address the burgeoning conflicts in the forest sector.[2]

Environmentalists and social activists are also opposed to the existing tenure system. They believe the system has had the effect of concentrating control of the timber resource in a very small number of large firms, making the industry less sensitive to the needs for both environmental and community sustainability.³ While these sorts of criticism have been substantial and persistent, the tenure system is the one major aspect of BC forest policy that has been stubbornly resistant to significant reform.

The Transformation of BC Forest Policy

Of the many issues involved in BC forest policy, this chapter focuses on four of the most important: (1) where to log and where to preserve, (2) how to log, (3) at what rate to log, and (4) how to maintain stable communities.⁴ Major initiatives in each of these areas will be outlined. Significant policy change has been achieved in each area, with the first three all moving toward greater environmental sensitivity and less timber harvesting. The fourth area is an effort to compensate for this shift, but the ability to do that in the long run is problematic.

Land Use Issues: The Crisis in Clayoquot Sound

The question of where to log and where to preserve has been one of the most divisive issues in BC politics over the past quarter century, the most prominent example being Clayoquot Sound. The Clayoquot Sound case gets its notoriety from the intensity of conflict over the ultimate decision, as demonstrated by the large number of people who engaged in civil disobedience to protest the government's action, as well as the international attention focused on the dispute. The case reveals a great deal about the politics of BC forest policy, and for that reason it is treated in some detail.

The Clayoquot Sound decision-making process was a failed test of an innovative and promising experiment in democratic governance. These experiments have emerged in response to a crisis of legitimacy in the Canadian administrative state that goes far beyond Clayoquot Sound or BC. Traditionally, government decisions garnered legitimacy through the norms of representative and responsible government. Governments were elected to office based in part on their policy positions. Policy was developed through consideration of expert analysis provided by bureaucrats and consultation with interested groups in society. Decisions on important matters were made by the cabinet, with elected politicians representing the views of competing interests. The government was held accountable for their decisions, and if the public disagreed with those decisions it had the right and duty to turf them out of office and replace them with a government more to its liking.

This view has fallen out of favour for several reasons. First, elections are extremely blunt instruments for representing the public's views on specific policy questions. People vote for parties for many different reasons, and it is extremely difficult to discern policy mandates for governments, especially on specific issues. Second, the nature of our electoral system and party system routinely produces results where parties control the govern-ment without winning a majority of popular votes. The provincial NDP government elected in 1991, for instance, received only 41 percent of the vote. Third, our norms of governance have changed so that people are demanding more direct participation by those most affected by decisions.

As a result of these problems, the legitimacy of representative, responsi-ble government has been undermined. The dilemma is that we have yet to settle on an alternative model of governance. BC has been in the forefront of developing one alternative model, known as consensus-based negotia-tion, or shared decision-making. These processes go beyond mere consul-tation with competing interests and actually devolve some authority over policy-making to a group of stakeholders. Rather than the majority rule common to legislatures, these new bodies operate under a decision rule of consensus. Clayoquot Sound was one of the first and highest profile at-tempts to use this new form of decision-making.

There were two attempts to reach consensus on land use decisions in the sound. Both of them floundered over the issue of what logging should proceed while the negotiations were in progress. The first, the Clayoquot Sound Sustainable Development Task Force, was formed by the provincial government in August 1989. It consisted of a broad range of interests, in-cluding labour, industry, environmentalists, Natives, and government. It was given the responsibility of developing a long-term sustainable devel-opment plan for the region, as well as approving short-term decisions about where logging would occur while the talks were going on. The process was a dismal failure because of the intense conflict over short-term logging issues.[5]

As a result, the task force recommended the creation of an alternative process, the Clayoquot Sound Sustainable Development Steering Commit-tee, which was established in October 1990. The key difference was that everyone agreed that the steering committee should focus on developing a long-term land use plan, and that the issues of short-term logging deci-sions would be delegated to a panel consisting of officials from the Minis-try of Forests and the Ministry of Environment.

It was the decision of that panel that created the major stumbling block for the consensus process. Environmentalists were outraged that the panel decided to permit logging in the Bulson Creek area, which they considered to be an unlogged watershed. To them, the decision to log a previously undeveloped watershed indicated the absence of a commitment to negoti-ate in good faith. There are differences of opinion about whether or not Bulson Creek was an unlogged watershed. The government and industry claim the watershed was already developed. Various documents list it as unmodified,[6] but apparently there had been some minor logging in the lower part of the drainage – on 160 hectares, or 2.2 percent of the watershed area. Whether that counts as developed or not, it seems, depends on your perspective.

From the view of the environmental representatives, at least, they saw irreversible decisions being made on the very issues they were supposed to be addressing at the table, proving their worst fears that they were falling into a 'talk and log' trap. They had already agreed to give up one unlogged watershed, Tofino Creek, when they entered into the original task force, and, not wanting to lend such a process any legitimacy, they resigned from the steering committee in May 1991. From the perspective of industry, labour, and government, the watershed had already undergone some development so additional logging there was not unreasonable. Moreover, timber supply in the region was sufficiently tight that in order to keep the workers of the Kennedy Lake Division employed, access to Bulson Creek was necessary.

The steering committee continued without the environmental representatives present. Environmental views were still represented in the committee by representatives from Tofino, the tourism sector, and the Ministry of Environment. But once the official environmental representatives left, the committee lost its most forceful and legitimate advocates of the preservationist position. The next major development occurred in January 1992, when, as discussed below, the new NDP government announced the formation of the Commission on Resources and the Environment (CORE). Despite CORE's mandate to develop a comprehensive land use planning process for the province – to move beyond the valley by valley conflicts that have plagued BC in the past decade – the Clayoquot Sound Steering Committee process was explicitly exempted. There is disagreement over the reason for this action. The official government explanation is that more than two years had already gone into the local process and it would have been unfair to the participants to preempt it at that point. A more cynical view is that the NDP was looking out for the interests of the International Woodworkers of America (IWA), which was concerned that CORE would become captured by environmentalists, and that it would be unfair to reward environmentalists for walking out on the steering committee. A view more charitable to the NDP is that it wanted CORE to succeed, and the last thing it should do is infect the CORE process from the start with the disaster-in-waiting that Clayoquot had become.

Even with the official environmentalists out, the steering committee could not come to a consensus. A number of parties had coalesced around the so-called 'Option 5,' but the greener members of the committee from Tofino and the tourism sector would not agree to it. As a result, the steering committee disbanded in October 1992 without coming to any consensus on the land use issues.

After the committee process ended, the coalition supporting Option 5 organized itself to present what it called the 'majority option.' This was supported by ten of the thirteen interest groups and communities, the thirteen not including Natives, who did not take a position on it, and the environmentalists who had walked out. Of the three dissenting groups, Tofino and tourism thought it wasn't preservationist enough, and mining thought it was too preservationist. Subsequently, the two co-chairs of the failed steering committee issued a report to cabinet in January 1993 laying out various options, including Option 5 and a more preservationist 'Tofino option,' as well as the option to refer all or parts of the decision to CORE.

With the failure of the innovative steering committee process, policy was then made the old-fashioned way, at the highest levels of government in a hard-fought, intense, and lengthy cabinet debate. The government announced its decision in April 1993.[7] The decision was more preservationist than the so-called 'majority option,'[8] but it did not protect nearly as much as environmentalists had sought, and massive protests began. During the summer of 1993, environmentalists conducted an impressive campaign of civil disobedience, with over 800 people being arrested for blocking logging roads into the sound.

The decision sparked the outrage of environmentalists not only in BC but across the continent and abroad as well. Despite opinion polls showing general public approval within the province for the government's compromise decision,[9] concerns raised by the internationalization of the issue forced the cabinet to have second thoughts. But reversal of such a highly public decision was politically impossible. The government has taken two major steps, however, that have produced something of a reversal in position without having to publicly acknowledge doing so.

First, at the prodding of CORE Commissioner Stephen Owen, the government appointed a Scientific Panel for Sustainable Forest Practices in Clayoquot Sound in October 1993, with the goal, as announced by Premier Harcourt, 'to make forest practices in Clayoquot not only the best in the province, but the best in the world.'[10] As an indication of his commitment, Harcourt appointed Dr. Fred Bunnell, a conservation biologist from the University of British Columbia with strong environmental credentials, and Dr. Richard Atleo, Hereditary Chief UMEEK, as co-chairs of the panel. Dr. Jerry Franklin, guru of the environmentally sensitive 'new forestry' paradigm in the US, was also appointed to the panel. As expected, in April 1995 the panel recommended extremely stringent forest practices that, while not forbidding logging altogether, will make it far more costly, in some cases prohibitively so.[11] In July 1995, the government announced that it was adopting all the recommendations of the scientific panel, most notably a reduction in the size of cutblocks to the point where the practice of clearcutting as it has been known in the region is prohibited, replaced by much smaller patch cuts. As a result, logging in environmentally sensitive areas has been reduced significantly without the government having to publicly reverse its land use decision.

Second, the province entered into an 'interim measures agreement' in March 1994 with the Nuu-chah-nulth tribes, creating what is essentially a co-management agreement between these First Nations peoples and the government. While the new governing arrangements have not been fully implemented, it is anticipated that the agreement will lead to less logging in the sound than would have occurred under the preexisting arrangement of government-industry bargaining. At the time of its announcement, the agreement was considered a shrewd political manoeuvre by the government to split the alliance between environmentalists and First Nations peoples in the region. – by coming to terms with First Nations peoples, the industry undercut environmentalists who claimed to be representing the interests of aboriginals. When Harcourt went on a European tour to defend BC forestry against international attacks by Greenpeace, he was accompanied by George Watts of Nuu-chah-nulth Tribal Council, much to the embarrassment of environmentalists. While Harcourt skilfully resolved the political problem of Clayoquot Sound for the time being, he may have created larger problems for future BC governments in creating a precedent for co-management arrangements.

Land Use Issues: CORE

In some ways, the crisis over Clayoquot is a classic example of what has always been wrong with BC forest policy: the ad hoc manner in which these issues have been addressed by focusing on particular contested areas, whether it be south Moresby Island, the Stein Valley, or Clayoquot Sound. Since its election in the fall of 1991, the NDP government has attempted to take a more comprehensive approach to land use planning through two major initiatives. The first is the Protected Areas Strategy, designed to double the province's wilderness areas from 6 to 12 percent by the end of the decade (see Chapter 16). The second, more controversial effort was the creation, in January 1992, of the Commission on Resources and the Environment (CORE), headed by Stephen Owen. CORE was given five functions:

- develop and implement a process to create a land use plan for BC
- initiate a regional process, starting with Vancouver Island, to resolve land use disputes by defining protected areas and providing greater certainty on lands available for integrated resource management
- apply mediation/facilitation dispute resolution techniques to land use issues
- advise on legislation to support the planning process;
- coordinate the development and dissemination of land information.[12]

The major activities of CORE have been three regional round tables to develop land use plans: Vancouver Island, Cariboo-Chilcotin, and Kootenay-Boundary. These CORE round tables attempted to succeed where the Clayoquot Sound Steering Committee failed: to bring all the relevant stakeholders together to reach a consensus on land use plans. Despite extraordinarily intensive and time-consuming negotiations, not one of the tables was able to achieve consensus on the most important issue of where to draw lines on the map to allocate land to wilderness and logging. As a result, that key task was left to CORE staff members, who developed plans and then submitted them to the cabinet. In each case, the government's ultimate decision made revisions to the CORE plans.

The most controversial plan was Vancouver Island, where the plan announced by CORE provoked a massive demonstration by loggers and their supporters. Approximately 15,000 demonstrators crowded the lawn in front of the parliament building and shouted down Premier Harcourt when it was his turn to speak. When the government announced its decision on the plan in June 1994, it bought thirty minutes of television time to explain the decision to the province. When Commissioner Stephen Owen went to interior towns to defend the Cariboo-Chilcotin plan, he was burned in effigy.

In some cases, the cabinet made significant revisions to the CORE recommendations on what areas were protected and what areas were left open to logging, but in all cases CORE plans were extremely influential in the government's decisions. As Table 15.1 demonstrates, in no cases were there significant changes in the aggregate amount of land allocated to the three major categories.

Because of its failure to achieve consensus among stakeholders, the CORE process failed to revolutionize governance in the forest sector. The most significant change in governance was the fact that environmental values were institutionalized in a new, effective way in the policy-making process. While cabinet had the final say – and did make some substantial alterations – the plans developed by the environmentally oriented CORE staff

Table 15.1

Comparison of protected areas in CORE plans and government decisions (% of area given protected status)

	CORE	Government
Vancouver Island	13.0	13.0
Cariboo	12.0	12.0
Kootenay-West/Boundary	11.3	11.3
Kootenay-East	16.0	16.5

were instrumental in shaping the final product. Aside from these institutional changes, the CORE process did result in major victories for environmentalists, who achieved significant additions to protected areas in the province, and advanced comprehensive land use planning by contributing to the resolution of a number of divisive conflicts across the province. In March 1996, Premier Glen Clark announced that CORE was being dismantled 'after fulfilling its mandate to help resolve land-use issues across British Columbia.'[13]

Regulating Forest Practices

Once the decision is made to allow logging in certain areas, the key policy questions then focus on forest practices, which include protecting fish habitat, the design of forest roads, techniques for falling and gathering timber, and reforestation. The most contentious issue is clearcutting, the practice of harvesting all the trees in one area at one time. Clearcutting results in barren landscapes that are hideous to look at, at least until new trees occupy the area, which takes approximately ten to fifteen years in BC. If done inappropriately, it can also lead to long-term environmental damage. Clearcuts have been the catalyst for the environmental movement in BC and elsewhere that are demanding an end to the practice. The problem for BC is that in most parts of the province clearcutting is the only way to economically harvest trees given current market conditions. In addition, professional foresters believe that it is the most ecologically suitable harvesting practice is many areas of the province. The major alternative to clearcuts – selection logging – raises significant safety problems for workers.[14]

Traditionally, forest practice regulations have been developed and applied in an ad hoc fashion with a significant amount of regional variation. Rather than a comprehensive set of rules for the province, policies have been contained in regional guides, management plans specific to a Tree Forest Licence or Timber Supply Area, and particular cutting permits. This regulatory style reflects not policy incoherence but rather the idea that appropriate forest practices differ depending on the area and situation, and that the best approach is to leave considerable discretion to professional foresters to do the right thing given the situation at hand. The problems with this approach, however, arc that it can result in inconsistent practices, it rests on faith in the expertise and judgment of professional foresters, and it raises problems for enforcement and government accountability to the public.

As a result of increasing concerns with the environmental effects of forestry and greater demands for accountability, the BC government has recently introduced a new Forest Practices Code that reduces the size of clearcuts and significantly strengthens the regulations of other forest practices. The Forest Practices Code of British Columbia Act was submitted to the legislature in May 1994 and proclaimed in April 1995. Regulations developed under the authority of the act began to take effect 15 June 1995, with full compliance required within two years. The Forest Practices Code strengthens environmental regulations of logging practices, which will result in significant increases in the cost of production. The government estimates the costs will be $500 million per year, but industry claims they will range from $1.1 billion to $1.9 billion.[15]

All Fall Down: The Timber Supply Review

The biggest change coming to BC forest policy is the recalculation of the annual allowable cut (AAC) levels. BC timber management policies have been premised on a relatively rapid liquidation of old growth forests and their conversion to more rapidly growing industrial forests, what Wilson calls the 'liquidation-conversion project.'[16] Because the volume of standing timber per hectare available from an old growth forest is larger than that expected from a second growth forest, the implication of this policy is that once the old growth is liquidated, sustainable harvest levels will have to decline, creating what has been termed a 'fall-down.'[17] Unbeknownst to most of the province, the policy assumed all along that there would be a fall down after the old growth stock diminished but before the second growth was ready to harvest.

The fall down is here. The province has initiated its so-called 'timber supply review,' which will result in significant reductions in the AAC in some areas. A report prepared for the industry estimates that the *average* reduction across the province will be 6 percent, but in some areas it will be much higher.[18] This will have a far bigger impact on timber-dependent communities than wilderness set-asides, but because it is basically a 'bad-news' policy it has been given far less public attention than other NDP forest policy initiatives. The NDP initiated the review in 1992, and it contains a four-stage process for each forest unit in the province: (1) a detailed timber supply analysis of the area; (2) a socioeconomic analysis of employment and economic implications of different harvest levels; (3) a discussion paper released to the public for feedback; and (4) the chief forester's decision and rationale statement.

The government committed itself in statute to completing the process by the end of 1995. The process has been slower than expected, however, for two reasons. First, the technical analysis involved has been far more resource intensive than anticipated, so the process has taken longer than expected. But even more important, it slowly dawned on the government that announcing significant cuts to harvest levels across the province shortly before an election was not an astute political move.[19] As of the end of December 1995 – the original deadline – the government had established new allowable cut levels for only nineteen of thirty-six TSAs and fifteen of thirty-five TFLs. The government has submitted, and the legislature passed, legislation to extend the statutory deadline to the end of 1996.[20]

The Big Promise: Forest Renewal Plan

As stated at the outset, the fundamental dilemma of forest policy is balancing the competing uses of forests between those who derive direct economic benefits from them and those who value them for environmental reasons. The three major initiatives discussed above will all result in reducing the amount of timber harvested, which will have a major economic impact on the province, in particular on those rural areas dominated by timber-dependent communities. This conflict is a vexing dilemma for the NDP, which has had the delicate task of trying to keep the union and environmental wings of its party together. The political tightrope was made even more perilous by the events on Vancouver Island, in particular in 1993 and 1994. As described above, the Clayoquot decision provoked the outrage of environmentalists in the summer of 1993 and put the government on the defensive. In response, an impressive grassroots mobilization of loggers and timber-dependent communities occurred, culminating in the massive demonstration in Victoria in March 1994.

In a skilful manoeuvre to solidify this apparently irreconcilable coalition, Premier Harcourt announced at the 1994 party convention in late March that 'not one forest worker will be left without the option to work in the forest as a result of a land-use decision.'[21] To back up this commitment, the government introduced its Forest Renewal Strategy in April 1994, three weeks after the loggers' protest in Victoria and two months before the government issued its first major decision on the CORE Vancouver Island plan. It promised to double stumpage payments – the amount the government charges timber companies per tree on crown land – and put the money in a fund to hire dislocated workers to help with more intensive management of second-growth forests, as well as environmental restoration projects such as cleaning logging debris out of fish-bearing streams and fixing degraded logging roads. The plan created a new crown corporation, Forest Renewal BC, to administer the fund (expected to be $2 billion over five years), and the government took the remarkable step of insulating the fund by statute from use for other purposes.

The agreement was announced with great fanfare and excitement, and with explicit endorsement from labour, industry, and environmentalists.[22] The plan seemed, at long last, to promise an end to the war in the woods. The economic consequences of environmental restrictions could be alleviated by using the fund to employ dislocated workers in forest 'renewal,' with the long-term promise of more intensive silviculture, which would ultimately produce more jobs in the woods. But on closer inspection, Harcourt's promise of no jobs lost is a carefully crafted commitment that ignores other fundamental changes in forest policy. Harcourt promised no job losses from 'land use decisions,' meaning decisions resulting from the CORE process and the Protected Areas Strategy only. Unfortunately, jobs are threatened at least as much – indeed, probably more – by the increased regulations from the Forest Practices Code, and especially from the reductions expected from the revision of annual allowable cuts resulting from the timber supply review. For instance, the wilderness set-asides in the Vancouver Island land use plan are expected to reduce harvest levels by 6 percent, but the timber supply review for the areas on the island is likely to result in reductions of 20 percent or more.[23]

While Harcourt's bold commitment was brilliant politics in the short term, it poses frightening long-term risks. By leading timber-dependent communities to believe that jobs and environmental protection are compatible, it threatens to raise false expectations and undermine preparation for the difficult transition that many rural areas of the province will confront in the decade ahead. This short-term truce may result in an even more bitter war in the woods than the province has already endured.

Taken together, these initiatives of the NDP government have resulted in substantial policy changes. Estimates of their impact on the forest industry and provincial economy differ. In a study for the industry-backed Forest Alliance, Price Waterhouse estimates a 17 percent reduction in harvest levels as a result NDP forest policies, resulting in between 23,000 and 71,000 jobs lost province wide.[24] The NDP government disputes these figures. It estimates an 8 percent reduction in harvesting, which, if there are no changes in the ratio of harvest levels to jobs (a very uncertain and controversial relationship), would mean a loss of 8,000 jobs in the forest sector alone (Forest Alliance estimates were for the entire provincial economy). However, the government argues that because of jobs created by the new regulations, as well as use of the Forest Renewal Strategy, current employment levels can be maintained or in fact increased.[25] Whatever the economic impacts, there is no doubt that the policies have resulted in bringing environmental values into much greater balance with developmental ones.

The Changing Political Landscape

In order to explain these dramatic changes, it is necessary to examine the interests, strategies, and resources of the major actors in BC forest policy.[26] At the risk of oversimplification, these core actors are essentially the BC Ministry of Forests, the forest industry, and, increasingly, environmental and First Nations groups.[27] Forest policy in BC is guided by a regulatory framework that has traditionally been minister-centred and highly discretionary. BC forest management is governed by the Ministry of Forests Act and the Forest Act, both of which set out broad general standards for forest management that do little to constrain the discretion of the minister of forests.[28] In recent years, other government departments have become increasingly relevant to forest management. The federal Department of Fisheries and Oceans has some jurisdiction because of the influence of forestry on salmon habitat, and the BC Ministry of Environment has become increasingly important both because of the greater concern for the environmental impacts of forestry and its jurisdiction over parks. Because of the significance of forest policy to the province, the cabinet typically plays a large role in most major decisions.

The government in power holds the over-riding objective of being reelected. As a result, their actions are constrained by public opinion. Bureaucrats, in particular those in the Ministry of Forests, seek influence and prestige, whether for their own sake or to pursue their policy interests. Politicians, particularly the cabinet, have the fundamental resource of authority that grants them the power to allocate costs and benefits to the other actors. Bureaucrats rely on a combination of authority and expertise to influence political actors.

The forest industry is represented both by individual firms and a trade association called the Council of Forest Industries in British Columbia (COFI). The principal interest of the industry is in making profits, and it has considerable economic clout as a result of its dominant position in the provincial economy. It controls a wide range of decisions that produce jobs and provincial tax revenues fundamental to the political survival of the government in power.

Forest workers are also an important actor, the largest union being the International Woodworkers of America (IWA). Their primary interest is in secure jobs, and their major political resource is the power of the vote and organized power through their unions, particularly through their ties to the NDP. While there is a history of bitter labour disputes in the industry, on most policy issues in the modern era the industry and workers, along with timber-dependent communities, share common political interests in opposition to environmentalists. A number of 'Share' groups have emerged around the province, which are grassroots alliances (with frequent industry backing) opposed to environmental restrictions. In April 1991, the BC Forest Alliance was formed to give a provincial voice to this coalition, with Jack Munro, long-time president of the IWA, as its president.

Environmental groups are an increasingly important actor in BC forest politics. There are a plethora of such groups across the province, some with a province-wide agenda, such as the Sierra Club of Western Canada and the Western Canada Wilderness Committee, and others with more local or regional agendas, such as the Friends of Clayoquot Sound and the Valhalla Wilderness Society. A major new actor entered the stage in 1990, when the Sierra Legal Defence Fund was formed to try to import some of the successful litigation strategies used to slow down logging in the US. The interest of environmentalists is in preserving wilderness and reducing the environmental consequences of forestry. They derive their influence primarily from their ability to represent significant parts of the electorate, and as we will see, they have developed increased economic power through their influence on consumers.

As Jeremy Wilson demonstrates, BC forest policy has traditionally been dominated by bargaining between forest companies and provincial ministries, centred around the Ministry of Forests. While environmentalists have played an active role in forest policy disputes since the late 1960s, as of 1989 they had not penetrated the core of the policy network. According to Wilson, 'These groups sit on the periphery of the subgovernment zone, closely enough connected to allow them to monitor and influence policy decisions but excluded from regular policy participation.'[29] Times have changed, however. Environmentalists have asserted themselves into the core of the policy regime, and forest policy has changed dramatically as a result.

First Nations are also an increasingly important actor. First Nations have been primarily interested in issues of aboriginal title, and since those concerns frequently interact with forest policy, First Nations have profound stakes in forest policy. Recent BC governments have been increasingly forced to recognize the interests of First Nations by changes in court interpretations of aboriginal title, and the NDP government has been conducting a treaty negotiation process to resolve some of these long-standing concerns.

The recent transformations of BC forest policy have resulted primarily from significant shifts in the resources available to these different actors. Beginning in the late 1960s, the political landscape began to change, with significant consequences for the structure of the forest policy regime and forest policy. Perhaps the most important change has been in public opinion. In the late 1960s, British Columbians, along with residents of other advanced industrial nations, began to place increasing importance on environmental values. In the context of forest policy, this change marked a shift from near exclusive focus on the economic benefits derived from logging to greater concern with preserving wilderness areas and regulating the environmental side effects of forestry practices. While this value change has been an enduring one, there have been several marked fluctuations in the salience of environmental issues, with one peak around 1970 and another around 1990.[30] The general effect of these changes has been to force politicians to give greater attention to environmental interests in policy-making.

Elections have also led to fundamental shifts in resources. The historical electoral dominance of the pro-industry Social Credit Party was interrupted briefly by the NDP in the early 1970s, and the NDP took over for a longer period in the wake of the collapse of the Socreds in 1991. Forestry policy creates interesting dilemmas for the NDP because it has both labour and environmentalists within its coalition. However, socioeconomic and demographic changes in the province – the decline of forest industry employment as a fraction of total employment, the rise of the service sector, and the dramatic growth of urban areas removed from any direct economic dependence on the forest sector – have served to increase the political importance of environmental interests to the NDP at the expense of forest workers. In both periods of NDP rule, the government was controlled by officials more inclined to represent environmental interests than their pro-business predecessors.[31]

One final change relates to the market within which the BC forest industry operates. As a commodity producer dependent on exports, the forest industry has been highly cyclical. The economic conditions of the industry have a significant impact on the distribution of political resources between various actors. In bad times, governments are particularly vulnerable to industry arguments that any regulatory action taken to increase the cost of production will reduce jobs and further threaten government approval ratings. In good times, arguments about the hardship imposed by new environmental requirements have less bite. Industry finds it harder to make compelling arguments that they cannot afford the additional costs, governments are less sympathetic to such arguments, and environmentalists – sensing the vulnerability of their opponents – press their case with renewed vigour. Structural changes in the market for softwood lumber in the early 1990s seem to have created a sustained period of high prices and expanded markets for BC wood products. The changes were caused in part by significant reductions in timber supply in the US Pacific Northwest as a result of environmental restrictions imposed there.

The significant transformation in power resources among the various actors over the past twenty-odd years – brought about by changes in public opinion, the government elected, and the market – account for much of the policy change described above. While the extent of change was limited, the reforms of the mid-1970s were largely the result of the NDP capturing the government in the early 1970s and the general shift toward environmental values. The pace of change began to increase considerably again in the late 1980s. The burst of public interest in the environment in that period forced the recalcitrant Socred government to undertake initiatives to improve the environmental image of the forestry sector, such as the Old Growth Strategy. But as long as a pro-business party remained in power, such efforts were likely to be largely symbolic or limited in their magnitude.

Policy change began to accelerate in 1991 as a result of a critical combination of factors. The most obvious was the election of the pro-environment

NDP government in 1991. The party's platform contained a number of environmental initiatives, including doubling the amount of protected wilderness area in the province from 6 to 12 percent. The NDP was forced to follow through on most of its environmental commitments in the interests of reelection. While the recession in the early 1990s produced a decline in the salience of environmental issues generally across Canada, BC forests continued to be an intense political issue, with support for preservation high in urban areas of the province. As the most important environmental issue in the province, developing a 'greener' forest policy was essential to the NDP's electoral strategy of moving beyond its core base of labour to capture white-collar, middle-class urbanites.[32]

While sustained public support for improved forest practices kept the pressure on the government, the incentives of the forest companies were changed dramatically by a brilliant strategic move by environmentalists. Moving beyond traditional strategies to influence governments by shaping public opinion, environmentalists began taking advantage of market forces to alter the incentives of corporations. Led by Greenpeace International, environmentalists began targeting industrial consumers of BC forest products, initially in Europe and then in the US, threatening to promote boycotts of their products if they did not stop purchasing BC forest products that environmentalists claimed were being produced in environmentally destructive ways.[33] While few contracts were actually cancelled, this campaign succeeded brilliantly in giving BC forest companies an economic interest in improving their environmental record. Despite the increases to their costs of production, the companies came to accept that additional regulation was essential to maintaining their market share. Concerns over the potential impact of this strategy on profits were assuaged by the structural changes in the markets for wood products discussed earlier. Because prices were high, demand robust, and both predicted to remain so, the forest industry was far less resistant to the dramatic policy changes than they would have been otherwise.

Conclusion

Thus far, this chapter has chronicled the transformation of BC forest policy and provided an explanation for that change based on the changing political resources of key participants. The remaining question is whether we should expect this move toward a more sustainable, environmentally sensitive forestry to continue. While it is always hazardous to speculate about the future, the analysis in this chapter at least provides us with a way of developing expectations about the resilience of these new policies. Policy change was made possible by the combination of pro-environment public opinion in the province, pro-environment values of some purchasers of BC forest products in the international market, a party in power committed to a more environmentally sensitive forestry, and favourable market conditions. There is little question that the party in power matters a great deal, but the implication of this analysis is that it is not sufficient for major policy shifts. Without sustained public support, the NDP would have lacked an electoral incentive to follow through on their pro-environment forestry initiatives, and without changing market conditions the industry would have been far more resistant to the changes.

Change in any one of these conditions would create pressure to weaken the new policy regime. A serious provincial recession could dampen public support for environmental restrictions and strengthen industry, worker, and community arguments about the economic toll of the new regime. If international markets become indifferent to BC's environmental performance, the major source of economic pressure to maintain the new policies will be relaxed. And, of course, the return to a more pro-business governing party would have substantial implications. Because none of these changes is implausible, the new forestry regime is vulnerable to retrenchment.

However, there are several reasons why significant retrenchment seems unlikely, although certainly not impossible. The first is simple policy inertia – it is more difficult to reverse policies put in place than to create new ones. Second, the reelection of an NDP majority government in May 1996 lends stability to the policy regime, even though Glen Clark is more labour oriented than Mike Harcourt. Even if the NDP were to lose power, however, a change in governing party is not a sufficient condition for significant policy shifts; other factors would have to change as well. Third, in some cases there are limited incentives for politicians of any political persuasion to reopen divisive political issues, such as land use disputes. While enthusiasm for the environment may wax or wane, an organized environmental constituency is most likely a permanent feature of BC politics, and efforts to reopen development areas now designated as protected would be met with fierce resistance. Finally, some of the change has been necessary and long overdue, such as the timber supply review, and even a resolutely pro-business party would be unlikely to attempt to perpetuate unsustainable harvest levels.

The transformation of BC forest policy achieved by the Harcourt NDP marks a profound change in BC politics and policy. While the forest industry maintains some profound advantages in terms of political resources, the environmental movement and its allies in the NDP have succeeded in bringing greater balance between values of environmental sustainability and the pro-development values that have historically dominated policy in this area.

Further Reading

Forest Resources Commission. *The Future of Our Forests*. Victoria: Forest Resources Commission, April 1991

Hoberg, George. 'Environmental Policy: Alternative Styles.' In *Governing Canada: Institutions and Public Policy*, edited by Michael M. Atkinson. Toronto: Harcourt Brace Jovanovich 1993

–. 'Putting Ideas in Their Place: A Response to Learning and Change in the British Columbia Forest Policy Sector.' *Canadian Journal of Political Science* 29 (March 1996): 135-44

Howlett, Michael, and Jeremy Rayner. 'Do Ideas Matter? Policy Subsystem Configurations and the Continuing Conflict over Canadian Forest Policy.' *Canadian Public Administration* 38, 3 (1995): 382-410

Kimmins, Hamish. *Balancing Act: Environmental Issues in Forestry*. Vancouver: UBC Press 1992

Lertzman, Ken, Jeremy Rayner, and Jeremy Wilson. 'Learning and Change in the British Columbia Policy Sector.' *Canadian Journal of Political Science* 29 (March 1996): 111-34

M'Gonigle, Michael, and Ben Parfitt. *Forestopia: A Practical Guide to the New Forest Economy*. Madeira Park, BC: Harbour Publishing 1994

Scientific Panel for Sustainable Forest Practices in Clayoquot Sound. *Sustainable Ecosystem Management in Clayoquot Sound: Planning and Practices*. Report 5. April 1995

Wilson, Jeremy. 'Wilderness Politics in BC: The Business Dominated State and the Containment of Environmentalism.' In *Policy Communities and Public Policy in Canada*, edited by William D. Coleman and Grace Skogstad. Toronto: Copp Clark Pittman 1990

16
Environmental Protection in British Columbia: Postmaterial Values, Organized Interests, and Party Politics
Kathryn Harrison

Environmental issues have enjoyed a prominent place on the North American political agenda in recent years. Environmental politics has been especially heated in British Columbia, where there is an inherent conflict between an economy heavily dependent on resource exploitation and a strong environmental movement intent on preserving those same resources. This tension has given rise to a series of high profile disputes over wilderness preservation. The arrest of over 800 protesters following the BC government's decision to allow logging in Clayoquot Sound is only the most prominent in a long series of disputes, including wilderness-logging conflicts in the Stein, Carmanah, and Walbran Valleys, and wilderness-mining conflicts in Strathcona Park and the Tatshenshini-Alsek wilderness area. These disputes over proposed developments are joined in rural communities by conflicts between environmentalists and operators of existing facilities, such as mines, smelters, and pulp mills. British Columbians also face a host of urban environmental problems characteristic of modern industrialized societies, including smog, sewage treatment, and hazardous waste generation and disposal.

The purpose of this chapter is to review the politics surrounding environmental issues in BC, using examples of recent controversies to illustrate efforts by provincial political parties to strike a balance between competing interests in environmental disputes. Forestry-related conflicts, and the emerging policy response, are discussed in Chapter 15 by George Hoberg, and will not be considered in detail here.

The Players
Sociologist Ronald Inglehart has theorized that the extended period of affluence that followed the Second World War in industrialized societies resulted in a fundamental shift in public values away from basic questions of survival and economic well-being toward 'postmaterial values' such as

equality and environmental quality.[1] Inglehart argues that such postmaterial values do not fit comfortably along the left-right spectrum represented by traditional political parties, both ends of which are preoccupied by economic growth and job creation. One result of this poor fit is that those concerned with postmaterial values have eschewed the party system and created alternative 'new social movements,' such as the environmental, feminist, and peace movements, to pursue their goals.

BC has a well-established environmental movement independent of the party system. Within the extremely diverse movement, 'expert analysts operate alongside skilled symbol mongers, [and] merry pranksters who are ready to consider a range of radical tactics alongside cautious birders who are convinced that progress requires diligent research and patient lobbying.'[2] Environmental groups in BC range from fish and wildlife clubs, such as the BC Wildlife Federation, to the radical Earth First!, and in between are naturalist and outdoor recreation groups, protest-oriented groups such as Greenpeace, wilderness groups such as the Western Canada Wilderness Committee and the Sierra Club of Western Canada, and the mainstream advocacy West Coast Environmental Law Association. Specialized groups, such as the Friends of Clayoquot Sound and Tatshenshini Wild, coalesce around particular environmental controversies. In addition, the 1990s have witnessed the emergence of the Sierra Legal Defence Fund, which pursues an innovative strategy of legal challenges on behalf of other environmental groups.[3] Finally, there are a plethora of smaller local groups, which coordinate their efforts with those of the better-funded, larger groups through the British Columbia Environment Network.

Environmentalists are not the only players in environmental debates. Typically, environmentalists are opposed by business interests, which resist environmental laws and regulations (or at least argue for less stringent standards) because they seek to minimize costs in the form of loss of access to resources, delays for environmental assessments, pollution control equipment, and waste disposal. Although any businessperson's initial inclination is to pass these costs on to consumers in the form of higher prices, invariably some fraction of the burden cannot be shifted to consumers without losing them to alternative suppliers or products. Like environmentalists, business interests are well represented in environmental debates in BC by individual firms, sector-specific associations such as the Council of Forest Industries and the Mining Association of British Columbia, and broader cross-sectoral organizations such as the Business Council of British Columbia.

As noted above, environmental politics do not fit easily along a left-right political spectrum, with labour pitted against business. Organized labour can come down on either side in debates between industry and environmentalists. On one hand, workers sometimes side with industry in opposing environmental controls because they fear that their jobs will be lost when their employers confront the costs of compliance with environmental standards. As Hoberg notes in Chapter 15, this has given rise to an alliance between forest companies and forest sector unions concerned with protecting access to the forest resource and thus jobs. In some cases, employers have actively tried to mobilize their employees in opposition to environmental controls by raising the spectre of job losses.[4]

On the other hand, workers in manufacturing may share environmentalists' concerns because they face occupational exposures to the same contaminants that are released into the air or water. Workers and their families may also have higher levels of environmental exposure than the population at large if they reside in the immediate vicinity of a polluting facility. For these reasons, organized labour sometimes forms alliances with environmentalists in demanding more stringent environmental controls, despite the threat of job losses. In contrast to the International Woodworkers of America (IWA), which has allied itself with the forest industry in opposition to calls for wilderness preservation, unions representing BC pulp and paper mill workers joined a coalition organized by environmentalists to lobby for strict controls of mill effluents. Moreover, non-industrial unions, such as the BC Government Employees' Union, which do not face an immediate threat of the loss of jobs as a result of industrial discharge regulations, tend to be quite progressive on environmental issues.

Finally, the role of labour can be unpredictable because environmental debates can pit one resource extraction industry against another. Thus, the United Fisherman and Allied Workers Union opposed Alcan's Kemano Completion Project on the grounds that it would irreparably harm the fishery, while the project received support from the trade unions working on the project.

First Nations are also frequent players in environmental debates in BC. Although they have often sided with environmentalists to pursue resource conservation, they have done so as part of a broader agenda to resolve claims to resource ownership. For that reason, First Nations have maintained a certain independence from the environmental movement. Thus, while Natives developed a joint strategy with the Rivers Defence Coalition in the Kemano dispute, they declined to actually join the coalition. As in the case of organized labour, the economic interests of aboriginal peoples create the potential for divergence between environmentalists and First Nations. As Hoberg notes in Chapter 15, Natives' desire not only to protect but to manage development of the forest resource in Clayoquot Sound resulted in a co-management agreement between First Nations and the provincial government, which threatened environmentalists' objectives by condoning logging in some areas of the sound.

The Environment and Party Politics

Environmentalism may not fit easily on the polarized left-right spectrum of BC political parties, but environmental politics nonetheless tends to be fought within the existing party system. While there is much truth to Paehlke's assertion that 'Environmentalism is inherently neither left nor right,' with environmental values finding supporters across the political spectrum,[5] in practice environmental activists have migrated to the left.[6] As in many other jurisdictions, the combination of absorption of green values by the left-most party, along with a first-past-the-post electoral system that rewards only competitive parties, has effectively precluded the emergence of a viable Green Party in BC.[7]

How can we explain the affinity between environmentalism and leftist parties? King and Borchardt believe that the answer lies in both environmentalists' and socialists' support for an activist state and willingness to regulate business.[8] The authors offer preliminary evidence from member countries of the Organization of Economic Co-operation and Development that suggests a correlation between a clean environment and a strong socialist party. Conversely, one would expect right-wing political parties, including BC's self-labelled defenders of 'free enterprise,' to have closer ties to the business community and thus to be more receptive to business opposition to environmental regulation.

Although environmental activists apparently feel more at home on the left, the alliance between the 'new left' (e.g., environmentalists) and the 'old left' (labour) is often an uneasy one. As Inglehart observes, 'the Old Left viewed both economic growth and technological progress as fundamentally good and progressive; the New Left is suspicious of both. The Old Left had a working-class social base; the New Left has a predominantly middle-class base.'[9] These potential tensions between organized labour and environmentalists are particularly acute within BC's New Democratic Party, which embraces both the trade unions fighting to maintain jobs in resource-extraction industries and the environmentalists intent on resource conservation. As Wilson has observed, the stakes are especially high since 'there are no second chances to win wilderness battles – once an area is logged it is lost as wilderness.'[10] In light of the prominence of wilderness conflicts in BC in recent years, these tensions have proved a special challenge for the NDP in government.

The concluding section of this chapter will revisit three issues raised by the foregoing discussion. First, how has the NDP addressed the inherent tension between its green and labour constituencies? Second, what impact did the affiliation between environmentalists and the NDP have on BC's environmental policy during the first term of NDP government? Finally, how do the positions of the opposition Liberal and Reform Parties differ from those of the New Democrats? Do their stronger ties with business pre-clude strong environmental positions?

Green Opposition, Green Government?

The BC NDP had staked out green policy positions well before its election in the fall of 1991. The party's strong position on environmental issues while in opposition reflects the predisposition of environmentalists to ally themselves with the left. However, the influence of environmental activists within the NDP was amplified by two factors. First, it was easier to make principled arguments about environmental protection, without apparent concern for short-term economic consequences, from the opposition benches. Second, the party was motivated by surging public concern for the environment in the late 1980s.[11]

As anticipated above, the party confronted profound tensions from within in developing its environmental positions. While the 'green caucus' within the party publicly pressed their leader for more aggressive policy positions,[12] resource-sector trade unions were increasingly uncomfortable with the party's environmental activism. A split between organized labour and environmentalists emerged at the 1990 convention over a proposed resolution concerning the Carmanah Valley. A walkout by the IWA was narrowly averted by artful politicking by the party leadership and a last-minute compromise that promised to labour a province-wide land use planning process to replace valley-by-valley conflicts, and to environmentalists the preservation of the valley (though without using the 'm word' – moratorium – which inflamed labour members).[13]

The response of the party leadership foreshadowed two key features of the party's electoral strategy. First, it emphasized procedural, rather than substantive, commitments regarding the most contentious environmental issue in the province: wilderness preservation. Rather than pledging to protect particular contested areas, the NDP promised a province-wide planning process to identify which areas would be preserved to achieve a goal of roughly doubling the extent of protected areas to 12 percent of the province. Second, the emphasis on consensual decision-making by 'stakeholders' in that planning process held out the promise of victory for both sides. Only after the election would the NDP be forced to confront its naivete in assuming that wilderness debates could be resolved without creating winners and losers.

Not surprisingly, in light of public attention to environmental issues, the NDP highlighted its environmental positions during the 1991 provincial election campaign. The party distributed a publication containing twenty-four private members' bills concerning the environment that it had introduced while in opposition. In addition, one third of the party's forty-eight-point election platform concerned forestry and environmental reforms. As a result, the NDP enjoyed strong support from environmentalists, to the extent that the Sierra Club of Western Canada sponsored full page ads in support of the party.

Despite what Wilson has described as a 'hypercapitalist ideology,'[14] the Social Credit Party had introduced a number of environmental policy reforms in the late 1980s in response to broad support for environmentalism across the political spectrum. However, in light of the NDP's persistent and stinging criticism of its performance on environmental issues, the environment clearly was not a winning issue for the Socreds. No mention of the environment was made in Social Credit campaign literature, and the environment minister at the time decried the NDP's 'pie in the sky' environmental platform as 'ignor[ing] economic reality.' The premier, Rita Johnston, promised to favour jobs over 'environmental terrorists.'[15]

After the NDP's victory in October 1991, the new government's first throne speech promised an ambitious program of environmental reforms, including the promised land use planning process, four major new environmental statutes (concerning wildlife, environmental protection, environmental assessment, and water management), action to clean up contaminated sites, waste reduction and recycling programs, and a clean air strategy for the province.[16] The government published an ambitious five-year environmental action plan within months of its election.[17] Although some of the items in the action plan had been initiated by the Social Credit government, efforts to reform BC's environmental policy were given new life by the NDP, who adopted many of the principles and catch-phrases of the environmental movement, such as 'zero discharge,' the 'polluter pays principle,' and the 'precautionary approach.'

Once in government, the NDP's relationship with environmentalists quickly soured, however, amid environmentalists' charges of betrayal on forestry issues.[18] The party's green reputation suffered a serious blow not only with activists but with the public at large in 1993 when it announced its decision to permit logging in Clayoquot Sound. That summer, over 800 protesters were arrested in acts of civil disobedience in Clayoquot Sound. Soon thereafter, the government had only a 22 percent approval rating on environmental issues.[19]

Despite this rocky start, the NDP government gradually rebuilt its reputation on the environment by proceeding with its five-year action plan and parallel land use planning process. Particularly successful was the government's addition of urban parks to its Protected Areas Strategy. The move was a conscious effort to win back the approval of urban voters disillusioned by the government's Clayoquot decision. The party thus was able to point to the ninety-nine new parks, many of which are in or adjacent to urban areas, established in an eighteen-month period between 1993 and 1995 as tangible and popular evidence of the NDP's environmental commitment at election time.[20]

Although progress on the government's ambitious legislative agenda was slow – only one of the four pieces of major legislation originally promised was proclaimed – the government made greater progress by relying on administrative discretion within existing laws: issuing innovative paint recycling requirements, promulgating new regulations concerning pulp mills, and creating new parks. In addition to these substantive measures, the government introduced significant procedural reforms. In 1990 Wilson described the profound cynicism of the BC environmental movement, quoting one activist who stated: 'I see the public participation process as a trap designed to exhaust the participants and to shield politicians and civil servants from discomforting confrontations.'[21] Since that time, the NDP government increased citizens' access to information and demonstrated a much stronger commitment to consultation than its predecessors. In fact, the extent of consultations undoubtedly contributed to the slow rate of progress of proposed legislative initiatives.

The new consultation processes invariably seek consensus among diverse 'stakeholders,' incorporating not only environmentalists, business, and labour but a wide range of interests including community representatives and youth. While consensus has often been elusive, particularly in the land use planning process described by Hoberg, these consultations have nonetheless fundamentally transformed environmental politics within the province. With the notable exception of the Clayoquot Sound controversy, environmentalists have in recent years channelled their efforts into consultation processes rather than protests and civil disobedience. It is striking that both business and environmental representatives interviewed for this chapter cited these procedural reforms as one of the most positive achievements of the first term of the NDP government. Moreover, it is likely to be a lasting one since, as one environmentalist observed, 'once you've involved the public and communities in meaningful ways, it's hard to then say "go home."'[22]

Case Studies of Environmental Politics

In order to examine environmental politics and party positions in BC more closely, three case studies are presented in this section: regulation of pulp mill effluents, and decisions concerning the Tatshenshini wilderness area and the Kemano Completion Projection. Each case study examines the constellation of organized interest groups involved in the policy debate and the corresponding positions adopted by the government and opposition parties.

Regulation of Pulp Mill Effluents

The forest industry is the economic lifeblood of BC, and also the source of the most heated environmental conflicts. In addition to reform of harvest practices, environmentalists have focused their efforts in recent years on reducing discharges from pulp and paper mills. The attention is not misplaced. The pulp and paper industry is the largest industrial source of conventional pollutants (i.e., pollutants other than persistent toxins) in Canada. However, it is also a major employer, providing 12,000 direct jobs in BC alone in 1987.[23] That fact, along with the tendency of pulp mills to be located in 'one industry towns,' has meant that no government undertakes environmental regulation of the industry lightly.[24]

Province-wide environmental objectives for the pulp and paper industry were first established in 1971 and revised in 1977. The impetus in recent years to reform those standards was the announcement in 1987 by the US Environmental Protection Agency that dioxins had been detected in pulp mill effluents and paper products.[25] Soon thereafter, Greenpeace released test results showing that dioxins were also present in sediments collected near a Vancouver Island pulp mill. In response, the federal government undertook a crash testing program, which resulted in closures of fisheries in the vicinity of mills along the BC coast after unacceptable levels of dioxins and furans were detected in shellfish.

In May 1989, BC's minister of the environment announced that the Social Credit government would regulate discharges of chlorinated organics, a class of chemicals that includes dioxins. Mills would be required to meet an AOX standard of 1.5 kilograms per air-dried tonne (kg/ADt) by the end of 1994.[26] In December 1990, the provincial cabinet approved a regulation to accomplish that goal. However, in response to industry lobbying, Premier Bill Vander Zalm vetoed the cabinet decision, stating, 'while I love the environment ... I also love those IWA and pulp mill workers and someone has to stand up for their jobs.'[27] Although the environment minister, John Reynolds, resigned from cabinet in protest, the remaining members of cabinet subsequently approved a weaker regulation requiring mills to meet an AOX standard of 2.5 kg/ADt.[28] Not surprisingly, the New Democratic opposition criticized the government's concession to the industry, taking full advantage of the prominence the issue received in light of the minister's resignation.

When the New Democrats were elected a year later, one of their first actions was to resurrect the more stringent AOX standard. In January 1992, the new government fulfilled a campaign promise to require that all mills meet an AOX standard of 1.5 kg/ADt by the end of 1995. Moreover, the new government outdid all other jurisdictions in Canada by adding a requirement that mills completely eliminate AOX discharges by 31 December 2002.[29]

Not surprisingly, the pulp mill controversy pitted environmentalists against forest companies. The latter, represented by the provincial Council of Forest Industries, had indicated their willingness to accept an AOX standard of 2.5 kg/ADt, but lobbied aggressively against the 1.5 standard on the grounds that the associated expenditure of hundreds of thousands of additional dollars was unwarranted since dioxins would be nondetectable in the mills' effluent at an AOX level of 2.5 kg/ADt. On the other side, environmentalists sought to widen the debate beyond dioxins, arguing for the complete elimination of all chlorinated organics. A coalition of over fifty groups was represented by the West Coast Environmental Law Association.

It is noteworthy that the coalition of regulatory advocates included both the fishers' and pulp mill workers' unions. The livelihood of the former was negatively affected by the fisheries closures. However, the support of the Pulp, Paper and Woodworkers Union is more surprising in light of the industry's claims of inability to afford the proposed control measures. The potential for exposure to hazardous substances in the workplace and in the communities surrounding pulp mills may explain the workers' activism in the face of threatened job losses. Native groups were also allied with the environmentalists. They had perhaps the highest stakes, since potentially contaminated fish and shellfish are a staple in the diet of coastal Native peoples.

BC's political parties responded quite differently to this constellation of interests. Consistent with the antipathy to environmental regulation associated with neoconservative parties, the Social Credit government clearly sided with the industry. Although the premier claimed to be protecting the interests of pulp mill workers, those same workers were in fact lobbying for stricter regulations.

In contrast, once elected, the NDP promptly delivered everything the environmental coalition had lobbied for. The support of the unions most directly affected undoubtedly made it easier for the labour-oriented party to take such a strong position. However, once in government, even a socialist party cannot ignore the voice of business. In response to ongoing industry objections that the requirement, not matched by any other jurisdiction, for 'zero discharge' by 2002 would render BC mills uncompetitive and effectively shut down the industry, the NDP government indicated its intent to reconsider the feasibility of the regulation.[30] Although the minister subsequently reaffirmed his commitment to the existing regulation,[31] it would not be surprising to see a future government of any political stripe relax the zero discharge requirement before the deadline of 2002.

The Liberal Party's statements on pulp mill effluents reveal the absence of a clearly articulated, consistent environmental policy. While the party's first environment critic made strong statements in support of the goal of zero discharge and called for an environmental bill of rights (a more radical step than even the NDP government has been prepared to take), one of her colleagues echoed industry arguments in depicting even the interim 1.5 kg/ADt AOX requirement as 'absolute and utter folly,' unaffordable, unsupported by scientific evidence, and harmful to the competitiveness of BC mills.[32] Two years later, a new Liberal environment critic cited the 1.5 AOX requirement as an example of a successful regulation![33] And by the time of the 1996 election, the party had come full circle, once again supporting the zero discharge requirement.[34]

The Tatshenshini Controversy

In 1958 a large copper deposit was discovered at Windy Craggy Mountain in the northwest corner of BC, wedged between the Alaska Panhandle and the Yukon in an area known as the Haines Triangle. That deposit gave rise to a conflict between wilderness preservation and mining in the late 1980s, when Geddes Resources proposed to build a combined open pit and underground mine to extract copper and other metals valued at $8.5 billion. The mine would involve an investment of more than $500 million over a twenty- to forty-year period, and create 500 direct jobs.[35] Other mineral deposits in the area have the potential to yield additional jobs and revenues.[36]

The catch was that the proposed mine would be located in a spectacular wilderness area, surrounded on three sides by Canadian and US national parks and wilderness areas: Kluane National Park in the Yukon, and Wrangell-St. Elias and Glacier Bay National Parks and the Tongass National Forest in Alaska. The area is relatively untouched by humans, with no permanent settlements, roads, or resource developments. The mountainous terrain supports a diverse wildlife population, including one of the last thriving grizzly bear populations in North America, which has several dens in the immediate vicinity of the proposed mine site.[37] The wild rivers of the region support spawning salmon, as well as offering what is considered one of the top fourteen wilderness rafting experiences in the world.[38]

Windy Craggy Mountain is located on Tats Creek, thirty kilometres upstream from the Tatshenshini River, which joins with the Alsek River before flowing through Glacier Bay National Park in Alaska to the Pacific Ocean. The central environmental issue in the Tatshenshini controversy was the potential impact of the proposed mine on those rivers. The Windy Craggy ore deposit contains a high concentration of sulphur, which forms sulphuric acid when exposed to air and water. Environmentalists were concerned that acid leachate from more than 300 million tons of waste rock would destroy aquatic life in the Tatshenshini and Alsek Rivers. As well, the construction and ongoing operation of the mine and access road could have detrimental impacts on wildlife species, such as the grizzly bear, which do not easily tolerate human disturbance. Geddes Resources welcomed a full environmental review of the project. The company acknowledged the potential for acid drainage, but expressed confidence that its proposal to construct huge disposal ponds for waste rock by damming Tats Creek would solve the problem. However, concerns about a potential breach of containment remained, since the tailing ponds would remain toxic long after the mine was abandoned, and because the mine would be located in one of the most seismically active areas of Canada.[39]

The project was further complicated by the potential for international impacts. The Alsek River supports one of the most productive salmon fisheries in Alaska, and also crosses Glacier Bay National Park. US environmentalists were joined in their opposition to the project by members of the US Congress, including Senator Al Gore, who continued his opposition to the project after he became vice president of the United States.[40] As a signatory to the World Heritage Convention, Canada was obliged not to take any deliberate measures that could directly or indirectly damage Kluane, Wrangell-St. Elias, or Glacier Bay National Parks, all of which had been designated world heritage sites.

Rather than proceeding with its usual Mine Development Assessment Process, in July 1992 the NDP government asked its land use planning commission, the Commission on Resources and the Environment (CORE), to assess Geddes's proposal. The resulting CORE report, issued in January 1993, concluded that the mining and wilderness options 'appear to be incompatible.'[41] Five months later, the premier announced his government's decision to create the Tatshenshini-Alsek Wilderness Park, effectively killing the Windy Craggy proposal as well as any others that might have come forward at a later date.[42] The government stated its intention to apply, along with the US, to the United Nations to have the 8.5 million hectare international wilderness area completed by the new park designated a world heritage site. The UN designation was subsequently granted in December 1994.

The dispute over Windy Craggy pitted Geddes Resources (a controlling share of which was later purchased by Royal Oak Mines) and the BC mining industry against environmentalists and river rafters intent on preserving the Tatshenshini wilderness. Environmental groups forged an international coalition of over fifty organizations to fight the project, led by the Canadian group Tatshenshini Wild and the US group American Rivers. The Champagne-Aishihik First Nation eventually supported the government's application for designation of the park as a world heritage site, but only after receiving a commitment from the government to engage in a separate land claims negotiation.

The Tatshenshini issue assumed symbolic proportions for the Mining Association of BC. The premier's announcement of the new park was met with jeers from placard-waving mining executives, who threatened an industry exodus to South America.[43] The industry argued that the mine and wilderness could coexist, that the economic benefits of the mine far outweighed the minimal impact on the wilderness experience of 1,000 wealthy river rafters per year, and that, in any case, 'all there is up there is a lot of rock and ice.'[44]

While the NDP government acceded to environmentalists' demands, both the Social Credit and Liberal opposition parties sided with the industry. Social Credit MLAs (who later joined the Reform Party) depicted the Tatshenshini decision as a sellout to 'preservationists' in compensation for the government's earlier decision to permit logging in Clayoquot Sound.[45] They emphasized the number of mining jobs lost, and the loss of confidence in the government by the BC mining industry.[46]

The Liberal opposition also depicted the decision as a payback to environmentalists for Clayoquot,[47] and decried the loss of mining jobs to Chile.[48] However, the Liberals were less willing to forswear environmental credentials than their Social Credit colleagues. The party had promised in the 1991 election to create a park in the Tatshenshini wilderness, and now adopted the controversial position that 'you can mine in parks in a responsible manner.'[49] The party also borrowed a leaf from the NDP's election manual in emphasizing procedural, rather than substantive, aspects of the decision: that the government bypassed its normal mine assessment procedures in evaluating the Windy Craggy proposal. Finally, the Liberals took advantage of the international features of the park proposal to argue that the NDP government's decision was a response to pressure from Americans, that joint Canada-US oversight of the proposed world heritage site would inevitably involve a loss of sovereignty to the US, and even that the provincial government may have entertained 'trading off that whole area for something else in the Alaska panhandle.'[50]

The story did not end there for the NDP government, however. Facing the threat of a lawsuit by Royal Oak Mines – even the CORE report had emphasized the need for compensation should the park option be adopted – and with an election looming nearer, the government undertook negotiations with the company. Coincident with the negotiations, the Mining Association of BC launched a $500,000 'mining awareness campaign,' with the intent of publicizing the positions of candidates in the next provincial election on issues related to mining.[51] In August 1995 the government reached an agreement with Royal Oak Mines to pay $26 million in compensation for cancellation of the Windy Craggy project.[52] The agreement also included $78 million in government funds to support Royal Oak's development of two proposed gold mines (the Kemess project near Sloane and Red Mountain near Stewart). The two new mines are expected to generate $500 million in investment and 550 direct jobs, conveniently matching what was lost with the cancellation of Windy Craggy.

In declaring a truce with Royal Oak, the NDP government sent a strong signal of reassurance to the BC mining industry, even at the risk of alienating its labour and environmental constituencies. Representing 5 percent of the provincial GDP and supporting 12,500 direct jobs,[53] the industry's views could not be dismissed. The fact that the agreement was announced jointly by the employment and investment minister and the president of Royal Oak Mines, Margaret Witte, is particularly noteworthy, since Witte was extremely unpopular within the organized labour movement for her decision to hire replacement workers to operate the Giant gold mine in Yellowknife during a strike in 1992. In stark contrast to the industry's rhetoric at the time of the Tatshenshini-Alsek park announcement, the president of Geddes Resources reflected that the compensation and investment agreement sent 'a very strong signal that, indeed, BC is open to mining.'[54]

Weighing the Impacts of the Kemano Completion Project

In 1987 Alcan began construction of a $1.3 billion hydroelectric development on the Nechako River in northern coastal BC. Eight years later, after the company had spent over $500 million on its Kemano Completion Project, the provincial government withdrew its approval, thus laying to rest the policy debate concerning the potential impacts of Kemano completion on the fishery.

As the name suggests, the proposed development was an extension of the original Kemano project built by Alcan in the 1950s. That project was made possible by an agreement between Alcan and the province granting the company rights to divert water from the Nechako and Nanika Rivers, as well as favourable water rental rates. The agreement allowed Alcan to dam the Nechako River and divert a substantial portion of the original flow through a tunnel to a hydroelectric facility at Kemano. The original Kemano project had the effect of reversing roughly three-quarters of the flow of the Nechako, which flows eastward, by redirecting it into the Kemano River, which flows to the west.[55] The electricity generated was then transported 82 kilometres to Kitimat to power Alcan's aluminum smelter.

The 1950 agreement guaranteed access to the water in perpetuity only if Alcan exercised its rights of access by the year 2000. The approaching deadline prompted Alcan to propose a second diversion from the Nechako for the purposes of electricity generation, even though the additional electricity was not yet needed by Alcan. Until such time as Alcan constructed a second smelter in Kitimat, it proposed to sell the surplus electricity to BC Hydro.

The environmental issue concerning the Kemano Completion Project was the impact of further reductions to the flow of the Nechako River.[56] Reduced flow rates result in warmer water temperatures in the summer, which are unfavourable for spawning salmon. The central question was whether the flow remaining after completion of the project would be sufficient to sustain the economically and ecologically important Nechako salmon fishery. Questions were also raised about the impact of reduced flows on other fish and wildlife species, and on downstream communities, industry, and agriculture.

Controversy over the impact of the project preceded construction in 1987. Throughout the 1980s, the federal Department of Fisheries and Oceans (DFO) had been critical of Alcan's project proposals. Federal objections were resolved in a three-way negotiation between Alcan, the province, and the federal government in 1987, which resulted in a settlement agreement signed by the three parties. In the agreement, Alcan relinquished its rights to water from the Nanika River and promised to take remedial measures to protect salmon stocks, including constructing a facility to release cold water from the Kenney Dam reservoir into the Nechako River. In return the federal government promised not to conduct environmental hearings, and the federal and provincial governments granted Alcan the necessary approvals to proceed with the Kemano Completion Project. Construction began soon thereafter. In 1990 the federal cabinet passed an order-in-council formally exempting the project from the federal Environmental Assessment and Review Process.

The 1987 settlement agreement did not satisfy project opponents. Controversy over the environmental impacts of the project continued when statements and leaked memoranda by retired federal scientists suggested that pressure had been brought to bear on DFO biologists to relax their criticism of the project. Having lost the first round with the federal and provincial governments, environmental groups and the Carrier-Sekani Tribal Council took their fight to the courts. They won an initial victory in May 1991, when the trial division of the federal court ruled that the 1990 order-in-council exempting the project from the federal Environmental Assessment and Review Process was invalid. Alcan suspended construction of the project pending appeal. Although the decision was reversed by the court of appeal a year later, Alcan declined to resume construction until the new NDP provincial government's position was clarified.

While in opposition, the NDP had strongly criticized the Social Credit government's refusal to conduct an environmental assessment of the Kemano Completion Project. After the election, the new government hired environmental lawyer Murray Rankin to examine the government's legal options. After Rankin concluded that the Kemano Completion Project would yield net economic benefits and that the government would, in all likelihood, be required by the courts to compensate Alcan should the project be cancelled as a result of an environmental review,[57] the government was slow to fulfil its campaign promise of a full environmental review. However, in January 1993 the premier announced that the government had directed the BC Utilities Commission to conduct public hearings.

In October 1994, before the commission could issue its report, Liberal leader Gordon Campbell announced his party's position that the Kemano Completion Project should be 'permanently shelved.'[58] Soon thereafter, in December 1994, the commission reported to the government that the project as proposed was likely to have a serious impact on the health of the salmon fishery.[59] Although the commission presented three alternatives that would mitigate to varying degrees the negative environmental impact of the project, the government announced in January 1995 that it was withdrawing its approval of the Kemano Completion Project.[60]

As in the Tatshenshini case, the Kemano Completion Project pitted the project proponent – in this case Alcan – against environmentalists. Joining Alcan in support of the project were the Kitimat and Terrace chambers of commerce, which foresaw economic benefits for local businesses. The strong support for the project in Kitimat, where Alcan employs 1,800 workers, is not surprising. However, support diminished the farther one travelled from Kitimat, with responses to the premier's announcement of the project's cancellation ranging from 'adulation in Prince George, to a stern lecture in Smithers, to disappointment in Terrace and, finally, to open anger and hostility in Kitimat.'[61] Province-wide polls showed that 64 percent of British Columbians opposed the project.[62]

The environmental attack on the project was led by the Rivers Defence Coalition. The coalition worked closely with First Nations in the region, who were concerned about the project's potential impact on the freshwater fishery, which is an important food source for Natives in the region. However, First Nations refused to participate in the BC Utilities Commission hearings because the narrow terms of reference precluded examination of the project's impact on the Fraser River, the impact of the original Kemano project, or the economic justification for the Kemano Completion Project.[63]

Organized labour was divided, reflecting the complex distribution of costs and benefits of such a large project. Members of the United Fishermen and Allied Workers perceived a threat to their livelihood and thus actively participated in the Rivers Defence Coalition. The position of workers in Alcan's Kitimat smelter was not so straightforward. The smelter workers originally joined the Rivers Defence Coalition in lobbying for a full environmental review of the project, but later withdrew from the coalition when Alcan suspended construction and laid off hundreds of workers after the 1991 federal court decision. The provincial labour movement sided with the fishers' union, passing a resolution in 1994 calling on the federal and provincial governments to cancel the project without compensation for Alcan.[64] However, the resolution was strongly opposed by the Allied Hydro Council, which represents the trade unions working on the project.

The most conservative party in the legislature, Reform, was the most supportive of Alcan and the Kemano Completion Project. The party's leader, Jack Weisgerber (at this point still a member of the Social Credit Party), stated that 'Real courage would mean standing up for the jobs that are being threatened or lost by this government's fear of decision-making ... Real courage would mean getting on with the Kemano completion project without further delay.'[65]

The Liberals' break with the business community in opposing the project came as a surprise to many, since the party was perceived as having moved to the right after choosing Gordon Campbell as leader. The Liberal Party's stand on Kemano sharply contrasted with its critiques of the government's pulp mill regulations and Forest Practices Code as being too harsh on business. It was also inconsistent with the party's position in the Tatshenshini debate that no decision should have been made prior to completion of a full environmental review. However, the party's own polls undoubtedly indicated the extent of public opposition to the project, mobilized at least in part by the prominent criticism of Kemano completion by open-line radio host Rafe Mair. It is probably no coincidence that the Liberal leader's announcement came on the eve of a scheduled appearance on Mair's program.[66] In addition, some have speculated that the Liberal Party chose the high profile Kemano issue to remake the leader's image as beholden to big business.[67]

Concerns had been expressed about the Kemano Completion Project by environmental activists within the NDP for many years. In fact, the chair of the party's Environmental Policy Committee, Pat Moss, also chaired the Rivers Defence Coalition. Once in government, the NDP was constrained by the previous government's legacy in the form of the 1987 settlement agreement. However, after the Liberal Party announced its opposition to the project and the BC Federation of Labour registered a similar position, it would have been surprising had the government not cancelled the project.

As in the Tatshenshini case, the high profile announcement was followed by discussions between the government and Alcan in an effort to reach a compensation settlement. In July 1995 the province and Alcan announced that they had reached an agreement to enter into negotiations to settle Alcan's claims for damages out of court, with the goal of finalizing an agreement by March 1996. Although the premier stressed that 'No cheque, no taxpayer money, is going to Alcan to compensate for cancellation of KCP,'[68] the framework agreement anticipates a provincial government guarantee to supply electricity to future Alcan developments in the long term and to purchase surplus electricity from the existing Kemano facility in the near term.[69]

Conclusions

The three foregoing case studies illustrate the divisiveness of BC environmental politics. Environmentalists and business clash, with organized labour and First Nations staking out positions in between. In light of these tensions, environmental policy-making invariably creates winners and losers, and thus friends and enemies for politicians. The NDP's land use platform in the 1991 election and the Liberals' procedural critique of the Tatshenshini decision both reflect a desire by politicians of all stripes to avoid making enemies, by committing to procedural, rather than substantive, reforms. However, when promised procedures reach a conclusion, those in government can no longer avoid making politically difficult decisions.

It is worth noting that the rural cases presented in this chapter may not be representative of urban environmental politics. Ironically, given the density of populations exposed, urban environmental problems may be less politically divisive because of obstacles to mobilization faced by both regulatory opponents and advocates. For instance, air quality problems in the Lower Mainland are caused by numerous and diverse sources. It is thus more difficult for interests that would be regulated to organize politically than in a rural case where one mill or mine is at issue. At the same time, it may be more difficult for beneficiaries of environmental regulations to organize, because more people are affected, and because urban beneficiaries do not know each other as well as they would in a small town. Moreover, there is no single 'enemy' to galvanize environmental opposition.

Environmental decisions present a special challenge for the NDP, which must reconcile tensions within its own ranks. Returning then to the first of three questions posed by this chapter, how has the party resolved internal tensions between environmental activists and organized labour? During their first electoral mandate, the NDP government has been quite successful at satisfying both labour and environmentalists. Satisfying both constituencies has not been difficult in cases such as the pulp mill regulations, where labour was allied with environmentalists. However, the government has had to confront a wide gulf between environmentalists and labour in forestry-wilderness debates.

As Hoberg describes in Chapter 15, the NDP government has managed to preserve significant tracts of wilderness for environmentalists, while simultaneously addressing labour's concerns by offering financial commitments for transition strategies. In effect, the NDP has moved away from the 'raw, redistributive politics' described by Wilson[70] by crafting distributive policies, such as the Forest Renewal Plan, to soften the impact of wilderness preservation on workers. Ironically, the internal tensions within the party may have been an asset, because a history of working together in the same 'political family' may have made it easier for a New Democratic government to forge compromises between labour and environmentalists.

While the government has managed to avoid deep rifts between its labour and environmental constituencies, it has often alienated the business community, which feels burdened by the cumulative impact of new environmental and land use regulations. However, as the government approached the end of its term, it sought to mend fences with business interests by defending the forest industry's image abroad against environmentalists' critiques, by reaching compensation agreements in the Kemano and Windy Craggy disputes, and by providing government subsidies for the development of new mines. While such compensation agreements have angered environmentalists within the NDP, it is unlikely that they responded by shifting their votes to political parties that opposed cancellation of the Kemano and Windy Craggy projects in the first place. In the end, the NDP government may succeed in satisfying three very diverse constituencies – organized labour, environmentalists, and industry – in effect by buying these organized interests' support with taxpayers' dollars.

The second question raised in the introduction was whether a green party necessarily provides green government. While the NDP government has made limited progress on its legislative agenda, it has accomplished a great deal through regulation, including passing the strictest pulp mill regulations in the country and promising a similar level of stringency for automobile emission standards. Although the government has not delivered everything the environmental community sought – bitterness remains over the Clayoquot decision – its subsequent decisions on Kemano, the Tatshenshini, and dozens of new parks throughout the province have won back the support of many environmentalists.

The NDP's record on the environment is also viewed favourably by the public. In a February 1995 poll, the government received the strongest favourable ratings on three issues: protecting the environment, getting tough with polluters, and protecting both jobs and the environment.[71] However, the party was hampered by the fact that environmental issues were no longer 'top of mind' as they were for voters in 1991.

Finally, how do the positions of the opposition Liberal and Reform Parties differ from those of the New Democrats? Do their stronger ties with business preclude strong environmental positions? All the Reform MLAs in the legislature were previously members of the Social Credit Party, and their positions on environmental issues are consistent with the Social Credit policy legacy. Reform MLAs sided with the business community in opposition to environmentalists in each of the three cases presented here. While the party acknowledges British Columbians' desire for environmental protection, the section concerning the environment in the party's policy statement begins by emphasizing the 'cost associated with environmental activism.'[72] As well, the leader of the party borrows forest industry rhetoric in labelling environmentalists 'preservationists.'

Consistent with their position on the political spectrum, the Liberal Party's environmental positions tend to be between those of the NDP and Reform. The Liberals joined Reform in criticizing the NDP's actions on the Forest Practices Code, the Tatshenshini decision, and pulp mill regulations from the perspective of affected business interests. However, the party is less consistent in its environmental positions than either Reform or the New Democrats.

This inconsistency can be explained by three factors. First, reflecting weaker representation of environmentalists within the Liberal Party and also the declining salience of the environment to the public at large, environmental issues simply are not a high priority for the Liberals. The party appears to have given little thought to its environmental platform. Second, the Liberal Party has been a victim of its own sudden success. After the 1991 election, the party only had limited policy research and development capacity. Liberal members of the provincial legislature were inexperienced and unencumbered by a record of party position statements, both of which help to account for inconsistencies in their statements on environmental issues. Finally, the Liberal Party is caught between its desire to ensure a favourable climate for 'free enterprise' and its desire to address even conservative voters' environmental concerns. The Liberals' posture on Kemano clearly signals that the party is not willing to completely sacrifice environmental values and environmental votes.

Addendum: The 1996 Election

Consistent with the low salience of environmental issues in public opinion polls, the environment was not a prominent issue in the 1996 election campaign, which revolved almost exclusively around three issues: the deficit, health care, and education. With polls showing the Liberals and NDP neck and neck at the mid-point of the campaign, the NDP began to devote greater attention to other issues, including the environment. However, the party's strong reputation on environmental issues was tarnished when BC Hydro drained a lake in the middle of the campaign, effectively relegating the environment to the back burner of the campaign once again.

The relative positioning of the three leading parties on environmental issues during the election was consistent with the preceding case studies. The NDP and Liberals adopted many similar positions, both expressing commitments to groundwater protection, stabilization of greenhouse gas emissions, and protection of 12 percent of the province as park land. In contrast, Reform had no position on many environmental issues, and argued that there was insufficient evidence to take action on global warming. The liberals diverged from the NDP, however, in promising to rewrite the Forest Practices Code, and they criticized the NDP government's reliance on regulation, to the point of likening the NDP government to an environmental policy state.[73] Not surprisingly, most environmentalists openly favoured the NDP,[74] although some environmental supporters of the Green Party were critical of their colleagues' almost exclusive emphasis on the mainstream parties. The 1996 reelection of the NDP thus promises a continuation of relatively progressive environmental policies for BC.

Environmental protection as a postmaterial value does not fit easily within the confines of the traditional left-right political spectrum, which is anchored by the competing forces of organized labour and business. However, in BC, where the emergence of a viable Green Party is hindered by a first-past-the-post electoral system, environmental conflicts are by necessity fought within the traditional party system. Environmentalists have tended to migrate to the left-most party – the NDP – while the business interests they commonly oppose have found greater receptiveness in parties farther right – Social Credit, Reform, and to a lesser extent the Liberals. The tensions between 'new left' environmentalists advocating resource conservation and protection and 'old left' trade unions fearful of resulting job losses have presented a special challenge for the governing NDP. However, it has been surprisingly successful in satisfying these two core constituencies and to some extent even the business community through distributive policies that compensate the 'victims' of environmental conservation and protection with taxpayers' dollars.

Further Reading

Boardman, Robert, ed. *Canadian Environmental Policy: Ecosystems, Politics, and Process.* Toronto: Oxford University Press 1992

Christensen, Bev. *Too Good to Be True: Alcan's Kemano Completion Project.* Vancouver: Talon Books 1995

Doern, G. Bruce, and Thomas Conway. *The Greening of Canada: Federal Institutions and Decisions.* Toronto: University of Toronto Press 1994

Harrison, Kathryn. *Passing the Buck: Federalism and Canadian Environmental Policy.* Vancouver: UBC Press 1996

Hoberg, George. 'Environmental Policy: Alternative Styles.' In *Governing Canada: Institutions and Public Policy,* edited by Michael M. Atkinson. Toronto: Harcourt Brace Jovanovich 1993

Inglehart, Ronald. 'Values, Ideology, and Cognitive Mobilization in New Social Movements.' In *Challenging the Political Order: New Social and Political Movements in Western Democracies,* edited by Russell J. Dalton and Manfred Kuechler. Oxford: Polity Press 1990

Paehlke, Robert C. *Environmentalism and the Future of Progressive Politics.* New Haven: Yale University Press 1989

Wilson, Jeremy. 'Wilderness Politics in British Columbia: The Business-Dominated State and the Containment of Environmentalism.' In *Policy Communities and Public Policy in Canada,* edited by William D. Coleman and Grace Skogstad. Toronto: Copp Clark Pitman 1990

17
The British Columbia New Democratic Party: Does It Make a Difference?

Richard Sigurdson

Does it make any significant difference whether British Columbia is ruled by a New Democratic Party (NDP) government rather than by a government of another political stripe? At one level, this is a version of an old political science question: Do parties matter? That is, we might wonder whether it makes any difference which of the main political parties holds office at any given time in a highly industrialized, urbanized, bureaucratized, pluralistic, and advanced capitalist society such as BC. At the same time, though, this topic is a variant of another equally popular political science concern: Can social democrats who gain power in a capitalist society successfully implement a social democratic program? On this score, we need to ask whether the NDP is truly social democratic, and, if so, whether the achievements of the two BC NDP governments fulfil their ideological expectations in such key areas as wealth redistribution, the growth of public ownership, the extension of public management and planning, or the advancement of democratic participation in decision-making.

In this chapter we will explore these issues, suggesting first that while parties do matter at the provincial level in Canada, there are limitations on what any provincial government can do – especially a social democratic one. This makes it difficult for an NDP provincial government to reform dramatically the social, economic, or political status quo. Yet this does not mean that it makes no difference which party rules BC. Even if we should not expect radical socioeconomic change from an NDP government, we should anticipate that the choices it makes will reveal the left-of-centre priorities that distinguish social democrats from their business-liberal counterparts in other political parties. An examination of the David Barrett regime of the early 1970s and the Michael Harcourt administration of the early 1990s will reveal that the NDP does make a difference, especially in the social policy and environmental arenas (rather than in the economic field, where structural obstacles to reform are greatest).

Do Parties Matter?

On the question of whether parties make a difference, there is strong support in some quarters for 'convergence theories' of various sorts, which emphasize the basic similarity of ideology and socioeconomic organization within the countries of the Western industrialized world. At bottom, some say, these places are really quite the same – all with advanced capitalist economies and liberal democratic political systems – and they can be expected, therefore, to have similar public policy needs that will be met regardless of the party in office at any given time. It is especially tempting to conclude that parties do not matter in Canada, since their ideological range, judged by international standards at least, is really quite narrow. There has long been a widespread suspicion that it makes very little difference which of the two national governing parties – the Liberals or Progressive Conservatives – holds office in Ottawa, since they both seek to appeal to the same conglomeration of interests, classes, and regions that is necessary to assemble a national government. These parties can be depicted, in Hugh Thorburn's words, 'as Tweedledum versus Tweedledee, the Ins versus the Outs: two brokerage parties or teams of office-seekers who rival one another in mounting and presenting programs calculated to attract the support of a majority of the electorate.'[1]

But even if the national governing parties have been quite similar, this does not mean that politics at the provincial level might not be more tolerant of ideological diversity and therefore of a wider range of public policy outcomes. Indeed, while the Liberals and Conservatives have been the only parties so far to rule the nation, various provinces have been controlled by a number of different parties, some quite unconventional by national party standards. In BC, in particular, idiosyncrasy appears to be a virtue, and for the last forty-odd years the two traditional parties have not formed a government (indeed, from 1952 until 1991, they were also excluded from the role of official opposition). In such a scenario, it is more likely that provincial ruling parties will diverge somewhat from the stereotypical brokerage party model, and that it will matter more which party controls the provincial state.

What is more, we should also remember that provincial politics is considerably more executive dominated than federal politics, with powerful party leaders staking personal positions in election campaigns that then form the core of government policy once the party is in power. Throughout the provincial political process, therefore, parties are closely identified with the leader and government policy is personified by the premier. An election victory tends to give provincial premiers a fairly broad mandate to put their own stamp on public policy. A strong premier can successfully redirect government policy without much fear of opposition from party or legislature. And BC has had a particularly striking history of flamboyant premiers. In such a setting, the choice of a governing party does ultimately matter in terms of policy outcomes.

Do Social Democratic Parties Make a Difference?

Neither of the two parties that have governed federally has been social democratic and that alone may make a great difference. One could argue that while non-socialist parties, whatever their official label, are all more or less the same, social democratic parties are different in kind from their 'bourgeois' competitors. At the minimum, social democrats can be expected to reject the status quo and offer progressive alternatives to the mainstream parties of the right and centre-right. A huge literature concerned with the assessment of social democracy in power exists, most of it based upon the experiences in those countries where social democrats have been a significant governing force in national politics – e.g., Britain, western Europe, Scandinavia, Australia, and New Zealand. Yet if one wants to find out what 'actually existing social democracy' looks like in a Canadian context, federal politics is not the place to look. For a variety of reasons, the federal NDP has never come close to forming a national government and appears extremely unlikely to do so in the foreseeable future. Yet NDP governments or the NDP's precursor, the Co-operative Commonwealth Federation (CCF), have been in office in several provinces over the years – in Saskatchewan the CCF ruled from 1944 to 1964, the NDP from 1971 to 1982 and again from 1991 to the present; in Manitoba the NDP was in power from 1969 to 1977 and again from 1981 to 1988; the Ontario NDP formed a government from 1990 to 1995; and in BC the NDP ruled from 1972 to 1975 and again from 1991 to the present.

Not surprisingly, the academic and journalistic opinion about the merits of New Democratic governments, including the two BC examples, varies widely. There are those, primarily on the political right, who feel strongly that the NDP is guilty of excessive socialist zeal, especially in its management of the economy. According to this point of view, it makes a big difference whether the NDP is in power, rather than a party more favourable to free market economics, limited government, and conservative social values. To these critics, New Democrats are by nature reckless spendthrifts hell-bent on raising taxes and exhausting the treasury in order to pay for extravagant social welfare programs. The NDP, the argument runs, is ideologically committed to policies that will stifle individual initiative, deter foreign investment, and hamper economic development. In addition, these criticisms of the NDP's socialism have been supplemented by the view that the contemporary NDP is beholden to 'special interests' – organized labour, radical feminists, environmentalists, and so forth. When the NDP is in power, therefore, these 'minority' interests exercise undue influence over public policy – and this comes at the expense of the 'silent majority' of citizens who do not want their tax dollars financing the pet projects of radical elites.

Seen from this perspective, the NDP is a dire threat to the capitalist way of life and must be stopped at all costs. Indeed, anti-socialist emotions can run high in BC and have encouraged an 'anything-but-the-NDP' attitude within certain segments of the population. As Donald Blake explains in Chapter 5, BC's bipolar party system – with the various 'free enterprise' parties on one side and the CCF/NDP on the other – has been structured around a perceived need to keep the 'socialist hordes' out of power. At first this took the form of a coalition government, initiated during the early 1940s as an alliance between the Liberals and Conservatives to block the CCF from forming a majority government. The end of this alliance in 1951 prompted the invention of an ingenious (or so it seemed) electoral device designed to extend the prohibition against a CCF government – i.e., an alternative vote electoral system that would allow Liberal supporters to cast a second place vote for the Tories, and vice versa. Yet, as fate would have it, in 1952 this system produced the unintended outcome of a narrow victory over the CCF by the upstart Social Credit Party and its leader, former Conservative MLA W.A.C. Bennett.

Thus began a new chapter in the history of BC's polarized party configuration, one that was characterized by a tenacious two-party system, with the Socred electoral coalition representing the free-enterprise right and the CCF-NDP's own coalition of socialist, labour, and progressive-minded liberal voters on the left. Throughout this period, BC's Socred leaders got a great deal of mileage out of warning that 'the Marxist-socialists are at the gates!' And when the NDP did form its first BC government in 1972, this shocking event precipitated attempts to form a unity party of the so-called 'free market majority' with the sole purpose of ensuring that the NDP could not win reelection.[2] Such a party proved unnecessary, however, since the Socreds were able to reestablish a dominant free-enterprise coalition under the leadership of William Bennett. The years have not cooled the highly partisan political climate in BC, and anti-socialist rhetoric can still run uncomfortably hot. An illustration of this is the April 1993 postbudget edition of the Vancouver business magazine *Equity*, with its cover photo depicting BC Premier Mike Harcourt and Finance Minister Glen Clark as brown-shirted, gun-toting Nazis standing over a screaming headline: 'The NDP Declares War on Success!'

For many other critics of the NDP, however, the problem has been that the Barrett and Harcourt governments were not socialist enough. Indeed, the NDP's record in office has been disappointing to many on the left precisely because these administrations fell well short of the goal of implementing a coherent social democratic program. For some of these observers, the reasons for the NDP's failures are mainly structural. That is, an NDP government, like any social democratic party government in a capitalist system, is simply unable to alter radically the prevailing social and economic institutions. NDP governments, committed though they may be to progressive reform, cannot but fail to make any significant difference.

For other leftist critics, however, the problem is less structural than personal. That is, NDP leaders and the top party brass – in contrast to the rank and file members or activists within the labour or other popular movements that support the party – are blamed for betraying the cause of social democracy and squandering the opportunity to make a difference. The accusations in this vein are numerous and often pointed, including that the party leadership is cowardly and unwilling to fight the good fight; that the NDP establishment has sold out to the powers of corporate capitalism; that the party, beholden to the financial power of big labour, has lost its creative will; or that the NDP has been rendered impotent as a social democratic force because of its systematic repression of the radical left in the 1970s and 1980s. For most who level these types of criticisms, the NDP should be primarily a vehicle for the advancement of the social democratic cause, and not just an electoral machine. NDP governments, according to this view, are the means and not the end, and should be judged on their ability to make a social democratic difference when they have the opportunity. By these standards, the NDP in power has been an utter failure, leaving behind a string of lost hopes and shattered dreams wherever it has taken power.

The BC NDP: Goals and Objectives

Are these fair assessments of the experience of NDP government in BC? What are the main objectives of the BC NDP and what sort of principles do they reflect? The BC NDP is part of a larger Canadian tradition of social democracy that is characterized by its moderate, relatively non-doctrinal approach. Unlike most of the socialist and labour parties of Europe, for instance, the CCF was never very strongly committed to orthodox socialist theories. Heavily influenced by the social gospel movement with its Christian concerns about social justice and by a moderate British Fabian socialist tradition, the CCF emphasized gradual reform through the institutions of parliamentary democracy. Inspired by Keynesian economics and welfare liberalism, party leaders advocated a greater role for the state in the regulation and control of the economy and saw some room for public ownership where the circumstances required it, but they never denied the preeminent role of private capital in the Canadian economy. The CCF in BC was more radical than in other parts of Canada – a reflection in part of the unique economic relations within a frontier, resource-based society characterized by sharp differentiations between labour and management – but it was never a vehicle for revolutionary socialism.

The NDP, formed in 1961 out of the CCF but with an institutionalized affiliation with the trade union movement, has been even less overtly socialist, and certainly less enamoured with public ownership, than was the CCF. Like its counterparts elsewhere in Canada, the BC NDP has continued to shift to the ideological centre as it attempts to broaden its electoral appeal and to keep up with changes that have redefined the nature of class politics in Canada. On economic issues, the party stands primarily for a full employment policy established along Keynesian, state-interventionist lines combined with a commitment to protect, if not expand, the existing web of social programs. This is supplemented by a generally progressive orientation across a variety of social issues, including human rights, women's equality, aboriginal rights, and environmental protection. Such an orientation means that NDP economic policy involves a willingness to use the power of the state in a positive way, both for regulatory and stimulative purposes. Nevertheless, no one should conflate the Canadian tradition of social democracy with free spending, high deficits, and the discouragement of private enterprise. Indeed, the icon most fervently revered by Canadian social democrats is Tommy Douglas; and we should note that his CCF governments in Saskatchewan (especially the post-1948 ones), as well as the NDP governments of Alan Blakeney from 1971 to 1982, were characterized by balanced budgets and sound, technocratic, fiscally prudent economic management.

While not a vehicle for radical socialism, the NDP is nevertheless a social democratic party and sees itself as such. While it does not aim at eradicating capitalism, it does hope to make capitalism more bearable for those who traditionally suffer when the market is left uncontrolled. The NDP adheres to the notion that popular pressure can be exerted through parliamentary means to win reforms that will have a real benefit to the less advantaged members of society. When in power, New Democrats generally attempt to redistribute wealth through such measures as progressive taxation or more generous social programs. While such measures do not transform the material relations of production, they do seek to influence the balance of economic and social power between the haves and the have-nots.

As an organization, the NDP attempts to institutionalize its left-populism by employing a more democratic set of internal party institutions than are common among its major rivals. This is sometimes explained in terms of the NDP's resemblance to a 'mass' style political party rather than the 'cadre' party model exhibited by the other mainstream parties. New Democrats are more likely than their cadre party opponents to focus on the 'many' rather than the 'few.' This is demonstrated, for example, by a larger role for the rank and file members as opposed to the party leadership. The NDP puts great store in the creation of party policy by voting members in conventions and generally emphasizes the party's principles over the leader's personality. Strictly speaking, though, the NDP does not fit all criteria for a mass party, primarily because it receives significant financial support from trade unions rather than relying solely on private donations. Still, the NDP remains unique in its ability to fund its activities without many large corporate donations. What is more, the NDP differs from other parties in its identification as the official mouthpiece for the larger social democratic and labour movements that it represents. For this reason, some tension has been caused by the dichotomy between the party's role as the vanguard of a political movement and its existence as a party like all the others.

By and large, however, the party side of the NDP personality has eclipsed its movement orientation. Though it is slightly more interested than other parties in political education and extraparliamentary activity, the BC NDP as an organization is concerned mainly with the mechanics of campaigning and with winning and maintaining power. Moreover, the experience of governing has led the NDP to conform more closely with other parties to the extent that the premier and cabinet are in effect very little constrained by party policy. Like other governments, the power rests in the hands of the executive, top-level civil servants, and a handful of expert advisors. Indeed, the BC NDP is a sophisticated and finely tuned operation, staffed by a unique band of political professionals. As party insider Brad Zubyk explains,

> Despite the public perception of the party as a grassroots driven, democratic organization which allows policy to be set by a convention of 'ordinary' members, the NDP is probably more dominated by entrenched power brokers and professional political staff than its competitors. Working for the party or NDP politicians allows the individual to enter into an exclusive, tight-knit fraternity which spans the entire country ... NDP activists typically come from one of the major interest groups that represent its core support – labour, the women's movement, the environmental movement or the gay community. Professional activists, whether government staff or party organizers, are generally linked to a series of patrons creating a complex web of alliances based on personalities, region and interest group affiliation. It is not unusual for an activist to have been employed by the party in four or five different provinces.[3]

The staffing of the BC NDP governments has been consistent with the experience of other NDP governments in Canada. Old networks have provided advisors and staffers from all parts of Canada, and the senior political players in the NDP administrations have relied heavily on the expertise of party professionals, drawn primarily from the major organizations that constitute the NDP's electoral and organizational coalition.

This coalition consists of a clearly identifiable set of interests, though there may be variations within the internal balance of power from time to time. Organized labour, of course, assumes pride of place within the NDP, because the party relies upon trade unions for financial support and organizational expertise. For historical and institutional reasons, labour is especially prominent within the BC NDP (compared, say, to the Saskatchewan party). The BC Federation of Labour is the key organization here, and its major players include the International Woodworkers of America (IWA) and the BC Government Employees' Union (BCGEU). Indeed, support for the NDP comes from both traditional blue-collar unions, largely operating in the private sector, and the increasingly influential white- or pink-collar unions, most prominent in the public services. At the same time, large numbers of party activists, members, and supporters come from the ranks of the so-called 'professional new middle class' – teachers, university professors, social workers, civil servants, and so forth. A common thread linking these individuals is a reliance upon the provincial government for employment or funding. As well, their educational and professional backgrounds tend to make them rather sympathetic to progressive reform, especially regarding social policy and equality issues. These middle-class professionals within the NDP are not always particularly keen on trade union matters, and this produces some tension within the ranks.

Women's groups, too, have long been a core constituency within the NDP coalition. As Lynda Erickson points out in Chapter 7, the BC NDP established a Women's Committee in 1962 with a mandate to stimulate interest among women and to encourage greater female participation. This committee was reconstituted in 1971, with a more overtly feminist orientation, as the Women's Rights Committee (WRC), and it plays a forceful role within the party – conducting workshops, organizing conferences, distributing information, and participating in party conventions under the auspices of the Women's Caucus. For many feminists, the NDP's social democratic platform offers the greatest hope for advancing the cause of gender equity. To be sure, not all feminists are social democrats (and not all social democrats are feminists), but there is a natural fit between the principles of social democracy and feminism, especially in their shared commitments to a communitarian ethos emphasizing social justice, equality, universal health care, and adequate income support for women and families.

Social democratic parties have also tended to attract support from environmentalists, and this is largely the case in BC. In theory, of course, environmentalism does not map neatly along left-right ideological lines. But, as Kathryn Harrison explains in Chapter 16, environmentalists tend to migrate to left-wing parties. Mainstream parties are more closely linked to major corporate interests than is the NDP and they are less sympathetic to calls for greater regulation of industry or stiffer environmental protection standards. The NDP, on the other hand, is in principle quite willing to use the power of the state to regulate business and impose restrictions on industrial activity. Hence, the BC NDP has been allied with the ecological protection movement and has usually enjoyed the public support of environmental groups. Yet environmental and land use issues are always controversial in BC, and the provincial NDP has had an increasingly difficult time reconciling environmental values with the need for continued economic growth and job protection, especially in the forestry sector. As George Hoberg points out in Chapter 15, forest sector unions have been allied with their employers, often against the NDP and its environmental faction, to fight attempts to restrict access to the forest resource.

Finally, the New Democratic coalition provides a political home for the representatives of a variety of popular sector movements. For some of these groups (e.g., antipoverty activists), the main issues are clearly material – food, shelter, income support, and so on. These are interests that fit well into the more traditional or 'old' left understanding of the world as divided most significantly along class lines. But for other members of the NDP coalition (e.g., civil libertarians, ethnocultural minorities, consumer groups, peace activists, gay and lesbian rights advocates), the key divisions in society may not be between capital and labour. The politics of these members is often motivated by lifestyle, equity, or quality of life issues. These individuals, along with many feminists and environmentalists, fall into the camp of the new, 'postmaterialist' left. The role of these new groups is increasingly important within the NDP, and this has complicated the task of achieving a balance between the competing needs of all members of the current NDP coalition.

Limitations on NDP Provincial Governments

It is useful here to bear in mind, as Peter Hall puts it, that government policy 'will be influenced most significantly, first, by what a government is *pressed* to do, and secondly, by what it *can* do in the economic sphere. To a large extent, the former defines what is desirable in a democracy and the latter defines what is possible.'[4] In BC we can see that much of what an NDP government finds desirable – what it is *pressed* to do by its supporters and clientele groups – reflects both traditional trade union and social democratic concerns (job creation, stimulation of the economy, progressive taxation, expansion of social services) as well as the more specific concerns (equality for women, environmental protection, aboriginal rights) of the popular sector movements that support the New Democrats. It is in these areas that we find the greatest difference between an NDP government and others. Meanwhile, NDP governments are pressed by the larger conglomeration of voters, including supporters and potential supporters who are not self-identifying NDPers, to do what all governments are expected to do – to provide 'good government.' At minimum, this is understood as providing the opportunities for the highest possible level of personal economic prosperity while also delivering an adequate level of public services.

At the same time, though, there are very real restrictions on what a government *can* do, especially in the economic field. For the most part, limitations are structural and have to do with the balance of power within societies with a capitalist economy and a liberal democratic political system. In such a case, the owners and managers of capital retain control over the lion's share of economic resources, and the representatives of business, therefore, have much greater political influence than those of the working class, even when there is a social democratic party in office. Indeed, such parties do not see themselves as servants of an exclusively working-class or social democratic constituency. A variety of factors contributes to this phenomenon, including cross-cutting cleavages that divide citizens along religious, ethnic, geographical, or ideological lines rather than class ones; the corresponding need to form broadly based electoral coalitions; the unequal access to funding, advertising, and especially media coverage during and between election campaigns; and the multiple and competing demands of interest groups.

Consequently, BC NDP governments, like the social democratic governments that have been in power during recent decades in other jurisdictions, do not regard themselves as enjoying a mandate to transform radically the relations of class power. In fact, any such bold redistributive initiative would be electoral suicide. Politicians at the helms of governments in capitalist economies, regardless of their political party affiliation, are loath to embark upon policies that might discourage the owners of capital from investing and expanding their operations. In order to secure reelection, politicians must be able at least to give the impression that their policies are creating employment opportunities and economic prosperity, both of which depend, in capitalist economies, on continued private investment and expansion of production. Business, in such a world, is not just another interest group competing with others for favourable consideration by policymakers, for it can trigger an automatic punishment against any unwelcome reforms by acting in such a way as to produce greater unemployment or sluggishness in the economy. Despite what leftists within the NDP might really wish to see done, then, no provincial government in Canada can afford to ignore the primary concerns of private capital. In fact, New Democratic governments are under even greater pressure than others (with the possible exception of Parti Québécois governments in Quebec) to demonstrate to the owners and managers of private capital that they will not transform too radically the economic status quo. In addition, they are scrutinized more closely than other governments by a media elite largely beholden to corporate interests.

New Democrats in Canada are further hampered by the fact that their only opportunities to wield governmental power come at the helms of provincial rather than national administrations. Unfortunately for the NDP provincial governments, many of the really useful levers of economic activity are controlled by federal governments, who have their own ideas about monetary policy, interest rates, currency exchange rates, tax incentives, job training, trade laws, and the like. Compared to the government in Ottawa, provincial governments have very little say over macroeconomic planning and not much more over industrial policy. Without the control of key economic instruments, then, social democratic provincial governments are limited in what they can expect to accomplish.

Furthermore, the organization of the bureaucratic state in Canada severely limits the scope for policy innovation by governing parties. Alan Cairns, for instance, has focused attention on the extent to which the national and provincial states in Canada are 'embedded' in society, leaving little room for gove:nments of any political stripe to manoeuvre. New governments inherit massive program commitments put in place by their predecessors, and these programs are entrenched in bureaucracies, supported by clientele groups, protected within existing budgetary procedures, and preserved by their sheer numbers and by cabinet's inability to deal with more than a fraction of the government's overall business at any given time. Hence, their existence is almost tantamount to their survival. Says Cairns: 'To turn around a huge loaded oil tanker steaming full speed ahead is child's play when contrasted with the difficulty of engineering a significant change of direction for the great ship of state. The latter task is beyond the capacity of particular governments between elections.'[5] For even the most ambitious new government, then, there is never enough time or expertise available to overhaul more than a minuscule fraction of the policies bequeathed by those who went before.

Finally, there is a new set of factors today that affects the ability of provincial governments to impose distinctive policy programs within their own jurisdictions. For one thing, trade liberalization has left governments very little economic policy room to manoeuvre. While governments are pressured to offer protection for workers or industries harmed by the transition to a lower-barrier trading environment, they have been largely unable to respond adequately due to the counterpressures of international business and finance. Increasingly, policies dealing with social welfare, environmental protection, or labour relations have become targets for international harmonization. And of course, these are the very policy areas central to the strategies favoured by NDP governments. What is more, the process of globalization has further hampered the ability of provincial governments to chart new directions within a world that is fast becoming one homogenous marketplace with uniform rules, regulations, and practices. The economics of globalization narrows the range of policy alternatives, shifts more power from governments and the state to the multinational representatives of capital, and undermines the ideological support for the sort of concerted government action necessary for carrying out a social democratic agenda in a capitalist economy. To make matters worse, the federal and provincial governments have been plagued for years by a crisis of high debts and deficits. Government restraint has become the policy mantra of just about every government in the Western world, and social democrats find themselves on the wrong side of an ideological war against the Keynesian ideas and practices that arose during the construction of the postwar welfare state in Canada. Given such a climate, it is hard to promote a social democratic strategy premised on the idea that there must be a more activist role for government.

NDP governments are thus limited in a number of ways in their attempts to implement social democratic policies. As a result, we cannot expect radical change from NDP governments in BC. And, to be sure, no such phenomenon has occurred. Nevertheless, there are indications that NDP provincial governments have attempted to manage their capitalist economies in ways that moderate business power in the name of working-class or labour interests. And they usually seek to justify their social and economic policies in left-populist terms, referring to the benefits for ordinary working people rather than the business elite. On several fronts, the BC NDP has been successful in its pursuit of new models for economic planning and has been particularly active in striving toward its broader goals of promoting social justice and equality. For many individuals, then, the election of a New Democratic government in BC does make a difference. Turning to the cases of the Barrett and Harcourt governments, we can identify the areas of labour relations, social policy, and environmental management as those where the New Democrats left their clearest mark.

The Barrett Regime

Dave Barrett's 1,200 days in office have been closely scrutinized over the years, and his personal performance, as well as that of his administration as a whole, have come in for a great deal of criticism.[6] In the opinion of many observers, the Barrett government attempted to do too much, too fast. As soon as he took office, according to Terence Morley, 'Barrett proceeded to govern as if there were no tomorrow – or, at least, as if there were little prospect of repeating the winning performance.'[7] Indeed, Barrett presided over a whirlwind of legislative activism – a record 367 bills were passed – but there was little evidence of the overall planning for which social democrats are famous. This was especially the case in economic policy, and much of the blame rests with Barrett himself, since he unwisely elected to assume the finance portfolio along with the position of premier. Moreover, early on the premier and his government gave the impression that they arrived at their policies in a chaotic fashion. The administration was ridiculed mercilessly for this by a hostile press that portrayed the NDP as a bunch of bumblers and incompetent do-gooders.

Academic observers have made similar arguments, pointing out that the BC NDP appeared to be afflicted with a 'minority party syndrome.' In other words, its years in opposition left it unprepared to govern effectively.[8] Paul Tennant's seminal analysis of the situation explained that Barrett's ministers – lacking experience, proper administrative support, or coherent leadership – were 'unaided politicians in an unaided cabinet.' For instance, there were no institutional mechanisms put in place to aid policy development, assist in the coordination between agencies and branches of government, or control expenditures. As a result, ministers were on their own to initiate policies and attempt to push them through. The innovative policies that did surface during this administration, therefore, were the products of separate and individual initiatives by forceful ministers.[9]

But despite its awkwardness and administrative ineptitude, the Barrett regime was responsible for a wide range of measures that transformed virtually every aspect of BC government operations. In many cases, these reforms simply brought BC up to speed with what had been going on in other provinces since the late 1960s. Having resisted many of the administrative and policy reforms that had become so fashionable elsewhere, W.A.C. Bennett left the new government with plenty of opportunity to make changes. In many instances, these were routine modernizations of the system and had nothing to do with social democracy. Nevertheless, the NDP governments in Manitoba and Saskatchewan provided positive examples of how changes could be made according to social democratic priorities.

Above all, the new government made a firm commitment to do what it could to improve the lot of the province's sick, disabled, poor, and elderly. Among the accomplishments in these fields was the construction of many new hospitals and nursing homes; the creation of a province-wide ambulance service; a dramatic increase in welfare rates; the hiring of many more social workers; the establishment of new day-care spaces and increased funds for low-income users; the creation of a new Department of Housing and a bold set of initiatives in public housing and rent control; the introduction of Mincome, an income security program for seniors and disabled persons; and the development of Pharmacare, a prescription drug subsidy plan similar to one recently set up in Manitoba. Social policy was the clear priority of the Barrett government, and it was here that we see the greatest degree of legislative activism. Barrett and his human resources minister, Norman Levi (both former social workers), were quick to approve a variety of new programs, in many cases without knowing fully what the costs would be. Not surprisingly, government spending on welfare sky-rocketed during Barrett's tenure, increasing both in actual dollars spent and as a percentage of overall government expenditures. At first this did not seem to be much of a problem since the province, buoyed by a robust export market, enjoyed a period of remarkable economic growth. By the fall of 1974, however, the economy started to nosedive, and the government's heavy spending on social programs made it a target for opposition sniping, especially when it was revealed that due to a 'clerical error' Levi's department had over-run its budget allocation by over $100 million (or almost 40 percent).

The Barrett government was also active on the economic policy front, raising taxes and natural resource royalties, increasing regulation, and extending public ownership. The most controversial moves involved the natural resources sector, which had remained largely unrestrained by Social Credit policies. The NDP wanted to tax windfall profits in the mining industry and regulate more effectively the process of natural resource extraction. The introduction of the Mineral Royalties Act led to howls of protest from the mining industry and assorted business interests. The NDP was unable to withstand the pressure exerted by industry on this issue, and had to back down not only on the royalties side of their strategy but on their plans for greater regulation as well. In other areas, the Barrett administration was more successful in its attempts to extend the role of government in the economy. They introduced a number of nationalization schemes in forestry, natural resources, and transportation, and established several new crown corporations and expanded old ones. The most famous (and popular) NDP experiment in public ownership was the creation of a government-run automobile insurance plan. The Insurance Corporation of BC (ICBC) was set up along the lines of equally popular plans in Saskatchewan and Manitoba and, like them, it became an important part of the NDP's legacy. Another controversial institution that was to prove its lasting power was the Land Commission, which brought to a halt the subdivision of prime agricultural land.

Like any NDP regime, Barrett's government came to power with the support of the labour movement and various popular sector organizations. Its record in these areas is mixed, and many of the NDP's traditional supporters became profoundly disillusioned. Labour was initially pleased with the new philosophy of labour relations espoused by the NDP government. The NDP was committed to full and free collective bargaining, and for the first time such rights were extended to the BCGEU. And in an effort to reverse BC's reputation as the jurisdiction with the most turbulent labour relations in Canada, the new government designed an innovative Labour Code and instituted a Labour Relations Board (LRB) to oversee most aspects of labour relations in the province. As well, the minimum wage was repeatedly increased and a lot of money was allocated to job-creating public works programs. In the end, however, labour turned against the Barrett government when, in 1975, back-to-work legislation was employed in the forest, supermarket, gas, and transportation sectors. Labour representatives publicly criticized the government and clashed with caucus members at party conventions, while some NDP backbenchers were moved to vote against their own government on labour matters.

Popular sector supporters of the NDP – especially feminists – also clashed with the government. As Erickson documents, the WRC had spearheaded resolutions at party conventions calling for a separate Ministry of Women's Rights. But Barrett publicly rejected the idea of a women's ministry on the grounds that he did not believe in giving any group 'special rights.' Even after the 1973 party convention reaffirmed its support for the establishment of such a ministry, Barrett immediately told the press that the resolution was not a priority and would not receive the government's support. While Barrett's attitude angered feminists throughout the country, and led many women's organizations either to work against the NDP in the 1975 election or to hold back the type of support they would normally give to an NDP campaign, these events were not taken very seriously by the cabinet, which endorsed the premier's decision. Some progress was made toward greater rights for women, though, with the introduction of a new Human Rights Code. And significant breakthroughs occurred in the health care field – e.g., BC became the first province to fund rape relief centres, women's health collectives, and shelters for battered women. The Ministry of Education struck a task force to eliminate sexism and racism from school textbooks, and a Women's Economic Rights Branch was established within the Ministry of Economic Development. Finally, in 1974, Barrett allowed the appointment of the government's first Coordinator on Women's Affairs, along with a small budget and staff.

In the end, the positive measures introduced by Barrett's government have been overshadowed – both in the academic literature and the political folklore of the period – by the negative impression of a disorganized, confused government led by a stubborn, incompetent premier. Yet the NDP did focus on a much different set of priorities than its Social Credit opponents. The Barrett regime made a difference in the lives of some of the most disadvantaged members of BC society – the elderly and the poor, in particular. And the role of government to protect the public's interest was expanded through new government agencies, public enterprises, and regulatory bodies. The Barrett regime also left a legacy behind in several major programs that survived the election of subsequent Socred governments – Mincome, Pharmacare, ICBC, the Land Commission, the LRB, and so on. While many of the more progressive elements of some of these initiatives were ultimately repealed or watered down, their longevity proved that alternatives to the strictly free market model could find a home in BC. Nevertheless, leftist observers have lamented the lost opportunity of the Barrett years. They argue that more could have been done to build a base of support for a deeper social democratic ethos in the province, or that the single term in office could have been used more productively to implement more explicitly socialist policies. As Philip Resnick saw things, this might not have secured the party reelection (indeed it might have led to a more devastating defeat), but at least it would have been a defeat for the 'right reasons.'[10]

The Harcourt Regime
The Harcourt government took office after an especially bizarre period, even for the theatre of the absurd that is normal for BC party politics. With Barrett's defeat at the hands of William Bennett's Social Credit Party, the BC party system was restored to its polarized but basically stable state of affairs. However, the strange events that followed Bennett's 1986 retirement from politics set the stage for the NDP's return to power in 1991. After a fiercely contested Socred leadership battle and a relatively easy electoral victory the same year, new premier William Vander Zalm proceeded to put his own stamp on BC politics and the result led directly to the downfall of the Social Credit Party. After a series of controversial policy moves and a succession of embarrassing scandals, much publicized in BC and throughout the country, the Vander Zalm government started to fall apart. Finally, amid revelations that the premier had used his own office to expedite the sale of his biblical theme park, Fantasy Gardens (and that he had accepted $20,000 in cash from a Taiwanese billionaire as partial payment), Vander Zalm stepped down as premier and leader of the party. He was replaced by Rita Johnson, who called an election only at the eleventh hour of the government's five-year mandate. As was inevitable, the once-mighty Socreds lost power to the New Democrats while the previously impotent Liberal Party, led by Gordon Wilson, formed the official opposition.

These events are crucial to an understanding of the nature of the BC NDP's second provincial government. For one thing, the Harcourt team knew well in advance of the election call that it would probably form the next government. As a result, the BC NDP (unlike Bob Rae's Ontario team in 1990) had plenty of time to plan its transition to power. The party was also well placed to recruit several outstanding candidates, which it did, and to attempt to broaden its base of support by ensuring that many of those individuals recruited did not fit the usual media- and business-generated stereotype of the highly ideological, radical, and labour-oriented BC New Democrat. Candidates with business and management experience were enticed to join the party, attracted both by the prospect of holding office and by the opportunity to work with Harcourt, himself an ideologically moderate and business-friendly NDPer.

Socred scandals and Vander Zalm's personal misconduct allowed the New Democrats to champion the causes of governmental accountability, ethics, and responsibility. Of course, none of this is exclusively social democratic – it speaks more to the general appeal of good government and sound management than to the ideals of socialism. Indeed, the Harcourt NDP was even able to promote itself as the party of fiscal constraint (at least compared to the Socreds, who had engaged in a preelection spending spree). This helped to blunt the traditional criticism of social democrats as wanton free spenders, and allowed Harcourt to distance himself from the already-tainted Ontario NDP government and its infamous $10 billion budget deficit. At the same time, however, Harcourt's party realized that it would inherit nothing but disorder from the previous government. Among other things, the NDP strongly suspected that the fiscal situation would be far worse than the Social Credit government had let on. Thus, while the NDP freely exploited the Socred's fiscal mismanagement as an election issue, it had to prepare to take office knowing that it would have to restore sound economic management practices to the government's operations.

Although party elders never said as much in public, there were also worries that the party's good fortune could cause difficulties down the road. One major concern was that a party in opposition tends to say things that might not be practical for a governing party. Another concern was that the activist members of the party – deprived for almost twenty years of the opportunity to put their ideas into practice – would have unrealistically high expectations about what could be done once the party was back in control. Thus, a key theme of the preelection preparatory stage, and of the campaign itself, was that a Harcourt government (unlike the previous Barrett one) would go slow, avoid spending more than BC could afford, and would plan to govern for two terms. Still, there was always the danger of a clash between the government and its party – reminiscent of the episodes during the Barrett years – that might politically damage Harcourt's administration.

One crucial prerequisite, therefore, was to initiate a comprehensive policy review. The party elite intended to smooth out certain troublesome policy areas but did not want to appear to be stepping on the toes of the rank and file members. For this reason, it set up a committee to consult widely and carry out a close inspection of existing policy with the goal of updating the party's many promises made while in opposition. In other words, to avoid having to renege on prior promises once in office, the NDP brass decided to give the party a chance to revamp its policies along lines more suitable for a governing party in the lean and mean 1990s. The result of the committee's consultation and review was a forty-eight-point election platform – distributed under the title *A Better Way British Columbia* – that committed the new government to a variety of specific legislative measures. Economic policy was clearly not the major focus of this document (issues such as the environment and gender equity figured into the greatest number of recommendations), yet an essential point was a promise to balance the budget over the business cycle. A New Democrat government, the document announced, 'will control government spending openly and responsibly ... programs will be affordable and within our means. We will not spend more than British Colombians can afford.' What is more, the platform confirmed that 'a prosperous British Columbia needs a dynamic market economy.' This sent the clear message that the BC NDP would not ignore the prevailing mood of economic restraint, and it was a theme that Harcourt returned to repeatedly throughout the 1991 campaign.

Taken on their own, these promises of economic austerity and the preservation of the free market status quo might lead leftist critics of the NDP to conclude that the party had sold out to the right in its desperation to win power. Yet a closer look at the document as a whole reveals that the call for fiscal restraint does not necessarily come at the expense of traditional social democratic concerns. Among other things, the NDP promised fairer taxes for 'ordinary people and small businesses' and higher taxes for 'profitable corporations and the wealthy.' Under a New Democrat government, the document says, workers will come first when decisions on plant closings or layoffs are made. And an NDP government would bring in a new labour code, increase spending on education and health, raise the minimum wage, stimulate the economy, and provide incentives for small business operators. Seven of the forty-eight points involve promises to improve the lives of women in BC by doing such things as legislating pay equity and guaranteeing access to abortions. And no fewer than seventeen points relate to the environment and its protection. So taken as a whole, the preelection policy package is consistent with the social democratic orientation of the NDP and it reflects the interests of the party's major constituencies. If carried out, this program would be significantly different from what the Socreds did while in office, and distinctive, too, from what Gordon Wilson was promising to do if the Liberals were elected.

Once in office, the Harcourt regime moved quickly to remake the structure of government in BC to ensure that appropriate planning bodies were in place and that they were staffed with competent party professionals. New and highly politicized bodies, such as the Policy Coordination Office (PCO), the Government Communications Office (GCO), the Premier's Outreach Office, and the Planning Secretariat, took over much of the policy-making responsibility of the regular bureaucracy. Key positions in the senior civil service and ministers' offices were filled by loyal New Democrats from all over Canada. It would be hard to accuse the Harcourt cabinet members of being 'unaided politicians' the way Barrett's were. John Walsh, aide to Yukon NDP Government leader Tony Penniket, had been brought to BC as early as 1990 to oversee a centralized system for recruitment and staffing. Although some ministers brought in their own people, the object was to build a coherent, well-experienced team that would be able to work together effectively. Manitoba and Saskatchewan provided important sources of experience for several of the leading backroom players in the Harcourt administration. To complement this solid core of top administrators, Harcourt was blessed with sufficient talent in caucus to select a well-balanced cabinet reflecting the major constituencies within the party's coalition.

As well as having competent people in positions of authority, the NDP enjoyed the benefits of a robust economy and a weak opposition. While recession gripped all of North America, BC was significantly less hard hit. Throughout the Harcourt years, BC's unemployment rate was comparatively low and economic growth was particularly impressive. BC maintained the highest credit rating of any province in Canada and received plenty of foreign investment. For all of its early term in office, moreover, the Harcourt administration faced a completely disorganized and distracted opposition. After its embarrassing electoral defeat, the Social Credit Party, attempting to regroup, managed only to humiliate itself further. Rita Johnson was replaced by the veteran Grace McCarthy, who then failed to win a by-election in a supposedly safe Socred riding. Ultimately, she resigned her party leadership but it no longer mattered – the Socreds were all but finished. Meanwhile, Wilson's Liberals, having leapfrogged over the Socreds to take over as the official opposition, became mired in a nasty internal dispute ignited by the leader's decision to appoint neophyte MLA Judy Tyabji as house leader. As it turns out, Wilson and Tyabji, both married to other people, were involved in a love affair. The resulting media controversy and caucus revolt not only revived BC's reputation for wildly flamboyant party politics but also rendered the Liberals unable to mount any serious campaign against NDP policies until Wilson was overthrown and replaced by Vancouver mayor Gordon Campbell. For a while, the new Liberal leader had to compete for right-of-centre support with the new BC Reform Party, which attempted to cash in on the popularity of Preston Manning's national Reform juggernaut (even though the federal party has no affiliation with the BC party). In the end, the Liberals emerged as the favoured free-enterprise alternative to the New Democrats, but it was not until quite late in the Harcourt term that they came together as anything like a real legislative opposition.

Given these favourable circumstances, the New Democrats could have been expected to exploit the situation by moving quickly, building public support, and implementing creative new policies before the economy soured or the opposition got its act together. Yet the Harcourt regime was relatively slow off the mark, obsessed as it was with avoiding the pitfalls that befell Barrett. Nevertheless, there were cautious attempts to redirect the government's approach in key policy areas, and after a major mid-term cabinet shuffle, the government became focused on a firm set of policy objectives: labour relations; health, education, and social policy; women's, multicultural, and First Nations matters; the environment and forestry. There were also some changes to be made in taxation policy, infrastructural investment, and public administration.

On the labour front, Harcourt's government managed to satisfy many of its supporters' demands without completely alienating business. Close affiliations between the government and key labour leaders – most significantly Ken Georgietti of the BC Federation of Labour and John Shields of BCGEU – helped in avoiding the type of confrontations that marred Barrett's relationship with labour. Moreover, at a time when the union movement was at odds with the NDP governments in Ontario and Saskatchewan, BC's unions refused to endorse the anti-NDP antics of their compatriots in other provinces. However, BC labour had little to complain about. The Harcourt government fulfilled its promise to replace Vander Zalm's much-despised Bill 19 with a new Labour Code. Unions won an anti-scab rule, a provision allowing secondary boycotts, an ease on the prohibition against common site picketing, an end to secret balloting on certification votes, and a provision for mandatory arbitration of first contract disputes. Labour did not get everything it wanted (e.g., sectoral certification) but the new bill restored union rights deleted in the blatantly pro-management Bill 19 and added a few new ones, thus improving significantly the ease of unionization in the province. As well, the BCGEU was rewarded early on with a generous contract settlement, and the government broke new ground with its Employment Security Agreement (ESA) with three militant health sector unions – the Nurse's Union, the Hospital Employees' Union, and the Health Sciences Association. An innovative deal, the ESA not only provided wage increases and employment security for health workers but it enhanced the role of employees in decision-making at the provincial and facility levels. The agreement also demonstrated the government's willingness to respond to the feminist and equality perspectives advanced by this coalition of unions, all led by women. In addition, the Harcourt regime improved the lot of workers by toughening employment standards legislation, increasing the minimum wage, and integrating the labour and postsecondary education portfolios to emphasize more strongly a 'skills and training' priority.

On health, education, and social policy, the Harcourt government was less accommodating to the demands of its popular sector supporters, especially when this might have cost a lot of money. Resolved to balance the budget before its term was up, the Harcourt government could promise only that its deficit reductions would not come at the expense of essential services. BC NDP politicians proudly asserted that there would be no 'slash and burn' approach akin to what Ralph Klein was carrying out next door in Alberta. However, the government was hard pressed to maintain service levels given that people continued to flood into BC in record numbers, driving up caseloads and increasing the demand for new schools and hospitals. There were progressive moves made – meals programs in some schools, a new Child, Family and Community Services Act, more social workers hired, assistance for those with special needs, and a few new programs for public housing. But while total spending on the core services of health, social services, and education went up, program spending per person declined steadily. In health, the government followed the lead of other provinces by attempting to rationalize and restructure the system through decentralization. While this was promoted as a populist move toward greater community democracy, the obvious priority was cost reduction. Similar cost-cutting operations occurred within the education system. As well, the government reacted to business and public concerns about reduced competitiveness in a new global economy by attempting to link education more closely to a 'skills development' model and by promoting a 'back to basics' approach normally associated with conservative politicians (the NDP even rolled back some of the more progressive educational initiatives enshrined in the 'Year 2000' program begun while the Socreds were in office). On social policy issues, the government made similar responses to reactionary public pressure. Prodded by a relentless series of reports about welfare abuse broadcast by BCTV and published in local newspapers, Harcourt publicly ranted about 'welfare cheats' and ordered the Social Services Ministry to crack down on welfare fraud and bureaucratic waste. In addition, the BC NDP took the controversial step of withholding for three months welfare payments for those who move to the province and then apply for welfare. Not surprisingly, these policies caused anger and resentment among the party's antipoverty activists and social reformers.

More impressive, from a progressive perspective, is the government's record on women's issues, gender relations, human rights, multiculturalism, and aboriginal affairs. Here we see a clear difference between the approach of the Harcourt government and what came before in BC (not to mention what goes on in provinces with non-NDP administrations). As well, developments in this area demonstrate the extent to which the postmaterialist left has gained greater leverage within the party. For instance, the Harcourt administration made real strides toward greater equality for women. As Erickson shows, the WRC pushed the party to encourage greater numbers of female candidates, especially in winnable ridings, and to give women a stronger voice at the cabinet table in the event of an NDP victory. In the end, sixteen women won seats for the NDP in 1991 (31 percent of the caucus) and Harcourt appointed seven of them to a cabinet of seventeen. Most significant, administratively, was the creation of a free-standing

Ministry of Women's Equality (MWE), Canada's first, with broad program responsibility as well as an advisory role. On the policy front, the Harcourt government increased the number of women at top levels of the public service; made available new funds for pay equity and affirmative action in the public sector (though there are no similar programs for the private sector); guaranteed access to abortion services and legislated 'bubble zones' around clinics to protect abortion service providers against harassment; launched a multifaceted Stopping the Violence Against Women Initiative; funded community women's centres and specialized women's health facilities; and doubled the available spaces in licensed day-care facilities.

The Harcourt government worked hard, as well, to accommodate the rapid social and cultural changes that have transformed BC into one of the most pluralistic and multicultural societies anywhere. For instance, the government strengthened the Human Rights Act to prohibit discrimination based on sexual orientation or family status and amended the adoption rules to allow equal rights for gay and lesbian couples; appointed more women and visible minorities to a variety of boards, agencies, and commissions; introduced BC's first Multiculturalism Act; amended the Police Act to allow Sikhs to wear turbans; increased funding for ESL programs; and initiated immigrant settlement grants for new Canadians.

The Harcourt regime also offered a new and more generous approach to the settlement of aboriginal land and treaty issues in the province. As Paul Tennant points out in Chapter 4, the election of the NDP in 1991 dramatically improved the climate for aboriginal treaty negotiations, since the new government was far more committed to resolving First Nations issues than the Socreds had ever been. The NDP government expanded the role and importance of the Ministry of Aboriginal Affairs, recognized aboriginal title, and advocated self-government. BC joined the First Nations and the federal government in implementing the BC Treaty Commission, and the NDP administration worked with First Nations to improve community involvement in education and skills training, justice and policing, forestry, resource management, and family and social services. Later in the Harcourt term, however, non-aboriginal constituents – egged on by opposition politicians, open-line radio hosts, newspaper columnists, and interest group representatives – protested that the government was caving in to unfair aboriginal demands for more land and special rights. It looked for a while as though the government, reacting fearfully to these complaints, would drag its feet on the treaty resolution issue until after a provincial election. Yet late in its first term, the NDP concluded a historic agreement with the Nisga'a Tribal Council and the federal government. The agreement-in-principle calls for a large cash settlement, a degree of self-government on over 1,900 square kilometres of land, Nisga'a ownership of resources, and entitlements to salmon stocks and wildlife. On this matter, the BC NDP truly sets itself apart from its rivals. The Liberal opposition threatened to scotch the agreement if it formed the next government, while the BC Reform Party called the deal 'racist' because of it grants special rights to Natives.

Another key area where the Harcourt NDP has made a clear difference is in the environmental field. New Democrats were vigorous in their attacks on Social Credit environmental policy while in opposition and a full third of the forty-eight points in *A Better Way British Columbia* related to environmental or forestry reforms. But could an NDP government make good on its 'green' agenda once in office? As both Harrison and Hoberg document, the Harcourt administration's toughest test came with its decision to allow clearcut logging in up to two-thirds of Clayoquot Sound. The resulting antigovernment protests, and counter-demonstrations by loggers and their families, inflamed opinion both inside and outside the party. Clayoquot quickly became an international *cause célèbre* and the Harcourt government spent much of the next two years in damage-control mode. The issue was finally (and quietly) resolved in 1995 with the government's adoption of the recommendations of the Scientific Panel for Sustainable Forest Practices in Clayoquot Sound – which called for changes to logging practices, including an end to conventional clearcutting. But the Clayoquot episode remains a harsh lesson in the politics of the contemporary NDP, highlighting as it does the rifts between labour and environmentalists, urban and rural members, the old leftists and the postmaterialists.

Because of the many conflicting interests involved in BC forestry issues, the Harcourt government determined early on to rely upon a consultative process for handling divisive land use questions. The Commission on Resources and the Environment (CORE) was established to help end 'watershed by watershed' conflicts and to secure public support for regional land use plans. A series of commissions would include various stakeholders – business, labour, First Nations, environmentalists, community representatives, and so on – in the process of hammering out agreements that defined the protected areas and working forests in each region. At the same time, the government implemented a Protected Areas Strategy aimed at protecting 12 percent of BC's representative ecosystems by doubling the amount of parks and protected wilderness areas. And where logging was to continue, it would now be regulated more carefully according to guidelines set out in the new Forest Practices Code. While it may have been presumptuous of the NDP to brag, as it did, about having 'ended the war in the woods,' the Harcourt administration nevertheless deserves to be commended, first, for confronting an issue that the previous government had done its best to avoid, and, second, for instituting a process that involved the public and communities in a meaningful way.

Initially, as we have seen, the Clayoquot Sound decision (which was made outside of the CORE framework) severely damaged the government's

image among environmentalists and the public. But the NDP's environmentalist reputation was largely rebuilt on the strength of its later approach
to forestry issues and its activist attitude toward ecological protection. As
Harrison's case studies demonstrate, the government made a series of pro-
environment decisions involving pulp and paper effluent, the Tatshenshini
wilderness area, and the Kemano Completion Project. As well, the Harcourt
administration was not afraid to beef up the province's antipollution regulations, imposing tough new measures protecting the air, water, wildlife,
and farmlands. These decisions further illustrate the NDP's commitment
to an environmentalist agenda – a commitment that sets it apart from
either the BC Liberal or Reform Parties. Indeed, if there is any lasting legacy
of the Harcourt years in office, it is the province's vastly improved environmental record, including the establishment of many new and spectacular
wilderness parks.

The BC NDP has been less successful, however, in staking out new territory on economic policies. Indeed, its main concern – deficit reduction – is
shared by all governments in Canada, and this preoccupation has earned it
the scorn of numerous leftist critics. Yet here, too, there is some evidence
that an NDP government makes a difference. In the 1990s, all provincial
governments face a squeeze from high debts, made worse by the reduction
of federal transfer payments and the pressures of globalization. Most opt to
meet these challenges primarily through cutbacks. They slash budgets, stop
spending on infrastructure, cut jobs in the civil service, reduce social benefits, limit access to medical services, and dismantle legislation that might
be seen as an impediment to the free market. This strategy has been extremely popular with business and media elites, who have made its top
cheerleader, Alberta Premier Ralph Klein, the poster boy of Canadian
neoconservatism. The Harcourt NDP has largely resisted these calls for radical
restraint, opting instead for what it calls a 'balanced approach' to deficit
reduction. Thus, it whittled away at the $2.4 billion deficit it inherited in
1991 (in fact, the deficit was eliminated in the 1995-6 budget and a surplus
is indicated for 1996-7), but it did so using a combination of new revenue
measures and cutbacks to lower-priority areas. Bucking the neoconservative
trend, the NDP increased taxes in each of its first two budgets, targeting in
particular higher-income earners and large corporations. As well, the government's immediate policy goals were achieved, in part, by heavy borrowing by government agencies and crown corporations to pay for all kinds
of capital projects – roads, ferries, local works, schools, hospitals, and so
on. Hence, the NDP remained true to its social democratic principles by
investing in economic stimulation and job creation.

In addition, the BC NDP government has been at the cutting edge of ad-
vances in computer and telecommunications technologies. While none of
this helped make BC a social democratic paradise, it did bring the province

in line with (and then to the vanguard of) developments in other highly advanced jurisdictions. The initiatives in this area reflect Harcourt's personal desire to see social democracy retooled for the postindustrial economy. He never tired of saying that BC must win the 'race to the top' in competition with the advanced economies of Japan and the European Community, rather than engage in a 'race to the bottom' with less developed economies in Mexico or the southern USA. The strategy was to attract high-technology employment opportunities rather than low-wage, low-skill jobs.

Despite all the hype about preparing the province for the twenty-first century, though, the Harcourt regime will not be remembered for its innovations. Those who expected a flurry of new programs or a radical break with the past were largely disappointed. Harcourt followed through on his promise not to move too far, too fast (as Barrett was accused of doing). There were noticeably few initiatives intended to redistribute wealth or extend the range of public ownership and control. Yet many would argue that breakthroughs in these areas cannot be expected in the tough economic climate of the 1990s; the most that can be expected in this era of fiscal constraint is that existing programs remain relatively unscathed. And on that score, the Harcourt regime managed to produce enough evidence of deficit reduction to keep investors happy without angering too many supporters by slashing programs. Indeed, Harcourt did not alienate labour (as Barrett did in the 1970s and Bob Rae did in Ontario in the 1990s) or his popular sector supporters (even environmentalists were back on board, despite Clayoquot).

Of course, some supporters argue that more could have been done – for example, new and more imaginative social policies, antipoverty measures, or some alternative economic strategies. Observers point out that given the enviable circumstances of a strong team, robust economy, and weak opposition, the New Democrats had a golden opportunity to promote a 'creative politics' and to build greater future support for the social democratic cause. Instead, they played it safe and, as a result, left behind few legacies that will not be easily undone by right-of-centre successor governments. Still, even leftist critics strongly prefer the NDP to the Socreds of the past or the present-day Campbell Liberals, the latter having inherited the role of free-enterprise saviours. The Harcourt government preserved, and in some cases expanded, the role for public management and planning – especially in the health field, social services, and the forestry sector. And it did so in opposition to general trends prevalent in most Western democracies.

Finally, the Harcourt regime made good on its promise to reform government operations by implementing tough new conflict of interest rules, passing sweeping legislation on freedom of information and privacy protection, reforming the public service's accountability guidelines, improving the appointment procedures for public agencies, and revamp-ing the province's electoral laws. It is ironic, then, that Harcourt was forced to resign over an embarrassing political scandal involving bingo revenues illegally diverted to the NDP by the Nanaimo Commonwealth Holding Society. Harcourt was himself never implicated in the long-running bingo scandal, which actually took place in the 1980s, before he became pre-mier. But his handling of the affair caused grumbling within the party, led to outrage on the opposition benches, drew scorn from the media, and garnered harsh disapproval from the public. Faced with evidence of internal party corruption, Harcourt refused to demand the resignation of any party officials, cabinet ministers, or caucus members. As the scandal festered, the NDP fell further behind the Liberals in the polls. With Harcourt's approval rating lagging behind his party's, and with Gordon Campbell comfortably ahead in the popularity race, there were fears that the premier's performance would sink the party, much as Vander Zalm's actions fatally wounded the Socreds in 1991. In the end, Harcourt threw himself on his sword, resigning as party leader and premier in order to allow a successor to rebuild the NDP's image before the next election, which had to be called in less than a year.

Glen Clark Takes the Helm

Glen Clark was an easy first-ballot victor in the February 1996 BC NDP leadership contest, and he then led the party to a narrow victory in the May election. This marks the first ever back-to-back NDP majority govern-ments in the province's history. Soon after becoming premier, and prior to the election, Clark set about distinguishing himself from his predecessor – at least in style if not in ideology. Harcourt is a rather plodding, techno-cratic, moderate conciliator who never quite seemed to be in control of his cabinet; Clark is a young, dynamic, scrappy partisan who gives every im-pression that he is firmly at the helm. When, for instance, it looked as if scandal was about to undermine the new premier before he even got going (just as Clark was being sworn in, a scandal broke involving well-placed NDP officials and friends who had profited handsomely from investments in a privatized BC Hydro project), Clark moved quickly and decisively to ward off further political damage – heads rolled and the new premier was back on track.

It is far too early to make any judgments about Glen Clark's premiership. But amid his many good-news preelection announcements – including a tax freeze until the end of the century, a freeze on auto insurance rates, a freeze on university and college tuition, a cap on doctors' salaries, and a twenty-month freeze on unionized government employee wages – there was some indication of the direction the Clark government will take. For one thing, the NDP under Clark will remain very much distinct from the other BC political parties, especially in terms of its attitude toward the government's role in the economy and social programs. Sensing that the public has grown weary of years of cutbacks, Clark announced a major initiative in the economic stimulation of the economy. Dubbed 'Investing in the Future: A Plan for BC,' this new strategy calls for increased spending on skills training, value-added natural resource projects, and investment in infrastructure. Clark promises to create thousands of new jobs, many in the forestry sector (there is some concern among environmentalists that Clark will be less proactive on ecological protection issues). Clark also signalled a strong commitment to the expansion of social programs through 'BC Benefits,' a plan for the renewal of the province's social safety net. With these two major initiatives, Clark – who came to power with the backing of all the key unions in BC, and who represents a working-class, east-end riding in Vancouver – reaffirmed the NDP's allegiance to its traditional coalition partners. Clark's campaign asked voters which side they were on, thus emphasizing the ideological difference between the NDP and its right-wing competitors. The strategy proved successful, and Clark will have an opportunity to put his own stamp on BC politics.

Conclusion

As a party committed to social and economic change, BC NDP governments face an entrenched extraparliamentary opposition in the business sector, and must shoulder the heavy burden of living up to their idealistic supporters' high expectations. It is thus not surprising that along with the expected business resentment of social democratic policies comes harsh criticism from party supporters and advocates of the social democratic principles endorsed by the NDP. Many of these critics argue that while NDP administrations act differently than non-NDP governments, they still do not distinguish themselves as much from their right-of-centre competitors as they promise or as much as their clientele groups hope. In the end, the critics will say, the BC NDP fails to capitalize on its opportunities either by building sufficient support for a new approach to provincial politics, or by putting in place innovative programs that might stand as a social democratic legacy for the future of the province.

In the eyes of some, moreover, the NDP is guilty of a shameless politics of appeasement. NDP administrations move to the centre once in power, hoping to avoid harmful confrontations with business and trying to make sure that moderate voters were not uncomfortable with the party. Barrett and Harcourt insisted that once empowered to govern, they had to rule for all the people of BC, not just the narrow interests that make up the NDP coalition. But critics of this strategy fear that 'playing it safe politically may be a dangerous game since it is unlikely to attract support from the right and will certainly lead to disaffection among traditional supporters.'[11] The

Barrett and Harcourt experiences seem to bear this out, at least to the extent that their moderation was not rewarded with increased electoral support from centrist or right-of-centre voters. Yet the leftist critics who want more from the NDP may be misinterpreting the reality faced by social democratic governments. For one thing, such governments cannot be expected to accomplish the task of altering radically a society that is dominated by capitalist economic institutions and governed according to the norms of parliamentary democracy. And in any event, these governments lack a clear mandate to make such far-reaching reforms. The NDP itself is a loose coalition of conflicting factions, and the policies applauded by one sector may be denounced by another. As a result, NDP governments simply do not have the green light to go forward with a uniform set of unmistakably social democratic policies.

Still, the BC NDP continues to chart its own course, even though it confronts enormous hostility from the province's business sector and from a variety of right-wing political groups and socially conservative institutions. From the ideological perspective of these organizations, the NDP in office makes a large difference, and an unwelcome one at that. And from the perspective of the average citizen, the NDP has made a difference, both in the level of government regulation to be confronted and the range of public services offered. In the end, BC's NDP governments have indeed left their imprint on the province's public life by expanding social services, promoting health and education reform, implementing civil liberties initiatives, protecting the environment, and modernizing the government's operations.

Further Reading

Barrett, David, and William Miller. *Barrett: A Passionate Political Life*. Vancouver: Douglas and McIntyre 1995

Berman, T., Maurice Gibbons, Löys Maingon, Gordon Brent Ingram, Ronald B. Hatch, and Christopher Hatch. *Clayoquot and Dissent*. Vancouver: Ronsdale Press 1994

Gawthrop, Daniel. *High Wire Act: Power, Pragmatism and the Harcourt Legacy*. Vancouver: New Star Books 1996

Kardam, Nükhet. 'Interest Group Power and Government Regulation.' *BC Studies* 60 (1983-4): 48-74

Kavic, Lorne, and Gary Brian Nixon. *The 1200 Days: A Shattered Dream, Dave Barrett and the NDP in BC, 1972-75*. Coquitlam, BC: Kaen Publishers 1978

Morley, Terence. 'From Bill Vander Zalm to Mike Harcourt: Government Transition in British Columbia.' In *Taking Power: Managing Government Transitions*, edited by Donald Savoie. Toronto: Institute of Public Administration of Canada 1993

Tennant, Paul. 'The NDP Government in British Columbia: Unaided Politicians in an Unaided Cabinet.' *Canadian Public Policy* 3, 4 (1977): 489-503

Young, W.D. 'A Profile of Activists in the British Columbia NDP.' *Journal of Canadian Studies* 6, 1 (1971): 19-26

Appendixes

BC governments, Confederation to 1996

Year	Premier	Party
1871	John F. McCreight	
1872	Amor de Cosmos (b. W.A. Smith)	
1874	George A. Walkem	
1876	Andrew C. Elliott	
1878	George A. Walkem	
1882	Robert Beaven	
1883	William Smithe	
1887	Alexander E.B. Davie	
1889	John Robson	
1892	Theodore Davie	
1895	John H. Turner	
1898	Charles A. Semlin	
1900	Joseph Martin	
1900	James Dunsmuir	
1902	Edward G. Prior	
1903	Richard McBride	Conservative
1915	Wiliam J. Bowsers	Conservative
1916	Harlan C. Brewster	Liberal
1918	John Oliver	Liberal
1927	John D. McLean	Liberal
1928	Simon Fraser Tolmie	Conservative
1933	T. Dufferin Pattullo	Liberal
1941	John Hart	L-C Coalition
1947	Byron I. Johnson	L-C Coalition
1952	W.A.C. Bennett	Social Credit
1972	David Barrett	New Democratic
1975	William R. Bennett	Social Credit
1986	William Vander Zalm	Social Credit
1991	Rita Johnston	Social Credit
1991	Michael Harcourt	New Democratic
1996	Glen Clark	New Democratic

Appendix A.2

Population of BC, Confederation to 1991

Year	Population (thousands)	As a percentage of Canada
1871	36.2	0.98
1881	49.5	1.14
1891	98.2	2.03
1901	178.7	3.33
1911	392.5	5.45
1921	524.6	5.97
1931	·694.3	6.69
1941	817.8	7.11
1951*	1,165.2	8.32
1961	1,629.1	8.93
1971	2,184.6	10.13
1981	2,744.2	11.27
1991	3,212.1	11.89

* As of 1951, BC had the third largest population of any province.

Appendix A.3

Religious and linguistic make-up of BC and Canada (%)

	BC	Canada
Mother Tongue		
English	80.2	61.5
French	1.6	24.3
Other	18.2	14.2
Religion		
Catholic	18.6	45.7
Protestant	44.5	36.2
No religion	30.7	12.7
Other	6.2	5.4

Source: 1991 census.

Appendix A.4

BC election results, 1920-96

Year	Total seats	PC % votes	PC # seats	Liberal % votes	Liberal # seats	CCF/NDP % votes	CCF/NDP # seats	Social Credit % votes	Social Credit # seats	Other % votes	Other # seats
1920	47	31.5	14	38.0	26					30.5	7
1924	48	29.6	16	32.3	27					38.1	5
1928	48	53.3	35	40.5	12					6.2	1
1933	47	–	–	41.7	34	31.5	7			26.8	6
1937	48	28.6	8	37.3	31	28.6	7			5.5	2
1941	48	30.9	12	32.9	21	33.4	14			2.8	1
1945	48		**37**	**59.7**		37.6	10	1.4	0	5.1	1
1949	48		**39**	**63.6**		35.1	7	1.2	0	2.3	2
1952	48	16.8	4	23.5	6	30.8	18	27.2	19	1.7	1
1953	48	5.6	1	23.6	4	30.8	14	37.8	28	2.2	1
1956	52	3.1	0	21.8	2	28.3	10	45.8	39	1.0	1
1960	52	6.7	0	20.9	4	32.7	16	38.8	32	0.8	0
1963	52	11.3	0	20.0	5	27.8	14	40.8	33	0.1	0
1966	55	0.2	0	20.2	6	33.6	16	45.6	33	0.4	0
1969	55	0.1	0	19.0	5	33.9	12	46.8	38	0.1	0
1972	55	12.7	2	16.4	5	39.6	38	31.2	10	0.2	0
1975	55	3.9	1	7.2	1	39.2	18	49.2	35	0.5	0
1979	57	5.1	0	0.5	0	46.0	26	48.2	31	0.3	0
1983	57	1.2	0	2.7	0	44.9	22	49.8	35	1.4	0
1986	69	0.7	0	6.7	0	42.6	22	49.3	47	0.6	0
1991	75	0	0	33.3	17	40.7	51	24.1	7	2.0	0
1996[a]	75	0	0	41.8	33	39.4	39	9.2	2[b]	9.6	1

Notes: The numbers in bold type, for the elections in 1945 and 1949, saw the Liberals and Conservatives run as a team to support the coalition government that they had formed after the 1941 election.

[a] Preliminary results.

[b] Both MLAs were elected for the Reform Party of BC, which was composed of remnants of the Social Credit Party. One of these MLAs, Jack Weisgerber, had been a cabinet minister in the last Socred government. For more details, see Chapter 5.

Appendix A.5

Summary of ministry responsibilities, government of British Columbia, June 1996

Premier

General Responsibilities
- Executive Council operations
- Minister responsible for youth
- Legislation program, corporate policy

Major Boards and Commissions
- Premier's Advisory Council on Science and Technology
- Transition Commissioner to implement new structures for child protection

Aboriginal Affairs

General Responsibilities
- Aboriginal land claims and self-government
- Interministerial and federal-provincial coordination of natural resource, economic, and social policies related to aboriginal issues

Major Boards and Commissions
- BC Treaty Commission
- Native Economic Development Advisory Board
- First People's Heritage Language and Culture Council

Agriculture, Fisheries and Food

General Responsibilities
- Agriculture, food, and beverage industry development, including the Buy BC Program
- Farm management, soil and water conservation, animal health, and crop protection
- Agriculture financial programs
- Economic development of BC's commercial fisheries and aquaculture operations

Major Boards and Commissions
- Agriculture Land Commission
- BC Egg Marketing Board
- BC Marketing Board
- BC Milk Marketing Board
- BC Agricultural Industry Development Council
- BC Aquaculture Industry Advisory Council
- BC Salmon Marketing Council
- Okanagan Valley Tree Fruit Authority
- BC Wine Institute
- Cattle Industry Development Council
- Columbia Power Corporation
- Columbia Basin Trust

Attorney General and Ministry Responsible for Multiculturalism, Human Rights and Immigration

General Responsibilities
- Criminal justice and family law
- Court administration, courthouse management, and sheriff services
- Public trustee
- Legal aid, victim assistance, and public legal education
- Sexual assault centres and women's assault centres
- Expropriation compensation
- Family maintenance
- Legal services to the government
- Land Titles Office
- Police and correctional services

- Emergency preparedness
- Coroner's service
- Film classification
- Liquor licensing and distribution
- Gaming enforcement
- Consumer legislation and investigations
- Landlord-tenant dispute resolutions
- Motor dealer, cemetery, and travel-agent operations
- Consumer debtors assistance
- Human rights and immigration
- Multicultural policy and services

Major Boards and Commissions
- BC Human Rights Council
- BC Parole Board
- BC Police Commission
- Expropriation Compensation Board
- Commercial Appeal Commission
- Law Foundation of BC
- Law Reform Commission
- Legal Services Society
- Liquor Appeal Board
- Multicultural Advisory Council
- Travel Assurance Board
- Motor Dealer Customer Compensation Fund Board
- Police Boards

Education, Skills and Training

General Responsibilities
- K-12 education programs, curriculum development, special education
- K-12 school funding
- Independent schools
- Training and skills development
- Universities and colleges
- Worker retraining strategies
- Community-based learning
- English as a second language
- Student financial assistance
- Training and job placement for social assistance recipients, UI exhaustees, and UI ineligibles

- Strategy for coordinating disabilities issues

Major Boards and Commissions
- Advanced Education Council
- BC college and institutes boards
- Open Learning Agency
- Private Post-Secondary Institutes Commission
- University boards of governors and senates
- College of Teachers
- Education Advisory Council
- Francophone Education Authority

Employment and Investment

General Responsibilities
- Development of economic framework for targeted strategies for growth and job creation in conjunction with Crown corporations, other ministries, and the private sector
- Creation of regional and community adjustment policies and vehicles
- Science and Technology
- Translation of BC 21 principles into the business plans of the Crown corporations and line ministries
- Public and private infrastructure development policy
- Trade development initiatives and actions
- International trade policies
- Crown Corporations Secretariat
- Trade and investment
- Energy and mineral resources management and policies
- Petroleum and mineral titles
- Geological studies
- Health, safety, and environmental approvals for exploration
- International Centre for Environmental Business

Major Boards and Commissions
- BC Ferry Corporation
- BC Hydro
- BC Buildings Corporation
- BC Rail
- Asia Pacific Foundation
- Job Protection Commissioner
- International Finance Centre Vancouver
- Science Council of BC
- Victoria Line Ltd.
- BC Community Financial Services Corporation

Environment, Lands and Parks

General Responsibilities
- Protected areas strategy
- Air, land, and water pollution control
- Water and flood plain management
- Fish and wildlife habitat and species protection
- Resource management, licensing, and permitting
- Environmental emergencies
- Crown land management
- Protection and management of parks and recreation areas

Major Boards and Commissions
- Environmental Assessment Board
- Environmental Appeal Board
- Fraser Basin Management Board
- BC Heritage Rivers Board

Finance and Corporate Relations

General Responsibilities
- Treasury Board
- Office of the Comptroller General
- Revenue collection, provincial treasury
- Economic and financial analysis and statistics
- Information Technology Services
- Financial institutions regulation
- Incorporation and registration

- Public Service Act
- Public Sector Employers Act
- Services to the Legislature, Executive Council, and the Office of the Lieutenant-Governor
- Information Technology Access Office
- Information and privacy
- Records and archives
- Government purchasing
- Queen's Printer, vehicle services
- Postal services
- Superannuation Commission
- Cabinet policy and Communications Secretariat
- Coordination of appointments to boards, agencies, and commissions
- Intergovernmental Relations

Major Boards and Commissions
- Vancouver Stock Exchange
- Financial Institutions Commissions
- BC Securities Commission
- Public Service Employee Relations Commission
- Public Sector Employers Council
- Purchasing Commission
- Real Estate Council
- Insurance Council of BC
- BC Utilities Commission
- Lottery Corporation
- Provincial Capital Commission
- BC Gaming Commission
- BC Racing Commission
- Insurance Corporation of BC

Forests

General Responsibilities
- Forest Practices Code implementation
- Harvest management, reforestation, forest research, resource inventory
- Integrated forest values
- Pest control and fire suppression
- Crown rangeland management
- Forest economics and revenue

Major Boards and Commissions
- Forest Sector Strategy Advisory Committee
- Forest Renewal BC
- Forest Practices Board
- Forest Appeals Commission
- Forest Land Commission

Health

General Responsibilities
- Health care reform
- Community and family health services
- Health promotion and education/ illness prevention
- Hospital and extended/ long-term care
- Public health
- Mental health, forensic psychiatric health
- Pharmacare
- Emergency care, ambulance services
- Birth, death, and marriage registration
- Medical services plan
- Alcohol and drug programs
- Seniors' programs and services

Major Boards and Commissions
- BC Health Research Foundation
- BC Mental Health Society
- Council of the College of Physicians and Surgeons
- Emergency Health Services Commission
- Hospitals Foundations of BC
- Medical and Health Care Services Appeal Board
- Medical Services Commission
- Seniors' Advisory Council
- Health Professions Council

Labour

General Responsibilities
- Labour relations
- Workers' compensation
- Employment standards
- Pension benefits standards
- Labour programs

Major Boards and Commissions
- BC Labour Relations Board
- Workers' Compensation Board
- Workers' Compensation Review Board
- BC Labour Force Development Board
- Pension Standards Advisory Council
- Employment Standards Tribunal
- Provincial Apprenticeship Board
- West Coast Express Ltd.

Municipal Affairs and Housing

General Responsibilities
- Affordable housing
- Local government services and finances
- Growth strategies
- Municipal organization, administration, engineering, and planning
- Islands Trust
- Downtown revitalization
- Safety standards and inspections
- Office of the Fire Commissioner
- Library services
- Environmental assessment of industrial projects
- Coordination of regional land-use planning

Major Boards and Commissions
- BC Assessment Authority
- Assessment Appeal Board
- Building Code Appeal Board
- Building Safety Advisory Council
- Courts of Revision
- Fire Safety Advisory Council
- BC Housing Management Commission
- Provincial Rental Housing Commission

Small Business, Tourism and Culture

General Responsibilities
- Implementing regional and community economic initiatives
- Small business policy and services
- Tourism marketing, promotion, services, and accommodation
- BC 21 community projects
- Government agents and access centres
- Cultural industries
- Artistic and cultural development
- Film industry
- Heritage conservation and historic sites
- Sports
- Recreation
- Cooperatives

Major Boards and Commissions
- Pacific National Exhibition
- BC Pavilion Corporation
- BC Arts Council
- BC Festival of the Arts Society
- BC Film Development Society
- BC Games Society
- BC Heritage Trust
- Pacific Rim Institute of Tourism
- Provincial Tourist Advisory Council
- Cultural Foundation of BC
- BC Transit

Social Services

General Responsibilities
- Family and child services
- Income support
- Adoption services
- Reunion registry
- Family maintenance
- Children with special needs
- Adults with mental handicaps
- Youth services for street kids

Major Boards and Commissions
- Board of Registration for Social Workers
- Child and Family Review Board

Transportation and Highways

General Responsibilities
- Highway construction and maintenance
- Air care program
- Traffic safety program
- Provincial highway policy and programs
- Vehicle safety and licensing
- Commercial transportation inspection
- Driver testing
- Creation of an integrated transportation plan

Major Boards and Commissions
- Motor Carrier Commission
- BC Transportation Financing Authority

Women's Equality

General Responsibilities
- Transition houses and emergency shelters
- Child care
- Equality in the workplace
- Initiatives to end violence and sexual assault against women
- Health services, including choice on abortion
- Access to post-secondary education, job and managerial training
- Community services which help women and their families

Major Boards and Commissions
- Provincial Child Care Advisory Council

Source: BC Government Communications Office, 17 June 1996.

Notes

Chapter 1: Value Conflicts in Lotusland

1 David Elkins, 'British Columbia as a State of Mind,' in *Two Political Worlds: Parties and Voting in British Columbia*, ed. Donald E. Blake (Vancouver: UBC Press 1985), 54.
2 Ibid., 57.
3 Quoted by Allan Fotheringham, 'Bennett the Second: Horatio Alger with a Head Start,' *Weekend Magazine*, 21 February 1976, 4.
4 This survey was conducted under the supervision of David Elkins, Donald Blake, and Richard Johnston. The data were made available by the UBC Data Library.
5 Elkins, 'British Columbia,' 63-4.
6 Ibid., 69-71.
7 These calculations are based on figures from British Columbia, *Profile of Provincial Electoral Districts, 1991*, 1994.
8 See Ronald Inglehart, *The Silent Revolution* (Princeton: Princeton University Press 1977).
9 Angus Reid Group, *The Reid Report*, Spring 1994, 111.
10 The survey was conducted by the author and Neil Guppy during the last two weeks of June and the first week of July 1995. The survey was part of a research project funded by a Tri-Council Grant from the Social Sciences and Humanities Research Council, the Medical Research Council, and the National Science and Engineering Research Council.
11 The data do not permit the construction of exact quartile boundaries. However, differences or similarities between social groups can be determined by comparing the values found in a given row of a table.
12 See, for example, Herman Bakvis and Neil Nevitte, 'The Greening of the Canadian Electorate,' in *Canadian Environmental Policy: Ecosystems, Politics and Process*, ed. Robert Boardman (Toronto: Oxford University Press), chap. 8.
13 In this study, a respondent was given a score of +1 for each postmaterialist value assigned high priority. An additional point was added for each materialist value considered to have low priority or no priority at all. Finally, a point was subtracted for each materialist value viewed as high priority. The scale has a theoretical range from -6 to +12. In fact, however, the highest score obtained in the sample was +8.

Chapter 2: From Timber to Tourism

1 See D.V. Smiley, 'Canada's Poujadists: A New Look at Social Credit,' *Canadian Forum* 40 (1963): 12-17; and Edwin R. Black, 'British Columbia: The Politics of Exploitation,' in *Exploiting Our Economic Potential: Public Policy and the British Columbia Economy*, ed. R. Shearer (Toronto: Holt Rinehart and Winston 1968), 23-41.
2 On the development of the United Nations system of Standard Industrial Classification (SIC) and the manner in which occupational categories are grouped into 'primary,' 'secondary,' and 'tertiary' or 'service' sectors, see Martin Wolfe, 'The Concept of Economic Sectors,' *Quarterly Journal of Economics* 69 (1955): 402-20; and Joachim Singelmann, *From*

Agriculture to Services: The Transformation of Industrial Employment (Beverly Hills: Sage Publications 1978).

3 On the impact of technological change in the forest sector, see Donald MacKay, *Empire of Wood: The MacMillan-Bloedel Story* (Vancouver: Douglas and McIntyre 1981).

4 Primary employment in the fishing, logging, mining, and agricultural sectors accounted for 27 percent of employment in 1911, declining to 14 percent in 1951 and just over 6 percent in 1991. Employment in secondary manufacturing and construction remained relatively steady over this period, accounting for 19 percent of employment in 1911, 24 per cent in 1951, and 19 percent in 1991. Employment in the variety of activities grouped into the tertiary or service sector – including transportation and communication, retail and wholesale trade, utilities, finance, insurance and real estate, and business, government, and public services – increased from 53 percent of jobs in 1911, to 63 percent in 1951, and then to just under 75 percent in 1991. See Canada, Dominion Bureau of Statistics, *Ninth Census of Canada 1951 – Volume IV: Labour Force — Occupations and Industries* (Ottawa: Queen's Printer 1953), Table II; and Canada, *Statistics Canada, ESTAT CD-ROM: 1991 Census CSD 2B Profile — Occupations by Canada – All Provinces by Industry* (Ottawa: Statistics Canada 1993).

5 By 1994, this 'battle' was largely over as the Lower Mainland and related southern Vancouver Island areas dominated the provincial population. Of the province's 3.7 million inhabitants, 1.8 million lived in the metropolitan Vancouver area along with another 312,000 in the nearby metropolitan Victoria area. See BC Stats, *Quickfacts about British Columbia: Population* (Victoria, 1996). Electronic document available at http://www.bcstats.gov.bc.ca/data/QF_peopl.HTM#pop

6 The latest manifestation of this ongoing struggle is related to aboriginal land claims in the province. The background to these claims, which cover most of the province, is discussed by Paul Tennant in Chapter 4, and in Frank Cassidy and Norman Dale, *After Native Claims? The Implications of Comprehensive Claims Settlements for Natural Resources in British Columbia* (Halifax: Institute for Research on Public Policy 1988).

7 R. Warburton and D. Coburn, eds., *Workers, Capital and the State in British Columbia: Selected Papers* (Vancouver: UBC Press 1988).

8 Black, 'British Columbia,' 23-41.

9 Until recent court decisions forced a major reapportionment of electoral constituencies, regionalism had some impact on provincial political life through the substantial overrepresentation of rural areas in the provincial legislature. See Norman Ruff, 'The Cat and Mouse Politics of Redistribution: Fair and Effective Representation in British Columbia,' *BC Studies* 87 (1990): 48-84.

10 R. Jeremy Wilson, 'Geography, Politics and Culture: Electoral Insularity in British Columbia,' *Canadian Journal of Political Science* 13, 4 (1980): 751-74.

11 On province-building, see E.R. Black and A.C. Cairns, 'A Different Perspective on Canadian Federalism,' *Canadian Public Administration* 9, 1 (1966): 27-44; Harold Chorney and Phillip Hansen, 'Neo-conservatism, Social Democracy, and "Province-Building": The Experience of Manitoba,' *Canadian Review of Sociology and Anthropology* 22, 1 (1985): 1-29; and Larry Pratt, 'The State and Province-Building: Alberta's Development Strategy,' in *The Canadian State: Political Economy and Political Power*, ed. L. Panitch (Toronto: University of Toronto Press 1977). For a critique of the term, see R.A. Young, Phillipe Faucher, and Andre Blais, 'The Concept of Province Building: A Critique,' *Canadian Journal of Political Science* 17 (1984): 783-818.

12 In 1995-6 the provincial government spent over $20 billion, of which 74.5 percent was spent in these three areas. See BC Stats, *Quickfacts about British Columbia: Provincial Government* (Victoria, 1996). Electronic document available at http://www.bcstats.gov.bc.ca/data/QF_peopl.HTM#pop

13 See, for example, Michael Howlett and Jeremy Rayner, 'Do Ideas Matter? Policy Subsystem Configurations and the Continuing Conflict over Canadian Forest Policy,' *Canadian Public Administration* 38, 3 (1995): 382-410.

14 H.C. Davis and T.A. Hutton, 'The Two Economies of British Columbia,' *BC Studies* 82 (1989): 3-15; R. Kunin and J. Knauf, *Skill Shifts in Our Economy: A Decade in the Life of British Columbia* (Vancouver: Canadian Employment and Immigration Commission 1992);

and W.G. Picot, *Canada's Industries: Growth in Jobs over Three Decades* (Ottawa: Ministry of Supply and Services 1986). The implications of this shift are manifold and some uncertainty surrounds their measurement and impact. See Robert L. Mansell, 'The Service Sector and Western Economic Growth,' *Canadian Public Policy* 11, Supplement (1985): 354-60.

15 See Thomas A. Hutton, *Visions of a 'Post-Staples' Economy: Structural Change and Adjustment Issues in British Columbia* (Vancouver: UBC Centre for Human Settlements Working Paper 1993); and D.F. Ley and T.A. Hutton, 'Vancouver's Corporate Complex and Producer Services Sector: Linkages and Divergence within a Provincial Staples Economy, *Regional Studies* 21 (1987): 413-24.

16 Margaret A. Ormsby, *British Columbia: A History* (Toronto: Macmillan 1958), chap. 4.

17 Robin Fisher, *Contact and Conflict: Indian-European Relations in British Columbia, 1774-1890* (Vancouver: UBC Press 1977).

18 The Terms of Union with Canada had granted ownership of all crown lands to the province, with the exception of a strip thirty-two kilometres wide on either side of the transcontinental railway line, which was ceded to the Dominion government. This arrangement avoided many of the federal-provincial disputes over natural resource control that plagued the other western provinces until they obtained control over their lands and resources in 1930. On provincial resource ownership and jurisdiction, see Gerard V. la Forest, *Natural Resources and Public Property under the Canadian Constitution* (Toronto: University of Toronto Press 1969), 3-47, 164-95; and Chester Martin, *The Natural Resources Question: The Historical Basis of Provincial Claims* (Winnipeg: King's Printer 1920), 17-26.

19 On the history of the forest industry during and immediately after construction of the transcontinental railway, see Joseph Collins Lawrence, 'Markets and Capital: A History of the Lumber Industry of British Columbia (1778-1952)' (Master's thesis, UBC, 1957), 38-100.

20 W.A. Carrothers, 'Forest Industries of British Columbia,' in *The North American Assault on the Canadian Forest*, ed. A.R.M. Lower (New York: Greenwood Press 1968).

21 MacKay, *Empire of Wood*, 153-81.

22 See Michael Howlett, 'Forest Policies in Canada: Resource Constraints and Political Conflicts in the Canadian Forest Sector' (Ph.D. diss., Queen's University, 1988).

23 Martin Robin, *The Rush for Spoils: The Company Province 1871-1933* (Toronto: McClelland and Stewart 1974).

24 See Robert E. Cail, *Land, Man, and the Law: The Disposal of Crown Lands in British Columbia 1871-1913* (Vancouver: UBC Press 1974).

25 See British Columbia, *Crown Charges for Early Timber Rights: Royalties and Other Levies for Harvesting Rights on Timber Leases, Licences and Berths in British Columbia – First Report of the Task Force on Crown Timber Disposal, February 1974* (Victoria: Ministry of Lands, Forests and Water Resources 1974).

26 Peter Pearse, *Forest Policy in Canada* (Vancouver: UBC Forest Economics and Policy Analysis Project Working Paper 1985). In 1910 the provincial government adopted the commission's proposal that a system of perpetual timber licences be established. Despite the concerns over the alienation of crown lands, the result of the new regulatory regime was to surrender control over large sections of the province, in one-square-mile parcels, to thousands of different owners. On the situation in BC between 1890 and 1925, see R. Peter Gillis and Thomas R. Roach, *Lost Initiatives: Canada's Forest Industries, Forest Policy and Forest Conservation* (New York: Greenwood 1986), chap. 6. See Chapter 15 by George Hoberg in this volume for a discussion of the province's forest management practices since the Second World War.

27 See Neil Swainson, 'The Public Service,' in *The Reins of Power: Governing British Columbia*, ed. J. Terence Morley, Norman J. Ruff, Neil A. Swainson, R. Jeremy Wilson, and Walter D. Young (Vancouver: Douglas and MacIntyre 1983), 119-60.

28 The provincial election of 21 October 1941 signalled this change in BC political life. The governing Liberals under Premier T.D. Pattullo declined from thirty-one to twenty-one seats in the legislature, while the CCF won fourteen seats and status as the official opposition. On this era generally, see Robin Fisher, *Duff Pattullo of British Columbia* (Toronto: University of Toronto Press 1991); George M. Abbott, 'Duff Pattullo and the Coalition

Controversy of 1941,' *BC Studies* 102 (1994): 30-53; and Dorothy G. Steeves, *The Compassionate Rebel: Ernest Winch and the Growth of Socialism in Western Canada* (Vancouver: J.J. Douglas 1977), 160-1.

29 Canada, *Proceedings of the Conference of Federal and Provincial Governments*, Ottawa, 4-7 December 1950 (Ottawa: King's Printer 1951), 117.

30 British Columbia, *Report of the Commissioner Relating to the Forest Resources of British Columbia*, 2 vols. (Victoria: King's Printer 1945). See also Philip Resnick, 'The Political Economy of British Columbia: A Marxist Perspective,' in *Essays in BC Political Economy*, ed. Paul Knox and Philip Resnick (Vancouver: New Star Books 1974); and Patricia Marchak, *Green Gold: The Forest Industry in British Columbia* (Vancouver: UBC Press 1983), 29-54.

31 Canada, *Proceedings*, 117.

32 See Donald Alper, 'The Effects of Coalition Government on Party Structure: The Case of the Conservative Party in BC,' *BC Studies* 33 (1977): 40-9.

33 In the forest sector, for example, by the mid-1970s, 70-90 percent of all timber leases were held by the ten largest forest companies in the province. The same companies owned 35 percent of provincial lumber mills, 74 percent of plywood plants, 90 percent of provincial pulp capacity, and 100 percent of provincial paper production. See Marchak, *Green Gold*, 30.

34 See the annual budget speeches presented by W.A.C. Bennett to the provincial legislature between 1955 and 1972 for an overview of the various benefits and concessions given to large resource industries.

35 On this period generally, see Stephen G. Tomblin, 'W.A.C. Bennett and Province-Building in British Columbia,' *BC Studies* 85 (1990): 45-61.

36 This increase occurred despite Social Credit's manipulation of provincial debt loads in 1955 by transferring debt and debt related expenditures to various crown corporations. See British Columbia, *A Review of Resources, Production and Governmental Finances* (Victoria: Department of Finance, various issues 1940-62).

37 Stan Persky, *Son of Socred* (Vancouver: New Star Books 1979).

38 See Paul Tennant, 'The NDP Government of British Columbia: Unaided Politicians in an Unaided Cabinet,' *Canadian Public Policy* 3, 4 (1977): 489-503; and Alan C. Cairns and Daniel Wong, 'Socialism, Federalism, and the BC Party Systems 1933-1983,' in *Party Politics in Canada*, ed. Hugh G. Thorburn (Toronto: Prentice-Hall 1985).

39 The mineral tax in particular provoked a major antigovernment public relations blitz and a threat of a province-wide capital strike by mining interests, proving the resource sector was not without influence even at this late date. See Raymond W. Payne, 'Corporate Power, Interest Groups, and the Development of Mining Policy in British Columbia 1972-1977,' *BC Studies* 54 (1982): 3-37.

40 On the Higgins Commission and the unionization of the public service, see Norman Ruff, 'Managing the Public Service,' in *The Reins of Power: Governing British Columbia*, ed. J. Terence Morley, Norman J. Ruff, Neil A. Swainson, R. Jeremy Wilson, and Walter D. Young (Vancouver: Douglas and McIntyre 1983), 172-7.

41 See P. Resnick, 'Social Democracy in Power: The Case of British Columbia,' *BC Studies* 34 (1977): 3-20.

42 Donald Blake, Richard Johnston, and David Elkins, 'Sources of Change in the BC Party System,' *BC Studies* 50 (1981): 3-28.

43 Nevertheless, it is true that BC exports to Asia, especially Japan, are much larger than the Canadian average and reduce the extent of BC's dependence on US markets to well below the Canadian average of over 80 percent.

44 See BC Stats, *Quickfacts about British Columbia: Export Trade by Commodity* (Victoria, 1996). Electronic document available at http://www.bcstats.gov.bc.ca/data/bus_stat/trade/netbwor.htm

45 Roger Hayter and Trevor Barnes, 'Innis' Staple Theory, Exports and Recession: British Columbia, 1981-86,' *Economic Geography* 66, (1990): 150-73.

46 See BC Stats, *Tourism in British Columbia* (Victoria, 1996). Electronic document available at http://www.bcstats.gov.bc.ca/data/bus_stat/tourism/bcbi9502.pdf

47 Overall, BC's development is in keeping with that of the other provinces, which have also shifted from an economy and social structure dominated by high primary sector employ-

ment in agricultural and/or resource-related pursuits to very high service sector employment. While not all the provinces have experienced the same rate of change, by 1991 they differed by just over 5 percent in terms of their dependence on service sector activities, ranging from a 'low' of about 68 percent in Prince Edward Island and Saskatchewan to a 'high' of almost 74 percent in Nova Scotia and BC. See Michael Howlett, 'De-mythologizing Provincial Political Economies: The Development of the Service Sectors in the Provinces 1911-1991,' in *Provinces: An Introduction*, ed. Christopher Dunn (Peterborough, ON: Broadview Press 1996).

48 See I.D. Horry and M. Walker, *Government Spending Facts* (Vancouver: Fraser Institute 1991); and F. Petry et al., 'Measuring Government Growth in the Canadian Provinces: Decomposing Real Growth and Deflation Effects' (paper presented at the annual meeting of the Canadian Political Science Association, Montreal, 1995).

49 Rennie Warburton and David Coburn, 'The Rise of Non-manual Work in British Columbia,' *BC Studies* 59 (1983): 23, 25.

50 In this case, elements of the growth of the service sector are somewhat more illusory than real, and arise as a result of the occupational classification system used by national statistical agencies rather than from a real change in occupational structures – although employment in smaller businesses has some significant consequences for employees in terms of reduced job security and other aspects of wages and working conditions. See Richard B. McKenzie, 'The Emergence of the "Service Economy": Fact or Artifact,' in *Conceptual Issues in Service Sector Research: A Symposium*, ed. Herbert G. Grubel (Vancouver: Fraser Institute 1987), 73-97; Herbert G. Grubel and Michael A. Walker, *Service Industry Growth: Causes and Effects* (Vancouver: Fraser Institute 1989); and James J. McRae, 'Can Growth in the Service Sector Rescue Western Canada?' in *Canadian Public Policy* 11, Supplement (1985): 351-3.

51 On gender divisions and segmentation in the contemporary provincial labour market, see Trevor Barnes and Roger Hayter, 'British Columbia's Private Sector in Recession, 1981-1986: Employment Flexibility without Trade Diversification?' *BC Studies* 98 (1993): 20-42.

52 See Marilyn Callahan and Chris McNiven, 'British Columbia,' in *Privatization and Provincial Social Services in Canada: Policy, Administration and Service Delivery*, ed. J.S. Ismael and Y. Vaillancourt (Edmonton: University of Alberta Press 1988), 13-40. On the similar situation found in other provinces, see Keith Brownsey and Michael Howlett, eds., *The Provincial State: Politics in Canada's Provinces and Territories* (Toronto: Copp Clark Pitman 1992); Rand Dyck, *Provincial Politics in Canada* (Toronto: Prentice Hall 1992); and Melville McMillan, ed., *Provincial Public Finances* (Toronto: Canadian Tax Foundation 1991).

53 Along with its 1983-4 budget, the government had introduced twenty-three bills that, among other things, limited the powers of municipalities and regional districts, extended compulsory review of wage levels of organized workers, expanded management rights in the workplace, abolished rent controls, and dissolved the provincial Human Rights Board. See W. Magnusson, Charles Doyle, R.B.J. Walker, and John De Marco, eds, *The New Reality: The Politics of Restraint in British Columbia* (Vancouver: New Star Books 1984).

54 By this time, membership in the IWA was in decline and that of the public sector unions was growing. By 1996 the four largest unions in the province were located in the public sector. These are: BC Government Employees' Union and affiliates (54,621); Canadian Union of Public Employees (51,707); BC Teachers Federation (41,525); and the Hospital Employees' Union (38,000). See BC Stats, *Quickfacts About British Columbia: Labour and Income* (Victoria, 1996). Electronic document available at http://www.bcstats.gov.bc.ca/data/QF_peopl.HTM#fed

55 See Donald E. Blake, 'The Electoral Significance of Public Sector Bashing,' *BC Studies* 62 (1984): 29-43; Philip Resnick, 'Neo-conservatism on the Periphery: The Lessons from BC,' *BC Studies* 75 (1987): 2-23; and Michael Howlett and Keith Brownsey, 'The New Reality and the Old Reality: Party Politics and Public Policy in British Columbia 1941-1987,' *Studies in Political Economy* 25 (1988): 141-56.

56 See William K. Carroll and R.S. Ratner, 'Social Democracy, Neo-conservatism and Hegemonic Crisis in British Columbia,' *Critical Sociology* 16, 1 (1989): 29-53; and Robert C. Allen and Gideon Rosenbluth, eds., *Restraining the Economy: Social Credit Economic Policies for BC in the Eighties* (Vancouver: New Star Books 1986).

57 On the decline of Social Credit during the Vander Zalm era, see Graham Leslie, *Breach of Promise: Sacred Ethics under Vander Zalm* (Madeira Park, BC: Harbour Publishing 1991); Stan Persky, *Fantasy Government: Bill Vander Zalm and the Future of Social Credit* (Vancouver: New Star Books 1989); and Gary Mason and Keith Baldrey, *Fantasyland: Inside the Reign of Bill Vander Zalm* (Toronto: McGraw-Hill 1989). On the conflict of interest charges related to the sale of his Fantasy Gardens theme park to Taiwanese investors seeking a provincial bank licence, see E.N. Hughes, *Report of the Honourable E.N. Hughes, Q.C. on the sale of Fantasy Garden World Inc.* (Victoria: Queen's Printer 1991).

58 On the government's worker-based Working Opportunity Fund (WOF), see David Smith, 'Harcourt Dangles Tax Break Investment Fund Carrot,' *Vancouver Sun*, 9 January 1992, D1.

59 On the general dynamics of the provincial party system, see Donald E. Blake, R.K. Carty, and Lynda Erickson, *Grassroots Politicians: Party Activists in British Columbia* (Vancouver: UBC Press 1991).

60 See P.W. Daniels, K. O'Connor, and T.A. Hutton, 'The Planning Response to Urban Service Sector Growth: An International Comparison,' *Growth and Change: A Journal of Urban and Regional Policy* 22, 4 (1991): 3-26. More specifically, see Trevor Barnes and Roger Hayter, 'Economic Restructuring, Local Development and Resource Towns: Forest Communities in Coastal British Columbia,' *Canadian Journal of Regional Science* 17, 3 (1994): 289-310; and Barnes and Hayter, 'British Columbia's Private Sector.'

61 This occurred in Ontario under the Rae government. See Neil B. Freeman, 'Budget Pink and Budget Blues: Fiscal Policy in the Ontario NDP Government, 1990-1994: A Preliminary Analysis' (paper presented at the annual general meeting of the Canadian Political Science Association, Calgary, 1994).

62 D.E. Blake and R.K. Carty, 'Partisan Realignment in British Columbia: The Case of the Provincial Liberal Party' (paper presented at the annual general meeting of the Canadian Political Science Association, Montreal, 1995).

63 H. Craig David and Thomas A. Hutton, 'Producer Services Exports from the Vancouver Metropolitan Region,' *Canadian Journal of Regional Science* 14, 3 (1991): 378-80; and Ley and Hutton, 'Vancouver's Corporate Complex.'

64 See H. Craig Davis, 'Is the Metropolitan Vancouver Economy Uncoupling from the Rest of the Province?' *BC Studies* 98 (1993): 4.

65 See Neil M. Swan, 'The Service Sector: Engine of Growth?' *Canadian Public Policy* 11, Supplement (1985): 344-50.

66 Irene Ip, 'An Overview of Provincial Government Finance,' in *Provincial Public Finances*, ed. M. McMillan (Toronto: Canadian Tax Foundations 1991).

67 On globalization in the forest products sector, see M. Patricia Marchak, 'For Whom the Tree Falls: Restructuring of the Global Forest Industry,' *BC Studies* 90 (1991): 3-24.

68 In the modern era, for example, the major increase in trade in the Pacific Rim among countries such as Hong Kong, Singapore, Korea, Thailand, Taiwan, and Japan has opened new markets for BC products, but has also led to an increase in immigration to the province of East and South Asians. This, in turn, has led to a resurgence in concerns centring on race. Despite press reports and public perceptions to the contrary, however, the number of foreign immigrants to the province remains a small percentage of the number of internal Canadian migrants, largely from Ontario. See Bali Ram, Y. Edward Shin, and Michel Pouliot, *Focus on Canada: Canadians on the Move* (Ottawa: Statistics Canada 1994).

Chapter 3: BC: 'The Spoilt Child of Confederation'

1 Norman J. Ruff, 'Pacific Perspectives on the Canadian Confederation: British Columbia's Shadows and Symbols,' in *Canada: The State of the Federation 1991*, ed. Douglas M. Brown (Kingston, ON: Institute of Intergovernmental Relations, Queen's University 1991), 201.

2 Margaret A. Ormsby, *British Columbia: A History* (Toronto: Macmillan 1958), chap. 5.

3 W. Kaye Lamb, 'A Bent Twig in BC's History,' in *A History of British Columbia: Selected Readings*, ed. Patricia E. Roy (Toronto: Copp Clark Pitman 1989). On the Terms of Union specifically, see Canada, *Extracts from Debates in Dominion Parliament and Columbia Legislative Council in 1871* (Ottawa: MacLean, Roger 1880), microfiche.

4 For discussions, see the periodical *Canada: The State of Federation* from 1985 on.

5 Drew Fagan, 'Softwood Hard on Free Trade,' *Globe and Mail*, 4 April 1996, B8.

6 The acronym refers to an established large particle physics enterprise called the Tri-Universities Meson Facility, and a proposal to expand on similar work at the same site.
7 Bev Christensen, *Too Good to Be True: Alcan's Kemano Completion Project* (Vancouver: Talon Books 1995).
8 Neil Swainson, *Conflict over the Columbia: The Canadian Background to an Historic Treaty* (Montreal: McGill-Queen's University Press 1979).
9 *R. v. Sparrow* (1990) in the Supreme Court of Canada.
10 See, among other sources, the following, all of which are in Roy's *A History of British Columbia*: Edwin R. Black, 'British Columbia: The Politics of Exploitation,' 129-42; R.M. Burns, 'British Columbia and the Canadian Federation,' 156-73; and Donald E. Blake, 'Managing the Periphery: British Columbia and the National Political Community,' 174-88.
11 Robert J. Jackson and Doreen Jackson, *Politics in Canada*, 3rd ed. (Scarborough, ON: Prentice-Hall 1995), 467-8.
12 Canada, *Bill C110*, 35th Parl., 1st sess. (December 1995).
13 Ruff, 'Pacific Perspectives,' 192.
14 W. Peter Ward, 'Class and Race in the Social Structure of British Columbia, 1870-1939,' in *British Columbia: Historical Readings*, ed. W. Peter Ward and Robert A.J. McDonald (Vancouver: Douglas and McIntyre 1981).
15 Ruff, 'Pacific Perspectives,' 201.

Chapter 4: Aboriginal Peoples and Aboriginal Title

1 Canada, 'Appendix No. 1; The Royal Proclamation, October 7, 1763,' *Revised Statutes of Canada 1970* (Ottawa: Queen's Printer 1970), 127-8.
2 The Indian Act defined 'Indian' to mean those enrolled on the Department of Indian Affairs' Register. Those entitled to be initially enrolled were the male members of Native communities recognized by the department, together with their wives and children; their descendants would similarly be 'registered.' Non-Native women became registered as Natives upon marrying a registered male; however, any registered Native woman was de-registered upon marrying a male who was not a registered Native. The definition was thus not racial, for many women with no Native blood became Natives, and many full-blooded Native women ceased to be Native. An amendment to the act in 1985 allowed those (mostly women and their children) who had lost their Native status to regain it, but the amendment did not de-register those whose status derived from marriage.
3 Indian and Northern Affairs Canada, 'BC Region Registered Indian Population by Residence Code' (Vancouver, April 1995).
4 For more detail on the 1849-71 period, see Robin Fisher, *Contact and Conflict: Indian-European Relations in British Columbia, 1774-1890* (Vancouver: UBC Press 1977), chaps. 3-8; and Paul Tennant, *Aboriginal Peoples and Politics: The Indian Land Question in British Columbia, 1849-1989* (Vancouver: UBC Press 1990), chaps. 2-4.
5 British Columbia, *Papers Connected with the Indian Land Question, 1850-1871* (1875; reprint, Victoria: Government Printer 1987), 5-11. The treaties also provided that Natives would have the rights to hunt on surrendered lands and to fish as they had in the past.
6 Ibid., 12.
7 Here was the fatal flaw in their approach, for eventually the Canadian courts would rule that aboriginal title continues to exist unless it has been explicitly extinguished.
8 George Stewart, *Canada Under the Administration of the Earl of Dufferin* (Toronto: Rose-Belford 1878), 492-3.
9 British Columbia, Legislature, *Sessional Papers, 1887* (Victoria: Government Printer 1887), 264.
10 At the turn of the century, however, to head off unrest relating to the flood of Yukon-bound prospectors, the federal government had unilaterally extended a Prairie treaty into northeastern BC, allotting reserves, at 640 acres a family, out of federally owned lands in the area.
11 *Indian Act*, Section 141, 1927.
12 Thus, the separate bands or First Nations composing a tribal nation would continue to administer their own local affairs, but would cooperate through the political structure of the tribal nation in pursuing major political goals.

13 Despite the differing organizational names, there was a continuity of leadership at the provincial level, provided principally by James Gosnell, Joe Mathias, Ed Newman, Sophie Pierre, Miles Richardson, George Watts, and Bill Wilson.

14 For more detail on this section, see Tennant, *Aboriginal Peoples and Politics*, chap. 16.

15 This argument rested on denying that the Royal Proclamation of 1763 had extended to the west coast of the continent.

16 *Calder et al.* v. *British Columbia (Attorney-General)* (1970), 13 Dominion Law Reports (3rd) (BC Court of Appeal).

17 An important legalistic consideration was that a BC statute (later repealed) required getting permission from the government before suing the province. That the Nisga'a had not done so meant that in legalistic terms the court was not issuing any formal ruling. What is important is that in later cases, (notably in *Guerin*, see below) the court was guided by the opinions expressed in *Calder*.

18 *Guerin* v. *Regina* (1984), 6 Western Weekly Reports, 495 (Supreme Court of Canada).

19 The Supreme Court of Canada declined to hear an appeal requested by the province.

20 *Martin et al.* v. *Regina in Right of BC et al.* (1985), 3 Western Weekly Reports, 583-93 (BC Court of Appeal).

21 Ibid., 607.

22 The FNC leaders had little to do with the blockades; one of them had even publicly dismissed them as 'knee-jerk reactions.'

23 The two names were used interchangeably until 'First Nations Summit' became official in 1992.

24 British Columbia Claims Task Force, *Report* (Vancouver, 1991).

25 That is, preexisting aboriginal rights were extinguished (although some were transformed into treaty rights) as a means of attaining 'certainty.'

26 British Columbia Claims Task Force, *Report*, 28-9.

27 Supreme Court of British Columbia, Mr. Chief Justice Allan McEachern, *Reasons for Judgment* [in *Delgamuukw* v. *The Queen in Right of British Columbia*] (Vancouver, 8 March 1991), 254.

28 Court of Appeal for British Columbia, *Reasons for Judgment* [in *Delgamuukw* v. *The Queen in Right of British Columbia*] (Vancouver, 25 June 1993), 65, 67.

29 Court of Appeal, *Reasons for Judgment*, 69.

30 Because they were already under way, the Nisga'a negotiations remained formally separate from the new treaty process and are not included in these figures.

31 Mel Smith's *Our Home or Native Land?* (Crown Western: Victoria 1995), a lawyer's case against aboriginal demands and government policies, provided further fuel and focus for those hostile to aboriginal demands.

Chapter 5: The Politics of Polarization

1 For the period until 1983, much of the following account is drawn from Donald E. Blake, ed., *Two Political Worlds: Parties and Voting in British Columbia* (Vancouver: UBC Press 1985), chaps. 2 and 3.

2 See F.W. Howay, 'The Settlement and Progress of British Columbia, 1871-1914,' in *Historical Essays on British Columbia*, ed. J. Friesen and H.K. Ralston (Toronto: Gage 1980), 25.

3 See W. Peter Ward, *White Canada Forever: Popular Attitudes and Public Policy toward Orientals in British Columbia* (Montreal: McGill-Queen's University Press 1978).

4 Howay, 'The Settlement and Progress,' 34.

5 See Edith Dobie, 'Party History in British Columbia, 1903-1933,' in Friesen and Ralston, eds., *Historical Essays*, 70-81.

6 Calculated from figures supplied in W. Peter Ward, 'Class and Race in the Social Structure of British Columbia, 1870-1939,' in *British Columbia: Historical Readings*, ed. W. Peter Ward and Robert A.J. McDonald (Vancouver: Douglas and McIntyre 1981), 21.

7 Ward, 'Class and Race,' 584-5.

8 Officially, the provincial Conservative Party took no part in the election, recommending that Conservative incumbents campaign as independents or under some other banner. Hence, the official record registers nine Conservative candidates with a popular vote of

2.1% and no seats. However, most of those elected as independents or 'other' party candidates had had Conservative Party affiliations.

9 Martin Robin, *The Rush for Spoils: The Company Province 1871-1933* (Toronto: McClelland and Stewart 1974), 260.

10 See Walter Young, 'Ideology, Personality and the Origin of the CCF in British Columbia,' in Ward and McDonald, eds., *British Columbia*, 567-70.

11 See Margaret Ormsby, 'T. Dufferin Pattullo and the Little New Deal,' in Ward and McDonald, eds., *British Columbia*, 533-45.

12 Alan C. Cairns and Daniel Wong, 'Socialism, Federalism and the BC Party Systems, 1933-1983,' in Hugh Thorburn, ed., *Party Politics in Canada*, 6th ed. (Scarborough, ON: Prentice-Hall 1991), 468-85.

13 Ibid.

14 A.L. Farley, *Atlas of British Columbia: People, Environment and Resource Use* (Vancouver: UBC Press 1970), 31, 65, 67, and map 30.

15 Ibid., 69, 71, maps 32 and 33.

16 Tax return series for the 1946-75 period are available in David K. Foot, ed., *Public Employment in Canada: Statistical Series* (Toronto: Butterworth 1970). Figures in the text are from pages 20-1 and 26-7. The analysis of public sector growth presented here was prepared by Richard Johnston.

17 For details, see Blake, *Two Political Worlds*, chap. 3.

18 For an account of events in the legislature and public arena during this period, see G.L. Kristianson, 'The Non-partisan Approach to BC Politics,' *BC Studies* 33 (1977): 13-29.

19 See Donald E. Blake, 'The Electoral Significance of Public Sector Bashing,' *BC Studies* 62 (1984): 29-43. Also see Chapter 1 in this volume.

20 Donald E. Blake, R.K. Carty, and Lynda Erickson, *Grassroots Politicians: Party Activists in British Columbia* (Vancouver: UBC Press 1991), 93.

21 Ibid., 99.

22 Norman Ruff, 'Redefining Party Politics in British Columbia: Party Renewal and Fragmentation,' in *Party Politics in Canada*, ed. Hugh Thorburn, 7th ed. (Scarborough, ON: Prentice-Hall 1995), 485.

23 Blake, *Two Political Worlds*, chap. 10.

24 Blake, Carty, and Erickson, *Grassroots Politicians*, 84.

25 Four of the seventeen Liberal MLAs subsequently left the party. Two sit as independents. Two others, including Gordon Wilson, the man who led the party during the election, formed a new party, the Progressive Democratic Alliance. The party amazed observers by winning nearly 6% of the vote in 1996 and electing one member, Wilson himself, to the legislature.

26 The leader of the party was chosen by a delegate-type leadership selection convention in 1987. Though it had involved members of both the (still united) federal and provincial wings of the Liberal Party in BC, that convention had involved only 240 delegates and Wilson was chosen by acclamation. For further details see Blake, Carty, and Erickson, *Grassroots Politicians*.

27 A significant redrawing of constituency boundaries and an increase in their number took place following the 1986 election. All double-member ridings (sixteen) were eliminated and the legislature expanded from sixty-nine to seventy-five members. The author's computation of vote shifts is based on a recalculation of the 1986 results using 1991 boundaries.

28 In all but eighteen of the ridings, Liberal gains were within one standard deviation of Social Credit losses. Parallelism between Liberal gains and Social Credit losses is also suggested by regression analysis using riding level data from the 1986 census of Canada. The correlation between average family income by riding and Social Credit vote dropped from .33 in 1986 to -.01 in 1991. Conversely, the correlation for the Liberals rose from .45 to .53.

29 Angus Reid Group, *BC Reid Report*, Autumn 1994, 32.

30 Donald E. Blake and R. Kenneth Carty, 'Televoting for the Leader of the British Columbia Liberal Party: The Leadership Contest of 1993' (paper presented at the annual meeting of the Canadian Political Science Association, Calgary, 1994).

31 The analysis of activist opinion draws heavily from Donald E. Blake and R. Kenneth Carty, 'Partisan Realignment in British Columbia: The Case of the Provincial Liberal Party,' *BC Studies*, 108 (1995-6): 61-74.

32 The following analysis is based on a public opinion survey conducted by the author and Neil Guppy during the last two weeks of June and the first week of July 1995. The survey was part of a research project funded by a Tri-Council Grant from the Social Sciences and Humanities Research Council, the Medical Research Council, and the National Science and Engineering Research Council.

33 See Blake, *Two Political Worlds*, 78-82.

34 See Chapter 1 for further details on the construction of these measures of populism, neoconservatism, and postmaterialism.

35 Angus Reid Group, *BC Reid Report*.

36 Current leader Gordon Campbell gave this figure in a speech in Vancouver on 26 April 1995.

37 See Vaughan Palmer, *Vancouver Sun*, 22 June 1995, A18.

38 Angus Reid Group, *The Reid Report*, 37.

Chapter 6: The BC Legislature and Parliamentary Framework

1 BC's own version of the British standard parliamentary reference by Erskine May, *Parliamentary Practice, London: Butterworths*, and the Canadian *Beauchesne's Parliamentary Rules and Forms* are to be found in E. George MacMinn, *Parliamentary Practice in British Columbia*, 2nd ed. (Victoria: Queen's Printer 1987).

2 To complete the charade, Tom Perry, MLA for Vancouver-Little Mountain, has taken to welcoming all those in the gallery who have not been recognized by himself or his fellow MLAs.

3 Ralph Miliband, *Capitalist Democracy in Britain* (Oxford: Oxford University Press 1982), 20.

4 Walter Bagehot, *The English Constitution* (Oxford: Oxford University Press 1942), 1.

5 See the BC attorney general's comments in the debate on Bill 36: Recall and Initiative Act, *Debates of the Legislative Assembly*, 6 July 1994, 12875.

6 Tina Loo, *Making Law, Order, and Authority in British Columbia, 1821-1971* (Toronto: University of Toronto Press 1994), 12-13.

7 See James E. Hendrickson, 'The Constitutional Development of Colonial Vancouver Island and British Columbia,' in *British Columbia: Historical Readings*, ed. W. Peter Ward and Robert A.J. McDonald (Vancouver: Douglas and McIntyre 1981), 245-74.

8 Sec. 14, British Columbia Terms of Union, *Order Admitting Colony to Canada, 1871* (16 May 1871).

9 Three BC premiers have been dismissed by lieutenant governors: Turner in August 1898, Semlin in February 1900, and Prior in June 1903. The choice of W.A.C. Bennett as premier in 1952 by Lieutenant Governor Clarence Wallace was the last time that there was any opportunity for independent action. The events in 1991 gave rise to the possibility of intervention by Lieutenant Governor Lam, but Premier Vander Zalm's resignation and the immediate selection of a new interim leader, Rita Johnston, by the governing Social Credit caucus and board made this unnecessary.

10 British Columbia, *Constitution Act*, R.S. 1979, chap. 62 (Consolidated November 1991), sec. 53. Often exercised by Trutch, the first lieutenant governor, bills were returned to the BC legislature a total of eighty-eight times up to 1944.

11 Campbell Sharman, 'The Strange Case of a Provincial Constitution: The BC Constitution Act,' *Canadian Journal of Political Science* 17 (1984): 87-108.

12 In the spring 1993 sitting there were, however, six notable exceptions to this rule: Bill 6, Property Taxation Statutes Amendment Act 1993, to reduce the homeowner grant and introduce a super tax on homes over $400,000, which did not go to second reading in the face of taxpayer demonstrations; Bill 32, Environmental Assessment Act, which went no further than second reading at that session; Bill 54, Constitution Amendment Act, an ordinary statute that proposed significant rewriting of sections 10-16 for the organization and definition of government ministerial structures and responsibilities, adding new references to responsibilities of provincial secretary, attorney general, and finance, and pro-

visions for the reorganizations and transfers of duties, which only received first reading; and Bills 10, Commercial Tenancy Act, 68, Health Council Act, and 70, Heritage Conservation Statutes Act. At the next session in 1994, all fifty-six government bills (excluding the traditional, symbolic, opening Bill 1, Act to Ensure the Supremacy of Parliament) became law.

13 The increased general competence in the press gallery over the last twenty years must also be ranked among the more significant instruments for improved political communications and informed debate within the province – despite the protests of premiers and governments who have become the objects of their attention.

14 Since the weekly capital city allowance ($100 per diem for outside members, $45 for capital electoral district members) is paid only for the first sixty sitting days of each session, one can anticipate a universal decline in enthusiasm among backbenchers commencing on day sixty-one.

15 C.J. (Chuck) Connaghan, *Official Report and Recommendations: 1992 Review of MLA Remuneration, The British Columbia Legislative Assembly* (Vancouver: Connaghan and Associates 1992).

16 E.H. (Ted) Hughes, *Final Report: Constituency Allowance Review* (Victoria: Conflict of Interest Commissioner 1993).

17 Connaghan, *Official Report and Recommendations*, 2.

18 Members choosing to be covered for a Legislative Assembly Pension contribute 9 percent of their total legislative allowance (annual indemnity, capital city allowance, and expense allowance). The monthly pension is calculated as 5 percent, multiplied by their highest four-year average legislative allowance, multiplied by years of pensionable service up to a maximum of sixteen years. It becomes payable to a former member having served for seven or more years, or two legislative assemblies, at age fifty-five, or when that member's age plus service is at least sixty years. See the Legislative Assembly Allowances and Pension Act. The Canadian Taxpayers Federation argue that fifty MLAs received $22 million from 1986 to 1992, of which only $3.4 million was covered by pension contributions.

19 In launching the first wave of reforms in 1973, the Speaker noted that 'A number of important changes are sought at last by this new legislature in procedures and practices which have remained practically frozen since 1893.' Gordon H. Dowding, Speaker, *First Report: Legislative Procedure and Practice Inquiry Act* (Victoria: Queen's Printer 1973), 1.

20 See David J. Mitchell, 'The Good Old days? W.A.C. Bennett and the Legislative Assembly,' *Canadian Parliamentary Review* 6, 1 (1983): 6-9.

21 The five reports published in 1973-4 included studies of parliamentary radio and television broadcasting, as well as such procedural matters as oral question period and Supply.

22 British Columbia, *Debates of the Legislative Assembly*, 16 June 1977, 2779-80. See overview by Jeremy Wilson in 'The Legislature,' in *The Reins of Power: Governing British Columbia*, ed. J. Terence Morley, Norman J. Ruff, Neil A. Swainson, R. Jeremy Wilson, and Walter D. Young (Vancouver: Douglas and McIntyre 1983), chap. 2.

23 Proposals for committee reform were presented by George MacMinn as part of the continuing study of procedure under the Legislative Procedure Review Act, 1972, in June 1979, and updated in Legislative Procedure Review Act, Report No. 2, *Committees of the Legislature* (Victoria: Legislative Assembly 1982). See also Carol Gamey, *Standing Committees of the BC Legislature: W.A.C. – Barrett-Bennett, 1955-79* (Victoria: BC Project Working Paper 1983). For a list of all select standing and special committees, see British Columbia, Legislative Assembly, Clerk of Committees, *Select Standing and Special Committees, Sessional Chronological Listing, 1872-1994* (Victoria, July 1994).

24 See British Columbia, *Debates of the Legislative Assembly*, 12 February 1985, 4913-15; and Jeremy Wilson, 'British Columbia: A Unique Blend of the Traditional and Modern,' in *Provincial and Territorial Legislatures in Canada*, ed. Gary Levy and Graham White (Toronto: University of Toronto Press 1989), 126-38.

25 See British Columbia, *Debates of the Legislative Assembly*, 26 March 1992, 195-6; and 31 March 1993, 4905-15; and amendments, 21 April 1993, 5315-17; 6 April 1994, 9771-81; and 10 April 1995, 13315-17. For 1994, the order was amended to increase the A Section committee from 22 to 24 members – 15 government, 6 Liberal, and 3 independents; it was modified in 1995, in keeping with opposition shifts, to 14 New Democrats, 6 Liberals; 2

Reform, and 2 others. The government had proposed that Section A be deemed a commit-tee of the whole so as to be able to consider bills after second reading. Legislation could already be considered in the house while estimates were in Section A, and estimates could be considered simultaneously in both sections, but this would have been a substantial extension of the scope of Section A. After opposition objections, the motion was amended to require unanimous consent before any such Section A committee stage referral. See also the Speaker's ruling on restrictions in membership to Section A of Committee of Supply in British Columbia, Legislative Assembly, *Votes and Proceedings* (12 April 1994).

26   Jim Hume, 'Democracy Inches Ahead?' *Times-Colonist*, 11 May 1993, A5.

27   See March 1994 amendment to section 11 of the Standing Orders.

28   British Columbia, Legislative Assembly, *Votes and Proceedings* (22 March 1994).

29   See the account in Norman J. Ruff, 'The Cat and Mouse Politics of Redistribution: Fair and Effective Representation in British Columbia,' *BC Studies* 87 (1990): 48-84.

30   Norman J. Ruff, 'The Right to Vote and Inequality of Voting Power in British Columbia: The Jurisprudence and Politics of the Dixon Case,' in *Drawing Boundaries*, ed. John Courtney, P. MacKinnon, and David Smith (Saskatoon: Fifth House 1992), 128-47.

31   *Dixon v. British Columbia [Attorney General]* (1989), 35 BC Law Reports (2nd), 300.

32   Reference re Provincial Electoral Boundaries (1991), 81 Dominion Law Reports (4th), 36.

33   British Columbia, *Report of Royal Commission on Electoral Boundaries* [Fisher Report] (De-cember 1988), Schedule G, 77-8.

34   British Columbia, Electoral Boundaries Commission Act, *S.B.C.* 1989, c.65.

35   E.N. Hughes, *Report of the Honourable E.N. Hughes, Q.C. on the sale of Fantasy Garden World Inc.* (Victoria: Queen's Printer 1991), 52-61; Graham Leslie, *Breach of Promise: Socred Ethics under Vander Zalm* (Madeira Park, BC: Harbour Publishing 1991), part 2.

36   For the pre-1993 debate and earlier attempt at direct democracy by the Oliver Liberals, see Norman Ruff, 'Institutionalizing Populism in British Columbia,' *Canadian Parliamentary Review* 16, 4 (1993-4), 24-32.

37   British Columbia, Report of the Chief Electoral Officer, *Referendum October 17, 1991.*

38   British Columbia, Legislative Assembly, Select Standing Committee on Parliamentary Re-form, *Report on Recall and Initiative* (November 1993).

Chapter 7: Women and Political Representation
This chapter has been adapted from Lynda Erickson, 'Women and Representation in Brit-ish Columbian Politics,' *In the Presence of Women: Representation in Canadian Governments*, edited by Jane Arscott and Linda Trimble. Copyright © 1996 by Harcourt Brace & Com-pany Canada, Limited. All rights reserved. Reprinted by permission. I would like to ac-knowledge the support of the Social Sciences and Humanities Research Council for its contribution to this research through its program grants, and I would like to thank Judy Morrison and Vicki Robinson for their assistance in the project, Brent Mueller for access to his research materials, and the women MLAs, cabinet ministers, and deputy ministers who shared their ideas and observations about women's programs and women in BC politics.

1   Sylvia Bashevkin, *Toeing the Lines: Women and Party Politics in English Canada*, 2nd ed. (Toronto: Oxford University Press 1993); Diane Crossley, 'The BC Liberal Party and Wom-en's Reforms, 1916-1928,' in *In Her Own Right*, ed. Barbara Latham and Cathy Kess (Victo-ria: Camosun College 1980).

2   Comparisons between the 1931 and 1991 census are difficult because the 1991 census allowed for multiple origins whereas the 1931 census did not. Clearly, however, the very British character of the population has changed dramatically.

3   Rand Dyck, *Provincial Politics in Canada* (Scarborough, ON: Prentice-Hall Canada 1991); Edwin R. Black, 'British Columbia: The Politics of Exploitation,' in *Party Politics in Canada*, ed. Hugh G. Thorburn, 4th ed. (Scarborough, ON: Prentice-Hall Canada 1979).

4   Daphne Marlatt, 'Subverting the Heroic: Recent Feminist Writing on the West Coast,' in *British Columbia Reconsidered: Essays on Women*, ed. Gillian Creese and Veronica Strong-Boag (Vancouver: Press Gang Publishers 1992), 296.

5 By 1951, 48.6 percent of the non-Native adult population were women. See Jean Barman, *The West beyond the West: A History of British Columbia* (Toronto: University of Toronto Press 1991), 369.

6 In the forestry and logging sector, which is by far the largest employer among the categories of mining, logging, and fishing, only 7.5 percent of the employees were women according to the 1991 census (Statistics Canada, 1993).

7 Daniel Kubat and David Thornton, *A Statistical Profile of Canadian Society* (Toronto: McGraw-Hill Ryerson 1974); by comparison, 42 percent of the Canadian population lived in urban centres in 1911 and 62 percent in 1951.

8 The 1921 census recorded the number of births per 1,000 women aged 15 to 49 in BC as only 84, compared to 98 in Ontario and 108 in the nation as a whole (Barman, *The West*, 370).

9 Statistics Canada, *Population Demographic Characteristics, 1976.*

10 Pippa Norris, *Politics and Sexual Equality: The Comparative Position of Women in Western Democracies* (Boulder, CO: Lynne Reiner 1987).

11 Ibid.

12 Hege Skjeie, 'Ending the Male Political Hegemony: The Norwegian Experience,' in *Gender and Party Politics*, ed. Joni Lovenduski and Pippa Norris (London: Sage Publications 1993); Diane Sainsbury, 'The Politics of Increased Women's Representation: The Swedish Case,' in Lovenduski and Norris, eds., *Gender and Party Politics*.

13 Sainsbury, 'The Politics.'

14 R. Darcy, Susan Welch, and Janet Clark, *Women, Elections and Representation*, 2nd ed. (Lincoln: University of Nebraska Press 1994); R. Darcy and Karen Beckwith, 'Political Disaster, Political Triumph: The Election of Women to National Parliaments' (paper presented at the annual meeting of the American Political Science Association, Washington, DC, 1991).

15 Sainsbury, 'The Politics.'

16 Linda Louise Hale, 'The BC Woman Suffrage Movement, 1890-1917' (Master's thesis, UBC, 1978); Michael H. Cramer, 'Public and Political: Documents of the Woman's Suffrage Campaign in British Columbia, 1871-1917: The View from Victoria,' in Creese and Strong-Boag, eds., *British Columbia Reconsidered*, 55-72.

17 Not all women in BC received the vote in 1917 when the female suffrage amendment was passed. Native, Japanese-Canadian, Chinese-Canadian, and Indo-Canadian women were not enfranchised until the provincial election of 1949.

18 Crossley, 'The BC Liberal Party.'

19 Barman, *The West*.

20 The Liberals had more general sympathy for issues that motivated the women's reform movement, something apparent both at the 1913 convention and later in the 1916 election campaign (see Crossley, 'The BC Liberal Party').

21 Judith Antonik Bennett and Frederike Verspoor, *British Columbia Executive Council Appointments 1871-1986* (Victoria: British Columbia Legislative Library 1989), 41.

22 Ibid.

23 Joan Sangster, *Dreams of Equality: Women on the Canadian Left, 1920-1950* (Toronto: McClelland and Stewart 1989).

24 Susan Walsh, 'The Peacock and the Guinea Hen: Political Profiles of Dorothy Gretchen Steeves and Grace MacInnes,' in Creese and Strong-Boag, eds., *British Columbia Reconsidered*, 73-89.

25 Hale, 'The BC Woman.'

26 Barman, *The West*.

27 In response to wartime conditions and the minority position in which the governing Liberal Party found itself, the Liberals and Conservatives formed a coalition government after the 1941 election. The experience of governing, reinforced by the very fact of the socialist CCF as the official opposition, led these two parties to continue the coalition until 1952 (see Donald E. Blake, *Two Political Worlds: Parties and Voting in British Columbia* [Vancouver: UBC Press 1985]). In that election, the use of a preferential ballot led to the unexpected success of the Social Credit Party, which then assumed the role of the dominant party for most of the

next four decades. During the two elections for which their agreement was in place, the coalition partners ran only one candidate in each riding.

28 With only three women in a caucus of forty-one, Johnston had few options available to her.

29 New Democratic Party Women's Committee, *Herstory and Policy*, 1977.

30 Ibid., 11.

31 Ibid., 12.

32 Officially, all women members in the party were entitled to be members of the Women's Rights Committee, although only a subset of women members were active in it. The committee's executive was chosen at convention by the women's caucus.

33 The specific issues targeted by the Equality Campaign were: 'choice on abortion; pay equity/economic equality for women; equality of opportunity for women; establishment of a Women's Equality Ministry; core funding of women's centres, sexual assault centres and transition houses; safe, affordable, non-profit childcare ...' See Vicki Robinson, *Women's Rights Organizer's Report to the Women's Rights Committee* (1991), 4.

34 In terms of diversity, none of the women elected were of minority racial background, but they were drawn from constituencies across the province, including the north, eastern regions, and Vancouver Island as well as the Lower Mainland.

35 British Columbia Social Credit Party, *Constitution and By-Laws of the BC Social Credit Party* (1990), 28.

36 Lynda Erickson, 'Political Women in a Partisan World: Women Party Activists in British Columbia in the 1980s,' in Creese and Strong-Boag, eds., *British Columbia Reconsidered*, 96-116.

37 McCarthy was a long-time Social Credit MLA who had sat in provincial cabinets since 1969, had held five different cabinet portfolios, and had been deputy premier for eight years in the cabinets of W.R. Bennett. She had contested the party leadership in 1986, the year that Vander Zalm won. She was appointed to Vander Zalm's first cabinet but had resigned from it in 1988 citing her unhappiness with the role the premier's advisers were playing in the government.

38 Justine Hunter, 'Scandal, Retirement Take Toll on Politicians Seeking Re-election,' *Vancouver Sun*, 24 September 1991, B7.

39 Donald E. Blake, R.K. Carty, and Lynda Erickson, *Grassroots Politicians: Party Activists in British Columbia* (Vancouver: UBC Press 1991).

40 Ibid.

41 News release, 5 November 1991.

42 For the new cabinet in 1993, the number of committees was reduced to five.

43 Judi Tyabji was Liberal house leader for four months but was replaced after a caucus revolt. Her personal relationship with the party leader, who was also subsequently forced out of the leadership by the caucus, was at the time an issue of public controversy.

44 Brent Mueller, 'Women and Politics in British Columbia: Obstacles and Barriers to Equal Participation' (honour's thesis, Simon Fraser University, 1994).

45 According to news reports of the case, the husband's lawyer cited Tyabji's career as the reason for the decision. See *Globe and Mail*, 4 March 1994, A5.

46 Mueller, 'Women and Politics.'

47 Personal interview with Jan Pullinger.

48 Mueller, 'Women and Politics.'

49 Ibid.

50 Janice D. Yoder, 'Rethinking Tokenism: Looking Beyond Numbers,' *Gender and Society* 5 (1991): 178-92.

51 Lyn Kathlene, 'Power and Influence in State Legislative Policymaking: The Interaction of Gender and Position in Committee Hearing Debates,' *American Political Science Review* 88 (1994): 560-76.

52 New Democratic Party Women's Committee, *Herstory and Policy*.

53 One of these task forces, on child care, was completed before the end of the government's term; the other, called the Task Force on Family Violence, was renamed the Task Force on Violence Against Women when the new government continued its mandate.

54 Ministry of Women's Equality, n.d.
55 Ministry of Women's Equality, February 1994.
56 *New Cabinet Submissions Format and Guidelines* (December 1993), 15.
57 One of the seven Social Credit members elected in 1991 stepped down in order for the party's newest leader, Grace McCarthy, to run. She lost that election.
58 An opinion poll taken on 13 and 14 May found that the NDP had the support of 44 percent of the female respondents compared to 33 percent of the male respondents. By contrast, the Liberals had support from 44 percent of the men and 35 percent of the women (Angus Reid Group poll, 15 May 1996).

Chapter 8: The Media and BC Politics

1 David Taras, *The Newsmakers* (Toronto: Nelson Canada 1990), 4.
2 Margaret A. Ormsby, *British Columbia: A History* (Toronto: Macmillan 1958), 124. In Taras's *The Newsmakers*, he describes similar developments elsewhere in Canada as 'the party press,' noting that during the first two decades of this century it was still the practice in Ottawa for reporters from Conservative papers to sit to one side of the speaker while reporters from Liberal papers sat on the other side (45).
3 *Victoria Colonist*, 24 January 1890, 2.
4 *Victoria Colonist*, 22 May 1898, 4.
5 Russell R. Walker, *Politicians of a Pioneering Province* (Vancouver: Mitchell Press 1969), 36.
6 Ibid., 16.
7 Ibid., 84.
8 Ibid., 83.
9 Jeremy Wilson, 'Government and Opposition Use of a Changing Legislature: An Analysis of the Battle for Media Coverage,' unpublished paper in legislative library (Victoria, University of Victoria Political Science Department: BC Project 1983), 17.

Chapter 9: The Government of the Day

1 Walter D. Young and J. Terence Morley, 'The Premier and the Cabinet,' in *The Reins of Power: Governing British Columbia*, ed. J. Terence Morley, Norman J. Ruff, Neil A. Swainson, R. Jeremy Wilson, and Walter D. Young (Vancouver: Douglas and McIntyre 1983), 54.
2 W.A.C. Bennett's story is lovingly and perceptively told by David Mitchell in his book *W.A.C. Bennett and the Rise of British Columbia* (Vancouver: Douglas and McIntyre 1983).
3 British Columbia, Cabinet Office, *Guide to the Cabinet Committee System* (December 1993), 6.
4 David E. Smith, *The Invisible Crown: The First Principle of Canadian Government* (Toronto: University of Toronto Press 1995), 22, 23.
5 See Herman Bakvis, *Regional Ministers: Power and Influence in the Canadian Cabinet* (Toronto: University of Toronto Press 1991).
6 The high-priced waterfront constituencies were Point Grey, West Vancouver, North Vancouver, Saanich, and Oak Bay, and these, during the W.A.C. Bennett years, often elected Liberals or Conservatives to the assembly.
7 For a description of the organizational chaos that characterized the Barrett government's deliberations and that reflected Barrett's own approach to reforming the system of government in place when he took office, see Paul Tennant, 'The NDP Government of British Columbia: Unaided Politicians in an Unaided Cabinet,' *Canadian Public Policy* 3, 4 (1977): 489-503.
8 Several Bill Bennett staffers went on to greater political glory (though often tarnished by excessive political calamity), including Norman Spector, who served as deputy minister and later became the key federal civil servant responsible for the ill-fated Meech Lake Accord (and was later consoled with the ambassadorship to Israel); Bud Smith, who served as Vander Zalm's attorney general until on-air revelations of an intimate friendship with a reporter turned him into a political liability; and Kim Campbell, who served as minister of justice in the Mulroney cabinet and was briefly prime minister of Canada before leading her party into the worst electoral debacle in the history of Canada.
9 For details of this planning, see Terence Morley, 'From Bill Vander Zalm to Mike Harcourt: Government Transition in British Columbia,' in *Taking Power: Managing Government*

Transitions, ed. Donald J. Savoie (Toronto: Institute of Public Administration of Canada 1993), 187-212.

Chapter 10: Provincial Governance and the Public Service

1 Popularized by US Vice-President Al Gore and taken from the blueprint sketched in David Osborne and Ted Gaebler, *Reinventing Government: How the Entrepreneurial Spirit Is Transforming the Public Sector* (New York: Plume 1993).
2 KPMG, *Report: Personnel, Shadow FTEs and Collective Bargaining* (Victoria, 1992).
3 Ibid., 15.
4 British Columbia, Office of the Premier, *Government Restructuring: Statement of Principles* (23 October 1987).
5 Graham Leslie, *Breach of Promise: Socred Ethics under Vander Zalm* (Madeira Park, BC: Harbour Publishing 1991), chap. 9.
6 British Columbia, *Public Service Act*, chap. 66, sec. 5 and 8 (1993). For earlier history, see Norman J. Ruff, 'The Provincial Bureaucracy,' in *The Reins of Power: Governing British Columbia*, ed. J. Terence Morley, Norman J. Ruff, Neil A. Swainson, R. Jeremy Wilson, and Walter D. Young (Vancouver: Douglas and McIntyre 1983).
7 British Columbia, *Matthew's Legacy*, vol. 2 of *Report of the Gove Inquiry into Child Protection* (Vancouver, 1995).
8 British Columbia, Ministry of Finance and Corporate Relations, *British Columbia Financial and Economic Review* (Victoria, 1995), 37-9.
9 British Columbia, Royal Commission of Inquiry into Employer-Employee Relations in the Public Service of British Columbia, *Report: Making Bargaining Work in British Columbia's Public Service* (Victoria, December 1972). See also committee report by R.D. Higgins, *The Higgins Report Revisited* (Victoria, March 1977).
10 Judi Korbin, Commissioner, *Report of the Commission of Inquiry into the Public Service and Public Sector*, 2 vols. (June 1993); and *Interim Report* (December 1992).
11 *PSERC NEWS* 5 (January 1995).
12 'Senior Public Servants Caught in Constant Cabinet Turmoil,' *British Columbia Politics and Policy* 5, 3 (1991): 1, 10-13.
13 'Special Report: The BC Public Service: Is Harcourt 'Politicizing' the Bureaucracy?' *British Columbia Politics and Policy* 5, 11 (1991): 6-9; 'Harcourt Risks Election Mandate: Patronage Appointments and Contracts Repudiate Campaign Pledge,' *British Columbia Politics and Policy* 6, 3 (1992): 1, 10-12, 15; Jane Doe and Rick Coe, 'Is Patronage Really Reborn in Harcourt's BC?' *New Directions* 7, 2 (1992): 8-14.
14 Patrick Dunleavy, 'Bureaucrats, Budgets, and the Growth of the State: Reconstructing an Instrumental Model,' *British Journal of Political Science* 15 (1985): 299-328.
15 The ORI was formed after the March 1995 budget and was originally composed of Jill Bodkin, former deputy minister and partner in Ernst and Young Consultants; Michael Phelps, CEO, Westcoast Energy; Jo Surich, chair and commissioner, Public Sector Employment Relations Council, the deputy to the premier; the deputy ministers of Finance and Education; and the secretary to the Treasury Board.
16 See Josephine Rekart, *Public Funds, Private Provision: The Role of the Voluntary Sector* (Vancouver: UBC Press 1993).
17 British Columbia, *Closer to Home: Report of the Royal Commission on Health Care and Costs* (Victoria, 1991).
18 British Columbia, Ministry of Health, *New Directions for a Healthy British Columbia* (Victoria, 1993); *New Directions Regional Health Forums* (Victoria, 1994); *Principles and Models for Representation and Voting on Regional Health Boards* (Victoria, 1994).
19 Its board of directors includes a representative group of forestry policy stakeholders through twelve private and six public sector appointees who administer designated stumpage revenue for investment in forestry related projects.
20 See British Columbia, Commission on Resources and the Environment, *Land Use Strategy for British Columbia* (August 1992); *Finding Common Ground: A Shared Vision for Land Use* (January 1994); *A Sustainability Act for British Columbia*, vol. 1 of *The Provincial Land Use Strategy* (November 1994); British Columbia Round Table on the Environment and the Economy, *Reaching Agreement*, vol. 1 of *Consensus Processes in British Columbia* (Victoria,

1991), A4-16; B70-114; and British Columbia Treaty Commission, *Annual Report*, 1994-5. Bob Nixon provides a critical account of BC's land use decision-making in 'Public Participation: Changing the Way We Make Forest Decisions,' in *Touch Wood: British Columbia Forests at the Crossroads*, ed. Ken Drushka, Bob Nixon, and Ray Travers (Madeira Park, BC: Harbour Publishing 1993), 23-66.

21 British Columbia, Auditor General and Deputy Ministers' Council, *Enhancing Accountability for Performance in the British Columbia Public Sector* (Victoria: Queen's Printer for British Columbia 1995), 32-3.

Chapter 11: Administering Justice

1 *Constitution Act, 1867*, sec. 92 (14). In 1867, when this act was passed by the Imperial Parliament at Westminster in London, it was called the *British North America Act*. Several generations of Canadians were raised to ponder the division of powers provided for in what they called the BNA Act, until Prime Minister Pierre Trudeau caused the name of the fundamental document of our constitution to be altered to his liking.

2 *Constitution Act, 1867*, sec. 91(27).

3 Peter H. Russell, *The Judiciary in Canada: The Third Branch of Government* (Toronto: McGraw-Hill Ryerson 1987), 54; and K.C. Wheare, *Federal Government*, 3rd ed. (London: Oxford University Press 1953).

4 *Constitution Act, 1982*, sec. 11(b).

5 Rainer Knopff and F.L. Morton, *Charter Politics* (Toronto: Nelson Canada 1992), 218.

6 Ibid., 50.

7 Ibid., 190.

8 For a justification of structural changes in the ministry during Gabelmann's time as attorney general, see the Hon. Colin Gabelmann, Attorney General of BC, 'The Attorney General's Page: New Structures, New Approaches,' *Advocate* 53, Part I (January 1995): 47-53.

9 Stephen Owen, *Report and Recommendations*, vol. 1 of *Discretion to Prosecute Inquiry, Commissioner's Report* (Victoria: Queen's Printer 1990), 111.

10 Gabelmann, 'The Attorney General's Page,' 51.

11 Before the Law Foundation was created, the banks and other financial institutions kept all the interest from these funds and, consequently, were eager to have law firms and lawyers as customers.

12 Government of British Columbia, Ministry of the Attorney General, 'Review of Legal Aid Services in British Columbia,' prepared by Timothy D. Agg, 28 August 1992.

13 In 1995 the benchers surrendered to modernity and North American usage and indicated their willingness to have the legislature change 'treasurer' to 'president.'

14 The benchers have always selected the treasurer from among their number. When the Legal Profession Act was last amended, a requirement was added that the assistant deputy treasurer, destined by those amendments to become treasurer, must be elected by the members of the Law Society. The benchers interpreted this change to mean that the benchers would put one name forward at the annual meeting of the society for the post of assistant deputy treasurer in the expectation that the individual named would be automatically ratified. Their hopes, in this regard, have so far been fulfilled.

15 Since the Legal Profession Act was mostly a creation of senior lawyers, the process of election is rather more complex than as outlined in this text. The benchers may choose to have two terms for the treasurer and his or her apprentices. An assistant deputy treasurer could be elected, at least under the law, not having served as a bencher. If a judicial county has the great good fortune to have one of its own serving as one of the 'treasury,' then the number of elected benchers from that county is reduced by one.

16 See the Law Society of BC, *1994 Annual Report*.

17 Ibid., 7.

18 David Lewis, once Canada's premier labour lawyer acting for the union side, later the national leader of the NDP, was fond of implying that lawyers were no better than labourers and had the same need as did those labourers for a trade union – so why should lawyers, as a class, pretend to anti-union sentiment given such a need?

19 See Russell, *The Judiciary in Canada*, for the most comprehensive analysis of the Canadian court system available.

20 The ancient office of Lord Chancellor represents the understanding, implicit in the English constitution, that men and women serving in high office will, in themselves, act decently and honourably to ensure that there is no bias in the system engendered by formal conflicts of interest. The Lord Chancellor plays many roles – roles which might be said to place him in conflict with himself. And so the Lord Chancellor is the senior judge in the United Kingdom, the equivalent of the Chief Justice of the United States Supreme Court. Unlike the chief justice, he is also a member of the government serving as a senior cabinet minister. Indeed, the Lord Chancellor's office, with direction from the Lord Chancellor, plucks from the ranks of the barristers certain of them to serve as judges in Her Majesty's various law courts. The Lord Chancellor is also the presiding officer of the House of Lords, a role analogous to that performed by the vice-president of the United States in his or her capacity as President of the United States Senate. Those with a taste for constitutional niceties will be pleased to note that in the event of an impeachment trial of the US president before the Senate, the chief justice presides. The Lord Chancellor has wider presidential powers in the British upper house that, in combination with his place at the cabinet table and his grave judicial dignity, may possibly justify his precedence at dinner and in other formal settings ahead of the prime minister of the United Kingdom.

21 It is difficult to reconcile this 1947 decision of the JCPC with the 1981 SCC decision setting out the constitutional rules for legitimately 'patriating' the major legal elements of the Canadian constitution. A majority on the Supreme Court decided that important changes to the Canadian constitution could only be produced with 'substantial' provincial consent.

22 There have never been close to eighty-four supernumeraries holding office. At the beginning of 1995 there were seventeen supernumerary judges, although that number is likely to increase over the next decade as more SCBC judges become eligible for this status.

23 British Columbia, *Supreme Court Act*, sec. 9(1).

24 Canada, *Criminal Code*, sec. 469.

25 Ibid.

26 *Constitution Act, 1982*, sec. 11(f).

27 See Martin L. Friedland, *A Place Apart: Judicial Interpretation and Accountability in Canada*, Canadian Judicial Council, May 1995, chap. 10.

28 So far, provincial court judges with this view have been unsuccessful in persuading superior court judges and the SCC of the merits of their case. In 1995 SCBC judges received a salary of $158,000 and provincial court judges a salary of $118,500. The judicial compensation committee set up by law to recommend salary adjustments for provincial court judges did in that year recommend a significant increase; however, the province's minister of finance quickly rejected the idea.

29 Section 99 of the *Constitution Act, 1867* provides that superior court judges may only be removed following a joint resolution of the Senate and the House of Commons until they attain the age of seventy-five. (Before 1961 superior court judges could stay in office for life, and some, such as Sir William Mulock, the Chief Justice of Ontario, continued to pronounce judgments well into their nineties.) No superior court judge has ever been removed from office, although some have quietly resigned in the reasonable fear and expectation that the joint resolution would be sought and obtained. Tenured professors in BC, by contrast, according to decisions of the tenured judges, may be forcibly retired at age sixty-five; moreover, since the Charter, according to the judges, does not apply to universities, it is to be presumed that the legislature could some day lower this retirement age.

30 Canada, Minister of Justice, *Federal Judicial Appointments Process* (April 1994), 3.

31 Peter H. Russell and Jacob S. Ziegel, 'Mulroney's Judicial Appointments and the New Judicial Advisory Committees,' in *Law, Politics and the Judicial Process in Canada*, ed. F.L. Morton, 2nd ed. (Calgary: University of Calgary Press 1992), 89.

32 The descriptions here are based on confidential interviews. If the judiciary comes to be seen as more politicized (as in the United States), it is likely that the process of appointment, and even the process of judicial decision-making in Canada, will become more transparent.

33 There are a number of tribunals that deal with specific areas of economic and social activity, including the Labour Relations Board, the Employment Standards Branch, the Worker's Compensation Board, the Gaming Commission, the Racing Commission, and so on.

Chapter 12: Lobbying and Private Interests

1 Column by Shelby Scates in the *Seattle Post-Intelligencer*, reprinted in the *Victoria Times*, 8 February 1979, 5.
2 Robert Salisbury, 'Interest Groups,' in *Handbook of Political Science*, ed. Fred I. Greenstein and Nelson W. Polsby (Reading: Addison-Wesley 1975), 175.
3 Robert J. Jackson and Doreen Jackson, *Politics in Canada* (Scarborough: Prentice-Hall 1994), 517.
4 Margaret A. Ormsby, *British Columbia: A History* (Toronto: Macmillan 1958), 117.
5 *Victoria Colonist*, 2 March 1892, 6.
6 *Victoria Daily Times*, 17 February 1921, 8.
7 *Victoria Daily Times*, 30 November 1921, 5.
8 *Victoria Times*, 16 February 1927, 1.
9 Russell R. Walker, *Politicians of a Pioneering Province* (Vancouver: Mitchell Press 1969), 107.
10 Ibid., 20.
11 *Vancouver Province*, 27 January 1928, 25.
12 *Vancouver Province*, 29 January 1928, 6.
13 *Vancouver Province*, 30 January 1953, 25.
14 British Columbia, *Closer to Home: The Report of the Royal Commission on Health Care and Costs* (1991). See especially 'Governance of the Health Care Professions: The Privilege of Self Regulation,' vol. 2, D30-7.
15 Joseph A. Gatner, 'In Pursuit of Public Opinion: Politics of Pressure Groups,' *Canadian Parliamentary Review* 3 (September 1980): 32-6.
16 A. Paul Pross, *Pressure Group Behaviour in Canadian Politics* (Toronto: McGraw Hill 1975).

Chapter 13: Public Finance and Fiscal Policy

1 C.L. Barber, *The Theory of Fiscal Policy as Applied to a Province*, Ontario Committee on Taxation (Toronto: Queen's Printer 1966), 27.
2 Ibid., 29.
3 See British Columbia, *Budget '95 Reports* (Victoria: Ministry of Finance and Corporate Relations, March 1995), 43, 56.
4 Allan M. Maslove, Michael J. Prince, and G. Bruce Doern, *Federal and Provincial Budgeting* (Toronto: University of Toronto Press 1986), chap. 2.
5 Ibid., 21-2.

Chapter 14: At the Edge of Canada's Welfare State

1 Ramesh Mishra, *The Welfare State in Society* (Toronto: University of Toronto Press 1990), 34.
2 Marsha A. Chandler and William M. Chandler, *Public Policy and Provincial Politics* (Toronto: McGraw-Hill Ryerson 1979), 180.
3 Peter F. Drucker, *Post-Capitalist Society* (New York: Harper 1993), 123.
4 Michael M. Atkinson, ed., *Governing Canada: Institutions and Public Policy* (Toronto: Harcourt Brace Jovanovich Canada 1993), 376.
5 James J. Rice, 'Social Policy, Economic Management, and Redistribution,' in *Public Policy in Canada*, ed. G. Bruce Doern and Peter Aucoin (Toronto: Macmillan 1979), 106.
6 Rod Dobell and Stanley Mansbridge, *The Social Policy Process in Canada* (Montreal: The Institute for Research on Public Policy 1986), 2.
7 Charles E. Lindblom, *The Policy-Making Process* (Englewood Cliffs, NJ: Prentice-Hall 1968), 4.
8 G. Bruce Doern, Allan M. Maslove, and Michael J. Prince, *Public Budgeting in Canada: Politics, Economics and Management* (Ottawa: Carleton University Press 1988), 154.
9 See Ronald Manzer, *Public Policies and Political Development in Canada* (Toronto: University of Toronto Press 1985); Andrew Armitage, *Social Welfare in Canada*, 2nd ed. (Toronto: McClelland and Stewart 1988); and Kenneth Bryden, *Old Age Pensions and Policy-Making in Canada* (Montreal: McGill-Queen's University Press 1974).

10   Quoted in Angela Redish, 'Social Policy and "Restraint" in British Columbia,' in *Restraining the Economy: Social Credit Economic Policies for BC in the Eighties*, ed. Robert C. Allen and Gideon Rosenbluth (Vancouver: New Star Books 1986), 156.

11   British Columbia, Speech from the Throne, *BC Debates*, 14 March 1994, 9418.

12   Dennis Guest, *The Emergence of Social Security in Canada*, 2nd ed. (Vancouver: UBC Press 1985), 93.

13   Harry Cassidy, *Public Health and Welfare Reorganization* (Toronto: Ryerson 1945), 62.

14   Lorne J. Kavic and Garry Brian Nixon, *The 1200 Days: A Shattered Dream, Dave Barrett and the NDP in BC, 1972-75* (Coquitlam, BC: Kaen Publishers 1978), 199. See also Michael Clague, Robert Dill, Roop Seebaran, and Brian Wharf, *Reforming Human Services: The Experience of the Community Resource Boards in BC* (Vancouver: UBC Press 1984); and William Cochrane, *Social Welfare Policy in British Columbia 1972-1975*, BC Working Paper (Victoria: University of Victoria 1983).

15   Josephine Rekart, *Public Funds, Private Provision: The Role of the Voluntary Sector* (Vancouver: UBC Press 1993); and Brian Wharf and Marilyn Callahan, 'Public Policy Is a Voluntary Affair,' *BC Studies* 55 (1982): 79-93.

16   Marilyn Callahan and Chris McNiven, 'British Columbia,' in *Privatization and Provincial Social Services in Canada*, ed. Jacqueline S. Ismael and Yves Vaillancourt (Edmonton: University of Alberta Press 1988), 13-39; and Allan M. Maslove, Michael J. Prince, and G. Bruce Doern, *Federal and Provincial Budgeting* (Toronto: University of Toronto Press 1986), chap. 8.

17   Stan Persky, *Son of Socred: Has Bill Bennett's Government Gotten BC Moving Again?* (Vancouver: New Star Books 1979), 303. That the media and a better-informed public are dubious of such programs, and that a new paradigm is needed, see Marilyn Callahan, Andrew Armitage, Michael J. Prince, and Brian Wharf, 'Workfare in British Columbia: Social Development Alternatives,' *Canadian Review of Social Policy* 26 (1990): 15-26.

18   In addition to the sources already noted, the academic literature on restraint policies in BC includes: Leslie Bella, 'Rhetoric and Reality: Health Care Cutbacks in Three Provinces,' in *Continuities and Discontinuities: The Political Economy of Social Welfare and Labour Market Policy in Canada*, ed. Andrew Johnson, Stephen McBride, and Patrick Smith (Toronto: University of Toronto Press), chap. 10; James Cutt, 'Budgeting in British Columbia, 1976-1986: Coping and Caring in Tough Times,' in *Budgeting in the Provinces: Leadership and the Premiers*, ed. Allan M. Maslove (Toronto: The Institute of Public Administration of Canada 1989), chap. 5; A.R. Dobell, 'Doing a Bennett,' *Policy Options* 5 (May 1984): 6-10; Warren Magnusson, Charles Doyle, R.B.J. Walker, and John De Marco, eds., *The New Reality: The Politics of Restraint in BC* (Vancouver: New Star Books 1984); M. Patricia Marchak, 'British Columbia: "New Right" Politics and a New Geography,' in *Canadian Politics in the 1990s*, ed. Michael S. Whittington and Glen Williams (Scarborough: Nelson Canada 1990), chap. 3; and Philip Resnick, 'Neo-Conservatism on the Periphery: The Lessons from BC,' *BC Studies* 75 (1987): 3-23.

19   Cutt, 'Budgeting in British Columbia,' 160.

20   Bella, 'Rhetoric and Reality,' 180. See also Robert G. Evans, 'Restraining Health Care: New Realities and Old Verities,' in *Restraining the Economy*, ed. Allen and Rosenbluth, chap. 9. Evans concludes that the Bennett government's health policy in these years was neither as generous as the language of budget speeches claimed nor as cutting as some critics charged.

21   Patrick J. Smith, 'British Columbia: Public Policy and Perceptions of Governance,' in *Canadian Politics*, 2nd ed., ed. James Bickerton and Alain-G. Gagnon (Peterborough: Broadview Press 1994), 506-26; and Stan Persky, *Fantasy Government: Bill Vander Zalm and the Future of the Social Credit* (Vancouver: New Star Books 1989).

22   Lynn L. Carter, 'Public Policy and Private Morality: The Abortion Debate in British Columbia,' *Canadian Review of Social Policy* 21 (1988): 7. On the issues of abortion, AIDS, and the family, see also Persky, *Fantasy Government*, chap. 9, and Gary Mason and Keith Baldrey, *Fantasyland: Inside the Reign of Bill Vander Zalm* (Toronto: McGraw-Hill 1989), chaps. 7 and 8. On the Vander Zalm government in general, see Graham Leslie, *Breach of Promise* (Sechelt, BC: BC Harbour Publishing 1991). Neoconservative governments in Canada responded differently to the Supreme Court's decision on therapeutic abortions. In contrast

to Vander Zalm's quick and determined action to prevent abortions, the Mulroney government appeared to dither, in search of a political compromise. See Leslie A. Pal, 'How Ottawa Dithers: The Conservatives and Abortion Policy,' in *How Ottawa Spends 1991-92*, ed. Frances Abele (Ottawa: Carleton University Press 1991), 269-306.

23 Public documents by the Premier's Forum include: *New Opportunities for Working and Living* (Victoria 1994); *Our Changing Economy and the Prospects for Work*, Background Paper 1; *Our Youth – Investing in Their Future*, Background Paper 2; *Children, Families and the Social Safety Net*, Background Paper 3; *Toward Retirement: Social Safety Net Issues for Older Adults*, Background Paper 4; *Persons with Disabilities: Directions for Dignified and Independent Living*, Background Paper 5; and *Opportunities for Renewal* (Victoria, 1995).

24 National Council of Welfare, *Poverty Profile 1993*, A Report by the Council (Ottawa: Supply and Services Canada 1995). This is the latest of a series of reports on poverty by the council, which analyzes factual material on national and provincial trends collected by Statistics Canada. For a look at the network of groups in Canada with a deep interest in, and knowledge of, poverty issues, see Rodney Haddow, 'The Poverty Policy Community in Canada's Welfare State,' in *Policy Communities and Public Policy in Canada*, ed. William D. Coleman and Grace Skogstad (Toronto: Copp Clark Pitman 1990), 212-37. Key groups in the BC policy community include the End Legislated Poverty Society, Together Against Poverty Society, and the Social Planning and Research Council.

25 Jean Swanson, 'BC: How Has the NDP Government Treated People Who Are Poor?' *Canadian Review of Social Policy* 31 (1993): 64-6; Michael Clague, 'Consumer Empowerment and the Community Voice,' *Perspectives* 16, 1 (1994): 8, 10; and Marjorie Griffin Cohen, 'British Columbia: Playing Safe Is a Dangerous Game,' *Studies in Political Economy* 43 (1994): 149-59.

Chapter 15: The Politics of Sustainability

Research for this chapter has been funded by the Social Sciences and Humanities Research Council. The author would also like to thank Edward Morawski for his research assistance and Clark Binkley, Ian Gill, and Murray Rankin for their comments on an earlier draft.

1 Forest Resources Commission, *The Future of Our Forests* (Victoria: Forest Resources Commission, April 1991), 35.

2 Ibid.

3 Michael M'Gonigle and Ben Parfitt, *Forestopia: A Practical Guide to the New Forest Economy* (Madeira Park, BC: Harbour Publishing 1994).

4 A similar scheme for the organization of forest policies is developed by Christopher Leman, 'A Forest of Institutions: Patterns of Choice on North American Timberlands,' in *Land Rites and Wrongs: The Management, Regulation and Use of Land in Canada and the United States*, ed. Elliot J. Feldman and Michael A. Goldberg (Lincoln Institute of Land Policy 1987). For another description of these policy changes, see Ken Lertzman, Jeremy Rayner, and Jeremy Wilson, 'Learning and Change in the British Columbia Policy Sector,' *Canadian Journal of Political Science* 29 (March 1996): 111-34.

5 Craig Darling, 'In Search of Consensus: An Evaluation of the Clayoquot Sound Sustainable Development Task Force Process' (Victoria: University of Victoria Institute for Dispute Resolution, n.d. [*circa* 1990]).

6 Clayoquot Sound Sustainable Development Strategy Steering Committee, *Clayoquot Sound Sustainable Development Strategy*, Second Draft of the Strategy Document, 3 August 1992, 6-12; Supplement to Second Draft, Table-19.

7 British Columbia, *Clayoquot Sound Land Use Decision*, April 1993.

8 It protected the Talbot drainage of the Megin watershed, which Option 5 did not, and imposed more stringent requirements on viewscapes.

9 Keith Baldrey, 'Public Backs Clayoquot Logging Plan,' *Vancouver Sun*, 3 November 1993, A3.

10 Scientific Panel for Sustainable Forest Practices in Clayoquot Sound, *Sustainable Ecosystem Management in Clayoquot Sound: Planning and Practices*, Report 5, April 1995, 1.

11 Ibid.

12 Premier's Office, 'Harcourt Unveils Comprehensive Land Use Initiative,' press release, 21 January 1992.

13 Remaining land use issues will be addressed by the BC Land Use Coordination Office. See Office of the Premier, 'Commission on Resources and Environment Winds Down,' news release, 7 March 1996.

14 Hamish Kimmins, *Balancing Act: Environmental Issues in Forestry* (Vancouver: UBC Press 1992).

15 Gordon Hamilton, 'Tab for Proposed Forest Practices Code Soars 4-fold,' *Vancouver Sun*, 3 March 1994, D1.

16 Jeremy Wilson, 'Wilderness Politics in BC: The Business Dominated State and the Containment of Environmentalism,' in *Policy Communities and Public Policy in Canada*, ed. William D. Coleman and Grace Skogstad (Toronto: Copp Clark Pittman 1990).

17 Peter Pearse, *Introduction to Forestry Economics* (Vancouver: UBC Press 1991), 161; Herb Hammond, *Seeing the Forest among the Trees* (Vancouver: Polestar Books 1992), 129-30; Forest Resources Commission, *The Future of Our Forests*, 81.

18 Forest Alliance of British Columbia, *Analysis of Recent British Columbia Government Forest Policy and Land Use Initiatives*, Report submitted by Price Waterhouse (Vancouver: Forest Alliance, September 1995).

19 Vaughn Palmer, 'Timber-Review Delay a Break for NDP,' *Vancouver Sun*, 9 February 1994, A10; Vaughn Palmer, 'Chief Forester Sets Cut, but Minister Bends Twig,' *Vancouver Sun*, 2 August 1994, A12.

20 Based on information supplied by Timber Supply Branch public information officer Karen Brant, 2 January 1996.

21 Vaughn Palmer, 'NDP Goes Out on a Limb for Forest Workers,' *Vancouver Sun*, 28 March 1994, A10.

22 Patricia Lush, 'BC Forest Plan Applauded,' *Globe and Mail*, 16 April 1994, B4.

23 Vaughn Palmer, 'For the Island, CORE Start of Bad News,' *Vancouver Sun*, 11 February 1994, A18.

24 Forest Alliance of British Columbia, *Analysis*.

25 BC Forest Service, 'Meeting the Employment Challenge in the BC Forest Sector – Response to the Forest Alliance/Price Waterhouse Report,' information bulletin, 3 October 1995.

26 See George Hoberg, 'Putting Ideas in Their Place: A Response to Learning and Change in the British Columbia Forest Policy Sector,' *Canadian Journal of Political Science* 29 (March 1996): 135-44.

27 In Chapter 16 of this volume, Harrison's characterization of 'players and their stakes' excludes government ministries. The difference in the relative significance of ministries to the policy field results from two factors. First, whereas the environment is a relatively recent policy field, forest policy has a much longer history as being central to the government and politics of BC. Second, whereas the Ministry of Environment brings together a diverse group of disciplines, the traditional professionalization of forestry provides a stronger sense of identity and mission for government employees in the Ministry of Forests.

28 Bob Nixon, 'Principles of Integrated Management Lack Legislative Authority in British Columbia, When Compared with US Forest Law,' *Forest Planning Canada* 6 (November-December 1990): 9-14.

29 Jeremy Wilson, 'Wilderness Politics,' 152.

30 George Hoberg, 'Environmental Policy: Alternative Styles,' in *Governing Canada: Institutions and Public Policy*, ed. Michael M. Atkinson (Toronto: Harcourt Brace Jovanovich 1993); Kathryn Harrison, *Passing the Buck: Federalism and Canadian Environmental Policy* (Vancouver: UBC Press 1996), chap. 6.

31 Donald E. Blake, R. Kenneth Carty, and Lynda Erickson, *Grassroots Politicians: Party Activists in British Columbia* (Vancouver: UBC Press 1991), 63-4.

32 See Chapter 16 in this volume.

33 W.T. Stanbury, I.B. Vertinsky, and Bill Wilson, *The Challenge to Canadian Forest Products in Europe: Managing a Complex Environmental Issue*, FEPA Working Paper 211 (Vancouver: Forest Economics and Policy Analysis Project, December 1994).

Chapter 16: Environmental Protection in BC
The author wishes to express her thanks to the politicians and interest group representatives who generously gave their time for interviews, to Gerry Kristianson and Brian Scarfe for helpful comments on an earlier draft, and to Willem Maas for superb research assistance.

1 Ronald Inglehart, *The Silent Revolution* (Princeton: Princeton University Press 1977).
2 Jeremy Wilson, 'Wilderness Politics in British Columbia: The Business-Dominated State and the Containment of Environmentalism,' in *Policy Communities and Public Policy in Canada*, ed. William D. Coleman and Grace Skogstad (Toronto: Copp Clark Pitman 1990), 150.
3 On the emergence of legalism, see George Hoberg, 'Environmental Policy: Alternative Styles,' in *Governing Canada: Institutions and Public Policy*, ed. Michael M. Atkinson (Toronto: Harcourt Brace Jovanovich 1993); and Michael Howlett, 'The Judicialization of Canadian Environmental Policy, 1980-1990: A Test of the Canada-United States Convergence Thesis,' *Canadian Journal of Political Science* 27 (1994): 99-127.
4 See, for instance, Bill Smith and Richard Watts, 'MacBlo Warns 200 Jobs May Go,' *Victoria Times-Colonist*, 24 January 1990, A1.
5 Robert C. Paehlke, *Environmentalism and the Future of Progressive Politics* (New Haven: Yale University Press 1989).
6 See Ian McAllister, 'Dimensions of Environmentalism: Public Opinion, Political Activism and Party Support in Australia,' *Environmental Politics* 3 (1994): 22-42; K.A. Rasinki, T.W. Smith, and S. Zuckerbraun, 'Fairness Motivations and Tradeoffs Underlying Public Support for Government Environmental Spending in 9 Nations,' *Journal of Social Issues* 50 (1994): 179-97. Even Paehlke rejects neoconservative parties as 'deeply hostile' to environmental protection (*Environmentalism*, 276).
7 Robert Rohrschneider, 'New Party versus Old Left Realignments: Environmental Attitudes, Party Policies, and Partisan Affiliations in Four West European Countries,' *Journal of Politics* 55 (1993): 682-701.
8 R.F. King and A. Borchardt, 'Red and Green: Air Pollution Levels and Left Party Power in OECD Countries,' *Environment and Planning C: Government and Policy* 12 (1994): 225-41.
9 Ronald Inglehart, 'Values, Ideology, and Cognitive Mobilization in New Social Movements,' in *Challenging the Political Order: New Social and Political Movements in Western Democracies*, ed. Russell J. Dalton and Manfred Kuechler (Oxford: Polity Press 1990), 46.
10 Wilson, 'Wilderness Politics,' 149.
11 For a discussion of trends in public opinion concerning the environment, see Kathryn Harrison, *Passing the Buck: Federalism and Canadian Environmental Policy* (Vancouver: UBC Press 1996), chap. 6.
12 Larry Kuehn, 'NDP Girds to Tackle the Threat,' *Vancouver Sun*, 30 November 1989, A15.
13 Justine Hunter, Keith Baldrey, and Doug Ward, 'Backroom-Forged Compromise Prevents Public NDP Squabble,' *Vancouver Sun*, 12 March 1990, A1, A2; Vaughn Palmer, 'Harcourt Shows How to Strike a Deal,' *Vancouver Sun*, 12 March 1990, A6.
14 Wilson, 'Wilderness Politics,' 164.
15 Glenn Bohn, 'Environmental Rhetoric Toxic,' *Vancouver Sun*, 8 October 1991, A11.
16 British Columbia, Speech from the Throne, 17 March 1992.
17 British Columbia, *Environmental Action Plan for British Columbia* (Victoria: Ministry of Environment, Lands, and Parks, n.d.); British Columbia, *New Directions in Environmental Protection: Five Year Action Plan (1992-1997)* (Victoria: Ministry of Environment, Lands, and Parks, n.d.).
18 Glenn Bohn, 'Turning Sour,' *Vancouver Sun*, 4 January 1992, B1, B8.
19 Personal communication, Moe Sihota, June 1995.
20 Ibid.; Larry Pynn, 'BC's Tranquil Legacy,' *Vancouver Sun*, 26 August 1995, B1, B4.
21 Wilson, 'Wilderness Politics,' 157.
22 Confidential interview, June 1995.
23 Canadian Pulp and Paper Association, *Reference Tables* (Montreal: Canadian Pulp and Paper Association 1989).
24 See, for example, William F. Sinclair, *Controlling Pollution from Canadian Pulp and Paper Manufacturers: A Federal Perspective* (Vancouver: Environment Canada 1988), 110.
25 Kathryn Harrison and George Hoberg, 'Setting the Environmental Agenda in Canada and the United States: The Cases of Dioxin and Radon,' *Canadian Journal of Political Science* 24 (1991): 3-27.
26 'BC Rules on Toxic Chemicals to Cost Pulp Firms $800 Million,' *Globe and Mail*, 13 May 1989.

27   Glenn Bohn, 'Phone Calls to Premier Reverse Tough Dioxin Law,' *Vancouver Sun*, 11 December 1990, A1.
28   Pulp Mill and Pulp and Paper Mill Liquid Effluent Control Regulation, BC Reg. 470/90, 13 December 1990.
29   BC Reg. 470/90, as amended 2 March 1992.
30   Robert Williamson, 'BC to Take a Second Look at Tough Pulp Mill Standards,' *Globe and Mail*, 1 October 1992, B1; Robert Williamson, 'BC Open to Change on Chlorine Ban,' *Globe and Mail*, 10 November 1992, B1.
31   'Pulp Emission Target Stands – Sihota,' *Vancouver Sun*, 11 December 1993, E9.
32   See statements by Judy Tyabji, *BC Debates*, 1 June 1992, 1948-1950; and Wilf Hurd, *BC Debates*, 27 May 1993, 6558; 31 March 1992, 381-2; 29 May 1992, 1941.
33   Personal interview, Mike de Jong, June 1995.
34   West Coast Environmental Law Association, 'From Candour to Cop-out: The Parties Respond to Key Environmental Questions,' *News from West Coast Environmental Law* 20 (23 May 1996): 1-2.
35   David Barr, 'An Industry Perspective on the TAT,' *Vancouver Sun*, 14 May 1993, A17.
36   British Columbia, *Report and Recommendations*, vol. 1 of *Interim Report on Tatshenshini/ Alsek Land Use* (Victoria: Commission on Resources and the Environment 1993), 40.
37   Ibid., 29.
38   Ibid., 34.
39   Ibid., 14.
40   Mark Hume, 'US Pressure Could Kill Copper Mine,' *Vancouver Sun*, 8 April 1992, B5.
41   British Columbia, *Interim Report on Tatshenshini/Alsek Land Use*, 7; Glenn Bohn, 'It's Mine or Wilderness, Report Says,' *Vancouver Sun*, 21 January 1993, E7.
42   Keith Baldrey, 'NDP to Name Tatshenshini as New Park,' *Vancouver Sun*, 22 June 1993, A1.
43   Ellen Saenger, 'Goodbye Vancouver, Hello Caracas,' *British Columbia Report*, 8 March 1993, 22; Robert Williamson, 'BC Chooses Green Over Copper,' *Globe and Mail*, 23 June 1993, B1, B19.
44   Williamson, 'BC Chooses Green'; and Barr, 'An Industry Perspective.'
45   See comments by John S. Weisgerber, *BC Debates*, 23 June 1993, 7715; and Robert Matas, 'NDP Government Trying to Win Back Friends,' *Globe and Mail*, 23 June 1993, B19.
46   See comments by Richard Neufeld, *BC Debates*, 23 June 1993, 7713, 7780.
47   Matas, 'NDP Government.'
48   Daniel Jarvis, *BC Debates*, 23 March 1993, 4757.
49   Daniel Jarvis, *BC Debates*, 23 June 1993, 7713.
50   Gary Farrell-Collins, *BC Debates*, 29 June 1993, 8030; Alan Warnke, *BC Debates*, 23 June 1993, 7714, and 29 June 1993, 8029; and Clive Tanner, *BC Debates*, 29 June 1993, 8029.
51   Joyce Nelson, 'Pro-mining Campaign Avoids Key Issues,' *Georgia Straight*, 1-8 September 1995, 11.
52   Gordon Hamilton, 'Windy Craggy Deal Worth $104 Million,' *Vancouver Sun*, 19 August 1995, A1-2; Miro Cernetig, 'NDP, Royal Oak Bury the Hatchet,' *Globe and Mail*, 19 August 1995, A1, A3.
53   British Columbia, *Interim Report on Tatshenshini/Alsek Land Use*, 39.
54   Cernetig, 'NDP, Royal Oak,' A3.
55   Murray Rankin, 'Alcan's Kemano Project: Options and Recommendations.' Submitted to Premier Mike Harcourt, 5 October 1992, 80.
56   The project and policy history presented here is based on British Columbia, *Kemano Completion Project Review: Report and Recommendations to the Lieutenant Governor in Council* (Victoria: British Columbia Utilities Commission 1994).
57   Rankin, 'Alcan's Kemano Project.'
58   Glenn Bohn, 'Liberal Leader Wants Kemano Project Killed,' *Vancouver Sun*, 12 October 1994, A3.
59   British Columbia, *Kemano Completion Project Review*.
60   Keith Baldrey, Peter O'Neil, and Rod Nutt, 'BC, Ottawa Bicker Over Alcan Payout,' *Vancouver Sun*, 24 January 1995, A1, A2.
61   Jeff Lee, 'Harcourt Blasted for Killing Kemano,' *Vancouver Sun*, 26 January 1995, A1, A2.
62   Barbara Yaffe, 'Greening Is the Rage in BC,' *Calgary Herald*, 28 January 1995, A6.

63 British Columbia, *Kemano Completion Project Review*, iii.
64 David Hogben, 'BC Fed Backs Kemano Battle,' *Vancouver Sun*, 3 December 1994, B12.
65 John S. Weisgerber, *BC Debates*, 22 March 1993, 4733.
66 Keith Baldrey, 'Campbell Pledge on Kemano Project Puzzles Pundits,' *Vancouver Sun*, 15 October 1994, A6.
67 Vaughn Palmer, 'Kemano a Makeover Tool for Campbell,' *Vancouver Sun*, 13 October 1994, A14.
68 Justine Hunter, 'NDP Banks on Green Peace. BC, Alcan Try to Settle on Kemano,' *Vancouver Sun*, 7 July 1995, A1.
69 Agreement between the Province of British Columbia and Alcan Aluminum Limited. July 1995.
70 Wilson, 'Wilderness Politics,' 144.
71 Sixty-six percent of those polled considered the government's performance at protecting the environment to be good or excellent. The comparable figures for getting tough with polluters and protecting jobs and the environment were 60 percent and 62 percent (personal communication, Moe Sihota, June 1995). See also Keith Baldrey, 'NDP's Pro-environmental Efforts "Growing on Public,"' *Vancouver Sun*, 2 November 1994, B5.
72 Reform Party of British Columbia, 'Policy Direction,' 33.
73 West Coast Environmental Law Association, 'From Candour to Cop-out'; Larry Pynn, 'Battling Over the Environment,' *Vancouver Sun*, 22 May 1996, D3.
74 A coalition of environmental groups formed and funded British Columbians for a Better Environment (BCBE) to disseminate information on the parties' environmental positions. BCBE's list of the '10 dirtiest candidates' was comprised of eight Liberals and two Reformers, including the two party leaders, Gordon Campbell and Jack Weisgerber. See Larry Pynn, 'Environmental Groups List Political Foes,' *Vancouver Sun*, 25 May 1996, A14.

Chapter 17: The BC New Democratic Party

1 Hugh G. Thorburn, 'Interpretations of the Canadian Party System,' in *Party Politics in Canada*, ed. H.G. Thorburn, 6th ed., (Scarborough, ON: Prentice-Hall 1991), 115.
2 See G.L. Kristianson, 'The Non-partisan Approach to BC Politics: The Search for a Unity Party – 1972-1975,' *BC Studies* 33 (1977): 13-30.
3 Brad Zubyk, *A Family Affair: Inside the Harcourt Government*, report by Brad Zubyk and Associates Ltd., Victoria (1993), 1.
4 Peter Hall, *Governing the Economy* (New York: Oxford University Press 1986), 232.
5 Alan C. Cairns, 'The Embedded State: State-Society Relations in Canada,' in *State and Society: Canada in Comparative Perspective*, Research Studies for the Royal Commission on the Economic Union and Development Prospects for Canada, vol. 31 (Toronto: University of Toronto Press 1985), 57.
6 For an overview, see Lorne J. Kavic and Gary Brian Nixon, *The 1200 Days: A Shattered Dream, Dave Barrett and the NDP in BC, 1972-75* (Coquitlam, BC: Kaen Publishers 1978). For his side of the story, see David Barrett and William Miller, *Barrett: A Passionate Political Life* (Vancouver: Douglas and McIntyre 1995).
7 Terence Morley, 'From Bill Vander Zalm to Mike Harcourt: Government Transition in British Columbia,' in *Taking Power: Managing Government Transition*, ed. Donald J. Savoie (Toronto: Institute of Public Administration of Canada 1993), 190.
8 Alan C. Cairns and Daniel Wong, 'Socialism, Federalism and the BC Party System 1933-1983,' in Thorburn, ed., *Party Politics*, 479.
9 See Paul Tennant, 'The NDP Government of British Columbia: Unaided Politicians in an Unaided Cabinet,' *Canadian Public Policy* 3, 4 (1977): 489-503.
10 Philip Resnick, 'Social Democracy in Power: The Case of British Columbia,' *BC Studies* 34 (1977): 19.
11 Marjorie Griffen Cohen, 'British Columbia: Playing Safe Is a Dangerous Game,' *Studies in Political Economy* 43 (Spring 1994): 159.

Contributors

Edwin R. Black is a professor of political science at the University of Northern British Columbia in Prince George.

Donald E. Blake is a professor and past head of the Department of Political Science at the University of British Columbia.

Keith Brownsey teaches political science at Mount Royal College in Calgary.

R.K. Carty is a member of the Department of Political Science at the University of British Columbia.

Lynda Erickson is an associate professor of political science at Simon Fraser University.

Kathryn Harrison is a political scientist at the University of British Columbia and teaches in both the political science and environmental studies programs.

George Hoberg is an associate professor of political science at the University of British Columbia.

Michael Howlett is an associate professor of political science at Simon Fraser University.

Gerry Kristianson is a semi-retired public affairs consultant and former visiting professor of political science at the University of British Columbia.

Barbara McLintock is a senior political reporter and columnist for the *Province* newspaper.

Terence Morley is a member of the Political Science Department at the University of Victoria.

Michael J. Prince is Lansdowne Professor of Social Policy at the University of Victoria and wrote this chapter while a visiting associate at the International Social Studies Institute at the University of Edinburgh.

Norman Ruff is an associate professor of political science at the University of Victoria.

Brian Scarfe is an adjunct professor at the University of Victoria's School of Public Administration and a professor of economics at the University of Regina.

Richard Sigurdson teaches political science and was formerly head of the Department of History, Politics, and Philosophy at the University College of the Cariboo in Kamloops.

Paul Tennant is a professor of political science at the University of British Columbia and director of the BC Legislative Internship Program.

Index

Set in Stone by Artegraphica Design Co. Ltd.

Printed and bound in Canada by Friesens

Copy-editor: Randy Schmidt

Proofreader: Anne Webb

Indexer: Karen Murray

Cartographer: Eric Leinberger